D1351516

# OXFORD ENGLISH MONOGRAPHS

# South Asian Writers in Twentieth-Century Britain: Culture in Translation

RUVANI RANASINHA

CLARENDON PRESS · OXFORD

# OXFORD
## UNIVERSITY PRESS

Great Clarendon Street, Oxford OX2 6DP

Oxford University Press is a department of the University of Oxford.
It furthers the University's objective of excellence in research, scholarship,
and education by publishing worldwide in

Oxford New York

Auckland Cape Town Dar es Salaam Hong Kong Karachi
Kuala Lumpur Madrid Melbourne Mexico City Nairobi
New Delhi Shanghai Taipei Toronto

With offices in

Argentina Austria Brazil Chile Czech Republic France Greece
Guatemala Hungary Italy Japan Poland Portugal Singapore
South Korea Switzerland Thailand Turkey Ukraine Vietnam

Oxford is a registered trade mark of Oxford University Press
in the UK and in certain other countries

Published in the United States
by Oxford University Press Inc., New York

British Library Cataloguing in Publication Data

Data available

Library of Congress Cataloging in Publication Data

Data available

Typeset by Laserwords Private Limited, Chennai, India
Printed in Great Britain
on acid-free paper by
Biddles Ltd., King's Lynn, Norfolk

ISBN 978–0–19–920777–0

1 3 5 7 9 10 8 6 4 2

For Senani

# *Acknowledgements*

This book began as a doctoral thesis at the University of Oxford, I am deeply indebted to Jon Mee for his enduring support and insightful guidance. Special thanks are due to Robert J. C. Young who offered much appreciated feedback on numerous drafts, and generously shared his knowledge with me. His input has been key to the preparation of this book. Rajeswari Sunder Rajan and Lyn Innes also kindly read earlier versions of several chapters and provided valuable suggestions. Similarly, I thank my anonymous readers, and at Oxford University Press Andrew MacNeillie, Tom Perridge, and copy-editor Katie Ryde (who by coincidence was interviewed by Tambimuttu for a post at the Lyrebird Press in the 1970s).

I am grateful to the British Academy for funding this doctoral study. Thanks also go to the board of Graduate Studies, Christ Church, Oxford and the Meyerstein Foundation for travel grants, which enabled me to present some of this material at the Third International Conference on Colonialism at the National University of Ireland, Galway, and to visit archives in the US. For their invaluable assistance I thank the librarians at the University of Bristol, Columbia University, Harvard University, Northwestern University, the University of Reading, the BBC Centre for Written Archives, the British Library, the Macmillan Archive, the National Sound Archive, Lake House Newspaper Archives, and the National Archives in Colombo. A special thanks to the late Nirad Chaudhuri, Hanif Kureishi, A. Sivanandan, and Meera Syal for answering my questions and for sharing their unpublished work with me, and to Shakuntala Tambimuttu for permission to cite her father's correspondence and unpublished work. I am also grateful to the BBC, Random House Group, and Jonathan Cape for permission to quote from their papers. Although every effort has been made to trace copyright holders and establish copyright before printing this has not always been possible. The publisher would be pleased to rectify any omissions or errors brought to their attention at the earliest opportunity. Some of the material on Hanif Kureishi in Chapter 5 has already appeared in Ruvani Ranasinha, *Hanif Kureishi: Writers and their Works* (Northcote House Publishers, 2002).

Friends and colleagues in the UK, Sri Lanka, and the US have inspired, encouraged and supported me in numerous ways, especially Elleke Boehmer, Paula Burnett, Neloufer de Mel, Lilamini de Silva, Alison Donnell, Priyamvada Gopal, Manique Gunesekera, Qadri Ismail, Arjuna Parakrama, and Sara Salih, My late father-in-law kindly copied out Tambimuttu's early poems by hand from the Colombo Municipal Library's only copy. Thanks also to Joe Aloysious, Singha Basnayake, Lola Chatterjee, Desmond Fernando, Pat Mylvaganam, Constance Ratnayake, Arun Tampoe, and Jeremy Vine for assistance in finding material on Tambimuttu and Nirad Chaudhuri. Lastly, my deep gratitude to my family for all their love and encouragement, and most especially to my beloved companions Senani, Rapti, and Pradeep for everything.

# Contents

# Introduction: Contexts of Literary Production and Consumption

In 1940, Mulk Raj Anand, a well-known and well-connected Indian author, hesitantly negotiated from his British publisher Allen and Unwin an advance of £50 for a reprint of his book, *A Hindu View of Art* (1932). Six decades later, Salman Rushdie earned an advance of £1 million for his seventh novel, *The Ground Beneath Her Feet* (1999). The hitherto unknown British Asian writer Hari Kunzru received a staggering £1.25 million advance for his celebrated first novel *The Impressionist* (2002), an exploration of culture, race, history, and identity. British Asian first-time novelist Monica Ali was offered a £30,000 advance on the basis of a few chapters of *Brick Lane*, a book that went on to dominate the best-seller lists for many months when published in 2003. Within this broad trajectory of the increasing marketability of 'South Asian' Anglophone writing, lies a complex history of shifting perceptions of cultural difference which forms the subject of this book.

*South Asian Writers in Twentieth-Century Britain: Culture in Translation* is the first book to trace a genealogy of the literary publication and reception of South Asian Anglophone writing in twentieth-century Britain, through a comparison of the changing contexts of literary production and consumption for succeeding generations of selected writers of South Asian origin, who emigrated to, or were born in, Britain. Comparing two or more writers of a similar 'generation' in each chapter, my study begins just before the second World War, a decade before the independence of the subcontinent.[1] This moment was the prelude to the mass emigration that would configure constructions of

---

[1] While I emphasise the way historical contexts inform this body of writing, this is not to suggest that a single writer is in any way representative of his or her generation. The construct of 'generation' does not totally contain or define any single writer or group of writers in a particular way. It is used as a heuristic tool rather than as a truth. As we shall see, differences are not only generational. Gender, race, class, religion, language,

South Asian identity in Britain. The writers discussed here include the early nationalist Indian writers, Anand and Raja Rao, alongside R. K. Narayan whose impact is compared to the contrasting receptions of Sri Lankan poet and publisher M. J. Tambimuttu (1915–83), and of Nirad Chaudhuri (1897–1999), the Bengali author of several idiosyncratic semi-autobiographical historical surveys of India's modern history, notably *The Autobiography of an Unknown Indian* (1951). Next, Kamala Markandaya (1924–2004), the Indian author of several explorations of the relationship between colonised Indians and their British rulers, from *Nectar in a Sieve* (1954) to *Pleasure City* (1982), is examined alongside her contemporary, Sri Lankan left-wing ideologue, and director of the Institute of Race Relations, Ambalavener Sivanandan (1923– ), who began to write fiction only late in life. Selecting these writers from an earlier generation that straddles the pre-war colonial era and the immediate post-war postcolonial period, enables an exploration of the transition between these epochs, and counters the relative neglect in our own times of pre-war migrant writers.

When questioning the traditional canon, contemporary postcolonial critics focus almost exclusively on narratives of contestation. In order to map a properly historicised genealogy of South Asian writing and its reception in Britain, however, the less resistant early voices also deserve attention. It is for this reason that I examine here the now neglected figures of Chaudhuri and Markandaya whose ideological orientation often evinces continuing oppression rather than opposition to colonial and neo-colonial tendencies. This enables a productive assessment of the varying achievements of the early authors who wrote in inimical cultural climates. In doing so, they were paving the way for younger writers who would work in very different conditions. Developing this idea, the following chapter considers Salman Rushdie's (1947– ) role in transforming the parochialism of the English novel, alongside the provocative satires on minority cultural identity authored by his contemporary, playwright and novelist Farrukh Dhondy (1944– ). The final chapter examines the ways in which British-born writers and filmmakers Hanif Kureishi (1954– ) and Meera Syal (1963– ) develop radical new dimensions to the space created for them by their precursors.

Although often defined within the broad framework of 'postcolonial literature', my concern is with the specific dynamics of South Asian

and region complicate minority identities and their representation, and intervene in the discursive production of the minority subject.

Anglophone migrant and minority writing. The immensely diverse backgrounds of these Asian writers, and the wide-ranging perspectives explored in their memoirs, poetry, fiction, essays, films, and dramas, make clear the limits of even this regional category. At the same time, South Asian Anglophone Literature itself is often equated with 'Indian Writing in English': authors from other countries in the Indian subcontinent are virtually ignored. My choice of several Sri Lankan writers seeks to rectify this imbalance. The historical, political, and cultural framework of this body of writing differs significantly from that of East African Asian Asian Caribbean, African, and Caribbean writing with their intimate connections to Britain's history of slavery and indentured labour. While the contested category 'Black British writing' has produced much fruitful literary criticism and anthologising, the establishment of the category of 'South Asian' writing within the British context is relatively new.[2] In this study, I consider the emergence and rise of the regional category 'South Asian', alongside the problems associated with such categorisation and the motivations that have fuelled the generation of categories 'South Asian', 'British Asian', and latterly and more specifically, 'British Muslim'. I will examine the ways in which South Asian identities and cultures in Britain were informed by the presence of large African, Caribbean, East African Asian, and Asian Caribbean communities, and briefly examine Indo-Caribbean V. S. Naipaul, and the impact of his construction of 'South Asian-ness' in Britain. We will see what roles these succeeding generations of writers play in the evolution of the shifting constructions of South Asians

---

[2] Existing work on Black Britain and Black British Literature includes the important scholarship of Peter Fryer, *Staying Power* (London: Pluto Press, 1984), C. L. Innes, *A History of Black and Asian Writing in Britain 1700–2000* (Cambridge: Cambridge UP, 2002), Sukhdev Sandhu, *London Calling: How Black and Asian Writers Imagined a City* (London: HarperCollins, 2003), James Proctor, *Dwelling Places: Post-war Black British Writing* (Manchester: Manchester UP, 2003), John McLeod, *Post-Colonial London: Re-Writing the Metropolis* (London: Routledge, 2004) among others. There is now a significant body of research specifically charting the cultural history of African Caribbean communities in Britain: Kwesi Owesu (ed.), *Black British Culture and Society* (London: Routledge, 2000), Bill Schwarz (ed.), *West Indian Intellectuals in Britain* (Manchester: Manchester UP, 2003), Alison Donnell, *Twentieth Century Caribbean Literature: Critical Moments in Anglophone Literary History* (London: Routledge, 2005) among others. In contrast, apart from Rozina Visram's pioneering *Ayahs, Lascars and Princes* (London: Pluto, 1986) and *Asians in Britain: Four Hundred Years of History* (London: Pluto, 2002), and Susheila Nasta's productive, wide-ranging discussion of South Asian diasporic writers, *Home Truths: Fictions of the South Asian Diaspora in Britain* (Houndmills: Palgrave, 2002), the varied and complex literary historiography of Asians in Britain remains little researched.

and other racialised groups from 'immigrants' to 'ethnic minorities'—a move that denotes a fuller participatory citizenship in Britain. How has this body of literature created wider public recognition of ethnic minorities in Britain? A generational comparison enables an analysis of the changes within the 'host' country to which migrant identity responds and, sometimes, conforms.

Placing the selected authors in the context of other writers of their generation situates them within the social and cultural contexts of the Britain of their day. Using a chronological scheme to show the evolving constructions of South Asian migrant or minority identity, each chapter takes a slightly later starting point than the preceding one, and then traces the varied development of these writers through the next few decades. I would argue that, broadly speaking, there are three things to be gained from such a generational comparison. First, studies of the diasporic identities of cultural communities tend to privilege space over time, compress distinct eras and produce more abstracted studies.[3] Braiding together diverse South Asian Anglophone writers from different periods provides a fuller understanding of some of the changing historical and cultural conditions that have shaped, and continue to shape, South Asian Anglophone writing within the historical framework of Britain's recasting itself over a transitional era, from the concluding decades of Empire through decolonisation towards a multicultural nation. Changing constructions of migrant identity across different periods, and the generational dynamics and differences in this body of writing, are rarely probed systematically. Examining these succeeding generations of South Asian Anglophone writers and their work in their historical moments provides a more nuanced and historically situated understanding of how migrancy, acculturation, and cultural difference have been experienced and conceptualised diversely at specific historical moments.

In the second place, my generational perspective conceptualises the cross-cultural interplay between these migrant or minority intellectuals and their 'host' and 'home' cultures as a process of cultural translation, a concept derived from the metaphoric use of linguistic translation.

---

[3] N. K. Wagle and Milton Israel (eds.), *Ethnicity, Identity, Migration: The South Asian Context* (Toronto: University of Toronto Press, 1993). Peter Van der Veer (ed.), *Nation and Migration: The Politics of Space in the South Asian Diaspora* (Philadelphia: University of Pennsylvania Press, 1995).

Positioning these writers as text and translator, translated and translating, object and agent, we will see the diverse ways these writers enact processes of inter-cultural transformation.[4] As in ethnographic studies, postcolonial fiction and criticism foreground the spatial mapping of cultural translation, especially in relation to migrancy, and tend to erase the complex question of the temporal. Consequently, tracing generational differences in succeeding generations of South Asian Anglophone writers' cultural translations, shows how the processes of translation are subject to different conditions at given specific historical moments: in every case, the metaphor of space, of carrying across, is mediated by the dimension of time. Such comparisons illustrate the changing assumptions that frame the translation of non-Western cultures into what is perceived as mainstream, metropolitan culture and the dominant code of English. Broadly speaking, up to the 1960s this phenomenon is studied most usefully in terms of the predicament of early 'minor' expatriate writers (such as Tambimuttu and Markandaya) who have moved from the colonies to the metropolis, and for whom the main concerns involve questions of authenticity, exoticism, East–West relations and anti-colonialism. The transfer of culture is inscribed by the dichotomy of centre and periphery. By the 1980s, a multicultural Britain produces a greater emphasis on questions of identity, sexuality, interracial romance, and race, all of which have different meanings and resonances in this later context. In the work of 'post-migrant' writers such as Kureishi we find a concern with wider questions facing multicultural Britain: how to accommodate cultural difference with the lived experience of diversity in both cultural and political terms. Here translation becomes a point where cultures merge and create new spaces, something closer to Homi K. Bhabha's description of multiple centres in which cultural differences are recognised, and which come to replace any centre–periphery dichotomy.[5] The book moves from tracing the first of these broad configurations to the second and shows how

[4] In postcolonial studies the term is used to describe the processes of the dissemination and transformation of cultures with colonial expansion, and now with the immigration of the global diasporas, within the host countries. For an understanding of postcolonial cultural translation see Vincente Rafael, *Contracting Colonialism: Translation and Christian Conversion in Tagalog Society* (Ithaca: Cornell UP, 1988). Tejaswini Niranjana, *Siting Translation: History, Post-Structuralism, and the Colonial Context* (Berkeley and Los Angeles: University of California Press, 1992). Homi Bhabha, *The Location of Culture* (London: Routledge, 1994).

[5] Homi Bhabha, 'The Third Space' in Jonathan Rutherford (ed.), *Identity: Community, Culture, Difference* (London: Lawrence and Wishart, 1990), 207–22.

Rushdie's and Dhondy's work forms a transformative bridge between the two.

Minority writers are often positioned by the dominant culture as authoritative mediators. Examining the different ways in which they negotiate the role of native informant reveals the centrality of notions of cultural ambassadorship in the processes of cultural translation. This role is linked to what is sometimes called 'the burden of representation', that is, the assumption that migrant or minority artists speak for the entire culture or community from which they come. This presumption impinges on these authors in different ways across the decades. In certain respects, the early writers such as Tambimuttu and Chaudhuri constructed themselves as native informants offering perspectives of their natal culture, largely for the majority population. Coming to Britain as the former colonies gained independence, Markandaya was similarly positioned as representing India in her work, more specifically feminised, exotic versions of India. As an organic intellectual integrated with populist anti-racist socialist movements, Sivanandan embraced a more politicised burden of representation in his activism and writing. Just as first-generation migrant writers are positioned as 'authentic' insiders and translators of Eastern *countries*, the British-born writers are often constructed by the dominant culture as privileged insiders and translators of minority *communities* who live in Britain. The large-scale post-war migrations transmuted the problems of representation from orientalist portrayals of the East to the West, to the politics of representing minority communities for the dominant gaze of the majority community, as well as to an increasing minority readership. The Other is no longer 'out there' but within Britain, while often remaining 'alien' for the majority population. By the time Rushdie, Dhondy, Kureishi, and Syal began to write during the late 1970s and 1980s, the increasingly vocal minority presence meant that the burden of representation had become increasingly politicised and intense. As we shall see in the final chapter, it took on a specific, precise political meaning during the 1980s. How do writers represent the ethnic community to which they belong? What are the possibilities and problematics of such kinds of representation? While contemporary minority writers such as Kureishi expand the space created for them by their forebears, we will also see the ways in which older writers, such as Rushdie, are influenced by younger contemporary writers.

Finally, I trace generational changes in this body of writing alongside a detailed analysis of its literary production and contemporary reception.

This is the first book to provide a historicised account of the publishing and reception of South Asian Anglophone writing in twentieth-century Britain.[6] Analysis of the conditions of production and reception affords a better understanding of the changing conceptions of racial Others and cultural difference, particularly with respect to minority writers, that configure contemporary Britain's racial politics. Taking writing and reading together shows the ways in which culture has been continually translated and transformed in the colonial and postcolonial contexts. The consumption of these texts also acts as a form of cultural translation. And if consumption is central to understanding processes of translation, publishing houses and reviewing apparatuses are important sites in which processes of 'domesticating' and 'foreignising' cultural translation come into play.[7] Publishers' considerations, perceptions of risk, sales, and reviews, reveal insights regarding perceptions of cultural difference, particularly in relation to questions of marketing and literary history, such as the commercial implications of a book's title, content, and format. Drawing on a broad range of original archival sources, including readers' reports and the early writers' previously unpublished correspondence with their publishers, I assess the role and impact of editors, readers, publishers, and reviewers who selected which narratives would be published, and shaped how they would be promoted and received in the predominantly metropolitan stronghold of English language publishing. In this way, the goal of my generational comparison involves not only the archaeological retrieval of neglected texts, but also illustrates the specific conditions that influenced why particular authors were acclaimed (or not), and why some have become comparatively neglected in recent years. While the literary reception of writers across the generations is analysed, the correspondence of most of the 'post-Rushdie' generation of contemporary writers is yet to be archived, or inaccessible because of copyright law.

[6] Graham Huggan examines the processes by which postcolonial literature is marketed as an example of 'the post-colonial exotic' and considers Indo-Anglian Fiction as a metonymic stand-in for India as an object of consumption during the 1990s in *The Post Colonial Exotic: Marketing the Margins* (London: Routledge, 2001).
[7] Lawrence Venuti terms the 'ethnocentric reduction of the foreign text to target-language cultural values' as 'domesticating' translation. Venuti advocates a 'foreignising method' that 'registers the linguistic and cultural difference of the foreign text, sending the reader abroad', where the target language (and by extension the target culture) becomes culturally hybridised and modified by the elements of source culture, although 'foreignising' translation does not always achieve this, as we will see. Lawrence Venuti, 'Translation as Cultural Politics: Regimes of Domestication in English', *Textual Practice* vii (1993), 208–33.

This history makes clear the degree to which publishers, attuned to the varying tastes of diverse, specific readerships, act as mediators between the writer and the reading public, raising important questions about the reception of migrant and minority writing. Such evidence influences and alters our present understanding of terms like translation, migration, hybridity, and multiculturalism by giving them a materialist history. It demonstrates the ways in which shifting political, academic, and commercial agendas in Britain and North America have influenced the selection, content, and consumption of many of these texts in specific ways across the generations. It becomes clear that the 'literary quality' of a book is not the only criterion that affects its trajectory and its success.

So while I would broadly agree with Sukhdev Sandhu's claim in his excellent study *London Calling: How Black and Asian Writers Imagined a City* (2003) that in contrast to customary representations metropolitan individuals and institutions 'have traditionally been very keen to encourage marginal voices', I would argue that such support is often offered on specific terms, in order to reinforce prevailing agendas. Sandhu's account of black and Asian migrants' encounters with literary London imbues their interaction with the dominant host culture with a neutrality that ignores the degree to which minority discourse is often shaped by the complex demands of various sections of the mainstream. Sandhu writes: 'They found in this old, old city a chance to become new, to slough off their pasts. London gave them the necessary liberty. It asked for very little in return. Certainly not for loyalty . . . they had free congress. They were emotionally and intellectually unshackled.'[8] While it is certainly true that many writers found moving to Britain a liberating experience,[9] many of the important shifts in migrant writing that a generational comparison makes visible, correspond to the pressures brought to bear by reader responses in the 'host' societies, and sometimes in the 'home' countries as well. These expectations vary over time, according to changing social and political factors. For example, as we will see in Chapter 2, the early South Asian migrants' writings were co-opted into larger propaganda movements against fascism and communism, during the 1940s and 1950s respectively. A more recent example would be

---

[8] Sandhu, *London Calling*, pp. xxiii, xxvi

[9] Markandaya, Attia Hosain, and Caribbean writer Sylvia Wynter among others have expressed that they would not have been able to become writers if they had not migrated to Britain. Firdaus Kanga and Suniti Namjoshi are examples of South Asian writers who felt freer to write about and live alternative lifestyles in the West.

Kureishi's distrust of Islamic separatists or 'fundamentalists' explored in the final chapter. These writers' cultural translations do not take place on neutral ground. Instead, South Asian Anglophone writers' penetration of white mainstream media and publishing institutions was and continues to be a contradictory, mutually affecting process. We will see how questions of literary fashion remain very much alive with younger contemporary writers. Agents of cultural transformation, creating the taste they were judged by, they also subserve as their predecessors did, an idea of British South Asian literature produced for the market by their publishers, producers, readers, and reviewers in Britain.

## TRANSNATIONAL CONTEXTS OF CULTURAL TRANSLATION: ASSIMILATION VERSUS RESISTANCE

My analysis focuses on South Asian Anglophone writers domiciled in Britain, and concentrates on the writers' own predicaments as expatriate, migrant, and later minority intellectuals, as well as on the question of what minority writing means to a white mainstream culture and minority communities.[10] It is also concerned, however, with an issue that is often ignored in discussions of migrancy in metropolitan postcolonial studies, preoccupied with acculturation and multiculturalism, namely the various and complex ways in which some of these texts are influenced by, respond to, intervene in, and are received within the changing contexts of the postcolonial country of origin from which they are spatially distanced. I locate any 'local' reception of these authors' work within a broader discussion of the politics of colonial and postcolonial literary production both nationally and internationally. Comparing the literary reception in Britain with responses within the countries of origin reveals some contradictions between the two. It raises questions about the transnational processes of book production, as well as how such a South Asian identity is produced within the community in Britain and outside it. We will see how South Asian writing, as with much

---

[10] 'Migrant' and 'expatriate' are contested terms. Commentators argue that the domicile of a writer alone is invalid as a category given that regardless of residence, both expatriate and resident writers have contested and conformed to roles of native informants reporting to the West. I would argue that the logic underlying the classification expatriate or migrant is the thematics of migrancy that emerge (implicitly or explicitly) in these texts, as well as the ways in which the changing cultural contexts of the place of domicile influence the work of migrant intellectuals.

nationalist literature written abroad, is also shaped by the nationalist discourses produced within the writers' countries of origin. These writers of South Asian origin are not just minority writers in Britain: they are also minority writers in South Asia because they write in English. For different reasons, therefore, they are *minor* writers—because of their miniscule readership—in both contexts; and yet because of the status of English as a world language they become highly visible as mediators, cultural translators, and spokespersons.

The contrasting ways in which succeeding generations of South Asian diasporic writers cope with changing questions of cultural difference informs the structure of this book. Nowadays postcolonial and minority writing is often considered as a form of 'resistance literature'.[11] The selected writers are examined in terms of the interplay between the processes and expectations of assimilation and resistance. Broadly speaking, early migrant writers were expected to assimilate, while later writers were better positioned to express difference in their own terms. Within the following chapters we will explore the refinements that complicate this broad trajectory, and the clear-cut notions of assimilation and resistance. Assimilation does not always involve downplaying one's cultural origins. Asserting cultural difference in pre-determined ways can equally amount to a form of assimilation. In distinct ways, across the generations, the more radical, innovative writers express cultural difference in a manner that challenges dominant or received conceptualisations of difference.

The first chapter offers a broad literary and structural history of South Asian Anglophone writing published in Britain, both to serve as a kind of map locating the specific writers discussed in the book, and also to provide a point for comparative and critical assessment. Early writers like Anand and Chaudhuri need to be seen in terms of modernist traditions, rather than what one might call the current literary apartheid of examining black and white modernist writers separately. For these early writers, modernity offered a way to transcend their sense of growing up in a secondary, provincial colonial culture, and to translate themselves into British or international writers. Chaudhuri assimilated into an Edwardian, imperial pre-modernist culture. While Anand appeared

[11] My use of the term 'postcolonial' in this study relates to Mukherjee's and Trivedi's understanding of 'postcolonial' as referring to both the historical break identifying the end of colonial rule, and ideological orientations that carry some resistance but not complete freedom from neo-colonial tendencies in Harish Trivedi and Meenakshi Mukherjee (eds.), *Interrogating Post-Colonialism: Theory, Text and Context* (Shimla: Institute of Advanced Study, 1996).

to assimilate into a form of modernism, he adopted and adapted an international counter-cultural discourse within the dominant culture. Here the impulses to assimilate and resist are closely interrelated. At one level, the decision to write novels in English stemmed from a motivated 'affiliation' and a bid for international recognition and readers. But at the same time, for Anand, Rao, and others, English was a weapon, as well as a key to the ideological arsenal in the struggle for independence: their writings in English reflected their emergent nationalism. Drawing on previously unpublished correspondence between Rao and his publisher Allen and Unwin, this chapter documents how Rao was requested to erase his cultural origins in his work so that he could assimilate and be accepted by the centre. Such demands are part of the metropolitan expectation for minority writers to conform to 'universalist' criteria. This amounts to a Eurocentrism, masked as the 'universality' of the human condition that neglects the local socio-political context of the country of 'origin' and conceals the refusal of Western audiences to engage with the unfamiliar. It results in de-radicalised, ahistorical readings.

At the same time, as the next chapter entitled 'Self-translation as Self-promotion' shows, these early 'Asiatic' writers, seen as exotic and oriental outsiders, were also often expected to embody 'foreignness', and provide 'alien' perspectives on Britain, usually in prescribed terms. This chapter explores the contrasting modes of 'domesticating' and 'foreignising' self-translation reproduced respectively in the writings of the self-Westernised Chaudhuri, and M. J. Tambimuttu. After coming to Britain in 1938, the equally anglicised Tambimuttu adopted a self-consciously 'Asian' cultural identity that embodied ideas about the East produced in the West. Such assertions of cultural difference, pre-shaped in orientalist terms for Western consumption, do not transform the centre, and offer a marked contrast to Anand and Rao's politicised efforts to nativise Standard English and to 'Indianise' the European novel. Unlike Anand who moved in radical political circles, on arrival in Britain Tambimuttu gravitated towards counter-cultural aesthetic movements. Tracing Chaudhuri's and Tambimuttu's varied development from the 1940s and 1950s onwards, we see that ironically Tambimuttu's self-reinvention as an 'Asian' allowed him to engage and be absorbed into his new environments to a far greater extent than the self-colonised Chaudhuri.

This pattern of assimilation by adopting prescribed versions of exoticism recurs with the Indian novelist Kamala (Purnaiya) Markandaya who settled in Britain in 1948 with her English husband Bertrand

Taylor. Markandaya, whose work is examined in the third chapter, launched a literary career during the mid 1950s in a climate where Indian material was a commercial liability in metropolitan publishing houses. Consequently Markandaya's work tends to embody a form of assimilative, 'domesticating' translation that suppresses cultural difference. At the same time, in a manner comparable to Tambimuttu, her work also contains forms of 'foreignising' translation based on received and already-established conceptions of cultural difference. In both cases we see these different forms of assimilation within the same writer. This third chapter entitled 'Assimilation and Resistance' examines Markandaya's work alongside the writings of her contemporary, Sri Lankan activist Ambalavener Sivanandan. Sivanandan migrated to England as a political refugee ten years after Markandaya in 1958, in the context of heightened racial intolerance exacerbated by the influx of post-war immigration. These biographical contemporaries could not be more different. On arrival, Sivanandan—following the trajectory of C. L. R. James and George Padmore—assimilated, not into dominant social formations, but into radical milieus that offered a politics of resistance. In different ways, Sivanandan's and Markandaya's responses problematise clear-cut notions of assimilation, and even of 'dominant' expectations and a monolithic 'centre'. Markandaya's fictional interrogation of the Raj forms a response to liberal humanist critiques of colonialism within Britain during the 1960s and 1970s, and was warmly embraced by the Eurocentric parameters of the discourse of Commonwealth Literature. Her work forms a sharp contrast to Sivanandan's radical and politicised Marxist polemics, evident in his later novel that was informed by his participation in anti-racist socialist struggles in Sri Lanka and Britain during this era.

These writers are not exact literary contemporaries. Markandaya's literary career spans the rise and eclipse of the Commonwealth Literature paradigm. Although virtually forgotten today, during the 1960 and 1970s Markandaya was acclaimed in Britain and the US as 'one of India's most able Anglophone writers'.[12] Her publishers even considered nominating her for the Nobel Prize. My discussion of Markandaya and her contemporary reception makes clear the presence of a dialectic of expectations between writer and publisher: this author writes what the publishers and critics suggest, while they in turn praise what she writes.

---

[12] Cited in John Wakeman, *World Authors, 1950–1970: A Companion Volume to Twentieth Century Authors* (New York: Wilson, 1975), 948.

Markandaya stopped writing in the 1980s when literary conditions in Britain were no longer receptive to her kind of fiction. Conversely, Sivanandan published his first novel *When Memory Dies* in 1997 when literary circumstances were more favourable for a novel interwoven with a history of Sri Lankan working-class self-organisation and participatory notions of community.

Markandaya's willingness to conform in her bid for mainstream acceptance, and the *conditions* that influenced her attitude, differ from subsequent writers. The mass immigration of the 1950s and 1960s changed the cultural dynamics of the host culture, and created new audiences. Later writers were more confident in self-consciously writing against the terms of dominant culture. Most prominent amongst these was Salman Rushdie, who contested stereotypical representations of India and of ethnic minorities in Britain in his fiction and criticism. Chapter 4, 'Writing back, Re-writing Britain', considers Rushdie alongside the figure of Farrukh Dhondy, who like Sivanandan began his career in Britain as a political activist. Their work is examined primarily in terms of the way they straddle the concerns of both first and second-generation writers. Rushdie's first three novels embody the movement from colonialism and anti-colonialism towards a project of re-writing multicultural Britain. Dhondy's early stories and plays form a transformative bridge between writing back and re-writing Britain in another way. They map out themes of generational conflict and class tensions within British Asian communities as well as the topical, vexed debates on the appropriate response to racism, particularly the role of violence in the anti-racist struggle. These are also issues that the younger Hanif Kureishi began to explore in his first plays in the early 1980s, written from the perspective of a second-generation 'Anglo-Asian' writer, as he was then quaintly referred to. The penultimate chapter, 'Staging Cultural Difference: Cultural Translation and the Politics of Representation', examines the emergence of British-born Asian writers in the 1980s and 1990s, focusing on the work of Kureishi and Meera Syal. Rather than offering forms of assimilation, in their work Kureishi and Syal can be seen to engage in a redefining of 'British-ness'. Locating their polemical and creative responses in the context of contemporary debates on the politics of representation, the chapter considers the different ways in which these writers contest 'the burden of representation'[13]

[13] An influential phrase coined by Kobena Mercer, *Welcome to the Jungle: New Positions in Black Cultural Studies* (London: Routledge, 1994), 214.

with portrayals that break decisively from what Ali Rattansi has called 'the stifling aesthetic of the positive image'.[14]

Like Dhondy and Rushdie, Kureishi's and Syal's works destabilise dominant constructions of 'black' or Asian identity. They disrupt notions of a monolithic, static Asian 'community' by dramatising how constructs of generation, class, sexuality, and gender impinge on the contested issue of what it means to be of Asian origin in Britain. Kureishi's subsequent move away from overtly politicised issues of race in his later novels can be read as contesting in turn the expectation that Asian writers should always address questions of race and identity in their work. The chapter ends with an analysis of the new directions in British Asian cultural production that have challenged the earlier models developed in the 1980s and 1990s.

The book concludes by tracing the tropes and motifs in this body of writing and its reception that recur across the decades in different circumstances. Taking in roughly equal periods of colonial and post-independence history (1900–50, 1950–2000) makes it possible to mark the shifts and changes that the 'postcolonial' introduces, and show subtle continuities that undermine the tendency to assume or overstate a radical discontinuity between colonial and postcolonial periods. Generational differences are not clear-cut: within continuity there is transformation. These indissoluble, nebulous tensions can be conceptualised as a form of intergenerational haunting. Adopting each other's concerns of the complexity of difference, assimilation, modernity, the issues change but also repeat, refusing to be laid to rest.

---

[14] Ali Rattansi, 'Changing the Subject: Racism, Culture and Education', in James Donald and Ali Rattansi (eds.), *Race, Culture and Difference* (London: Sage Publications in association with the Open University, 1992), 34.

# 1

# Shifting Conditions: The Changing Markets for South Asian Writing in Britain during the Twentieth Century

This chapter considers the shifting political, literary, and socio-economic conditions that influenced the writing and reception of the diverse continuum of South Asian Anglophone writing in Britain during the course of the twentieth century. The steady interchange between mainstream and minority codes can be conceptualised as a process of cultural translation. In particular, my discussion highlights the role of publishers and reviewers as socio-historical filters through which culture is transmitted. A target audience that creates a demand also supplies a framework of reference that accompanies the subsequent interpretation of the text. What were the British target culture's local priorities and conditions, tastes and convictions that influenced the subtle modifications expected? How did these differ from the contexts of reception in the Indian subcontinent? By tracing the selected writers' frequently contradictory reception in both contexts, we can examine the ways in which they adapted to, or contested the expectations of their multiple readerships.

## EARLY CROSS-CULTURAL ENCOUNTERS

The Indian subcontinent has fed the Western imagination since ancient times, but India took on a new role at the end of the nineteenth century when Europeans became convinced that Western civilisation itself was caught in a degenerative decline. The Theosophical Society inspired many writers and thinkers in Europe and North America to look to the East for a source of cultural renewal, in contrast to what they experienced as the spiritual barrenness of modern civilisation in the

West. In London, the publications of John Murray's *Wisdom of the East* series from the 1900's, marks the period of such interest. During the following decades, spiritual versions of the subcontinent continued to preoccupy British readers, and it was this that conditioned and determined the reception of South Asian writers. A striking example of this would be the enormous impact of Rabindranath Tagore's visit to Britain in 1912, when William Rothenstein, W. B. Yeats, and Ezra Pound launched him as an Eastern mystic in the West. The impact of the Theosophical Society, the *Bhagavad Gita* and Hindu and Buddhist teachings on T. S. Eliot has been well attested.[1] Eliot was then subsequently to play an instrumental role in initiating Mulk Raj Anand's and Tambimuttu's entrée into literary life.[2]

In this period, reports of the colonial territories remained popular amongst metropolitan readers.[3] Alongside the British descriptions, notably Leonard Woolf's *The Village in the Jungle* (Edwin Arnold, 1913), an increasing number of Indian and Ceylonese (Sri Lankan) accounts appeared, such as a translation of T. N. Ganguli's *Swarnlata* (Macmillan, 1915), Lucian de Silwa's *Dice of the Gods* (Heath Cranston, 1917), or J. Vijaya-tunga's *Grass Beneath my Feet* (Edwin Arnold, 1935). While some, such as Rosalind Mendis' fictionalised portrait of Ceylonese native elite, *The Tragedy of a Mystery* (Arthur H. Stockwell, 1928), were written by writers who had never visited Britain, since the eighteenth century Asian (then referred to as 'Asiatic' or 'Oriental') writers visiting or domiciled in the 'mother country' had also offered converse views of Britain in their memoirs. This kind of book flourished at the beginning of the twentieth century, notably T. Ramakrishnan's *My Visit to the West* (T. Fisher Unwin, 1915), Sunity Devee's *The Autobiography of an Indian Princess* (1921), and Cornelia and Alice Sorabji's writings which were published by John Murray. Their perceptions were not chiefly directed at subcontinental audiences. Instead they provided defamiliarising perspectives of British society for British readers. This defamiliarising trope recurs across the decades. In the following pages, we will encounter migrant intellectuals who fall into what Abdul JanMohamed refers to as 'traps of specularity', and articulate and affirm hegemonic notions of

---

[1] Paul Foster, *The Buddhist Influence in T. S. Eliot's 'Four Quartets'* (Frankfurt: Haag und Herschen, 1977).

[2] Reported in several accounts of the era including J. Maclaren-Ross, *Memoirs of the Forties* (London: Alan Ross Ltd., 1965),136.

[3] For instance Caroline Corner, *Ceylon the Paradise of Adam* (London: Bodley Head, 1908). Samuel Baker, *Eight Years Wandering in Ceylon* (London: Longmans, 1890).

'Englishness', but we will also find those who challenge them and offer a transforming reflection.[4]

## SOUTH ASIAN ANGLOPHONE WRITERS OF THE 1930s AND 1940s AND THEIR RECEPTION: MULK RAJ ANAND (1905–2004), R. K. NARAYAN (1906–2001) AND RAJA RAO (1908–2006)

During the early part of the twentieth century, most of the South Asian Anglophone writing published in Britain was broadly anthropological non-fiction. Art-historian Ananda K. Coomaraswamy's (1877–1947) early publications in Britain, focused on Hinduism and Buddhism, alongside interpretations of Hindu culture (*Suttee, a Vindication of the Hindu Woman*: London Sociological Society, 1912), with an emphasis on insurmountable cultural difference: *The Deeper Meaning of the Struggle between Englishmen and Indians* (Essex house Press, 1907). Later fictional narratives would be seen through such an anthropological lens. The Allen and Unwin archive makes clear the publisher's primary interest in historical and political material about India rather than fiction.[5] Under Stanley Unwin's stewardship, Allen and Unwin published several autobiographies, biographies, and historical texts by Indian writers in the decade prior to independence. These include the first English edition of Gandhi's *My Experiments with the Truth* (under the title *Mahatma Gandhi: His Own Story*) and *Mahatma Gandhi at Work* edited by C. F. Andrews, Mulk Raj Anand's *The Hindu View of Art* (1932), but significantly, not his novel *Untouchable* (1935), Professor Sarvepelli Radhakrishnan's (1888–1975) *An Idealist View of Life* (1932), Jawaharlal Nehru's (1889–1964) *India and the World* (1936), a collection of essays edited by Raja Rao and Iqbal Singh entitled *Changing India* (1938) and R. P. Masani's *Dadabhai Naoroji: Grand Old Man of India* (1939). The list included just one notable novel, Raja Rao's *Kanthapura* (1938). In later years, Allen and Unwin continued to publish historical books by

---

[4] Abdul JanMohamed, 'Worldliness-Without-World, Homelessness-as-Home: Towards a Definition of the Specular Border Intellectual' in Michael Sprinker (ed.), *Edward Said: A Critical Reader* (Cambridge, Mass.: Blackwell, 1992), 105.

[5] Stanley Unwin states this preference in his autobiography *The Truth about a Publisher: an Autobiographical Record* (London: Allen and Unwin, 1960). Rao later reprinted *Kanthapura* with OUP.

South Asian writers, such as Khuswant Singh's *Ranjit Singh* in 1962 and political essays *Colour, Culture and Consciousness: Immigrant Intellectuals in Britain* edited by Bhikhu Parekh in 1974. A few other publishers took on literary topics. Oxford University Press published Iqbal Singh's book on Mohammed Iqbal's poetry after Allen and Unwin rejected his proposal. The Hogarth Press published Ahmed Ali's novel on Indian Muslim culture, *Twilight in India* in 1940. But as we shall see, on the whole, it was also much harder for South Asian writers to be taken seriously as fiction writers than as social historians in the British context.

It was, in fact, the advocacy of established English authors that brought about the publication of two founding fictional texts of the Indo-Anglian tradition, Mulk Raj Anand's *Untouchable* (1935) and R. K. Narayan's *Swami and Friends* (1935). Prior to this, in the space of a few years, Anand had published four non-fictional, explicitly anthropological works on Indian art and culture: *Persian Painting* (in *Criterion*'s Miscellany Series, Faber 1930), *Curries and Other Indian Dishes* (Harmondsworth, 1932), *A Hindu View of Art* (Allen and Unwin, 1932), and a critical study *Studies of Five Poets of the New India* (John Murray, 1934). During this time, Anand published only one fictional collection, *The Lost Child and Other Stories*, significantly with a smaller publisher, J. A. Allen, in 1934. Meanwhile, nineteen publishers rejected his novel *Untouchable*. It was E. M. Forster who eventually secured Anand's socialist realist story of the deprivations suffered by a young outcaste sweeper and latrine cleaner, with Lawrence and Wishart. While *Untouchable*'s cultural background played a part in publishers' negative responses to Anand's novel, presenting such 'squalor'—the grim details of a latrine cleaner's daily routine—as the subject of fiction constituted a daring, groundbreaking step for any writer at this time.[6] Their editor Edgill Rickward describes Forster's preface and recommendation as 'the book's passport through the ordinary reviewer's latent hostility'.[7] Domiciled in Britain between 1925 and 1945, Anand moved closely with the leading writers of the day. Patronised by some,

[6] E. M. Forster, letter to Anand, where he describes publishers' objections to 'squalor not length', 5 May 1934, Lawrence and Wishart Archive, Uncat. MSS 13 Beinecke Rare Book and Manuscript Library, Yale University. I am grateful to Susheila Nasta for this reference. See Susheila Nasta, 'Between Bloomsbury, Gandhi and Transcultural Modernities: the Publication and Reception of Mulk Raj Anand's *Untouchable* (1935)', unpublished paper, The Colonial and Postcolonial Lives of the Book Conference, 3–5 Nov. 2005.
[7] Edgill Rickward, letter to Anand, 30 Nov. 1934, Lawrence and Wishart Archive, Uncat. MSS 13 Beinecke Rare Book and Manuscript Library, Yale University.

he was supported by the likes of Forster, Stephen Spender, and Leonard Woolf, and employed by T. S. Eliot to write for his *Criterion*. Founded by Ernest Wishart in the early 1920s and amalgamated with Martin Lawrence (1936) and the Communist Party's Press, the liberal, anti-fascist publisher, Lawrence and Wishart provided a fitting platform for Anand. Involved with British trade unions and the 1926 General Strike, he fought with the International Brigade in the Spanish Civil War in the 1930s. He helped found the All-India Progressive Writers' Union in London, calling upon Indian writers to incorporate a socialist vision in their work. Lawrence and Wishart went on to publish Anand's *Coolie* (1936) and *Two Leaves and a Bud* (1937).

R. K. Narayan sent his manuscript of *Swami and Friends* from Mysore to London. Similarly rejected by several publishers, including Allen and Unwin, his comic realist evocation of a middle-class South Indian childhood attracted the attention of Graham Greene in 1934, thanks to Narayan's friend Purni who was at Oxford University. Greene recommended it to Hamish Hamilton for publication, suggesting the writer shorten his surname from Narayanaswamy to Narayan, no doubt to lessen the difficulty of his South Indian name for his English audiences. However, despite 'a few enthusiastic reviews' there were almost no sales. Hamish Hamilton rejected Narayan's next novel, *The Bachelor of Arts*, responding: '*Swami* was a sad failure. I don't think *Chandran* [working title for *Bachelor*] is going to do any better. I hope someone will prove me wrong.'[8] Greene's mentoring of Narayan and editing of his work continued. He found fresh publishers for Narayan's next two books. Recommending *The Bachelor of Arts* (1937) to Nelson, Greene wrote the introduction. He then persuaded Macmillan to publish Narayan's subsequent novel *The Dark Room* (1938), which met with a similar critical but not commercial success in Britain. Yet such acclaim furthered Narayan's career in India. The sale of the Tamil rights of his novels in Madras led to a regular column in *The Hindu*. In contrast, Anand's *Untouchable*, translated into over twenty languages, was initially better received in Britain than in India, where some Indian commentators critiqued the novel as communist propaganda.

These writers' early reception in Britain reveals the awkward position of South Asian fiction in English at this point. The future success of Indian English as a literary style seemed inconceivable. Reviewing Anand's *The Sword and the Sickle* (1942), George Orwell predicted that:

---

[8] R. K. Narayan, *My Days* (New York: Viking Press, 1974), 111–12.

'[English] might survive in dialect form as the Mother Tongue of the small Eurasian community, but it is difficult to believe it has a literary future.'[9] The internationalisation of English and its ownership outside Britain was yet to be recognised: a review of *Two Leaves and a Bud* in 1937 describes Anand as 'a veritable artist in a language which is not his own'. The same reviewer suggests that 'The easy apt style would be praiseworthy in an Englishman, since Mr Narayan is writing in a language that is not his own, his mastery of English [in *Bachelor of Arts*] appears as something more than praiseworthy.'[10] British reviewers tend to emphasise any evidence of assimilation to Standard English, rather than comment on Anand's Punjabi-inflected English and the expression of Indian sensibilities through local images and metaphors. Today, Anand's pioneering efforts to subvert Standard English in his works have been eclipsed in the post-Rushdie literary landscape: but from the first his writings demonstrate the use of literal translations of Indian swear words, original vernacular words without translation and a modification of traditional English spellings. Anand's recollections in *Conversations in Bloomsbury* suggest how, encouraged by Gandhi and inspired by James Joyce, he aspired to modify Standard English to an even greater degree: 'I had been daring to use words like *ghaoon maoon*. In fact I would have liked to play about with words like Joyce in such a way that no English words could communicate our feelings. I could introduce vibrations as speech, never mind if the English didn't understand.'[11]

The reviews of the time reveal the gradual emergence of a critical apparatus grappling to evaluate these challenging, 'different' fictional texts, alongside motifs that persist today in the reception of black and Asian fiction: even now, interest in the novel's anthropological function eclipses its literary qualities. In 1938 the *Times Literary Supplement* (*TLS*) reviewer claims 'The story [of Narayan's *The Dark Room*] is of no great importance, it is the picture of Brahmin life in South India that gives the book its value.'[12] Reviews often define Narayan's and Anand's reading constituency as 'those who know or remember India' or 'those

---

[9] George Orwell, 'Review of Anand's *The Sword and the Sickle*', *Horizon* (1942).

[10] John Chartres Molony, 'Review of *Two Leaves and a Bud*', *Times Literary Supplement* (15 May 1937), 379. John Chartres Molony, 'Review of *Bachelor of Arts*', *Times Literary Supplement* (12 June 1937), 446.

[11] Mulk Raj Anand, *Conversations in Bloomsbury* (London: Wildwood House, 1981), 142.

[12] John Chartres Molony, 'Review of *The Dark Room*', *Times Literary Supplement* (22 Oct. 1938), 679.

English readers who are anxious to understand Indian life'.[13] They foreground both writers' credentials as native informant: 'Mr Anand, a high caste Hindu [writes] with sympathy and intimate knowledge of the details of Indian customs.'[14] Even E. M. Forster's introduction to *Coolie* emphasises Anand's insider–outsider perspective: '*Untouchable* could only have been written by an Indian and by an Indian who observed from the outside.'[15] As we will see, such sociological interpretations stem in part from a suspicion as to whether these Indian writers could write fiction: while a number of Indians had recently published sociological treatises on village life in India, these early novels mark British readers' first *fictional* encounter with such topics.[16] One review described *Untouchable* as 'suitable for those who have felt some interest in the Indian Untouchables as a result of Mr Gandhi's efforts . . . but who have little knowledge of how they live'. Thus *Untouchable*'s critique of India's caste system receives praise, marking the first time English readerships encountered such criticism of India from an 'Indian novelist's' perspective. Significantly the reviewer appears gratified by the description of cultural colonialism, particularly Bakha's rejection of 'his life, his home, his street, his town because he had been to work at the Tommies' barracks and obtained glimpses of another world, strange and beautiful: he has grown out of his native shoes'.[17]

Concurrently, the reviews confine the designated native informant's brief to depictions of the native population, discouraging a parallel scrutiny of the British in India. A review of Anand's novel *The Village* (1939) praises the writer for 'some penetrating perceptions of Indian character' and suggests that 'he wisely avoids that stumbling block the "European"'.[18] For another reviewer the author's censure of British characters in *Coolie* renders it 'less successful' than *Untouchable*. He suggests that Anand 'would have done better to leave out the English characters, for all of them are caricatured'.[19] Anand's unflinching portrayal of

[13] Molony, 'Review of *Bachelor*'.

[14] Samuel Townsend Sheppard, 'Review of *Coolie*', *Times Literary Supplement* (20 June 1936), 520.

[15] Forster, Preface to Anand, *Coolie* (Lawrence and Wishart, 1936), 9.

[16] Such as Mahadev Desai, *Gandhiji in India* (1927) and G. G. Mukhtyar, *Life and Labour in a South Gujarat Village* (1930)

[17] Anonymous, 'Review of *Untouchable*', *Times Literary Supplement* (2 May 1935), 298.

[18] Hilton Brown, 'Review of *The Village*', *Times Literary Supplement* (15 Apr. 1939), 215.

[19] Sheppard, 'Review of *Coolie*'.

British tea companies' exploitation of plantation workers in a tea-estate in Assam proves too unpalatable for the Times Literary Supplement reviewer of *Two Leaves and a Bud* (1937) to accept. Incredulous that the labourers can be as 'underpaid, starved, bullied, beaten', as Anand depicts, the reviewer claims it is 'against commonsense' for a company to mistreat the labour on whom it depends for its profit. Anand becomes an unreliable informant in the reviewer's insistence that 'Penny wise, pound foolish is an Indian rather than an English characteristic.' Preferring to dismiss the fictionalised possibility that a English-dominated jury would overturn the charges against a British officer, guilty of brutally murdering the protagonist Gangu, and attempting to rape his daughter, the reviewer claims 'it is . . . unlikely that English jurymen in disregard of their oaths would return a manifestly iniquitous verdict; it is much more unlikely that an English judge would concur'.[20] This myopic nationalism refuting the possibility of a difference in conditions between Britain and India, points to some of the prevailing attitudes circulating at this time, giving us a fuller picture of the sociological and ideological conditions surrounding the emergence of these writers. In contrast to the incredulous British reception, the Bengali translation of *Two Leaves and a Bud* sold well, as did the Czech and Polish versions: socialist readers were more ideologically attuned to Anand's critique of the exploitation of peasants lured into working in such appalling conditions. The critical material of Anand's novel led to the banning of *Two Leaves and a Bud* in Britain and colonial India, which had implications for Rao's novel *Kanthapura* (1938), a legendary history of a small village's participation in Gandhi's Civil Disobedience Movement in the Kara district of Karnataka in the 1930s.

While these early authors placed their books according to their mentors' contacts, it was also the case that certain publishers were particularly associated with publishing South Asian material and South Asian writers, some since the nineteenth century. We have already noted the role of the non-conformist and liberal thinker, Stanley Unwin, the principal of publishers Allen and Unwin, who also published books by Bertrand Russell and J. A. Hobson that questioned imperialism.[21] His support of Indian writers can be seen as an extension of this effort, and perhaps stems from his desire to increase understanding of

---

[20] Molony, 'Review of *Two Leaves and a Bud*'.
[21] Unwin observes 'I had read J. A. Hobson, *The War in South Africa* and realised that Britain was not necessarily in the right', *The Truth about a Publisher*, 49.

Indian affairs. Always keen to introduce foreign works to Anglophone readers, he published many translations throughout his career. The best known publisher of Indian material, Macmillan and Co. (1843– ) produced the first edition of Kipling's *Plain Tales from the Hills* in 1890, and was one of the earliest publishers of Indian authors, from the early works of Maharshi Devendranath Tagore, Rabindranath Tagore, to Narayan, Nirad Chaudhuri, and Zulfikar Ghose. Other key publishing institutions in this regard included John Murray and OUP, with established offices in Delhi, Chennai, Mumbai, and Kolkata from 1912. Journalist and lawyer V. K. Krishna Menon (1896–1974) worked as an editor for Bodley Head whilst immersed in politics and pamphleteering as secretary for the India League campaigning for Indian self-government.[22] Allen Lane, a director of Bodley Head, set up Penguin, a separate enterprise, publishing paperbacks that were cheap but of high quality; Menon became the first editor of the non-fiction Pelican series launched in 1937, obtaining books by Roger Fry and H. G. Wells. According to Menon's biographer T. S. J. George, the partnership failed because his idealism clashed with Lane's business sense. George suggests it was Menon's idea to flood the market with cheap paperback versions of worthwhile books so that people with limited funds, like him, could benefit from them.[23] Menon's close political association with Nehru and Anand no doubt contributed to Bodley Head's publication of Nehru's autobiography in 1936, and the republication of Anand's *Untouchable* as a Penguin Modern Classic in 1940. Chatto and Windus published Indo-Irish Aubrey Menen's first novel *The Prevalence of Witches* (1947) and went on to publish the greatest number of South Asian writers in English, as we shall see.[24]

---

[22] See also Rozina Visram, *Asians in Britain: Four Hundred Years of History* (London: Pluto Press, 2002), 290.

[23] T. J. S. George, *Krishna Menon* (London: Jonathan Cape, 1964).

[24] Chatto and Windus published Attia Hosain (*Phoenix Fled*, 1953, *Sunlight on a Broken Column*, 1961), Khushwant Singh (*Train to Pakistan*, 1956), Nayantara Sahgal (*Storm in Chandigarh*, 1969), Narayan (*The Ramayana*, 1973, *My Days*, 1975) and as well as Chaudhuri (*The Continent of Circe*, 1965) and Markandaya's novels between 1972–82 after her first publisher Putnam, later Bodley Head, merged with Chatto. Chatto merged with Jonathan Cape (1969) and Virago (1982). The companies retained editorial control until Random House purchased the group in 1987. What made Chatto and Windus publish so many Indian writers? One factor may have been Chatto's acquisition of a controlling interest in the Woolfs' Hogarth Press in 1947, given this circle's close connection and support of South Asian Anglophone writers. Moreover, Cecil Day-Lewis, one of Hogarth's prize authors became an editor at Chatto and edited Attia Hosain. Literary agents also clearly played a key role. Hosain's agent Joyce Weiner approached

## TRANSNATIONAL PUBLISHING CONTEXTS: PUBLISHERS AND THE IMPORTANCE OF COLONIAL MARKETS

Longmans', Macmillan's, and Allen and Unwin's trade history selling textbooks to schools in the Indian subcontinent (either directly, or through local agents) formed an important prelude to publishing Indian authors of non-fiction and fiction and identified an important market for these publishers. Macmillan's particularly long trade history with India dates back to the 1860s, exporting textbooks and then novels through its Colonial Library Series, and opening branches in Mumbai (1901), Kolkata (1907), and Chennai (1913).[25] As Priya Joshi has shown, it was in fact Indian and colonial readers who shaped Macmillan's English fiction list towards the late nineteenth century. Macmillan's reliance on the high sales of English fiction to readers in India made them willing to provide the 'anti-realistic' fiction sought by these readers, and to neglect and ignore audiences in Britain.[26] Shafquat Towheed reveals how Rudyard Kipling's first six texts were popularised by the burgeoning mass market of Indian readers when published by A. H. Wheeler's successful Indian Railway Library texts.[27] Reliance on Indian sales evidently influenced Macmillan's subsequent decision to commission Kipling, who was simultaneously placed on their British and colonial lists. The latter sold cheaper copies with only 10 per cent of the royalty received in Britain. Initially the sales were higher in Britain but with several re-printings in India the sales evened out.

Chatto; David Higham represented Narayan. Nirad Chaudhuri and Markandaya were both represented by Innes Rose.

[25] For an account of Macmillan's trade in India, see Rimi Chatterjee, 'Macmillan in India', in Elizabeth James (ed.), *Macmillan: a Publishing Tradition* (Houndmills: Palgrave, 2001), 153–70. Other publishers, such as OUP *Heritage of India Series* (1915– ) catered to the missionary interests of Christianity in India: the Calcutta YMCA and Associated Press published its later volumes.

[26] Priya Joshi, *In Another Country: Colonialism, Culture and the English Novel in India* (New York: Columbia UP, 2002).

[27] Shafquat Towheed 'Two Paradigms of Literary Production: a brief comparison of the production, distribution, circulation and legal status of Rudyard Kipling's *Departmental Ditties* (1886) and Indian Railway Library Texts', unpublished paper, The Colonial and Postcolonial Lives of the Book 1765–2005 Conference, Institute of English Studies, University of London, 3–5 Nov. 2005.

Following Maurice Macmillan's lead, Stanley Unwin was also conscious of the importance of cultivating foreign, especially colonial, markets. In 1912, Unwin visited the dominion countries South Africa, Australia, Singapore, and Sri Lanka (then Ceylon) to obtain first-hand knowledge of the customer requirements of overseas markets. He subsequently visited India. In his autobiography, Unwin perceives the 1912 trip as 'one of the best investments' he ever made. He writes 'the fact that fifty five per cent of my firm's turnover is represented by export sales, demonstrates that my travelling has not been altogether in vain.'[28] These reconnaissance visits allowed him to identify topics of interest particularly to readers in Britain and South Asia, and stimulated the flood of non-fictional writings by Gandhi and Nehru, among others published by Allen and Unwin during the 1930s, listed above. Clearly, it made commercial sense to publish the works of India's foremost intellectuals in the years leading up to Independence. The archive of Allen and Unwin contains other examples of the way that reading communities and consumers in South Asia fuelled the publication of South Asian Anglophone writing in Britain. In 1949 Allen and Unwin stated they had no interest in reprinting Anand's *A Hindu View of Art* (1932) since there were over a hundred unsold copies in the UK.[29] However, when Anand, together with Allen and Unwin's local agents in Bombay, brought the demand in India to the publisher's attention, they became 'quite ready to consider producing a new edition of the book'.[30] This pattern recurs with Narayan's and Attia Hosain's fiction published subsequently by Chatto and Windus.

Allen Lane of Penguin also visited India and Sri Lanka in 1939 to promote Menon's Pelican series, popular amongst Anglophone readers in those countries. The literary supplement of the progressive monthly *Young Ceylon* (published in Colombo during the 1930s and modelled on Gandhi's *Young India*) reports Lane's visit amidst a host of notices of the latest books published in Europe.[31] The local interest in his visit, and in books published abroad, reveals the existence of vibrant, cosmopolitan, transnational reading communities, as well as offering insights into the circulation of print

[28] Unwin, *The Truth about a Publisher*, 112–13.
[29] Allen and Unwin, letter to Anand, 22 March 1949, Allen and Unwin Correspondence, University of Reading.
[30] Allen and Unwin, letter to Anand, 11 Oct. 1949.
[31] *Young Ceylon* 7.2 (1939), Sri Lanka National Archives.

and ideas between metropolis and periphery at this time. Lane's visit reinforces the importance of South Asian readers to British publishers, particularly in the context of the publishing agreement between the US and Britain that gave British publishers exclusive rights throughout the Empire. Just before Indian independence in 1947, Bill Withers advised Allen Lane to expand Penguin's publishing activities in the Commonwealth, particularly in Australia and India: 'Every conversation I have with intelligent Indians confirms me in the belief that, once they have cast off the political shackles to Great Britain, they will be all the more culturally receptive to us.'[32]

## NARRATIVES OF NATIONALISM

Published simultaneously in Delhi and London, Rao's *Kanthapura* (1938) addresses these dual readerships, in a manner comparable to Anand's *Untouchable*. The previously unseen Allen and Unwin correspondence reveals, however, that Rao and Anand's primary interest was in reaching Anglophone Indian readerships rather than British ones. This transnational dimension to the publishing of South Asian writing in English in Britain during this period, contrasts with more recent South Asian Anglophone writers' alleged disregard for local audiences. In a letter to his publisher, Rao comments that he originally suggested the idea of a foreword to *Kanthapura* by Professor Sarvepalli Radhakrishnan—the Indian philosopher in Eastern religions and ethics at Oxford University (1936–52)—rather than E. M. Forster, because 'Radhakrishnan could understand both the social and the religious side of my book'.[33] As publishers, however, Allen and Unwin preferred E. M. Forster: 'That we should regard as the more valuable introduction from the commercial point of view. This matter you will of course regard as confidential.'[34] While Rao was happy for the publisher to approach Forster, he nevertheless made his point again: 'I should believe too that for the *Indian market* [Radhakrishnan's] *introduction might even be more useful*.'[35] In their letters to Allen and Unwin, both authors

[32] Bill Withers, letter to Allen Lane, 14 July 1947. Cited in Steven Hare, *Portrait of a Publisher* (Harmondsworth: Penguin, 1970), 48.
[33] Rao, letter to Allen and Unwin, 24 Feb. 1937.
[34] Allen and Unwin, letter to Rao, 20 Feb. 1937.
[35] Rao, letter to Allen and Unwin, 24 Feb. 1937 emphasis mine.

reiterate their concern to reach Anglophone Indian readers by proposing that the price of their texts be kept as low as possible for the Indian market.[36]

This correspondence is particularly illuminating in its support of Rumina Sethi's sophisticated account of *Kanthapura*'s construction of a pan-Indian bilingual nationalist intellectual as its implied reader.[37] Allen and Unwin employed an editor to identify potentially inflammatory material because the colonial government censored books before publication in India. The correspondence suggests that Rao prudently accepted this pre-publication vetting in the interest of the dissemination of his work amongst nationalist intellectuals. In 1937, in the immediate context of the banning of Anand's *Two Leaves and a Bud* (1937) in Britain and by the colonial government in India, Rao writes: 'As I am myself keen that the book [*Kanthapura*] should circulate freely and largely in India, I should be glad to accept all toning down of the text, which would unnecessarily bring down the heavy hands of the Censors on my book.'[38] Since Rao wants to engage Indian intellectuals on the Left, a similar prudence can be found at work in relation to his choice of title. Rather than foreground his religious treatment of Gandhian nationalism in his novel, he rejects an alternative title with religious overtones that could alienate this particular reading community: 'The title "Soul Forces" or "soldiers of the soul", though in a way significant would *put away readers of the Left parties to whom also the book is destined.*'[39]

With the backing of an enlightened principal of a publishing house, Indian writers themselves played an extremely influential role in shaping the content of South Asian Anglophone writing published in Britain during this period.[40] What was produced under the sign of India at this time reflects these bilingual, Westernised writers' emergent nationalism.

[36] Anand asked for a cheaper reprint of his *A Hindu View of Art* so that it would be affordable to Indian readers. See Anand, letter to Allen and Unwin, 17 Mar. 1949. Similarly Rao and Singh propose that a series of new editions of Indian classics should 'not exceed one rupee eight annas for the Indian public'. Rao and Singh, letter to Stanley Unwin, 12 Jan. 1939. Rao's *Kanthapura* was sold at 5 rupees in India in the 1930s.

[37] Rumina Sethi, *Myths of the Nation: National Identity and Literary Representation* (Oxford: Clarendon Press, 1999).

[38] Rao, letter to Allen and Unwin, 24 Feb. 1937.

[39] Ibid., 5 Mar. 1937, emphasis mine.

[40] Iqbal Singh co-edited the All India Progressive Writers' Association (AIPWA) literary magazine *Indian Writing* with Ahmed Ali between 1936–8. Ali and Anand published work in Lehmann's *New Writing*.

Allen and Unwin published a selection of writings by 'great Indians' including Nehru, Gandhi, Tagore, and Vivekananda entitled *Changing India* (1938) at Rao and Iqbal Singh's instigation.[41] Some of their proposals were not accepted because Allen and Unwin's objectives did not always coincide with their own. Particularly invested in the task of nation building in the lead-up to independence, through what they term 'a rediscovery' and revaluation of India's past and contemporary culture, Singh and Rao proposed a series of new editions of Indian classics, such as Kalidasa's *Shakuntala*, to fulfil what they called the 'growing desire among the younger generation in India today to know more of the sources of Indian thought . . . and cultural heritage'. Reprinting the classics was to be followed by editions of nineteenth- and early twentieth-century works: the writers suggest 'that existing collections or editions of classical and contemporary Indian writers do not cater for the needs of the modern Indian or Western reading public'.[42] Promoting local reappraisals of India's past did not, however, necessarily match British readers' interest in 'modern' India, and this is likely to have been the reason why Allen and Unwin chose not to publish Singh and Rao's projected series of Indian classics, but expressed interest in, and eventually published a selection from modern writers.

As the example of Krishna Menon at Penguin and the Bodley Head demonstrates, there can, of course, be no simple distinction between South Asian writers and British publishers. Allen and Unwin themselves employed Sarvepalli Radhakrishnan as a consultant on book proposals by Indian authors. Radhakrishnan supported Rao and Singh's idea of a collection of modern writers, but even he doubted the 'wisdom of . . . embarking upon the publication [in Britain] of a series of reprints of the Indian classics'.[43] In contrast to Singh's and Rao's nationalist aspirations, Radhakrishnan appears to have been primarily concerned with Allen and Unwin's commercial interest. While we must allow for differences of opinion between Radhakrishnan and Rao et al., it would seem that South Asians such as Radhakrishnan and, as we shall see, Z. A. Bokhari at the BBC, employed by and working within cultural or academic institutions within Britain were positioned differently from those more tangentially linked to such establishments: in practice, Rao, Singh, and Anand were more successful in imposing their own agenda,

[41] Allen and Unwin, letter to Singh, 26 Apr. 1939.
[42] Rao and Singh, letter to Stanley Unwin, 12 Jan. 1939.
[43] Cited in Allen and Unwin, letter to Rao, 6 Feb. 1939

whereas Radhakrishnan and Bokhari were more ready to conform to British expectations.[44]

## THE PUBLICATION OF *KANTHAPURA* (1938)

Given the often patronising, imperialist attitudes of the era, Allen and Unwin was ahead of its time in giving South Asian writers a platform. This was not, however, always offered to them on their own terms. Despite the broad support offered chiefly by Stanley Unwin, the Allen and Unwin correspondence—particularly between Rao and his editor Malcolm Barnes—reveals a resistance to Rao's stylistic experimentation in *Kanthapura* with a non-Standard English inflected with Kannada cadence, expressions, and figures of speech, together with the integration of myth, history, realism, and fable. As Meenakshi Mukherjee argues, this generation, in its anxiety to compensate for writing in English, deployed such formal and thematic devices 'to tether their texts to indigenous contexts'.[45] The opposition identified here stems in part from Barnes' accurate predictions of the commercial implications of a parochial reading public not prepared to engage with forms of cultural difference that challenged their own reading practices. It is worth noting that at this juncture the literary conditions in the US appear to have been even more resistant to non-standard English: Allen and Unwin unsuccessfully approached eleven firms in North America to place an American edition of *Kanthapura*.

In dealing with Rao, Barnes initially insisted that his suggestions are 'tentative rather than imperative'.[46] He expressed his concern that towards the end of *Kanthapura*, as the tempo changes, 'the colloquial style of the book also becomes a little trying to English readers'.[47] Barnes further encouraged Rao to find an alternative, more anglicised title: 'we fear *Kanthapura* would not give the book its best chance.'[48] Subsequently, Barnes became increasingly frustrated with Rao's refusal

---

[44] See also Ranjee Shahani's criticism of Anand for 'creating bad blood between Indians and the English' at a critical point during the Second World War in his 'Review of Anand's *The Sword and the Sickle*', *Times Literary Supplement* (2 Apr. 1942), 221.

[45] Meenakshi Mukherjee, *The Perishable Empire: Essays on Indian Writing in English* (Delhi: Oxford UP, 2000), 170.

[46] Barnes, letter to Rao, 12 June 1937.         [47] Ibid., 19 May 1937.

[48] Ibid., 3 Mar. 1937.

to modify his text for English readers. His tone became increasingly peremptory and patronising: 'even when I make allowances for the high colours of the *oriental* imagination, I feel that for the benefit of literature some curb has to be made on the misuse of words.'[49] Rao remained willing to concede only revisions of 'grammatical and idiomatic order', defending at length his use of metaphor, such as the 'road hisses', on the grounds that it is appropriate to the cultural context. Rao objected to the deletion of phrases such as 'Oh have you seen the gods, sister?' or 'Oh how inauspicious!' Far from pleading for concessions, Rao underlined the editor's ignorance of other cultures. He confidently argued 'that anyone in the least acquainted with Indian psychology and superstition would know that people are supposed to bring unhappiness when they yell. It is quite understandable that you are ignorant of them, but they happen to be an integral part of the book.'[50]

Barnes attempted to pressurise Rao by arguing that they shared the same goal. He claimed both writer and publisher 'may be held up to ridicule' for producing a book with the disputed passages.[51] An early review describing *Kanthapura* as 'disappointing... despite the author's comprehensive knowledge' of his subject confirms Barnes' forecast. As Barnes anticipated, the reviewer criticises Rao's style and implies the novel has not been edited sufficiently, in his assertion that Rao 'has not discovered how to present the vitally interesting material... in the form of fiction. *As it stands* [the novel is] too difficult for the impatient Western reader to tackle.'[52] One could suggest that the correspondence manifests the customary tussles between the competing agendas of publisher and author. Yet these disputes represent the pressures of the literary culture with which this generation of South Asian Anglophone writers had to contend. Rao fused both the political and personal, the national and the individual in his steadfast defence of his original text: 'for an author his book is part of his life and his *blood*, and he cannot see it so sadly disfigured.'[53] Ultimately Barnes conceded, because 'one party has to give way'. Rao was able to maintain his stand because Allen and Unwin contracted *Kanthapura* for publication before

[49] Barnes, letter to Rao, 10 Nov. 1937 (emphasis mine). Chaudhuri and Aubrey Menen were similarly described as 'orientals', a term subsequently used to denote East Asians. The term was used interchangeably with 'Asiatic' at this time.
[50] Rao, letter to Barnes, 6 Nov. 1937.       [51] Barnes, letter to Rao, Nov. 10 1937.
[52] Anonymous, 'Review of *Kanthapura*', *Times Literary Supplement* (26 Mar. 1938), 122, emphasis mine.
[53] Rao, letter to Barnes, 6 Nov. 1937, emphasis mine.

'actual revisions [were] agreed upon in close detail'.[54] This exchange and Rao's refusal to accept all the modifications suggested highlights his generation's achievement, not simply in penetrating mainstream metropolitan publishing houses, but in resisting their demands to conform to Eurocentric standards. This hitherto unseen correspondence gives a fascinating insight into the pre-publication debates behind the scenes, the impact of editors, and illuminates the impulse behind Rao's famous foreword and self-reflexive commentary on *Kanthapura*, which begins 'My publishers have asked me to say a few words . . .'.[55] The context is particularly relevant to an introduction now read as a manifesto for the practice of Indian writing in English. Such a framework illuminates a text—long enshrined as one of the foundation texts of Indian writing in English—that enacts these cultural contestations, and challenges the formal and generic expectations of the Western novel in the 1930s.

Commercial pressures aside, the archived comments on Rao's work always assume the inferiority of South Asian writing in English, and invoke British, or sometimes European standards, as the only important touchstone. Aware of this bias, Rao named 'parallels taken from the classics of English and European literature' in response to Barnes' complaint 'that one starves people not stomachs'. Arguing that such criticisms are 'contrary to all conceptions of peasant literature', Rao cited Faolin, Synge, Ramuz, and Silone.[56] Similarly he maintained that the writer Pearl Buck uses the 'archaic expressions' such as 'sate', 'spake' or 'a-lit' that Barnes objects to. A contemporary review of Anand's *The Village* (1939) judges the novel according to the same European standards: Anand, we are told, 'avoids altogether two of the besetting sins of the Indian novelist—melodramatic incident and over-plotting; almost avoids a third—those long wit-sharpening conversations that get us

---

[54] Barnes refers to this 'mistake in the management' of *Kanthapura* in Barnes, letter to Rao, 10 Nov, 1937. Clearly Barnes felt most strongly about the changes necessary: Rao cites Philip Unwin's letter (16 Dec. 1936) stating that corrections would involve 'nothing beyond the slight change of a turn of phrase here and there', Rao to Barnes, 15 Nov. 1937.

[55] Rao's comments reveal the reason for the foreword: 'In fact nobody could hold you up to ridicule for whatever ridiculous parts you still think there are, as they are all covered up by my foreword', Rao, letter to Barnes, 15 Nov. 1937.

[56] Rao's Francophone influences suggest he needs to be examined beyond his Anglophone and Indian contexts. Anand comments that his lack of French further excluded him from the literary currents of modernism at this time in *Conversations in Bloomsbury*, 18.

"no forrader"; but succumbs to the fourth—the lack of any story. His book is mainly a picture-album: fifty views of the Punjab.'[57] This last comment also reinforces the argument that South Asian Anglophone writers were not taken seriously as fiction writers: the novel is turned into topographical descriptions. In Rao's case, the underlying assumption that comes across in the correspondence is the firm's generosity in allowing Indian writers into the exclusive world of metropolitan publishing. In a later rejection of Rao's subsequent book *Indian Nation*, Rayner Unwin observed 'if one wanted to be very charitable an Indian could read it and give a report, but I fear it is beyond hope'.[58]

In this way, reviewers and publishers both initiate and impede the translation of cultural difference. This kind of conflictual dynamic is evident also in the mechanics of book production. The Rao correspondence demonstrates the pressure of an indisputable push towards Anglicisation, so that the implied English reader will not be over-taxed. At the same time, as Anand suggested in a fascinating letter to his publisher Penguin, the practice of italicising Indian words (a practice that still operates today, although now a bone of contention) heightens their foreignness and serves as a barrier:

I have taken this opportunity to suggest putting many of the Indian words, which were originally in italics [in the proofs sent to Anand] into Roman lettering. Italics seem, from my experience to confuse the English reader and to increase the gulf between him and my alien subject matter, when all my efforts are calculated to show, not how queer the Indians are but how human and like everyone else, *inspite of their particular norms* . . .[59]

As a humanist writer, Anand emphasised commonality, alongside a bid for the recognition of cultural specificity that does not involve hierarchies of difference. Italicising Indian words marks the language as different and Other and not equal to English. (This resonates with contemporary arguments made by commentators like Kenan Malik who argues that the more recent emphasis on diversity and difference militates against equality, and plays into the hands of the exclusionary tactics of the British National Party.[60])

[57] Brown, 'Review of *The Village*'.
[58] Rayner Unwin, Report on Raja Rao's *Indian Nation*, 1954, Allen and Unwin Archive.
[59] Anand, letter to Mr Maynard, 30 Oct. 1940, Special Collections, University of Bristol, Penguin 00.0312.6 [DM 1107], emphasis mine.
[60] Kenan Malik, *The Meaning of Race: Race, History and Culture in Western Society* (Houndmills: Macmillan, 1996).

Anand's self-conscious desire to contest perceptions of Indians as 'queer' explains his generation's emphasis on common humanity, in the context of prevailing notions of racial inferiority. In the same way, Narayan also emphasises universal humanity and experiences. In the classic Commonwealth Literature tradition, these are mediated through 'English, a language . . . which has destroyed the barriers of geography'.[61] Anand's letter underscores his concern to address and engage with European readers and to challenge their partial, long-distance perceptions of India. His memoir *Conversations in Bloomsbury* registers his disappointment when he arrived at the literary capital of the English-speaking world and found that he only encountered parochialism and ignorance of India's diversity. In his novels, memoirs, and private correspondence, he challenges what he considers the Bloomsbury circle's—particularly T. S. Eliot's—metaphysical versions of India and their uncritical readings of Kipling. At the same time, in a passage that underscores his espousal of a version of modernism, he admits to the internalisation of certain forms of denigration that impinged on even such a radical, outspoken critic of colonialism:

Suddenly, I felt that there was an uncanny gap between me and people, as though I was inferior and others were superior. I realised that all of them, being older than me, and part of a metropolitan world, had been privileged to take part in a living culture, whereas, apart from two Shakespeare plays and Thackeray's *Henry Esmond*, I had only read the books of poetry which Professor Harvey used to lend me. . . . I came from a world where everyone was hampered, where desires were frustrated, and happiness thwarted by the elders who were all important. And inside me was the longing to be free, to expand my consciousness, to live and to be on equal terms with the men of learning like those Bonamy Dobrée was familiar with.[62]

When Tambimuttu arrived in London in 1938, he encountered many of the same literary figures, such as T. S. Eliot, who aroused such conflicting emotions in Anand. One can only imagine their impact on a far less politicised consciousness such as Tambimuttu's. At that time, London—the nerve centre of a colonial Empire about to be shattered by a second World War—was a hotbed of radical, anti-colonial activity. Yet Tambimuttu rather gravitated towards the metropolitan literary elite, not towards the nationalist activists at India House who sought to disrupt and overturn colonial rule. Anand and Krishna Menon, by contrast, with

---

[61] Narayan, interview with Hallam Tennyson, 4 Oct. 1961, BBC WAC.
[62] Anand, *Conversations in Bloomsbury*, 18.

their involvement within the India League, and with the Congress party, were to be found at the centre of these activities. The synergy between Anand's politics and writings characterises his early work. As we will see in the following chapter, Tambimuttu's primarily aesthetic concerns with reviving poetry in wartime London contrast sharply with the nationalist, anti-colonial agendas of militant, politically motivated South Asians. They formed their own cultural institutions such as the Tagore Society, and forged ties with Harold Laski, George Bernard Shaw, and other British and Irish sympathizers with Indian independence, as this letter to Shaw from the secretary of the Tagore society suggests:

Greetings on your 88th birthday. It is on this occasion, which reminds us how deeply India is indebted to you for your support and sympathy to the cause of Indian independence. The India struggle draws its inspiration from the people of Eire whose common enemy is British imperialism. Eire is fortunate to have De Valera, as we were Gandhi. Indians are fortunate to be inspired by the greatest poet of the East, Tagore, just as the people of Eire drew inspiration through your immortal oeuvre.[63]

Anand's fiction exemplifies this affinity between Indian and Irish nationalism at a literary and political level, as well as staging a dialogue between nationalism and modernism. Moreover, while Anand's depictions of the ordinary, rural reality of India were intended to counter the spiritual, mystical versions of India endorsed by writers such as Eliot, as we will see, Tambimuttu's later self-translation had the effect of reinforcing such received ideas, aptly exemplifying Abdul JanMohamed's 'trap of specularity'. In contrast, as Sethi has argued, Rao's treatment of spirituality in *Kanthapura,* and the increasingly metaphysical concerns of his later fiction, can be read as 'an assertion of the persistence of a fundamental Hindu tradition in a period of internal dislocation following independence'.[64] These three distinct, concurrent assertions of cultural difference stem from and result in radically contrasting politics.

## TALKING TO INDIA: SOUTH ASIAN BROADCASTERS AT THE BBC

During the Second World War, former civil servant Malcolm Darling, Z. A. Bokhari, and later George Orwell who became Talks Producer of

---

[63] B. B. Chaudhuri, letter to George Bernard Shaw, 27 July 1944, British Library, Dept. of Manuscripts, Add 50524, f.109.
[64] Sethi, *Myths of the Nation,* 153.

the Indian section of the BBC Eastern Service (1941–3), encouraged South Asian writers living in Britain (such as Anand, Tambimuttu, and Venu Chitale) to participate in the *Talking to India* radio programme. This was a series designed to impart propaganda to Anglophone South Asians to encourage support for Britain's war effort. It was aimed at India's opinion-forming intelligentsia in the hope of maintaining the conditional allegiance of the nationalists, especially the two million soldiers, in the fraught context of the Quit India movement of the early 1940s, and in order to counter the Axis propaganda offensive voiced by Subhas Chandra Bose on Radio Azad Hind (Free India). The easy successes Japan and Germany achieved between 1939 and 1943, above all the fall of Singapore in 1942, which resulted in the formation of an Indian National Liberation Army, compounded the need for propaganda. As we will see in the following chapter, translating and refracting versions of England to India prompted these writers to take on a doubly 'specular' role.

The disjunction between the aims of British cultural institutions, and the aspirations of some of the Indian nationalist participants, which we saw in relation to Allen and Unwin, finds direct expression in Anand's letter of 1941 to Malcolm Darling.[65] Anand explains his personal ideological conflict in being associated with the broadcasting service rallying Indians to fight in the War, in the context of the colonial government's suppression of Indian nationalists in the Quit India movement, and the British government's evasion of the question of India's independence, promised before the war:

Since the breakdown between the Viceroy and Gandhiji, the position of Indians in this war has become very invidious. Particularly is this so with regard to the Indians resident in England at the moment.

Because, even those who have the most distant affiliation with Congress, are bound to feel a certain sense of national humiliation if, with full awareness of the internment of hundreds of their compatriots and the savage sentence on Pandit Nehru, they do anything to help the war effort.

My own connections with the Congress are rather more intimate. I am afraid the British Government has done nothing, which may help to solve the

---

[65] In marked contrast to Anand and Nehru who supported Gandhi's policy of non-co-operation during the Second World War, G. V. Desani broadcast several talks urging fellow Indians to resist Japanese and German armies on behalf of the British army and the Imperial Institute.

dilemma, which faces some of us. It has declared neither its war aims nor its peace aims,—and India seems to be its one blind spot.[66]

The indeterminacy of Anand's position at this point is complex. The supposed agent of propaganda becomes closer to its object. At the same time, his stance makes him particularly valuable to the Eastern Service, precisely because he shares the sceptical nationalism of their target audience. Anand seems to have been more important to the BBC than fellow contributor Tambimuttu who shared none of these misgivings, as we shall see. Orwell made several bids to involve Anand. Z. A. Bokhari suggested to Anand that: 'it is important for you to broadcast. As you know, you are well known in India.'[67] Perhaps it was because of the apparent contradiction between Orwell's opposition to imperialism, and his involvement in a series that served to preserve the hegemony of British imperial power in India, that Orwell was clearly able to sympathise with Anand's reluctance and dilemma. In his letter 'India Next' to the *Observer* (22 Feb. 1942), Orwell exhorted the British government to give 'concrete, unmistakable action on independence: Dominion Status with the right to secede after the War'.[68]

Subsequently in 1942, Bokhari (now mainly concerned with Hindi broadcasts to India) rejected Anand's proposal to broadcast Hindi poetry on the BBC's Eastern Service. His response identifies further contradictory objectives, alongside Anand's potentially multiple specular functions as a border intellectual and cultural translator. Bokhari writes:

Our object in our English broadcasts [to India] particularly, and in the Hindustani broadcasts in general is to *project England to India, and not India to India*. . . . If our Poets were translated into the English language and an English poet paid a tribute to our Poets or criticised them, it would be of some value,

[66] Anand, letter to Malcolm Darling, 22 Mar. 1941. Cited in W. J. West (ed.), *George Orwell: The War Broadcasts* (Harmondsworth: Penguin, 1987), 15. Anand experienced other such conflicts when he applied for a scholarship to continue his studies in Britain for if he were successful he would be 'hating British rule in India and living on its dole', cited in *Conversations in Bloomsbury*, 29.

[67] Bokhari, letter to Anand, 4 Dec. 1941. Some months later Anand participated in the BBC Indian Section's Open Letter series with his 'Open Letter to a Chinese Guerrilla' broadcast on 30 July 1942. His contributions were in keeping with the socialist concerns that animate his fiction. He also interviewed a soldier on 13 Nov. 1942, and a member of the merchant navy on 20 Nov. 1942, a canteen worker on 18 Dec. 1942 for the 'A Day in the Life' series.

[68] Peter Davison (ed.), *The Complete Works of George Orwell: Two Wasted Years* (London: Secker and Warburg, 2001), 187–8.

but unfortunately practically none of our Poets have been translated into the English language.[69]

As we saw with Radhakrishnan's dismissal of Rao's and Singh's idea to produce a series of Indian classics, South Asian figures employed by mainstream cultural institutions occupied ambivalent positions. Correspondence with Bokhari suggests his very presence within the BBC encouraged Asian writers to contribute. At the same time, Bokhari's own sought-after position in a key institution was most probably dependent on the extent to which he promoted the goals of the BBC, whilst being a reassuring figure to Asian contributors and listeners in Asia. The implicit solidarity in Bokhari's invocation of 'our Poets' is perhaps intended to soften his rejection to Anand, so as not to deter him from future contributions.

Once the Japanese threat receded, Orwell resigned from the BBC in 1943 arguing that in 'the present political situation [the failure of the Cripps mission and internment of nationalist leaders] British propaganda in India is an almost hopeless task'.[70] *Talking to India* reached few listeners and was poorly received in India. An intelligence report cites an Indian professor explaining 'If we want to hear Indians speaking on intellectual subjects . . . we can hear far better ones on All India Radio.'[71] It was Orwell's innovative monthly literary radio programme *Voice* launched in August 1942, featuring Asian writers Anand and Prem Chand, alongside T. S. Eliot and other key figures of the day that became a forerunner of the Third Programme. The Eastern broadcasting service to South Asia remained, but it was *Caribbean Voices* (1945– ) featuring literary and cultural contributions by Caribbean writers that came to the fore. The Jamaican poet and journalist Una Marson initially conceived the programme with institutional support from Henry Swanzy and Grenfell Williams, Director of the African and Caribbean Service. The failure in *Talking to India* in relation to the success of *Caribbean Voices* needs to be seen in the context of the active, vociferous nationalist movement that skewed Indian cultural output in Britain during this era. As Anand's letter showed, those nationalist participants in *Talking To India* were positioned very differently to the Caribbean contributors who did not generally share the same political

---

[69] Bokhari, letter to Anand, 9 Sept. 1942, BBC WAC, emphasis mine.
[70] For a fuller account of Orwell's reasons, see West, *War Broadcasts*, 57–8.
[71] Cited in Davison (ed.), *Two Wasted Years*, 347.

agenda. This partially explains the *Caribbean Voices'* accommodation and relative success.

It is difficult to ascertain how far Asian contributions to the Eastern service raised the profile of 'Asian writing' in Britain. For many years, sharp distinctions were drawn between Home and Overseas Broadcasting Standards. A BBC memo dismissing Narayan's radio plays as 'the products of a relentlessly Oriental pen' lacking in 'distinction' with 'nearly non-existent plots by Western standards' concludes: 'None of them is the slightest use to us. The writing is stilted and foreign like. They might do for one of our Far Eastern Services, but would not come up to Home Broadcasting standards at all.'[72] Challenging this hierarchy, Indo-Irish Aubrey Menen (1912–89), born and brought up in London, and Sindi writer, actor, and critic G. V. Desani (1909–2001), who first came to Britain from the Punjab as a student, published their first novels in Britain in 1947 and 1948. Championed by Eliot and Forster, like Anand and Rao before them, Menen and Desani's exuberant, boisterous satires stand out against their forerunners' construction of 'Indian-ness' in their novels. Victor Sassoon introduced Menen to Chatto and Windus who went on to publish all his novels and autobiographies. Based on his experiences as an education officer in India, Menen's satire of religion and imperialism *The Prevalence of Witches* (1947) is staged in the mythical Indian state of Limbo where the native community's beliefs in witches thrive, and appear at odds with Western notions of morality. Desani's parodic, eclectic, picaresque *All About H. Hatter* (1948) contests narrow notions of nationalism and Standard English much in the manner of Joyce. As Nasta and Innes have suggested, although their works were well received as specifically Anglo-Indian or Indian phenomena, they did not form the subject of serious critical scrutiny in terms of their impact as modernists.[73] (The first printing of 5,000 copies of Menen's *The Prevalence of Witches* sold within the first four months and like the other South Asian writers he made money from North American sales.[74]) Significantly, the first reviews of *The Prevalence of Witches* focused on the more obvious exposure of Limbo's superstitious

[72] P. Hughes and Mollie Greenmalgh, Memo to Script Editor, 9 Nov. 1956, Narayan R cont 4, BBC WAC.

[73] See Nasta, *Fictions*, 23 and Innes, *A History*, 231–2.

[74] Hugh Walpole and H. G. Wells advised Menen on the importance of North American sales which financed his books according to Menen, letter to Curtis Brown, 9 Oct. 1948. Similarly Markandaya's and Narayan's sales were much higher in the US than in Britain.

natives and paid little attention to Menen's satire of imperialism and of the British residents, interpreting his portrayal of the European colony as 'a queer but agreeable lot [who] sit talking, talking and talking'. The object of satire constantly shifts in the text leading the same reviewer to observe: '*The Prevalence of Witches* is a diverting squib. I must confess I was not always quite sure whom or what it is aimed at; but the general effect was to leave me vaguely stimulated.'[75]

Unlike most of the South Asian writers living in Britain at this time, Anand returned to India after the war, where he encouraged other Indian writers, notably Attia Hosain, to join the Indian Progressive Writers Association. He became actively involved in local publishing, founding the Kutub publishing house, and editing the arts journal *Marg* with Anil de Silva. This era saw the establishment of the *Illustrated Weekly of India* (1950), *Imprint* and *Quest* (and later *Venture* in Pakistan) and P. Lal's Calcutta's Writers Workshop (1958) which became the Writers Workshop Press in 1959. The press published the monthly *Miscellany* giving locally based Indian Anglophone writers an alternative forum for publishing, reducing to some extent their dependence on publishers in Britain. However, after Anand moved to Bombay, British interest in his subsequent work published in India dwindled. Alistair Niven recalls the indifference he encountered from the British media when he tried to set up an interview with Anand on what, given his advanced age, turned out to be his last visit to Britain in the 1990s. Niven was repeatedly asked 'when did Anand last publish in Britain?'[76] The *location* of publishing and its implications for writers from developing countries becomes particularly relevant to the next wave of writers to arrive in Britain. These Caribbean, African, and Asian writers saw their domicile and presence in the metropolis as vital to securing a publisher, a readership, and a critical apparatus. Caribbean writer Derek Walcott, and perhaps Narayan, present the only exceptions.

## POST-WAR AND POST-IMPERIAL BRITAIN

In the wake of Indian independence, the Nationality Act of 1948 gave citizens of the former colonies rights of residence in Britain. Perceived links to the 'mother country' made Britain with its open door policy,

---

[75] Peter Quennell, 'Review of *The Prevalence of Witches*', *Daily Mail* (22 Nov. 1947).
[76] Alistair Niven, address, Oxford Brookes University, 5 Oct. 2003.

fuelled by its need for labour, a natural choice for migrants: not just the 492 'West Indian' arrivals on the *Empire Windrush*, but also many South Asians fleeing from the turmoil of partition. Riots in London, Liverpool, and Birmingham against the newly arrived 'coloured' immigrants followed. As Mike Phillips observes, 'This period marked the establishment of a 'black' British population, and ensuing violence such as the Notting Hill race riots in 1958 became a central issue of political and social life in Britain. The 1950s marked an important shift particularly in London's identity. Received ideas on race, citizenship, and nationality began to be dismantled'.[77] During the late 1950s and early 1960s large numbers of economic migrants arrived from India and Pakistan. The latter settled mainly in the northern industrial towns. Bangladeshi communities followed in the 1970s, leaving floods and civil war at home.

Among the successive waves of Asian, African, and Caribbean immigrants, emerging from distinct historic and cultural circumstances, were the writers who went on to chronicle the profound transformation that Britain was undergoing. This mass post-war migration initiated the shifting reconstruction of the 'expatriate' or 'migrant' writer into 'minority' writer. The occasional expatriate writer does not constitute a category. Minority literature is however a matter of mass—it becomes a *phenomenon* when substantial numbers of writers constitute the literary scene, if their work has an impact, and is regarded as significant. In this way post-war immigration was to radically change the context for appreciation and consumption of minority culture in Britain.

With its distinctive style, and affinity to native British dress and customs, Caribbean culture, particularly fashion, strongly influenced British youth culture, becoming increasingly synonymous with urban culture; on the other hand, Asian culture was persistently seen as alien.[78] Similarly, in an extraordinary burst of literary productivity, it was the Caribbean writers Sam Selvon, George Lamming, Andrew Salkey, Sylvia Wynter, and the Indo-Caribbean writer Naipaul, who emerged on the literary scene of this era with novels about their Caribbean environments and new London homes. Most of these Caribbean writers first worked with the BBC Colonial Services as broadcast journalists, before publishing their first novels. While studying at Oxford, Naipaul prepared scripts and teachers' notes for the Overseas Schools Certificate for the Colonial Schools Unit. In 1954, relieved to escape what he describes as the stifling atmosphere of Trinidad,

---

[77] Mike Phillips, 'From slaves to straw men' *The Guardian*, August 30 2003
[78] Dick Hebdige, *Subculture: the Meaning of Style* (London: Methuen, 1979).

Naipaul's literary career in Britain seemed uncertain. The future winner of the Booker Prize, the Nobel Prize for Literature, and the David Cohen award, writes to the Head of the BBC Colonial Services:

One thing I certainly do not want to do is go back to Trinidad or any other island in the West Indies if I can help it. I very much want to go to India, but there are many difficulties. I cannot be employed on the Indian side because I am British, and on the British side I cannot be employed because I am not English. *I think it is almost impossible for me to do anything worthwhile in this country for reasons, which you doubtless know.*[79]

Revealing the multiple displacements that Naipaul was to explore fictionally over the next decades, this letter equally expresses his sense of frustration and cultural exclusion from literary Britain, in spite of his elite education. Three years later André Deutsch would publish his first novel, locating the socio-literary currents of this historical juncture as a crucible of radical change. Published by Longman and Faber, as well as newly established presses keen to attract new voices in the context of a post-war publishing boom, Caribbean writers were reviewed to critical acclaim by leading periodicals and the mainstream press.

Their South Asian contemporaries, Markandaya and Hosain, also published their first novels in 1950s Britain, achieving quieter critical success. As we will see in the discussion of Markandaya, Chatto and Windus took a financial risk in providing a platform for many of the South Asian authors writing at this time. Correspondence shows that Harold Raymond, Cecil Day Lewis, D. J. Enright and Norah Small-wood at Chatto worked closely with their South Asian authors using a variety of means to raise their profile, and make their work palatable in an inimical climate. Due to poor sales in Britain Markandaya's and Hosain's novels had to be remaindered after a few years. In the aftermath of Britain's withdrawal from India in 1947 and Sri Lanka in 1948, there was not a wide constituency or readership for writing on India or Empire, which was no longer an immediate concern, and subsequently became a painful reminder of Britain's declining global power. There were exceptions. As the following chapter shows, Nirad Chaudhuri's laudatory account of British rule in his *Autobiography of an Unknown Indian* (1951) influenced his favourable reception in Britain, as it adjusted to its post-imperial status. Elsewhere, in the context of the new socialism

---

[79] V. S. Naipaul letter to Grenfell Williams, 14 May 1954, File R cont 1 1950–62, BBC WAC, emphasis mine.

of the post-war Labour government and the Welfare State, the working class was identified as a new and significant area on the literary map. The 1950s and early 1960s saw the rise of white working-class culture as a legitimate subject for middle-class art. Social realism was the dominant form of the novel in the 1950s employed by both Indian writers such as Anand and Markandaya, and British ones like Allan Sillitoe, John Braine, and John Wain. Wain and Kingsley Amis were also part of the anti-conservative, if not socialist, 'Movement' poets who negated the neo-romanticism championed by Tambimuttu's *Poetry London*. Some of the first post-independence South Asian poetry in English published in Britain (before the emergence of the local publishers such as the Calcutta Writers' Workshop) matches this shift. Nissim Ezekiel (1924– ) lived in London between 1948 and 1951, and published his first book of poetry *A Time of Change* (1952) with Fortune Press, which had previously published Tambimuttu's *Out of this War* (1941). As Rajeev Patke argues, Nissim Ezekiel's first five volumes, *A Time of Change, Sixty Poems* (1953), *The Third* (1960), *The Unfinished Man* (1960), *The Exact Name* (1965) were 'armed with a more hard-headed set of assumptions which corresponded to the mood reflected concurrently by poets writing in England, in which the neo-romanticism of poets like Dylan Thomas was being overtaken by poets like Philip Larkin'.[80]

Indian writer Dom Moraes' poems, on the other hand, were reminiscent of the early Spender. Bombay-born Moraes (1938–2005) went up to Oxford University in 1956. In 1957, at the age of nineteen, his collection *A Beginning* won the prestigious Hawthornden Prize, given to the best work of imaginative writing by a writer under 41. Other winners included Graham Greene and Robert Graves. Before winning, *A Beginning*, which was privately published with Parton Press, sold only 400 copies. The *TLS* review emphasised Moraes' 'formal poise' and 'supple confidence in the handling of rhythm' rather than innovative content. His contemporary at Oxford, Bengali writer Ved Mehta (1934– ), gives an evocative account of Moraes in his memoir *Up at Oxford* (John Murray, 1992) as a well-connected, 'bohemian' figure who stood out in 1950s Oxford. Like other Hawthornden Prize winners, Moraes went on to be published in the Penguin Modern Poets Series, alongside Kingsley Amis and Peter Porter in 1962. The series traditionally published British and American writers. Australian Porter,

---

[80] Rajeev Patke, 'Poetry Since Independence' in Arvind Krishna Mehrotra (ed.), *A History of Indian Literature in English* (London: Hurst and Co., 2003), 247.

Indian Moraes, and later Zulfikar Ghose (resident in Britain from 1952 to 1969 and published in Penguin Modern Poets, 25) seem to have been included partly because they had assimilated themselves into the London scene. These volumes contain no reference to their place of birth or cultural origins. However, Moraes soon began to be championed as a rare Indian writer of poetry in the context of an emerging interest in Commonwealth writing in Britain in the mid-1960s promoted by publishers, writers, and reviewers who were also readers at publishing houses.

## THE RISE OF COMMONWEALTH LITERATURE IN BRITAIN AND ITS CRITICS

The 1960s saw the development of a liberal university interest in Commonwealth Literature, coinciding with the questioning of the cultural assumptions of the imperial era. This interest was characterised by the promotion of Commonwealth Literature in higher education—particularly at the Universities of Kent and Leeds, where it was taught as a subject from the early 1960s. The interest in Commonwealth Literature sprang up as the product of particular pioneering individuals, notably the late A. Norman Jeffares, then Professor of English Literature at Leeds University (1957–74). Leeds held the first Commonwealth Literature conference in 1964, attended by Narayan and Chinua Achebe. The university housed *The Journal of Commonwealth Literature* launched in the same year. The Caribbean Artists' Movement's (1966–72) first meeting was held at the University of Kent. Partly as a result of new funding from the Labour government, this era saw several Commonwealth Literature publications (particularly of poetry, in contrast to the predominance of postcolonial fiction today),[81] readings and festivals, such as the Cardiff Commonwealth Arts Festival and 'Verse and Voice: Poems and Ballads of the Commonwealth' held at the Royal Court Theatre in London in September 1965, and broadcast on the BBC's Third Programme. *The London Magazine* devoted its September issue in 1965 to a special Commonwealth number. Such events and publications indicate the level of interest in Commonwealth Literature, particularly poetry, in mainstream cultural institutions at this juncture.

---

[81] Howard Sergeant (ed.), *Commonwealth Poems of Today* (London: John Murray, 1967). See also Gail Low's discussion of the formative role of public libraries and London-based publishers in the dissemination of Caribbean writing in 1950s London in Gail Low, 'A West Indian Literary Capital?' *Journal of Commonwealth Literature* (2002), 37, 21–38.

African and Caribbean writing was the primary focus, although *Young Commonwealth Poets' 65* contains poems from India, Pakistan, and Sri Lanka edited by Nissim Ezekiel, Zulfikar Ghose, and Patrick Fernando respectively. A number of these Asian poets, Ghose, Adil Jussawalla, Moraes, and Adrian Hussain, lived in Britain at the time.

Despite some of the fraught ideological assumptions behind the label, the emergence of 'Commonwealth Literature' as a literary subject in its own right gave these African, Caribbean, and Asian writers a category that enabled them to be anthologised and canonised in this way, marking a first vital step towards establishing a canon of postcolonial literature, a paradigm that remains in organisations such as ACLALS (Association for Commonwealth Literature and Language Studies), founded at Leeds University in 1964. The emergence of a critical apparatus to examine these texts in relation to each other, rather than against English Literature, marks a concretised shift from expectations of assimilation to European literary conventions to an acknowledgement of a diversity of cultural and literary practices. At the same time such a paradigm reinvigorated critical assumptions about an 'Indian worldview' versus an English one in the reception of South Asian Anglophone texts.[82]

The emphasis of Commonwealth Literature, however, was still on writing in English to an implied Western reader. Douglas Cleverdon's foreword to *Verse and Voice* sets the tone with his emphasis on unity in diversity by the use of the English language: 'The Festival will engender a much greater awareness of what they have in common—notably the English language itself, which is responding with its usual flexibility to new modes of expression from Africa and Asia and the West Indies.' Cleverdon brushes aside the dilemma facing Commonwealth writers 'of choosing to write in English or in a native language' at a time in which some in the newly independent colonies such as Ngugi hotly debated writing in English, considering it unpatriotic but also unhistorical. In contrasting 'older' civilisations with the 'newer', 'emergent' countries of the Commonwealth, an exclusive emphasis on the latter's contemporary Anglophone writing ignores their rich cultural heritage in indigenous languages.[83] Despite the interest in difference, the elision of universal and Western standards still persists, alongside literary commentary devoid of political context: 'Good writing is something which transcends borders whether local or national, whether of mind or spirit'

[82] Narayan, Interview with Hallam Tennyson, 4 Oct. 1961, BBC WAC.

[83] Douglas Cleverdon (ed.), *Verse and Voice: Poems and Ballads of the Commonwealth* (Commonwealth Arts Festival, 1965), 11–13.

remarks Jeffares.[84] As we will see in the discussion of Markandaya (Chapter 3), many liberal humanist critiques of colonialism written in Britain during this period remained within some of the parameters of the discourse of Commonwealth Literature, outlined here.

It was also a time of colonial reassessment. Naipaul's travels in India in 1962 recounted in *An Area of Darkness* (1964) provided an early revisionist view of Empire in the post 1960s context. (Later fictional texts such as *A Bend in the River* (1979) would thematise the colonial power's idealism of effort and monstrous postcolonial abuse, and would rationalise colonial rule more explicitly.) Naipaul's *An Area of Darkness* (1964) and Chaudhuri's controversial *The Continent of Circe* (1965) share illuminating affinities: the tendency to extrapolate cultural traits from individual examples and the emphasis on postcolonial decay, alongside the staging of their different predicaments of alienation within India. Yet Chaudhuri's even more extreme pronouncements and infamous Anglophilia meant his work was not taken as seriously as Naipaul's. As we will see in the following chapter, Chaudhuri faced some difficulty publishing *Circe*. Correspondence concerning his break with Macmillan indicates that while certain circles privately endorsed his revisionist accounts of empire, they also recognised such views were becoming marginal and unfashionable in Britain.

Naipaul began to be increasingly celebrated in Britain. His winning the Booker Prize for *In a Free State* in 1971 marked a turning point in post-war British fiction.[85] Simultaneously, Sivanandan and Rushdie, alongside, some Caribbean and India-based critics, interrogated his uncompromising representations: Nissim Ezekiel's essay 'Naipaul's India and Mine' (1965), formed an immediate rejoinder to Naipaul's *An Area of Darkness* (1964). Subsequently Ezekiel describes Markandaya's novel *Two Virgins* (1974) as 'an Indian novel for non-Indian readers. It evokes the India of their imagination even if it makes ours impatient' in an article in the *Illustrated Weekly of India* in 1975. He complains that Markandaya is 'over-conscious of her audience. A style... functions according to a formula. Descriptive passages about village habits and mores, which ought to merely fill out the crevices of a novel, become

---

[84] A. Norman Jeffares, introduction, in Cleverdon (ed.), *Verse and Voice*, p. xviii.
[85] For a discussion of the impact of literary prizes on marketing, promotion, sales, reading habits, constructions of canons, and the formation of literary identities, see Richard Todd, *Consuming Fictions: the Booker Prize and Fiction in Britain Today* (London: Bloomsbury, 1996) and Graham Huggan, *The Postcolonial Exotic: Marketing the Margins* (London: Routledge, 2001).

its very substance.' With some justification Ezekiel argues 'The writing may be as wretched as the village life, but readers in London, New York and similar places are fascinated by its exoticism.'[86] These pertinent criticisms published in India did not receive wider attention, yet Ezekiel's comments form part of an early, important critique of such South Asian Anglophone texts by local critics. Such critics contested in particular the way that Commonwealth literary critics in Britain such as William Walsh, and C. D. Narasimhaiah in India, tended to de-politicise these writings, mainly wanting to showcase Narayan and others in a universal, humanist light.

A similar transnational effort to dismantle different, but equally stereotyped views of India produced in England, emerged from a close associate of Ezekiel's, poet and critic Adil Jussawalla, resident in Britain from 1957 to 1970 before returning to India. Like Ezekiel's, his poetry was committed to revising orientalist versions of India. In the opening paragraphs of Jussawalla's introduction to *New Writing in India* (1974), he contests Cyril Connolly's preference for representations of India as a non-violent, loving, wise, erotic paradise. He cites Connolly's resistance to engage with Indian literature on its own terms because of its ' "unpronounceable names, the too numerous deities, the unfamiliar geography, the long-windedness and dullness of translations" '. Jussawalla suggests this kind of response is representative of 'the view of the liberal section of the British public to which Mr Connolly belongs'.[87] In contrast to the dominant strands of the discourse of Commonwealth Literature, Jussawalla does not naturalise the use of English and discusses writing in India's many other languages, anticipating debates and issues now entrenched in contemporary metropolitan postcolonial literary studies.

## PUBLISHING 'INDIAN WRITING IN ENGLISH' IN 1960s AND 1970s BRITAIN

By the late 1960s and early 1970s, British university courses on Commonwealth Literature, and now more specifically on 'Indian writing in English', were sufficiently established to have made an impact on the publishing of South Asian writing in Britain. Publishers looked

---

[86] Nissim Ezekiel's essay 'Naipaul's India and Mine' (1965) reprinted in Nissim Ezekiel, *Selected Prose* (Delhi: Oxford UP, 1992), 144–5.

[87] Adil Jussawalla (ed.), *New Writing in India* (Harmondsworth: Penguin, 1974), 17–19.

to the male elder writers domiciled abroad rather than to Indian women writers Markandaya and Hosain living in Britain. The Oxford University Press (OUP) archive underlines academics, and publishers' overlapping interest in Commonwealth writers during this period. OUP employees attended Commonwealth Literature conferences at Leeds University, and Leeds' lecturer Arthur Ravenscroft was the OUP reader for proposals on South Asian Anglophone texts.[88] In 1972, OUP decided to bring out a new edition of Raja Rao's collection of short stories *The Cow of the Barricades*, partly on the recommendation of Professor C. D. Narasimhaiah, at that time a visitor to Leeds University on a sabbatical from India. The impetus for this new edition, renamed *The Policeman and the Rose*, also stemmed from OUP's identification of British universities as a potential market in the early 1970s: 'The great point about Raja Rao is that he is likely to get prescribed for examinations.'[89] Originally published by OUP (India) in 1947, *The Cow of the Barricades* had in fact received little critical attention in the West: Rao's reputation had not been sufficiently established. Ravi Dayal (then at OUP, Delhi) reports that of the 2,000 copies printed in 1947, London took 94 copies, New York 29; the total exports over 23 years stopped at 146.[90] By contrast, it sold well in India where Rao's work was included in the honours and graduate courses of many Indian universities.

British schools emerged as another potential market for South Asian Anglophone writing in the 1970s. Increasing awareness of the considerable number of minority children in schools led community councils to recommend the inclusion of Asian and African writers on reading lists.[91] Heinemann followed OUP's lead, reprinting all Narayan's novels in the late 1970s. Yet such interest was short-lived. Narayan's *Ramayana* (1973) and *My Days* (1975) had to be remaindered and taken off Chatto-Hogarth's list by 1979. It was only in the late 1980s that the firm reprinted *My Days* in the context of the renewed media interest in Narayan and Indian writing in general, fuelled largely by the success of Rushdie's *Midnight's Children*.

Several publishers' commitment to publishing Commonwealth writers contributed to creating and showcasing a postcolonial canon

[88] Arthur Ravenscroft, Reader's Report, 2 Oct. 1973, OUP Archive.
[89] P. J. Chester, memo to Ron Heapy, 13 Apr. 1972, OUP Archive.
[90] Ravi Dayal, letter to Ron Heapy, 14 Apr. 1972, OUP Archive.
[91] W. Owen Cole (ed.), *Religion in Multi Faith Schools* (The Yorkshire Community Council, 1973).

to wider, more general readerships, particularly Heinemann's African Writers Series (which was started in 1964), Penguin, Peter Owen, Macmillan, and the *London Magazine*.[92] A few mainstream contemporary writing anthologies such as *Writing in England Today* (1968) included writers such as Naipaul and Achebe. The editor observed: 'The emergent cultures have provided much talent and *as far as literature is concerned Britain and her empire are now one*. British writers treat colonial themes; colonial writers like Naipaul have come to Britain and see it in new, true colours.'[93] As far as the immigrant population from the former colonies was concerned, the equation between 'empire' and Britain was less straightforward. A palpable disjunction existed between the liberal university interest in African, Caribbean, and Asian writing, and the prevailing racism directed towards people from these countries living in Britain. For these reasons Kamau Brathwaite (then Edward Brathwaite), co-founder of the Caribbean Artists' Movement, urged writers to fuse political and creative action in 1968. A writer like Markandaya, protected from racism by class privilege, was nevertheless prized for shedding light on the 'race problem', in her novel *The Nowhere Man* (1972). In many instances racism operated beyond class lines. Shiva Naipaul describes his 'initiation in the subworld of "racial prejudice"' when he came to Britain as a student and faced difficulty finding lodgings.[94] Yet at this point racism was not a major factor affecting how these particular Indian and Indo-Caribbean writers wrote.

Paradoxically, despite the dismantling of imperial ideologies in some Commonwealth writing, the 1970s saw a renewed interest in Empire literature, and nostalgia for the British Raj. In the first decade of its inception, three Eurocentric novels on the Raj won the Booker Prize: J. G. Farrell's *The Siege of Krishnapur* (1973), Ruth Prawer Jhabvala's *Heat and Dust* (1975), and Paul Scott's *Staying On* (1977). Markandaya's novel exploring the colonial encounter, *The Golden Honeycomb* (1977) received greater acclaim than many of her other novels. Perhaps this nostalgia operated within a desire for difference. This literary revival

---

[92] Peter Owen published Anita Desai's first novels *Cry the Peacock* (1963) and *Voices in the City* (1965). See also Jessica Gardner, 'Where is the postcolonial London of London Magazine?' *Kunapipi* 21.2 (1999), 93–101.

[93] Karl Miller (ed.), *Writing in England Today: the Last Fifteen Years* (Harmondsworth: Penguin, 1968), 27, emphasis mine.

[94] Shiva Naipaul, *Beyond the Dragon's Mouth: Stories and Pieces* (London: Abacus, 1988), 209.

prefigured the cult of Merchant Ivory films and documentaries on India in the 1980s.

## THE EMERGENCE OF BLACK POWER AND 'BLACK' AS A POLITICAL CATEGORY

Against a backdrop of burgeoning sexual revolution, and possibilities of social mobility and change, for many of Britain's African, Caribbean, and Asian populations, the 1960s represented the growth of joint struggles against the increasing racism facing their communities in a climate of proposed repatriation and xenophobia. Legislation labelled 'ethnic minorities' (a term adopted from the US and widely used in Britain from the 1960s to define a group of people differentiated from the rest of the community by racial origins or cultural background) a problem, fanning this hostility. This period of national anxiety over immigration to Britain resulted in three restrictive immigration acts. The first Commonwealth Immigration Bill of 1962 revoked free entry to Britain from the Commonwealth: riots occurred in the Midlands in the same year. The year 1968 saw the first expulsion of Asians from East Africa, leading Enoch Powell to make his infamous speech predicting that rivers of blood would flow if such immigrants were not repatriated: a speech that politicised minority writers such as Kureishi. During this time of heightened racial tension, the Commonwealth Immigration Act of 1968 was passed which was designed to keep out expelled Asians. The Immigration Act of 1971 made the right of dependants to join not an automatic one, and severely restricted immigration from Asian and African Commonwealth countries.

In the face of escalating racial attacks and the coalition of far right organisations into the National Front in 1967, the late 1960s was a period of heightened militancy in African, Caribbean, and Asian struggles (or as sometimes labelled at the time 'Afro-Asian'), strongly influenced by the 'Black Power' movement in the US. The Black Panthers sought to recruit African, Caribbean, and Asian activists in Britain. Stokely Carmichael and Angela Davis addressed black power meetings in London. Among its predominantly African-Caribbean members, was Indian writer Farrukh Dhondy. Arriving in Britain as a student in 1964, Dhondy joined the movement in the late 1960s. He describes this period as 'the era of black publication . . . the explosive, provocative defiant writings of George Jackson, Malcolm X, Eldridge

Cleaver, Bobby Seale and Angela Davis'.[95] He has pointed to
C. L. R. James' influential role during this era in his biography of the great
Caribbean writer.[96] Although less potent than its American counterpart, this movement politicised a range of minority activists, prompting
angry, coruscating voices. The year 1969 saw what was presented as
the first black political trial of the Mangrove 9. Dhondy's task was to
document the trial for minority readerships and the black socialist press.

The toothless Race Relations Acts of 1965 and 1968 (ineffectual
because they did not legislate against racism) reinforced minority political activists' perceptions of the inadequacy of mainstream institutions,
and the need to reshape them to present their interests. It was only
in 1976 that the Race Relations Act made it unlawful to discriminate
on the grounds of race in housing and employment. It established and
empowered the Commission for Racial Equality (CRE) to take legal
action in 1977. In 1972, a staff-led rebellion transformed the Institute
of Race Relations. Formerly a forum aimed at exploiting Third World
resources, it became the first anti-racist, anti-imperialist 'think-tank' in
Britain, with Sivanandan at the helm. In 1974 members of the Black
Panther Movement founded the Race Today Collective of African,
Caribbean, and Asian activists. Its members included Leila Hassan and
Dhondy.

During the 1960s and 1970s, many Asian activists and writers
embraced the single collective term 'black' as a political identity, a
term adopted from the Civil Rights movements in the USA. By their
involvement in these struggles against entrenched racism, older first
generation Asian and Caribbean activists Sivanandan, Tariq Ali, and
Stuart Hall also adopted the nomenclature 'black', which for them
represented a new identity. In this way the term 'black British' gained
currency in the mid-1970s, primarily, as a political signifier, although
not without ambivalence. Despite divergent traditions, certain activists
and writers from different diasporic communities supported common
political and cultural projects in relation to cultural exclusion, and the
discrimination they faced in housing, work, and education. For instance,
Hall and Dilip Hiro collaborated on BBC Radio programmes on Asian
teenagers.[97] Dhondy's prose depicted both African-Caribbean and Asian

[95] Farrukh Dhondy (ed.), *Ranters, Ravers and Rhymers: Poems by Black and Asian Poets*
(London: Collins, 1990), 13.
[96] Farrukh Dhondy, *C. L. R. James: A Life* (London: Weidenfeld and Nicolson, 2001).
[97] Dilip Hiro and Stuart Hall, *Asian Teenagers 2*, Radio 4, 28 Feb. 1968, BBC WAC.

characters. He based his novel *Siege of Babylon* (1978) on the Spaghetti House siege of 1975. During this period, diverse Asian, African, and Caribbean feminists formed anti-racist, sexist, and socialist collectives such as the Organization of Women of Asian and African Descent (1978–83) and the Southall Black Sisters (1979– ) who are in fact Asian. These groups, alongside a number of interventions from women scholars Amrit Wilson and Hazel Carby, brought feminist perspectives to the male-centred African-Caribbean dominated black politics of this era, as well as contesting Eurocentric, middle-class models of 1960s feminism.

## THE EAST AFRICAN ASIANS

Colonial administrators in Kenya in 1930 originally coined the term 'Asian'.[98] Widespread use of 'Asian' as a collective category for all sub-continentals in Britain dates from the arrival of the 'Indian' (originally from the Gujarat) communities expelled from Kenya in 1968, and subsequently from Uganda in 1972.[99] The innovative and pervasive use of 'Ugandan/Kenyan Asians' in the 1970s, moved into the space created by the offensive, informal use of 'Paki' to denote Pakistanis and anyone of South Asian descent from the mid-1960s.[100]

Although legal citizens of Britain, the Ugandan and Kenyan Asians were termed and treated as refugees, and rejected from cities, notably Leicester, where they are now celebrated as the city's most vibrant entrepreneurial population; a history retrieved in Parita Mukta's East African Asian family memoir *Shards of Memory* (2002).[101] Others became particularly active in the waves of strikes during the mid 1970s, especially at Dagenham Ford and Imperial Typewriters in

[98] Kenyan Legislative Council Debates 1930 cited in Oxford English Dictionary, online edition. Previously only 'Asiatic' as in 1929 2nd edition COD.

[99] In official discourse the term 'Asian' was first used to replace the archaic term 'Asiatic' considered offensive: thus the *Asiatic Review* was renamed as the *Asian Review* in 1953. Cited in OED, online edition. Although not generally a current term in Britain until the arrival of the East African Asians in the 1970s, individual uses of Asian occur; such as the *West Indian Gazette: African and Asian News* (1958–64) edited by Claudia Jones.

[100] OED cites the first entry in 1965 in Scotland. Entries include 'Paki-shop' and 'Paki-basher'.

[101] Parita Mukta, *Shards of Memory: Woven Lives in Four Generations* (London: Weidenfeld and Nicolson, 2002).

Leicester in 1974, and at the photo processing plant at Grunwick in North London in 1977, a particularly long-drawn-out strike led by spokesperson Jayabehn Desai. Many of the writers and commentators who revitalised British arts and cultures in the 1980s and 1990s come from this diasporic community, notably Gurinder Chadha, Jatinder Verma, Yasmin Alibhai-Brown, Pratibha Parma, and Avtar Brah.

But throughout the 1970s the 'East African Asians' were in the public eye in terms of the ensuing 'refugee crisis', which involved resettlement, the reunification of separated families, and employment. In early 1973 *The Times* reported that of the 90,000 arrivals, 70,000 refugees remained in camps, while many of those who had left camps were unemployed.[102] A group of Caribbean and East African Asian writers attempted to contest the media construction of this exiled community as 'a problem to be solved—a foreign element to be tolerated', by producing *The Ugandan Asian Anthology: Merely A Matter of Colour* in 1973:

This emphasis in our opinion was wrong. What is now needed is to allow people to present their image in their own way. The gap . . . created between the Ugandan Asians and the British public cannot be bridged merely by statistics published by the Ugandan Resettlement Board. The gap . . . will only be bridged at the grass-roots level. People to people. We hope this book is one step in that direction.[103]

The humanist appeal invoked in 'people to people', and the self-distancing from constructions of 'a foreign element' suggest the terms in which the discourse of cultural differences was debated. Here we see an attempt to contest the white-dominated media's representation of minorities that defined the period, one that is explored fictionally in Dhondy's early stories.

With excerpts from the most accomplished Anglophone writers from East Africa, notably Peter Nazareth's novel *In a Brown Mantle* (1972), and Mahmood Mamdani's novel, *From Citizen to Refugee* (1973), appearing alongside children's poems, the anthology offers poignant insights into the problems of race and exile. Mamdani's novel, based on the months he spent in a refugee camp in London, narrates the conflicts he and others experienced with the camp administrators, and 'their refusal to act as refugees: as helpless well-behaved children, totally devoid of any initiative, indiscriminately grateful for anything that may come

---

[102] Editorial, *The Times* 8 Jan. and 5 Mar. 1973.
[103] E. A. Markham and Arnold Kingston (eds.), *The Ugandan Asian Anthology: Merely a Matter of Colour* (London: Q books, 1973), 11.

their way; in other words as dependence personified'.[104] Mamdani's account directly contrasts with Shiva Naipaul's interpretation in his article based on his interviews with refugees at Plasterdown Camp that appeared simultaneously in the *Sunday Times Magazine*.[105] In this essay, Naipaul argues that British passports gave the Ugandan Asians an 'illusory sense of security and identity of being British, and hypnotised them into paralysis, when they should instead be examining their place in English Culture and what it means to be a "British Asian" '. His discussion represents an early debate about key contested, shifting terms 'English', 'British', and 'British Asian', the latter usually considered to have emerged only in the 1980s when its usage became more widespread—a debate engendered in part by the arrival of these Asian populations. Mamdani and Naipaul's contrasting representations reveal some of the conflicting perspectives and agendas amongst this undifferentiated group of 'Asians'. The differential impact of a little-known publication and Naipaul's widely circulated article underscores the uneven access to the means of representation within minority groupings in this period.

## BUILDING A COMMUNITY: COMMUNITY PUBLISHING AND JUVENILE LITERATURE

During the 1970s the immigrant communities settled: the integration of their often British born children into education and society became their shared, most pressing need, particularly when racial violence escalated in the playground as well as on the streets. Asian, African, and Caribbean parents and activists protested against the bussing of their children to schools far away to reduce the concentration of minority children in borough schools in London. During the 1970s and early 1980s, many of the minority writers trying to establish and promote a 'black' cultural movement that reflected Britain's pluralist culture, were also involved with the education of minority children. Drama critic Akua Rug founded the Black Parents Association in 1975 and the independent black education movement. Asian writers and filmmakers

[104] Mahmood Mamdani, *From Citizen to Refugee* (London: Francis Printer, 1973), 126.
[105] Shiva Naipaul, 'Passports to Dependence', *Sunday Times Magazine* (30 Dec. 1973), 228–9.

Dhondy, Debjani Chatterjee, and Parma actively engaged in these debates on minority education. Dhondy taught English in inner-city London comprehensives until he gave up teaching to pursue writing in 1982. The Race Today Collective published Leila Hassan, Dhondy, and Barbara Beese's response to the 1981 Committee of Enquiry into the Education of Children from Ethnic Minority groups.

At the same time, minority groups began facing specific problems and different cultural questions. Describing them all as black no longer felt useful, partly because the label 'black' was rooted in African-Caribbean identity. The term became the subject of more sustained questioning in the 1980s when the bureaucratic classification 'Asian' emerged as a collective, cultural term for all subcontinentals.[106] Beyond its strategic use in terms of contesting racism directed towards Asian communities, for the Indian, Pakistani, Bangladeshi, and Sri Lankan populations themselves this overarching identity meant little: from the time they arrived they established their diverse, distinct communities through places of worship, and English and bilingual community newspapers that combined international news with a special focus on the subcontinent and news of Asian communities in Britain, such as the, Hindi *Navin Weekly* (1966) and *Amar Deep* (1971), the Panjabi *Des Pardes* (1965), and Urdu *Daily Jang* (1971). During this period language theatre groups performed occasional plays by and on behalf of particular language communities in Marathi, Gujarati, and Urdu, partly as an attempt to recover threatened languages amongst communities who had come to settle. These groups did not attract mainstream funding and declined, revealing perhaps mainstream funding agencies' foremost interest in promoting assimilation at this time.

Multiculturalism emerged as an alternative to assimilation.[107] In keeping with this new agenda, Macmillan commissioned Dhondy to write his first stories. His *Come to Mecca* won the Fontana/Collins Book Prize for Multi-Ethnic Britain in 1978. This achievement and the existence of this prize indicates the recognition by mainstream publishers

[106] The first use of Asian as a British term to describe people of subcontinental descent in COD appears in the 6th edition of 1976 stating Asian (native or inhabitant frequently preferred to 'Asiatic'). The 7th edition (1982) only includes Asian signalling the term came into official and general use in this period.

[107] A definition of integration such as Roy Jenkins' 'not as a flattening process of uniformity, but cultural diversity, coupled with equal opportunity, in an atmosphere of mutual tolerance' needs to be distinguished from integration as assimilation and 'soft' forms of multiculturalism, a subject of intense debate.

and the Community Relations Council of the need to create a body of literature for and about minority children. In the same year, the ACER (African-Caribbean Educational Resource) Black Penmanship award was launched to promote young African-Caribbean writers. Similarly, Methuen commissioned Jamila Gavin to write a series of stories for children that would reflect Britain's cultural diversity in 1979. Later Ravinder Randhawa was commissioned to write *Harijan* for Bijlee, a teen series for young Asian women.

This era witnessed the development of community publishing projects across the country. School based publishing schemes provided important creative outlets for young minority children, and enabled a wider distribution of their work. Such endeavours need to be seen within the context of a wider working-class and minority writing movement that took root across the country from the early 1970s, largely due to the extremely successful Centerprise Bookshop established in Hackney in 1972 by Glenn Thompson, providing the impetus for a national writing movement. Alongside the community newspapers, these projects promoted the growth and coalescing of minority audiences and readerships, the building of regional networks, and a sense of a wider 'imagined' community across Britain. For instance, Centreprise published the anthology *Breaking the Silence*. In sometimes non-standard English, a range of young Asian women, powerfully express various responses to growing up in Britain. Some preferred to remain anonymous. Others like Diljeet were defiant: 'I cannot and will not let my family interfere in . . . my studies and career.' Parveen, on the other hand, writes 'I wish I was in India just as I was.' The impulse animating such a publication is not simply to make visible what is hidden in the dominant white culture, but to encourage dialogue, to be 'of value and interest within the community' and 'thought provoking outside of it'.[108] In seeking to generate debate within South Asian communities, this set the tone for much of the second-generation British Asian writers' work that was to follow: raising the question, 'South Asian for whom?'

An earlier publication, *Small Accidents* (1977), the autobiography of an East African Asian schoolboy Sabir Bandan, published jointly by Tulse Hill School and the Inner London Education Authority English Centre, is an example of the commitment to inclusion of certain mainstream educational institutions. At the same time, as Bandan's

---

[108] *Breaking the Silence: Writing by Asian Women* (London: Centerprise Trust, 1984), 6, 11, 1.

teacher points out, those involved in 'multi-racial' (as it was then referred to) education often wanted such texts to support their own political agendas. Bandan's criticism of African children in Uganda brought 'anguish' to such educators who suggested 'Bandan should have been directed'. Their understandable concern that 'this kind of writing can harm others' feeds into the wider privileging of the sociological function of minority literature.

His teacher goes on to identify the relative 'dearth of Asian material for use in schools' at this juncture that texts like Bandan's serve to counter. She comments 'There is far less material which supports and reflects Asian culture than for the West Indian for whom the black studies movement has raised consciousness.'[109] In the following year, 1978, ACTAL was founded to promote the teaching of Asian, African, and Caribbean and Associated Literatures, and to persuade exam boards to incorporate *all* these literatures into the curriculum. Despite this kind of unity, the shifting relativity between evolving African-Caribbean and Asian cultural forms—the way one appeared to flourish, divisively, at the expense of the other—was to persist across the decades.

## THE RISE OF ASIAN YOUTH POLITICS AND THE EMERGENCE OF URBAN THEATRE AS POLITICAL PROTEST

In the mid-1970s, Asian youth became increasingly disaffected by the rise in racially motivated attacks on their communities. The repeated assaults on Asians in Spitalfields in East London between 1976 and 1978, led to the formation of the Anti-racist Committee for the Defence of Asians in East London. Syed Manzurul Islam's comic-fantastical short stories in *The Mapmakers of Spitalfields* (1997) revisit this era. Mild brands of liberal anti-racism seemed inadequate, particularly for younger Asians with a keener sense of their rights.[110] The summer of 1976 witnessed a new phenomenon. Young Asian workers and students moved *en masse* to challenge the increasing racial attacks on Asians. By

---

[109] Carol Dix, 'Reaching a Wider Audience', *Times Education Supplement* (3 June 1977), 29.

[110] This is not to diminish the first generation's activism, for instance in factories in Preston and Southall during the 1950s.

mid 1979 young Asians were the major participants in mass movements such as the Indian Workers' Association.

The emergence of vigilante groups and demonstrations characterised this period. The murder of Gurdip Singh Chaddar in Southall in 1976 prompted huge demonstrations, while the murder of Altab Ali two years later promoted the local community of all ages to march in protest to Downing Street. Finding theatre the best medium to articulate their responses, Jatinder Verma's Tara Arts theatre company was founded in 1976 in response to the racist murder of Chaddar, kick-starting British Asian theatre. Harwant Bains' (1963– ) and Jyoti Patel's (1970– ) plays and theatre workshops, pitched to young Asians born or brought up in Britain, soon followed. The mid 1970s saw a flowering, of urban theatre groups as a form of political protest: notably, Tara Arts, Temba, and The Black Theatre Co-operative.

These kinds of response were themselves overtaken by the explosive 'black' urban uprisings in Southall in 1979, followed by those in St Paul's in Bristol in 1980, and Toxteth and Brixton in 1981, that forced the British establishment to wake up to an awareness of white British racism and to the extent to which black and Asian people were alienated. British-born Meera Syal describes the impact of watching the Southall uprising on TV as having a decisive effect on her own politicisation. For Syal it marked 'the end of our image as victims, the beginning of a new pride in ourselves'.[111] However her metaphor tends to downplay the role of the preceding generation when she writes: 'I knew for the first time I was not alone and I did belong. A whole new generation had sprung up, nurtured in the hard soil of urban Britain and not in the soft loam of their parents' Punjab, who burned with the fury of the dispossessed.'[112] Tariq Mehmood's novel *Hand on the Sun* (1983) describes the politicisation of Bradford's South Asian community during this period, together with his more direct involvement with the 1981 disturbances in Bradford: he was put on trial as one of the Bradford 12. The novel also provides a sympathetic critique of both first-generation Asian immigrants and second-generation Youth Movements' co-option by the state.

---

[111] Meera Syal, 'Influences', *New Statesman and Society* (19 Apr. 1996), 21.

[112] Meera Syal, 'PC: GLC', in Sarah Dunant (ed.), *The War of Words: The Political Correctness Debate* (London: Virago, 1994), 120. Hereafter *PC* pagination will appear in the text.

BRITAIN IN THE 1980s: THE EMERGENCE
OF 'BRITISH ASIAN' IDENTITY AND
THE VISUALISATION OF ASIAN CULTURE

The radicalisation of blacks and Asians in the inner cities (and the subsequent Scarman Enquiry and Report) was accompanied by a shift from commercial to state funding, which promoted their work on their own terms as could never have happened before, and increased minority artists' access, although unevenly, to a national literary and cultural apparatus. The work produced by this means itself helped to lay the groundwork for the broader cultural acceptance of minority writing, which enabled the mainstream commercial successes of South Asian Anglophone writing. In the final chapter we will see how the British born Asian writers both benefited from and contributed to these spaces created for minority representation: particularly the creation of Channel 4 in 1982 by Margaret Thatcher's government, with its remit for minority representation, in response to the Scarman Report. The Labour-controlled Greater London Council (GLC) and other councils had already begun to promote ethnic and sexual minorities and their demand for representation, although Thatcher in turn abolished the GLC in 1986. Naseem Khan's influential report *The Art Britain Ignores* (1976) had argued for better-structured funding for minority art in Britain, including dance. This report paved the way for the establishment of agencies promoting specifically South Asian Arts in Britain in the 1980s. Her account instigated the setting up of the Minorities' Arts Advisory Service which published *Echo*, and then the intercultural arts quarterly *Artrage*, which alongside *Bazaar* and *Eastern Eye* (founded in 1989 and published by the Ethnic Media Group) created a space for review and comment on South Asian cultural production.

The 1980s marked a watershed for Asian arts in Britain, with the emergence of the British Asian Theatre Company, the Asian Theatre Co-operative and Tamasha bringing marginalised stories to mainstream audiences. The emergence of postcolonial literary studies in British and American universities also fuelled interest in diasporic and minority writing, with intellectuals from the former colonies re-interpreting the Western cultural canon that had once represented the non-European world. As we will see in Chapter 4, the phenomenal success of Rushdie's *Midnight's Children* (1981) after it won the Booker Prize propelled

South Asian Anglophone writing into the mainstream. Asian women's writing in Britain came to the fore in the mid 1980s: a body of writing provoked by the politics of Thatcherism, was supported at first by the GLC and then by the newly established feminist publishing houses like The Women's Press who published several Asian women writers, such as Leena Dhingra's *Amritvela* (1986), Ravinder Randhawa's *A Wicked Old Woman* (1987), Suniti Namjoshi's *The Blue Donkey Fables* (1988), and later Farhana Sheik's *The Red Box* (1991). Virago re-published Attia Hosain's *Sunlight on a Broken Column* (1988), out of print for many years, along with Shashi Deshpande's *That Long Silence* (1988), published by the Calcutta Writers' Workshop, but ignored outside India. Similarly Bloodaxe Poetry helped propel young poets like Moniza Alvi to the fore and commissioned Ketaki Kushari Dyson's translations of Tagore. Lokamaya Press, set up by British Asians, published several volumes of poetry. Hanif Kureishi identifies the paradoxical nature of this decade: 'the cultural interest in marginalized and excluded groups' was 'one plus of the repressive eighties'.[113] Salman Rushdie argued that the popularity of the spate of films about the British Raj in the mid 1980s—*Gandhi* (1982), *A Passage to India* (1984), and the repopularising of the 1970s Raj novels with TV screenings of Paul Scott's *The Jewel in the Crown*, Jhabvala's *Heat and Dust*, and M. M. Kaye's *Far Pavilions* in 1984—were the 'artistic counterpart of the rise of conservative ideologies'. In an important essay of 1984 that marked his emergence as an influential political and cultural commentator from the vantage point of a borderline intellectual, Rushdie cites Thatcher's speech justifying white British fears of being 'swamped' by 'people of other cultures' made on television in 1978 as a prime example of the relation of the rise of the new conservatism to issues of race and immigration.[114] This kind of xenophobia was translated in political terms into the flurry of new anti-immigration legislation passed in the 1980s.[115] Rushdie noted that the 'continuing decline, the growing poverty and the meanness of spirit of much of Thatcherite Britain encourages many Britons to turn their eyes nostalgically to the lost

---

[113] Hanif Kureishi, *Sammy and Rosie Get Laid* (London: Faber and Faber, 1988), 63.

[114] Salman Rushdie, *Imaginary Homelands* (London: Granta, 1991), 131.

[115] The 1981 British Nationality Act removed the automatic right of all children born in the UK to be citizens. Subsequently, in 1987, the Carriers' Liability Act cut the number seeking asylum by half. In the same year, visa requirements were introduced for visitors from five Asian and African countries. Most controversial was the new bill introduced to restrict family reunion.

hour of their precedence', and that this has led to 'refurbishment of the
Empire's tarnished image'.[116] He argued that Thatcher's attempts to
revivify notions of imperial glory in the Falklands War excluded Britain's
minority populations who felt differently about the empire. This was
very different from their parents' situation, some of whom had fought
for Britain in the Second World War. In this way, the first generation
of British-born Asian writers were shaped by British 1980s' political
culture when questions of national identity and national belonging
were fraught issues. Kureishi suggests that his rough, wild early films
on contemporary London were consciously formulated against both
Raj revival 'lavish films in exotic settings' and genteel Merchant Ivory
representations of Thatcherite heritage culture evoking an image of
Englishness that encapsulated the identity only of its elite, ruling class
and nothing of the Britain he experienced.[117]

This fertile dialectic between repression and the production of resistance can be seen in the proliferation of black film collectives, such as
Sankofa, where diverse minority artists galvanised around protest against
the Tory Government's Section 28's prohibition of portrayals of gay
sexuality in Britain. By the late 1980s and during the early 1990s, however, many Asians began to contest their being subsumed in the category
'black', and to critique the 'black' anti-racist model.[118] Black British
cultural projects such as BBC2's *The Real McCoy* tended to be rooted
in African-Caribbean experiences, sidelining Asian cultural identity. At
this point, the earlier political unity in action began to fragment into its
various constituent elements, and into more particularistic conceptions
of cultural difference. The solidarity that prompted diverse African,
Caribbean, and Asian feminists to form publishing co-operatives such
as Blackwomantalk and Sheba Feminist publishers, began to founder.
In 1987 the Asian Women Writers' Collective decided not to include
the term 'black' in their organisation. The term 'Asian' was retained
because it was felt a forum for specifically Asian women writers in Britain
was necessary. Similarly, in 1988 Shivanandan Khan set up SHAKTI
(South Asian Lesbian and Gay Network) to address issues of homo-
sexuality 'specific to Britain's 1.5 million South Asian communities'.

---

[116] Rushdie, *Imaginary Homelands*, 91–2.

[117] Elyse Singer, 'Hanif Kureishi: A Londoner, But Not a Brit', in Melissa Biggs
(ed.), *In the Vernacular: Interviews at Yale with the Sculptors of Culture* (Jefferson, NC:
McFarland and Co., 1991), 109.

[118] Tariq Modood, *Not Easy Being British: Colour, Culture and Citizenship* (London:
Trentham Books Ltd., 1992), 20.

Pratibha Parma's documentary *Khush* (1991) traces an emerging South Asian diasporic queer movement in the late 1980s and early 1990s. In 1988, the Commission for Racial Equality recommended that people of South Asian origin in Britain should no longer be classified as black. (The geographical and political category 'South Asian' comes from Area Studies and International Relations. It emerged as a term in Britain fairly recently in the late 1980s, originating in the US, where 'Asian' refers to Chinese, Japanese, and Korean populations, so South Asian is used for subcontinentals because 'Asian' is not available for them.) In this context, some Asians embraced the double identity 'British Asian'. Others, particularly the British-born generation, articulated their claim to be British without qualification, in opposition to a dual identity that they felt perpetuates the idea that they are permanent foreigners, forever racialised and identified with countries they may never have seen.

Sivanandan attributed this rejection of unified notions of blackness, and shift from the politics of solidarity to ethnic pluralism, to the policies of multiculturalism, which he dismissed as the celebration of 'some pre-ordained, congealed set of artefacts, folklore' and 'the promotion of cultural separatism'. While several anti-racists and minority intellectuals criticised multiculturalist policies for paternalism, and the failure to address inequalities of power and resources, unlike Sivanandan they welcomed the disruption of the common black subject. Stuart Hall's influential essay expands upon this cultural shift delineating how the category 'black' has been destabilised by other affiliations to ethnicity, class, gender, and sexuality, particularly in the work of the British-born writers.[119]

However, as Sivanandan implies, Asian contestations of the label 'black' do indeed need to be seen in relation to an ethnicised competition for public space and resources in the subsidy battles of the late 1980s and 1990s.[120] However, the competition was also partly regional. The large numbers of Asians settled in the Midlands and north of England meant funding was diverted from London-based arts of the late 1980s, now crippled by the Tory abolition of the Greater London Council. This

---

[119] Stuart Hall, 'New Ethnicities', in Kobena Mercer (ed.), *Black Film, British Cinema* (London: Institute of Contemporary Arts, 1988), 27–31.

[120] A. Sivanandan, *Communities of Resistance: Writings on Black Struggles for Socialism* (London: Verso, 1990), 7. Tracing the causes of tensions between black and Asian communities in 2006, Kenan Malik argues that the policy of funding on ethnic lines fermented divisions between different ethnic groups. Kenan Malik, *30 Minutes: Multiculturalism*, Channel 4, 10 Feb. 2006.

led to the formation of SAMPAD, the South Asian Arts Development organisation in the Midlands, and ADITI, the national organisation for South Asian Dance. Organisations such as London's Horizon Gallery, once *the* platform for Asian visual artists in Britain, lost its funding. The politics of funding and the impact on minority arts deserves wider exploration, as Gurinder Chadha's observation implies: 'The funding game is a war of manoeuvres—and I'm constantly changing my positions.'[121] Nevertheless, state funding for theatre and TV enabled Asian artists to move into more popular cultural forms, which were also appreciated by now more diverse mainstream audiences, even while many of them were also writers in a more traditional sense.

Emerging into a cultural scene that had already been decisively altered by the presence of migrants, the British-born generation contributed to the revival of British film, poetry, and drama in the 1980s in specific ways. As far as fiction was considered, publishers favoured established first-generation migrants such as Salman Rushdie and Ben Okri until the mid 1990s when the novels of 'second-generation' writers Caryl Phillips and Hanif Kureishi, with their explorations of class, sexuality, and race in Britain, came to the fore. Writers such as these swiftly joined Rushdie as key cultural commentators. As we will explore in Chapters 4 and 5, Dhondy's and Rushdie's work forms a transformative bridge between first- and second-generation Asian writers and thus complicates any clear generational divide. If Dhondy and Rushdie anticipate Kureishi's destabilisation of dominant representations of Asians, his work in turn stimulated their own.

Dhondy's early stories and Kureishi's portrayal of a Thatcherite Uncle Nasser evicting ethnic minority tenants in his screenplay *My Beautiful Laundrette* (1986) portray the emergence of an Asian community divided on class lines. These divisions came to a head in the general election of 1979 when many middle-class Asians voted for Thatcher despite the racist ethos of her government. For their part, Dhondy and Kureishi helped to create the foundations for British Asian cinema. Their early plays, TV dramas, and films, were not just narratives of integration, but material and social practices that gave work at a time when Asian actors had limited professional opportunities. They provided exposure to some amateurs appearing in commercial performances for the first time, as well as boosting actors established in India. They

---

[121] Emma Brockes, 'Laughing all the way to the Bank', *Guardian* (19 July 2004), online edition.

were instrumental in the creation of a small pool of experienced British Asian performers who in turn went on to produce more, diverse British Asian narratives. Rita Wolf, who acted in Dhondy's *Romance, Romance* (1983) and in Kureishi's *My Beautiful Laundrette*, co-founded the Kali Theatre Company with Rukhsana Ahmad in 1989. Kureishi's *Sammy and Rosie get Laid* (1987) provided Meera Syal with her first film role. Ayub Khan-Din, who acted as Sammy, went on to write the celebrated play and film *East is East* (1999). This move into popular media suggests the extent to which British Asian writers began to redefine British mainstream culture, and raised the profile of Asians in Britain. Such a move was made possible, in part, by the specific socio-political and economic conditions that influenced the creation, dissemination, and reception of minority cultural forms in Britain in the 1980s and 1990s.

## THE 1990s AND BEYOND: MOVING CENTRE STAGE; IS BROWN THE NEW BLACK?

During the 1990s the international success of writing by Salman Rushdie, Vikram Seth, and Rohinton Mistry among others, spawned more and more talented writers, and fuelled interest in lesser known British-based South Asian writers, such as Sunetra Gupta and Romesh Gunesekera whose novel *Reef* was short listed for the Booker Prize in 1994. These writings, augmented by the phenomenal talent of Arundhati Roy, who also received a legendary advance for her first book from HarperCollins and went on to win the Booker Prize in 1998, led critics to claim that 'The future of English Literature is Indian'. In time this success would even produce a backlash against South Asian Anglophone writing in relation to the Booker Prize. Despite these successes, the interest in Asian writing remains confined to Anglophone writing. The British reading public still resist translated literature, which even today forms only 4 per cent of literature published in Britain, in sharp contrast to other European countries. Any translated literature tends to be from European languages, together with Spanish writing from South America. In order to 'dispel this narrow perspective and place modern Asian writing within the broad spectrum of contemporary world literature', and to build on its success with its African Writers Series, in 1993 Heinemann launched a new Asian Writers Series intended to introduce English language readers to translations of novels from

Indian languages.[122] The series, edited by Ranjana Ash, who had long emphasised the Anglocentric nature of interest in South Asian writing, produced six novels translated from Bengali, Hindi, Malayalam, Tamil, and Urdu including Tagore's *Quartet* and Ishmat Chughtai's *The Crooked Line*. The series was much publicised and received Arts Council funding. It also benefited from a new interest in literary awards for translated works, such as the *Independent*'s Foreign Fiction Awards and Prize for translation. However the initial interest was short-lived and by 1995 sales had dipped. In 1996 the Heinemann Asian Writers Series in the UK was taken over by Heinemann Inc. in the US. The initial focus on South Asian writing was now replaced by South East Asian writing, given the market for such literatures in the context of large populations of South East Asians in North America. India has differentially resisted metropolitan dominance with the emergence of Ravi Dayal's publishing house Penguin India, Rupa, and IndianInk producing affordable fiction in English for local readers. Within Britain, small publishers and distributors Lokomaya, Sangam, and Mantra nurtured minority writing. More recently Serpent's Tail, Peepal Tree Press, Redbeck Press continue their efforts. Aamer Hussein writes to audiences in Pakistan and Britain in his works published by Saqi Books.

In the aftermath of the Rushdie Affair (1989) and the Gulf War (1991), the 1990s ushered in an era of religious revivalism, and the emergence and racialisation of 'British Muslim' identities, that prefigured the more intense scrutiny of Muslim identity as a result of 9/11 and the London bombings of 7 July 2005. As Tariq Modood suggests, from the early 1990s Britain's shifting racialised boundaries had begun to include certain culturally assimilated South Asian and African-Caribbean (middle-class) values, but continued to exclude culturally 'different' Asians, Arabs, and non-white Muslims.[123] Britain's South Asian Muslims, particularly its Pakistani and Bangladeshi communities, continue to be the most alienated, socially deprived, and racially harassed group. South Asian identity is now increasingly rooted in religion rather than culture, in part as a bid by Hindus and Sikhs to be differentiated from racialised Muslim identities. At the same time this shift has meant that distinct identities and intricacies in the

[122] Ranjana Ash, address, launch of the Asian Writers Series at the Asian Literature in Translation Conference, Commonwealth Institute, 19 Nov. 1993.
[123] Tariq Modood, '"Difference", Cultural Racism and Anti-Racism', in Pnina Werbner and Tariq Modood (eds.), *Debating Cultural Hybridity: Multi-Cultural Identities and the Politics of Anti-Racism* (London: Zed Books, 1997), 164.

previously homogenised 'Asian community' have begun to be explored creatively. Similarly, simple generational divides between traditional first-generation South Asians and their acculturated children are no longer tenable, with some young Muslims becoming increasingly more conservative than their parents, as Kureishi captured strikingly in his screenplay *My Son the Fanatic* (1997). The varied responses to Monica Ali's portrayal of the predominantly Sylheti community in her novel *Brick Lane* (2003) testify to the inadequacy of monolithic constructs of 'British Bengali' or 'Bangladeshi', and the presumption of representation that continues to haunt this latest symbol of twenty-first century multicultural Britain.

The last decade has witnessed the seismic ascent of British Asian cultural forms in popular culture. Music provides the key catalyst in developing cultural identity and visibility for British Asian youth from Bhangra in the mid 1980s, the initially 'underground' music scene, Nitin Sawhney, Talvin Singh, Taz, Cornershop to Bobby Friction and Nihal's prime-time show on national radio showcasing British Asian music. [124] The phenomenal success of *Goodness Gracious Me* in 1998, a satirical exploration of racial stereotypes in Britain, created a new genre of 'Asian comedy', instigating the inclusion of 'chuddies' (underpants) in the OED. The pioneering format of the Bafta-nominated spoof chat show *The Kumars at No 42* (2001– ) spawned localised versions of 'customised Kumars' sold to American and Australian networks. These diverse artists can be described in Paul Gilroy's words as 'celebrants of the ordinary multi-culturalism that distinguishes' Britain and mark its 'conspicuous gains'.[125]

The recent impact of transnational Bollywood cultural forms led to the surprising alliance of conservative Andrew Lloyd Webber, Shekhar Kapur, and Meera Syal in the West End musical *Bombay Dreams* that opened in London in 2002 before transferring to Broadway. This hugely profitable £4.5 million extravaganza created a new market of Asian audiences for the waning British musical. Far from being a commercial liability, British Asian writing has shown itself far more successful in popular rather than literary culture, as for example is demonstrated by the global success of *Bend it Like Beckham* (2002)

---

[124] See S. Sharma, J. Hutnyk, and A. Sharma (eds.), *Dis-orienting Rhythms: the Politics of New Asian Dance Music* (London: Zed Books, 1996).

[125] Paul Gilroy, *After Empire: Melancholia or Convivial Culture* (London: Routledge, 2004), p. xi.

grossing over $75 million, the most successful of a series of British Asian films marketed as mainstream comedy not art-house viewing, over the last decade. The commissioning of formulaic Asian teen novels *Chapatti or Chips* by Nisha Minhas is another example of this trend. Like their precursors, these younger writers feed market-driven demands: today the heightened interest in Asian culture and British Asian lives. In contrast to their forerunners who received critical but not commercial success, some of these profitable enterprises received a mixed critical reception. Syal's least acclaimed script *Bombay Dreams* propelled her into the super-league and contributed to her nomination as the second most influential Asian in the British media. The backing of these projects—Lloyd Webber's invitation to write a treatment, and in effect to meet the craze for all things Bollywood—suggests how questions of literary fashion, commodification, and co-option persist today, and qualifies the extent to which these contemporary artists make projects on their own terms. For example, unable to find backers for cutting-edge, realist documentaries, Chadha 'set out to make the most commercial film I can' with the formulaic *Bend it Like Beckham*; its unprecedented box-office success made her one of Britain's most successful female directors, enabling her to direct a £2 million Bollywood-style musical *Bride and Prejudice*.[126] While British Asian cultural production becomes increasingly mainstream, the popularity of satellite Asian networks and the international turn taken by contemporary Bollywood has seen some British Asian viewers move from a BBC and Channel 4 that does not reflect their interests to specialist international TV stations. Others argue that minority programming is outdated.

Over the last decade British Asian writers, notably Kureishi, have justifiably begun to refuse to speak only to minority interests, and have begun to contest particularly the requirement to discuss race imposed by both ends of the political spectrum. Kureishi has asserted his right to comment on wider British society, now focusing on contemporary mores and modern urban experiences and relationships. Some younger British fiction writers of Asian origin reflect this trend in a defiant rejection of ethnic pigeonholing, and a bid to secure more mainstream readerships: Bidisha Bandyopadhya's tale of white middle-class men in London's media world, *Seahorses* (1997) is one instance.

---

126  Brockes, 'Laughing all the way to the Bank'.

On the other hand, writers like Syal, have refuted this trajectory of effacement. Equally concerned to comment on and speak to wider society, Syal thematises the role of her cultural heritage as a creative resource, particularly in her novel *Life Isn't All Ha Ha, Hee Hee* which was recently dramatised into a primetime TV drama. Syal claims the high numbers of Asian viewers of *Goodness Gracious Me* identified an audience for whom the communal references resonated, in contrast to her mainly white audience's 'warm, puzzled' response to her early stand-up comedy during the 1980s. At the same time, it was *Goodness Gracious Me*'s widespread appeal to the white majority that ensured its success. Yet it also eroded preconceptions of what 'crossed over', and how much culturally specific humour mainstream audiences could share and enjoy. Most importantly, it now did not matter if the predominantly white audience did not immediately understand all the cultural references. In this way, the popular success of Asian writers challenges definitions of mainstream success. In contrast to predictions of assimilation (on the assumption perhaps that as these populations become increasingly integrated, the generational conflicts that fuel these narratives may decrease in intensity with each generation), stories such as Pakistan-born Nadeem Aslam's dramatic and moving portrayal of Muslim life in an unnamed English town in *Map for Lost Lovers* (2004) suggest that the complexities of multicultural Britain continue to be fertile ground for novelists. Many second- and third-generation novelists, dramatists (Indu Rubaisingham, Tanika Gupta, Ash Kotak), and filmmakers (Asif Kapadia) continue to straddle two or more cultures and foreground bilingual and bi-cultural experiences and a cross-cultural conduct that is not necessarily Westernisation.

# 2

# Self-translation as Self-promotion:

## I: Nirad C. Chaudhuri

Though recent historians have pointed to the increasing stream of black and Asian visitors and settlers throughout the nineteenth century, it remains the case that during the pre- and immediate post-war period, literary London considered 'Asiatic' writers from the colonies as exotic outsiders, solitary figures, and objects of curiosity. Perceived as native informants who could tell the secrets of their native culture, this generation's burden was to embody foreignness, to describe the colonies, and provide 'alien' perspectives on British culture, largely, though not exclusively, for the majority population. Different writers in various ways negotiated this role, created by the dominant culture. Such identification heightens notions of cultural ambassadorship in the processes of cultural translation, particularly in the reception accorded to this generation in Britain. The blurb on the first edition of Aubrey Menen's first novel *The Prevalence of Witches* (1947), for example, presents the Indo-Irish author as an informed mediator between two widely divergent, incompatible cultures, and accentuates the anthropological, referential content of his fictional text: 'The author puts to good use his first hand knowledge of India. *The Prevalence of Witches* is in some ways a novel of fantasy; but it is firmly tied to real human beings, and throws a sharp light on the gulf between European and Oriental morality and ways of thinking.'

A reviewer suggested that 'among Menen's strong qualities is an insight into the primitive mind'.[1] Menen, who worked in India for several years, but was born and educated in England, wryly distanced

---

[1] Maurice Lane Richardson, 'Review of *The Prevalence of Witches*: Tribal Affairs', *Times Literary Supplement* (6 Dec. 1947), 625.

himself from such a construction in private correspondence to his publishers, Chatto and Windus:

On the whole, I prefer not to be called 'Indian'. I am *not Indian*; I don't speak a word of any Indian language (except achcha). I am not Hindu or Muslim and I don't kill people who are [he converted to Catholicism in 1949]. I am by birth, language and inclinations English, in fact so English that I do not like embarrassing other Englishmen by saying so.

Menen was well aware of European predilections for stereotyped versions of India. With reference to publicity for the forthcoming book, he wrote in the same letter: 'journalists will be disappointed if you don't assure them that I write my books sitting on a bed of nails.'[2] *The Prevalence of Witches* satirises such attitudes in its depiction of the Governor of Limbo, who instructs the native community to create specifically crude drawings in order to establish a trade in primitive artefacts. Alongside this savouring of 'otherness', reviews and reports reveal a simultaneous relishing of the spectacle of assimilation apparent in other texts. Anglicised Asian writers' familiarity with Western culture proved a particular source of incredulous fascination and gratification for some British consumers; as a reader's report on Chaudhuri's impressionistic travelogue of his first visit to Britain in 1955 suggests: 'There are passages [in *A Passage to England*] showing a greater awareness of the English character and the English past, as well as the English landscape, than I have ever encountered in any book by any foreigner, let alone an Asiatic.'[3]

Exploring the processes of cultural translation, and the ideological construction of cultural difference within the contexts of the literary production and consumption of South Asian writing during the 1940s and 1950s, this chapter focuses on the contrasting modes of assimilative and 'foreignising' self-translation, reproduced respectively in the writings of self-Westernised Chaudhuri (1897–1999), and M. J. Tambimuttu (1915–83), who reinvented his 'Asian' cultural identity after coming to Britain in 1938. The notion of *self*-translation is particularly relevant for this generation, whose persona and writings are so closely intertwined, particularly in the minds of their first readers, and whose colonial experiences are defined through the processes of being translated and hybridised. Both writers' self-Westernisation testifies to

---

[2] Menen, letter to Peter Cochcrane, 16 Oct. 1947, File Aubrey Menen, 1947–8, Chatto and Windus Archive.
[3] J. C. Squire, Reader's Report on *A Passage to England*, undated, Macmillan Archive.

the colonialist interpellation of the indigenous elite, an outcome of a colonial education and values that are imposed but also 'chosen' to some extent. Tambimuttu's later 'false' self-transformation from a 'brown Englishman' to an Eastern mystic represents a different kind of self-translation and assimilation.

Listlessly occupied in colonial Sri Lanka as a poet, Tambimuttu seized an opportunity to come to Britain when a relative offered to pay for his fare in 1938. On arrival, Tambimuttu soon established himself in the literary and artistic circles of London's Soho and Fitzrovia. Within two years, at the age of 23, he founded *Poetry London* (1939–51) with Anthony Dickins. Originally launching the poetry magazine on money raised by subscriptions, Tambimuttu eventually secured the financial backing of publisher Nicholson and Watson. He edited the first fourteen numbers of *Poetry London* as well as a number of books (an anthology of poems, *Poetry in Wartime* (1942), commissioned by T. S. Eliot, together with *Out of this War* (1941) and *Natarajah: a Poem for Mr. T. S. Eliot's Birthday* (1948)), while participating in the BBC Overseas Service to India during and after the Second World War.[4] In 1952 Tambimuttu moved to New York with his second wife Safia Tyabjee, where he published semi-autobiographical short stories in *The Reporter* and the *New Yorker,* and the long poem *Gita Sarasvati.* In 1954 he co-translated and edited a collection called *India Love Poems* illustrated by John Piper, and began the short-lived *Poetry London–New York* (1956–60). Tambimuttu returned to Britain in 1968. His final reworking of *Poetry London, Poetry London/Apple Magazine,* had a first issue in 1979, and a second in 1982. He died in 1983.

In contrast to Tambimuttu's cosmopolitan career, Nirad Chaudhuri published his memoirs, *The Autobiography of an Unknown Indian* (1951), with Macmillan while he was living in Delhi, working as a political and military commentator for All India Radio. His best-known and finest achievement evokes in loving, intense detail 'the conditions in which an Indian grew to manhood in the early decades of the twentieth century'.[5] Chaudhuri devotes a chapter to each of the four environments that had the greatest influence on him: his birthplace Kishorganj, his ancestral village Bangram, his mother's village Kalikutch, and 'imagined'

---

[4] The full publication details of the texts of the selected writers will be given with the first citation of the text.

[5] Nirad C. Chaudhuri, *The Autobiography of an Unknown Indian* [1951] (Bombay: Jaico Publishing House, 1997), preface. Hereafter *Autobiography* pagination will appear in the text.

England. The *Autobiography* concludes with a consideration of Calcutta and the Indian Renaissance, advancing Chaudhuri's critique of the early nationalist movement and contrasting his experience of the arrogance of colonial Englishmen with his idealised conceptions of English civilisation, for him 'the greatest civilisation on earth'.[6] Chaudhuri did not actually visit Britain until he was 57, when he came under the sponsorship of the BBC. He moved to England in 1970 (originally, to research Max Müller's papers at the Bodleian Library) at the age of 73. He and his wife eventually settled in Oxford, where they spent the rest of their lives. His prolific writing career includes two biographies, the second volume of his autobiography, *Thy Hand, Great Anarch! India: 1921–57* (1987) that tells of his experiences as a student of history in Calcutta, and as a secretary to Congress leader Sarat Chandra Bose, and several books on Indian culture and national history, all suffused with his personal history. He writes as a witness to the 'decline' of Bengal as a force in Indian culture and politics, which he regards as matched by the failure of British imperialists to bequeath a lasting cultural legacy in India. Chaudhuri wrote his last book *Three Horsemen of the New Apocalypse* (1997) when he was 100 years old.

At first sight, Chaudhuri and Tambimuttu are not obviously comparable in terms of age, individual cultural background, or formative influences. This chapter seeks to make visible a hidden series of connections between these fascinating figures who published their work in Britain and North America contemporaneously. Their literary careers span periods of colonial rule, the Second World War, independence, the Cold War and the advent of multicultural Britain, and at all points illustrate their times. Both writers share an undeniable elitism, a patriarchal, anti-national cosmopolitanism and Eurocentric universalism, in sharp contrast to their more radical Asian, Caribbean and African contemporaries, such as Anand or C. L. R. James. At the same time, their different responses to their historical conditions, dissimilar experiences of alienation within their natal culture, contrasting modes of self-translation and distinct reception in Britain, suggest more diverse realities.

Tracing the different trajectories of Chaudhur's and Tambimuttu's literary careers as cultural translators and specular border intellectuals over time reveals shifting constructions of migrant identity and perceptions of cultural difference. Tambimuttu's chameleon-like self-translation tended to mirror the desire for exotic 'otherness' amongst

[6] Nirad C. Chaudhuri, interview, *Everyman*, 26 June 1983, 7, BBC WAC.

the counter-cultural circles of liberal aesthetes that he entered on his arrival in Britain (1938–49), and then in the US (1952–68). He self-consciously manipulated the prevailing orientalist discourses of cultural difference amongst his various immediate social contexts at different historical junctures.[7] In contrast, Chaudhuri's self-Westernisation remained static and fossilised throughout his long career. At first, Chaudhuri's negative views of post-Independence India in his *Auto-biography*, and his effusive praise and intense delight at the continued existence of 'Timeless England' in *A Passage to England*, found favour amongst his conservative publishers, journalists, and readers in Britain. A reader's report on *A Passage to England* recommends publication of this 'extraordinary story' of Chaudhuri's visit 'where he found what he had been absorbing for half a century was a reality'. According to the reader, this visit fortuitously enabled Chaudhuri 'to overcome his doubt that we had really weathered the storms of the last generation and were still capable of enough national energy to continue developing in the present the brilliant civilisation which he admitted in our past'.[8] His self-Westernisation played an important role in his initial acclaim in Britain in the 1950s. A letter he received from his hosts after his visit in 1955 suggests that his Anglicisation and desire to assimilate made him popular and non-threatening, and reveals his circle's particular attitudes towards 'coloured' immigrants during this era. The letter reads: 'Everyone was pleased to have met you, especially as you fell in with all our habits and customs as if you had lived among us for years.'[9] However, in clinging to obsolete notions of 'Englishness' and subscribing to largely discredited imperial ideas, Chaudhuri increasingly became an anachronism. He continued to reproduce outdated colonial ideologies throughout his long lifetime, in ways that were critical of what he perceived as an unsatisfactory, decadent present. In this sense his dislocation was quite extreme and possibly unique. The comparison between the two writers reveals that paradoxically, despite the extent to which Chaudhuri was self-colonised, he was a far more isolated figure than Tambimuttu, and

---

[7] The parallels between Tambimuttu and the reception of his literary predecessor Sake Dean Mahomet (1749/59–1851) underline the resilience of this desire for difference across the centuries.

[8] B. W. Swithunbank, Reader's Report on *A Passage to England*, Macmillan Archive, undated.

[9] Cited in Nirad C. Chaudhuri, *A Passage to England* [1959] (Delhi: Orient Paperbacks, 1971), 119. Hereafter *Passage* pagination will be given in the main body of the text.

never actually assimilated in Britain. Perhaps this is to be expected given his advanced age at the time he settled in England in 1970. Paradoxically, Tambimuttu's literal and metaphorical self-fashioning as an 'Asian' allowed him to engage with, and be absorbed into his new local environments in London and New York to a far greater extent than Chaudhuri: he altered in response to changing expectations of cultural difference of different eras, whereas Chaudhuri did not.

Throughout this book we will see that this paradox continues to inhabit migrant and minority identities, in terms of the formations of 'foreignising' and 'domesticating' cultural translation that emerge in the works of affiliated writers later in the century, such as Kamala Markandaya, whose work is discussed in the next chapter. The distinct responses that Chaudhuri and Tambimuttu evoked amongst their individual reading constituencies undo monolithic representations of 'the host community', show that 'dominant' expectations can be complex, and furthermore complicate totalising conceptions of the metropolitan centre as a stable and universal phenomenon by disclosing the centre as internally variegated and ideologically nuanced, as well as temporally differentiated. These authors brought global perspectives to bear on their perceptions of England that were shaped by the forces of Empire and colonisation, by metropolitan centres and social peripheries. Examining the way their contributions to a cosmopolitan literary landscape were co-opted into the overarching political agendas of Britain and North America at different historical moments, allows the development of a notion of consumption as a different form of cultural translation.

The writers under discussion reflect the complexities, contradictions, and ironies of colonial and postcolonial situations, as products of the tensions arising out of historical circumstances and political actions. These conflicts create interesting aesthetic choices and ethical challenges. This is particularly true for Chaudhuri, as well as for the younger Indo-Caribbean author V. S. Naipaul who was writing contemporaneously in the 1950s and 1960s, and whose writings bear a complex dialogic relationship to Chaudhuri's. Born in East Bengal, Chaudhuri wrote in Bengali for some years, and only later (encouraged by his English teacher) in English. He published a monograph on the organisation of the Indian army (*Defence of India*, 1935) before writing his autobiography at the age of 54. Naipaul's earliest encounters with the English language were filtered through the Creole patois of his father's Caribbean English. To a greater extent than Tambimuttu who spoke only English, both Chaudhuri and Naipaul stand, in a sense, at a certain distance from the language they chose for their imaginative explorations and intimate medium of expression.


## MODES OF SELF-TRANSLATION: VOLUNTARY AFFILIATION

From an early age, Chaudhuri embarked upon an active process of self-Westernisation, exemplifying the process of affiliation in an extreme form: identification through culture, where the colonised replace filiative (that is, by descent) connections to indigenous cultural traditions, with affiliations to the social and political culture of the colonising power. Although Chaudhuri grew up in a Bengali-speaking household, he read English and French literature and philosophy extensively (including Shakespeare, Pascal, and Racine) in order to emulate and become part of his idealised conception of English civilisation, which he defined as 'an accumulation of products of the intellect and ways of behaving'.[10] In Frantz Fanon's words, Chaudhuri typifies the colonised who wants to be white, who 'will be proportionately whiter—that is, he will come closer to being a real human being—in direct ratio to his mastery of the [coloniser's] language'.[11] Yet, Chaudhuri was painfully aware of the limits of his self-translation. He constantly sought to compensate for the absence of 'blood ties' that the white inhabitants of the settler colonies could lay claim to (*Passage* 22).[12] Chaudhuri reinforces Macaulay's paradigm where knowledge of literature and language is a privileged means of affiliation, whilst simultaneously underscoring an unbridgeable gulf.[13] In the absence of 'blood ties' he argues that only a cerebral interest in English culture and fluency in the language can validate a non-English person's claim to 'their share in English greatness': 'The only ties felt in the heart that we can have with England are those created by things of the mind' (*Passage* 22).[14] It is no

---

[10]  Nirad C. Chaudhuri, *Everyman*, 1983, 7.

[11]  Frantz Fanon, *Black Skin, White Masks* [1952], trans. Charles Lam Markmann (London: Pluto Press, 1986), 18.

[12]  Chaudhuri was not unique in seeing Standard English as the preserve of the native English. Attia Hosain observes that she 'grew up with the English language but not the culture behind it. Not bred in one's bones, one missed certain subtleties' in *Writing in a Foreign Tongue*, Third Programme, 8 May 1956, BBC WAC.

[13]  G. M. Young (ed.), *Macaulay: Prose and Poetry* (London: Hart-Davis, 1952), 722.

[14]  See also Chaudhuri, 'Why I Mourn for England', *Daily Telegraph* (20 Feb. 1988), 1.

coincidence that Chaudhuri admired, and later wrote the biography of, Max Müller—entitled *Scholar Extraordinary: The Life of Professor the Rt. Hon. Friedrich Max Müller* (1974)—a German by birth, who, like Chaudhuri, later consciously adopted English cultural norms and the English language as his medium of expression.

In the absence of connections by descent, Chaudhuri's fluency in English led him to claim what Fanon has called an 'honorary citizenship' in lieu of the citizenship the British Empire 'withheld', when it only 'conferred. . . subjecthood' (*Autobiography* 171).[15] Chaudhuri follows Macaulay in projecting what he perceives as the liberal or progressive ideologies of England's native speakers onto the English language. He discusses the 'impact of English Literature on the mental make-up of Indians', suggesting that 'it revolutionised the Bengali peoples' relationship to God, and the relations between men and women in India'. He identifies the English language as the medium through which he and others were transformed:

We could not write in English without changing mentally. . . . the Indian mind had become dependent on the English language for all its highest functioning. . . .

In fact, there was no subject on which the human mind could dwell at any level above the practical tasks of life. . . about which we did not think and feel differently under the impact of English.[16]

This passage suggests the influence of ideas derived from Victorian linguistic theories (which claimed that the languages of a 'primitive' society showed a corresponding lack of sophistication) on Chaudhuri.[17] As a product of late Victorian intellectual culture himself, Chaudhuri describes imperialism in terms of a social Darwinism: 'The historical process [of Empire] was only the continuation of a biological process, through which from age to age, new classes and orders of animals have emerged. . . dominating the earth in succession.' (*Thy hand* 776)

Chaudhuri's own language symbolises his self-translation. His ornate English is distinctly formal, late Victorian: words such as 'larceny', 'mendacity' and 'besmirched' abound in his prose. The style is almost neo-classical with long balanced sentences and a masculine tone. He uses archaic, colloquial terms resonant of those used by an upper-class

15 Fanon, *Black Skin*, 38.
16 Nirad C. Chaudhuri, 'Opening Address', in Maggie Butcher (ed.), *The Eye of the Beholder: Indian Writing in English* (London: Commonwealth Institute, 1983), 10, 16.
17 George Stocking, *Victorian Anthropology* (New York: The Free Press, 1987).

elite: 'not a whit', 'bragging fellow', 'pilfering', or 'Acquired a violent prejudice against Muslims and wanted them to get a *licking everywhere*' (*Autobiography* 124). Colloquialisms are important 'touchstones of intimacy with English', but these terms give his work an anachronistic feel.[18] As Sara Suleri writes of Naipaul, it is perhaps the 'anguish of affiliation [that] dictates the grimly perfect grammar' of Chaudhuri's work.[19] Ironically, this apparent polish is the only feature that suggests Chaudhuri is not an English author.

Chaudhuri's 'anguish of affiliation' over his command of an English that was his second language, was partly a response to the demands of the publishing market and not simply a consequence of his internalisation of inferiority. He perceived it to be imperative to conform to the norms of the native speakers born to the language. He recalls:

... an acute anxiety troubled me when I was writing my first book, *The Autobiography of an Unknown Indian*, in 1947 and 1948. I asked myself whether what I was writing would sound like English to *those who were born to the language*. I knew, unless it did, no English publisher would accept my book.[20]

His anxiety was not unfounded: he had to prove his mastery of English.[21] His own publisher at Macmillan marvelled at Chaudhuri's 'freedom, amplitude, and allusiveness' in a language 'which is not, in the ordinary sense, your own'.[22] It was only to be later Asian writers whose facility in English was not in question who were in a position to abrogate Standard English.

In Chaudhuri's work the former coloniser's tongue is not used as an arena for confrontation or resistance. There is no attempt to challenge the competence of metropolitan readers. His texts are replete with untranslated Latin and French quotations, but there are no untranslated Bengali words, which reflects the subordinate position it occupies in the

---

[18] Arjuna Parakrama, *De-Hegemonizing Language Standards: Learning from (Post)-Colonial Englishes about 'English'* (Basingstoke: Macmillan, 1995), 98.

[19] Sara Suleri, *The Rhetoric of English India* (Chicago: Chicago UP, 1992), 149.

[20] Nirad C. Chaudhuri, 'My Hundreth Year', in Ian Jack (ed.), *Granta 57 India! The Golden Jubilee* (London: Granta, 1997), 208, emphasis mine.

[21] As Meenakshi Mukherjee observes, 'For a long time "Indian English" used to be a term of disapprobation, implying an insecure grip on English idiom or an infelicitous use of English vocabulary.' Meenakshi Mukherjee, *The Twice Born Fiction: Themes and Techniques of the Indian Novel in English* (Delhi: Heinemann, 1971), 170.

[22] See Thomas Mark's letter to Chaudhuri cited in Nirad C. Chaudhuri, *Thy Hand, Great Anarch! India, 1921–52* (London: Hogarth Press, 1987), 903. Hereafter *TH* pagination will appear in the text.

language hierarchy. Chaudhuri does not try to inscribe difference onto Standard English, or to formalise the cross-cultural character of the linguistic medium, unlike subsequent postcolonial writers whose language variance is a privileged metonymic figure for their cultural difference.[23] In contrast to the emphasis on cultural and linguistic hybridity in later writers, above all Rushdie, Chaudhuri insists on the absence of a cultural nexus between English and Bengali language and culture, even though he himself embodies their cultural synthesis: 'The . . . bilingual . . . writer has to forget that he knows the other language when he is writing in one. . . . English and Bengali stand in utterly different worlds, not only as languages, but also as embodiments of the mind.'[24] Postcolonial theorists have stressed untranslatability as a positive quality for minority cultures and languages.[25] This is very different from Chaudhuri's emphasis on untranslatability, which is based on an essential difference that must be held apart because the secondary language can never aspire to the status of the first. Chaudhuri writes that he is grateful that as a child his father never allowed him 'to translate . . . Bengali passages into slipshod English smacking of Bengali' (*Autobiography* 173). He never allowed translations of his works into English or Bengali and critiqued attempts to translate Tagore's poetry.[26] Chaudhuri's desire to separate his English and Bengali identities suggests his internalisation of the idea of the inferiority of Bengali culture. As Albert Memmi observes, 'colonial bilingualism cannot be compared to just any linguistic dualism . . . but actually means participation in two psychical and cultural realms . . . in conflict. The colonized's mother tongue . . . which holds the greatest emotional impact, is precisely the one which is the least valued.'[27] Just as Chaudhuri feels there should be no linguistic contamination in the writing of the bilingual writer, he rejects all models of integration based on hybridised mixtures, and instead promotes assimilation into the

---

[23] Bill Ashcroft, Gareth Griffiths, and Helen Tiffin, *The Empire Writes Back: Theory and Practice in Post-Colonial Literatures* (London: Routledge, 1989), 53.

[24] Nirad C. Chaudhuri, 'Why I Write in English', *Kunapipi* 3.1 (1981) 2.

[25] Bhabha argues that global 'border culture' or diaspora makes translation in the traditional sense impossible because cultures are always already mixed, and at the same time make it a crucial, undeniable part of life. 'How Newness enters the World: Postmodern Space, Postcolonial Times and the Trials of Cultural Translation' in *The Location of Culture*, 212–35. See also Gayatri Chakravorty Spivak, *Outside in the Teaching Machine* (London: Routledge, 1993), 191.

[26] Nirad C. Chaudhuri, 'Tagore the True and the False', *Times Literary Supplement* (27 Sept. 1974) 1029–31.

[27] Albert Memmi, *The Colonizer and the Colonized*, trans. Howard Greenfield (London: Earthscan Publications, 1990), 173.

host culture. In a personal interview in 1997, given after twenty-seven years in England, he complained that 'the problem with Indians in this country is that none of them have assimilated'.[28]

## CONDITIONS OF EXILE VERSUS MIGRANCY

Chaudhuri's own immersion in late Victorian intellectual culture shows how he (like others of his generation of 'educated' writers) was conditioned by the imported culture from the centre, long before visiting or choosing to settle in England, suggesting a distinction between metaphoric and physical exile. Chaudhuri claims that his sense of metaphorical, internal exile led to his literal exile, although both he and Tambimuttu are better described as expatriates who chose to live abroad.[29] For culturally colonised 'natives' such as Chaudhuri and Tambimuttu, the sense of dislocation or separation from the native place is not a result of physically crossing the border from one national group to another, but of motivated, voluntary affiliation. It was Chaudhuri's liberal Hindu parents who initiated the major severance from native values, abandoning the extended family and traditional religious rituals, to set up a nuclear family in a new town where his father practised law in English. Following his parents' lead, Chaudhuri distanced himself from what he perceived as the 'native', 'barbaric' elements of Hinduism, adopting the 'Christianised' monotheistic Brahmoism characterised by the ethical demands and values of the Low Church Protestantism of Victorian England to which his parents adhered. Influenced by the Bengali-dominated Brahmo 'reform' movement that sought to purge Hinduism of 'medieval' practices such as an idol-focused ritual pantheon, this group saw British rule as a deliverance from Muslim tyranny.[30] Chaudhuri recalls that his father 'intuitively imbibed the humanistic spirit . . . of a school of *Bengali humanism* in the nineteenth

[28] Nirad C. Chaudhuri, interview with the author, 27 Oct. 1997.

[29] Chaudhuri writes: 'The only loyalty, which I admitted I owed to my people, was that I should warn them about the danger that faced them . . . even at the risk of being unpopular. This duty I have performed all my life, and therefore, I have now to live in exile' (*TH* 656). Chaudhuri was not actually exiled but chose to settle in England. However he describes how he was 'punished', by nationalists for his pro-British views when his books were banned in India. This is confirmed in P. C. Chatterjee, *The Adventure of Indian Broadcasting* (Delhi: Konarck Press, 1998), 63.

[30] Sumit Sarkar, *Modern India, 1885–1947* (Basingstoke: Macmillan, 1989), 70–6.

century . . . and tried to make it the spiritual heritage of his children'
(*Autobiography* 171, emphasis mine).[31]

Chaudhuri greatly admired nineteenth-century Bengali reformers
such as Ram Mohan Roy, who argued for English education in
India from 1823, and positioned himself alongside the Bengali novelist Bankimchandra Chatterjee (1838–94) and Swami Vivekananda
(1863–1902) as a similarly objective critic of Hindu culture.[32] The
hybrid nature of this reformist tradition is clear.[33] It is important to
locate Chaudhuri in terms of this modernising tradition within India,
and not simply to see him as an eccentric Anglophile. At another level,
this tradition also produced rationalists such as Nehru. Chaudhuri,
by contrast, appeared anachronistic as a latter-day nineteenth-century
reformist. In this way, Chaudhuri's self-translation needs to be seen
in relation to his hopes for a European-inspired renaissance in India.
As Tejaswini Niranjana suggests, the interpellation of colonised Indians functioned through forms of translation: 'European translations of
Indian texts prepared for a Western audience provided the "educated"
Indian with a whole range of Orientalist images.'[34] Influenced by Max
Müller's (and later Hindu revivalists Vivekananda's and Chatterjee's)
glorification of ancient Aryans, Chaudhuri mourns the passing away
of India's distinguished past. He writes 'we shall never again achieve
anything like the greatness and individuality of the Hindu civilization.
That civilization is dead forever, and cannot be resuscitated' *(Autobiography* 521). This reinforces the degree to which Chaudhuri was himself
a translated man, imbibing a Westernised social formation that was
already a translation. Chaudhuri's internalisation of orientalist images
extolling India's past ('The Wonder that was India') was inextricably
entwined with notions of India's present decay, and consequently the
positive force of an imperial, civilising mission.

---

[31] Reformist Hinduism also influenced Naipaul's father.

[32] Nirad C. Chaudhuri, *The Intellectual in India* (Delhi: Associated Publishing House, 1967) 10–13. Hereafter *Intellectual* pagination will appear in the text.

[33] Nandy provides an important corrective to Chaudhuri's account of these men as supposedly ideologically neutral reformers. Nandy argues that by the time Vivekananda 'entered the scene' because of 'the widespread internalization of Western values by many Indians . . . an over-emphasis on the reform of the Indian personality could only open up new, invidious modes of Westernization'. Nandy suggests this rendered 'exogenous categories of self-criticism' as 'indirectly collaborationist'. Ashis Nandy, *The Intimate Enemy* (Delhi: Oxford UP, 1983), 24, 26.

[34] Tejaswini Niranjana, *Siting Translation: History, Post-Structuralism, and the Colonial Context* (Berkeley and Los Angeles: University of California Press, 1992), 31.

Chaudhuri's voluntary affiliation to English culture, particularly his stance as a passionate apologist for the British Raj and his assertions of India's need for English rule, recall Octavio Mannoni's theory of the 'dependence complex' (*Intellectual* 26). Mannoni claimed particular races experience a psychic need to be colonised because they suffer from an unresolved dependence complex. Mannoni argued that colonisation was 'expected—even desired by the future subject peoples'.[35] Chaudhuri's denigration of his 'own' society manifests itself in these terms. Suggesting British and Indian cultures are not composed of factors of 'equal strength and maturity', he speculates as to whether India's 'curiously naïve . . . childish society . . . left to itself . . . would have reached the adult stage in its own way' (*Intellectual* 43). He asserts that India can only be saved by Western domination and that the British 'abandoning India' amounted to an abrogation of responsibility for those they ruled (*TH* 26): 'in the light of what has happened since India became independent . . . [British] doubts about the capacity of the Indians to govern their country and [their] residual loyalty to the imperial idea of protecting the Indian people from anarchy were justified' (*TH* 70). Chaudhuri's articulation of this theory about India is part of his desire to affiliate. Equally, Chaudhuri's views need to be read in the context of Fanon's critique of Mannoni's theory and theorisation of resistance. Fanon counters that if there is any evidence of this complex, it is indeed the 'pathology' of the colonised but represents the effect, not the cause. He contends that the colonised subject lives in a society that makes his 'inferiority complex' possible and derives its stability from the perpetuation of this complex: '*It is the racist who creates his inferior.*'[36] The irony of Chaudhuri's praise for the imperial legacy is that he illustrates and perpetuates the denigration that imperialism bequeathed. He dramatises the predicament of the culturally colonised 'native' in his lament at the elimination of the last traces of civilising Western influence. As Naipaul comments on Chaudhuri's autobiography, 'No better account of the penetration of the Indian mind by the West—and by extension, of one culture by another—will be or can now be written.'[37]

---

[35] O. D. Mannoni, *Prospero and Caliban: The Psychology of Colonisation*, trans. Pamela Powesland (New York: Praeger, 1964), 86.

[36] Frantz Fanon, *Black Skin*, 84, 85, 93, emphasis in original.

[37] V. S. Naipaul, *The Overcrowded Barracoon and other Articles* (London: Andre Deutsch, 1972), 59.

In contrast to Tambimuttu's (probably exaggerated) claim that he grew up with a fragmented sense of identity, oscillating between his multiple inheritances of Hinduism, Roman Catholicism, local and imperial culture, Chaudhuri never expresses any such sense of conflict about the complexity of his intellectual inheritances.[38] The almost schizophrenic duality of Chaudhuri's personality that observers immediately perceived did not seem to present any personal conflict for the writer himself. When a British friend asked him in 1974 'which is the *real* Nirad Chaudhuri? Is it the person dressed in Indian style, talking of the old Delhi that he loved, or the person dressed impeccably in Savile Row suits talking knowledgeably about English literature?', Chaudhuri immediately and confidently replied 'both'. He asserted that he was, as he put it, 'probably one of the few Bengalis to be as much English as I am Bengali . . . both in the marrow'.[39] Later he insists, 'I have never been under the compulsion to go on that wild goose chase which in these days is called "discovering one's identity". I never lost mine, and never had any doubts about it' (*TH* p. xxviii). While Chaudhuri's identification of himself as 'Bengali' becomes more simplified over the years in England as opposed to when he was in Bengal, the absence of conflict may also be because Western traditions had become so assimilated into the culture of certain Bengali social formations, such as the 'Bengali humanism' identified above.

Chaudhuri's native culture is a hybrid anglicised Bengali culture, modelled on Western norms. His birthplace, Kishorganj, although remote, was itself an outcome of such cultural contact, created in the 1860s as a sub-divisional headquarters of the local government system set up by the British. He lived and studied in Calcutta from 1910 to 1942, a city dominated by the British. However, the main reason Chaudhuri appears not to experience tension is that he values so little of the indigenous culture, which is tied up with his desire to be British. Long before he came to Britain, Chaudhuri recalls the Second World War as a turning point in his political and ideological identification with

[38] However, Chaudhuri's powerful recreation of the Hindu festival, the Durga Puja, conveys a conflictual attraction and repulsion towards his native culture. He is both 'aghast and awestruck' by the 'orgiastic . . . devotional' nature of the 'bloody sacrifices' of the buffalo (*Autobiography* 77–8). On the one hand, he wants to distance himself from the 'savage' native customs, on the other, the immense detail and loving particularisation betray his fascination.

[39] Nirad C. Chaudhuri, interview with D. Barlow, BBC *Profile*, 3 Oct. 1974, BBC WAC.

Britain and being British: 'As for myself, during the war I became and remained, except in birth, an Englishman.' He felt particularly inspired by 'the bravery of the British . . . it has left a permanent legacy behind' (*TH* 534). This identification suggests the extremity of his estrangement from India even whilst he still lived there.

What were the causes of Chaudhuri's sense of alienation? His intense, cerebral relationship with England fuelled his sense of internal exile in India. Until he left India for the first time in 1955, Chaudhuri had a fascinating, imaginary relationship with England and its intellectual culture. This was so much so that as a reviewer of *A Passage to England* suggests, 'Mr. Chaudhuri does not appear to be seeing [England] for the first time, but returning after years of exile' (cited in *Intellectual* 77). The implied presence of the 'absent yet real' England shadows Chaudhuri's formative years and is a central symbol of a series of paradoxes of his life (*Autobiography* 115). He describes the imaginary presence of England as 'an intangible and exotic element in the ecology of our lives'. The '. . . extraordinarily uneven knowledge . . . of England' meant that 'what we did not know was so dark that we could easily people the void with phantasms evoked out of our ignorance' (*Autobiography* 115–16). The literature of exile is often characterised by its propensity to place remembered realities above immediate, referential ones. For the culturally colonised the imagined 'realities' also sometimes take on a greater significance than immediate ones. 'England evoked by the imagination' exerted as great an influence on Chaudhuri as Bangram and Kalikutch were 'sensibly experienced' (*Autobiography* xiv). This process anticipates Naipaul's protagonist Ralph Singh's description of 'calendar pictures of English gardens superimposed on our Isabellan villages of mud and grass' in *The Mimic Men*.[40]

The Indian critic K. Chellapan suggests that Chaudhuri's 'obsession with what India is not made him seek an aggressive Western identity'.[41] Chaudhuri's autobiography opens with his description of his village, 'Kishorganj', in terms of what it is not, that is to say an English country town, which immediately indicates that he is addressing a Western audience (*Autobiography* 1). This is one instance in a general process of attempting to define India in relation to England. However, it is

---

[40] V. S. Naipaul, *The Mimic Men* (London: Penguin, 1967), 89.
[41] K. Chellappan, 'The Discovery of India and the Self in Three Autobiographies', in H. H. Anniah Gowda (ed.), *The Colonial and the Neo-Colonial: Encounters in Commonwealth Literature* (Mysore: University of Mysore, 1983), 99.

just as likely that the converse is true: Chaudhuri's obsession with the West radically separated him from the culture into which he was born. Whatever its cause, this severe estrangement from his environment caused the writer to be perceived in India as one of Macaulay's freakish progeny: '. . . Indian in blood and colour but English in taste, in opinions, in morals and in intellect'.[42] The way Chaudhuri presents his negative personal qualities as specifically *Indian* reinforces the extent of his disaffection. When as a child he destroyed his neighbour's prize flower we are told he succumbed to 'the ancient malice to which [he] was heir' (*Autobiography* 344). Chellapan suggests that Chaudhuri 'projects his psychic malady upon India—he seems to hate India because it is an image of himself, reflecting his own incapacity for dynamism and expansion'.[43] Indeed stagnation is a governing metaphor for Indian identity in Chaudhuri's autobiography, a way of thinking about India that has a long colonial history. However, the strongest evidence of Chaudhuri's psychic alienation is his racist attitude towards 'coloured' immigrants in Britain. Ironically, this was expressed in an extreme form after his own emigration to England.

Where Tambimuttu emphasises divisions within the self, Chaudhuri foregrounds the division between self and others. At the end of his autobiography, Chaudhuri retraces the trajectory of his alienation and 'intellectual isolation' from the nationalism espoused by his 'country-men and contemporaries' that, according to him, became increasingly 'impenetrable' (*Autobiography* 414): 'During the years of my education I was becoming a stranger to my environment and organizing my intellectual and moral life along an independent nexus; in the next ten years I was oppressed by a feeling of antagonism to the environment; and in the last phase I became hostile to it' (*Autobiography* 607–8). In order to justify this sense of alienation, or to make it coherent, elsewhere Chaudhuri even repeats Max Müller's suggestion that all Aryans in India are as transplanted and dislocated as colonial Englishmen, because they themselves were immigrants to India. This thesis is developed further in his notorious *The Continent of Circe* where he delineates the 'degeneration' of Aryans in India. Chaudhuri's emphasis on his 'Aryan heritage' is symptomatic of the colonialist interpellation of the elite. The

[42] Young, *Macaulay*, 722. Narasimhaiah describes Chaudhuri in these terms. C. D. Narasimhaiah, *Essays in Commonwealth Literature: Heirloom of Multiple Heritage* (Delhi: Pencraft International, 1995), 61.

[43] Chellapan, 'The Discovery of India', 99.

parallel is a way of constructing affinities between the British and the Indians. Chaudhuri claims that, as he puts it, 'this historical thesis has emancipated me from a malaise that had haunted me throughout my life'.[44] Describing his writing as cathartic, he presents his alienation as liberating and ultimately resolved in freedom: 'my intellect has indeed at last emancipated itself from my country.' This sense of liberty and autonomy was achieved without uprooting himself 'from the native soil by sojourn in a foreign country or schooling' (*Autobiography* 607).

## MODERNIST CONTEXTS AND THE GENERIC IMPLICATIONS OF ALIENATION

Although he describes it in terms of a personal experience, Chaudhuri's self-conscious separation from his own culture can also be understood in terms of the wider context of modernism, particularly the potentially liberating nature of modernist alienation. Ashis Nandy has characterised Chaudhuri as 'the last of the great Edwardian modernists of India'.[45] While he is part of Indian modernising traditions, Chaudhuri draws on a wide range of literary influences. His sense of dislocation and spiritual exile from his contemporary culture is similar to that expressed by early twentieth-century European modernist writers. In European nostalgia for a supposedly organic past, alienation is presented as temporal rather than spatial, whereas Chaudhuri seems to see himself—as an Aryan—permanently dislocated, living a form of exile that operates in both time and space. With modernism, the notion of exile as a precondition to being a writer became ingrained, so that it came to stand for the critical distance in the act of writing itself. Virginia Woolf describes a sense of internal exile as 'feeling outside . . . *alien and critical*'.[46] Although Woolf refers to her sense of exclusion from a male-dominated literary world, as Randall Stevenson suggests, 'all modernist exiles may have found the experience of being "outside . . . alien and critical" a

---

[44] M. K. Naik refutes Chaudhuri's claim, arguing that 'it is the other way round . . . it is the "malaise" that explains the historical thesis'. M. K. Naik, *A History of Indian English Literature* (Delhi: Sahitiya Akademi, 1982), 265.

[45] Ashis Nandy, *The Savage Freud and Other Essays on Possible and Retrievable Selves* (Delhi: Oxford UP, 1995), dedication.

[46] Cited in Randall Stevenson, *Modernist Fiction: An Introduction* (London: Harvester Wheatsheaf, 1992), 187, emphasis mine.

provocative, shaping influence in the evolution of their art'.[47] This sense of alienation from one's own familiar culture and criticism emerges in obvious ways in Tambimuttu and Naipaul as well as Chaudhuri. Taken collectively, these writers' modernist sense of exile and alienation challenge the more familiar representations of 'postcolonial' alienation in colonial and postcolonial writing as the experience of loss and alienation in migrating to a new culture.[48]

The cultural alienation produced by colonialism encouraged many of Chaudhuri's and Tambimuttu's generation to respond to their situation through autobiography.[49] This was not a new phenomenon. Dean Mohamet (1749 (or 1759)–1851), Parsi journalist, and poet Behramji Merwanji Malabari (1853–1912), and Cornelia and Alice Sorabji wrote travel and conversion narratives in part in response to existential crises. The autobiographical form can be a strategy for creating the illusion of unity and coherence, despite the fragmentation of identity. Anand, a contemporary of both writers, observes that his adaptation of the European novel form into an autobiographical narrative is 'the kind of creativeness from which I have had to make myself into some kind of wholeness'.[50] Equally, it is a form where the self is seen and explored as Other and draws attention to the divisions internalised by the author. The autobiographical form, a genre shaped by history, is an apt vehicle to treat the impact of colonialism: it is intimately connected to the emergence of a historical consciousness in Western culture.[51] Showing how the colonised modified this imported form, Sunil Khilnani interprets the spate of autobiographies in this era as an example of Indians' conformity with universal demands of modernity. He goes on to argue that Indian nationalists 'created and expressed . . . their public selves . . . through that literary genre which Indians embraced in the nineteenth and twentieth centuries, the didactic autobiography: a genre that in Indian hands . . . conveniently fused picaresque personal adventures with the odyssey of the nation'.[52]

[47] Stevenson, *Modernist Fiction*, 191.

[48] For instance Andrew Gurr, *Writers in Exile: The Identity of Home in Modern Literature* (Sussex: Harvester Press, 1981).

[49] For an indication of the large number of autobiographies published during this era by South Asians see Naik, *A History of Indian English Literature*, 270–2.

[50] Cited in Jane Williams (ed.), *Tambimuttu: Bridge Between Two Worlds* (London: Peter Owen, 1989), 198. Hereafter *Tambimuttu* pagination will appear in the text.

[51] Laura Marcus, *Auto/biographical Discourses: Theory, Criticism and Practice* (Manchester: Manchester UP, 1994), 167.

[52] Sunil Khilnani, *The Idea of India* (London: Hamish Hamilton, 1997), 7.

Similarly Dipesh Chakrabarty observes that 'many of the private and public rituals of modern individualism became visible in India in the nineteenth century. One sees this, for instance, in the sudden flourishing in this period of the four basic genres that help express the modern self: the novel, the biography, the autobiography, and history.' Chakrabarty shows that Indian autobiographies are altered to their new contexts: citing Chaudhuri as an example, he suggests the difference is that 'Our autobiographies are remarkably "public" . . . when written by men . . . they seldom yield pictures of an endlessly interiorized subject.'[53]

However, Chaudhuri's text complicates such characterisations that present the self and the communal as intertwined, 'where the telling of the individual story and the individual experience cannot but ultimately involve the whole laborious telling of the experience of the collectivity itself'.[54] Of course at one level, the telling of Chaudhuri's autobiography is a way of telling a larger story. In descriptive, analytical prose he recreates the village life of the East Bengal of his childhood, the Calcutta and Delhi of his adulthood, and the first decade of independent India. As Chaudhuri observes, 'even if I had intended to write only an autobiography I could not have excluded the public and collective themes because they were part and parcel of the personal lives of all Indians of that age' (*TH* p. xvi). Yet although Chaudhuri, like Nehru, draws significant parallels between the discovery of modern India and the discovery of self, employing the autobiographical form to unveil the history of self and project a political platform, his text differs significantly in one aspect from Nehru's and Gandhi's autobiographies.[55] Where they chart the movement away from a Westernised upbringing to a positive 'discovery of India', Chaudhuri is extremely critical of the native culture that he 'discovers'. His work is characterised by the opposite impulse: he is anxious to differentiate his own identity from 'a primarily social identity' and mark his distance from his native 'psychosocial context'.[56] In contrast to the didactic autobiographies Khilnani identifies, Chaudhuri's

[53] Dipesh Chakrabarty, 'Postcoloniality and the Artifice of History: Who Speaks for "Indian" Pasts?', in Padmini Mongia (ed.), *Contemporary Postcolonial Literary Theory* (London: Arnold, 1996), 230–1.

[54] Fredric Jameson, 'Third-World Literature in the Era of Multinational Capitalism', *Social Text* 15 (1986), 85–6.

[55] Jawaharlal Nehru, *The Discovery of India* (London: Meridian Books, 1946).

[56] Chaudhuri challenges Gurr's suggestion that non-metropolitan exiles consistently put self in its diminished place in the broad social context of a primarily social identity. Gurr, *Writers in Exile*, 139.

use of the genre is an attempt to chart not fusion with the nation at large, but separation. His emphasis on himself somewhat obscures the nation, as his claim '*L'Inde, c'est moi*' suggests (*Autobiography* 553). Whether Chaudhuri writes memoirs, travelogue or social and political commentary, he refracts his vision of historical reality through himself. His over-identification with his material differs from the other writers treated here who wrote both autobiographically *and* fictionally. This particularly contrasts with Naipaul's ability to translate his singular personal experience into a series of mesmerising novels, a characteristic that in part explains their different levels of literary success.

It could be said that Chaudhuri chose the autobiographical form in order to assert his autonomy and detachment from his surroundings. Western autobiography is largely predicated on a belief in the autonomous self: the fully constituted male subject who pre-exists the language into which he casts his story. Autobiography is the genre most closely associated with the idea of the potency of self-identity and separate selfhood.[57] As Philippe Lejeune suggests, this individualist ideology and the performance of an autobiographical act lends itself to a belief in the possibility of self-creation, masking the agency of cultural institutions at work in the life history that determines our stories and our selves.[58] So Chaudhuri claims to have 'lived by imposing my own terms on the world' (*TH* p. xxviii). He is always anxious to emphasise his self-determination: 'I have never been carried away by the currents of history, I have navigated through them' (*TH* p. xxvi). In this way, far from expressing angst about his alienation, Chaudhuri self-consciously asserts the extent to which he embraced and relished it. He had at first a great respect for Rabindranath Tagore because he perceived Tagore as 'very hostile to his own people, maladjusted—exactly like me!'[59]

Chaudhuri adopts the stance of outsider for many reasons. First, it offers a convenient way of rationalising his situation: he is already excluded from dominant nationalism, and may have felt alienated in caste and class terms. He was of the *Kayastha* caste, not of the Brahmin caste, which is significant in the context of his idealisation of the Bengali Renaissance, which was dominated by Brahmins. The *Kayastha* caste,

---

[57] Anne McClintock, *Imperial Leather: Race, Gender and Sexuality in the Colonial Context* (London: Routledge, 1995), 313.

[58] Philippe Lejeune, *On Autobiography*, trans. Katherine Leary (Minneapolis: University of Minnesota Press, 1989), 192.

[59] Duncan Fallowell, 'Nirad C. Chaudhuri: At Home in Oxford', *The American Scholar* 60.2 (1991), 245.

it should be added, is not one of the oppressed castes; its members are often educated and wealthy. Chaudhuri's position in terms of class is also ambivalent. He is very conscious of his *bhadralok* status: education in English and middle-class origins. His anxiety to assert these origins is clear. In an article on Jane Austen, he writes 'I saw nothing wrong in Darcy's pride, because I came from a landowning family, which would not even dine in any house connected with trade.'[60] His position on the decline of Bengal, like his attitudes to underclass immigrants, typifies what Partha Chatterjee describes as the 'anxiety of an entrenched but now somewhat beleaguered literati about the effects of . . . democratization'. Chatterjee exposes the theory of Bengal's decline as one that 'easily lends itself to a social conservatism that justifies class privilege by dressing it up as a meritocracy and a celebration of the nineteenth-century "synthesis" of West and East'. Chatterjee names Chaudhuri as 'the most extreme . . . proponent of this view'.[61] At the same time, Chaudhuri's family was not particularly affluent. He endured penury for many years as a 'scholar-gypsy' and painfully recalls being treated like a provincial 'country bumpkin' when he first went to Calcutta (*TH* 31). Class consciousness signals loudly in his self-conscious declarations of chosen exile. He eagerly insists his alienation is self-imposed and not borne out of being socially marginalised:

I was against historical trends, not any people. . . . the class which dominates India today is some sort of an extension of the Bengali class to which I belonged. Thus, if I speak of alienation from a world, that does not mean social or personal alienation.

Although I have rejected the whole ideology of the dominant order in India, I am socially at home among them. I could have shared their position and prosperity if I had wanted that, and if I have not, that has been my free choice. (*TH* pp. xxvii–xxviii)

In this way, Chaudhuri maintains that he is also a privileged *insider*.

In his defiant separation from his countrymen, Chaudhuri insists his location as an intellectual outside the dominant group enabled him to be free from ideological constraints or allegiance to any particular national constituency. Echoing Chaudhuri, Naipaul observes that as 'a colonial' one had to first distance oneself from the familiar and

---

[60] Nirad C. Chaudhuri, 'Woman of the World' *Times Literary Supplement* (16 Jan. 1976), 55.
[61] Partha Chatterjee, *The Present History of West Bengal: Essays in Political Criticism* (Delhi: Oxford UP, 1997), p. vii.

focus on personal achievement before one could assume responsibility for others. The writer's responsibility was his 'honest' dialogue with his own 'undeveloped' society.[62] Chaudhuri's (self-)construction as an objective outsider anticipates the privileging of the migrant intellectual's perspectives in postcolonial studies. Ironically, and to very different ends, just as Said claims that 'the intellectual [is a] dissenter from the corporate ensemble', Chaudhuri positions himself as such an intellectual outsider who dares to transcend provincial limits and put criticism before solidarity.[63] He dismisses 'patriotic passions' as 'blind Xenophobia' (*Intellectual* 16). Drawing on Julian Benda, Chaudhuri critiques any form of unquestioning allegiance to one's countrymen as the 'trite dictum of pseudo-morality. My family, right or wrong' (*TH* 62). To protect himself from accusations of partiality, Chaudhuri suggests that detachment of the one from the many is the precondition of all original thought, again anticipating Said's description of the intellectual inhabiting 'an ascetic ode of willed homelessness'.[64] Accordingly, *The Intellectual in India* (1967) can be read as a defence of Chaudhuri's criticisms of India. He implicitly positions himself as one of 'a small number of historians whose intellectual integrity would not succumb to nationalism, however patriotic they might be'. He contrasts his stance unfettered by communal loyalties with the 'openly partisan . . . general tone of historical writing' (*Intellectual* 52). However, various historical, political, class, and gender determinations result in the different articulations of this subject-position of intellectual as outsider. In view of the impositions of imperialism, can Chaudhuri claim to be truly free? Chaudhuri's work, like Naipaul's, raises questions about the formation of consciousness and subjectivity. Can we preserve a sense of autonomy and self-respect even though we may be the oppressed subjects of colonial powers? Furthermore, can we stand apart from the ideological and cultural circumstances that shape our worldviews and make impartial judgements and assessments of other cultures, or of our own? Naipaul's travelogues both continue in the convention of British travel writing, and establish their own tradition of the displaced writer of Third-World origin as the detached, 'objective' observer of 'other' cultures.

[62] Adrian Rowe-Evans, 'V. S. Naipaul: A Transition Interview 1971', in *Conversations with V. S. Naipaul*, ed. Feroza Jussawalla (Jackson: University Press of Mississipi, 1997), 24–36, 27.

[63] Edward Said, *Representations of the Intellectual* (London: Vintage, 1994), 24.

[64] Edward Said, *The World, the Text and the Critic* (Cambridge, Mass.: Harvard UP, 1983).

Both Chaudhuri and Naipaul have been taken to task for their negative cultural evaluations of formerly colonised peoples, a position frequently interpreted as reflecting the writers' colonised minds and reactionary conservatism. Throughout his life Chaudhuri had 'complete confidence' in his objectivity concerning his appraisal of British rule. He maintained that his hostility to the dominant cultural orthodoxy of Gandhian nationalism did not result in an uncritical appreciation of Western ideologies (*Intellectual* 31). Despite this assertion and his acknowledgement of colonialism's 'shortcomings and positive evils', the overriding emphasis of his work is on his 'loyalty to English life and civilization' and 'identification with British greatness' (*TH* 27). This claim to objectivity dissimulates the imperial discourse that Chaudhuri has internalised. His analysis is locked into a Manichean structure of a valorisation of England and a reciprocal devaluation of India as Other. With Chaudhuri, the 'objectivity' of his criticism of India remains questionable. How far is it a result of his internalisation of the colonial denigration of his culture? It is not surprising that, until recently, responses to his work and questions over his objectivity were partly explicable in terms of the location of distinct readerships.

As the following discussion of Chaudhuri's reception shows, early Western reviewers and publishers emphasised his objectivity. One reader's report describes Chaudhuri as an 'observant, broad-minded, receptive and utterly unprejudiced inhabitant of Eastern Bengal'.[65] But while British and American critics describe him as a 'scholar of great intelligence, learning, and subtlety and a courageous, wise and honest man', Chaudhuri's characteristic attitude of the denunciation of India has meant that his claim to be objective has not been accepted by many locally based Indian critics.[66] From the 1950s to the 1970s, these critics argued that his stance, loaded with value judgements, was far from dispassionate. (In contrast, the migrant writers Naipaul and Rushdie both comment on the 'analytic and *detached*' style of Chaudhuri's autobiography.)[67] An early review of the *Autobiography* in the *Sunday Times* interprets local Indian hostility to Chaudhuri as *their* inability to be as 'objective' as he is. The reviewer argues that 'it is only a solidly established society that crowns its detractors: a people in the fever of

---

65  J. C. Squire, Reader's Report on *A Passage to England*, Macmillan Archive.
66  Edward Shills, 'Citizen of the World', *The American Scholar* 57 (1988), 550.
67  Naipaul, *The Overcrowded Barracoon*, 64, emphasis mine.

resurgent nationalism never feel robust enough to profit by a scolding'.[68] Interestingly, in contrast to Chaudhuri's initial reception in India, some early British commentators saw Chaudhuri as a nationalist. A reader for Macmillan observes: 'It would seem to us difficult to doubt the nationalist feeling of the author of the *Autobiography*, but he has been criticised in India for being too partial to the West, and too critical of his own countrymen.'[69] In fact, Chaudhuri's correspondence does suggest that his criticisms stem from desperate concern, rather than from professed and perceived detachment. However, as we will see, the British reviewers' focus on Chaudhuri's ambivalent 'criticisms' of the British in India only serves to give credibility to, and effectively reinforce, his conservative views in general. The frequency with which these critics foreground Chaudhuri's 'criticisms' of the British, and his assumed divergence from dominant views, suggest paradoxically that such supposed assertions of difference constitute an integral part of his affiliation. Later, we will see this paradox in relation to Tambimuttu in a more pronounced form. However, because Tambimuttu's mostly liberal left supporters represented the opposite political pole to Chaudhuri's, Tambimuttu's assimilation demanded a different kind of self-translation.

## CHAUDHURI: AFFILIATION IN BRITAIN (1951–99)

In Britain, the hitherto 'unknown' Indian emerged from obscurity onto the pages of the *Illustrated London News* with the publication of his *Autobiography* in 1951. As suggested earlier, Chaudhuri's description of the 'atavisation' of the nationalist movement, and lament at the withdrawal of British imperialism, emerging at a time when the country was trying to come to terms with the loss of Empire and its post-imperial status, boosted the initial success of his *Autobiography* in Britain. The influential J. C. Squire (1884–1958)—of the *London Mercury*, chief literary critic of the *Observer*, and reader for Macmillan—recommended Chaudhuri's *Autobiography* to Macmillan for publication. Squire's subsequent review of Chaudhuri's first book illustrates its appeal to a readership very different from that of the Bloomsbury Group who had championed Anand and celebrated Tambimuttu. Squire's 'appreciation' in the *Illustrated London News* focused on Chaudhuri's laudatory account of British

[68] Raymond Mortimer, 'The Square Peg', *Sunday Times* (9 Sept. 1951), 3.
[69] Francis Watson, First Reader's Report on *Circe*, 28 June 1961, Macmillan Archive.

rule which reinforced Squire's own views. Squire believed that, as he put it:

we had justified ourselves in India by our policemanship, our care for the forestry, our irrigation works, our precautions against plague and famine, Lord William Bentinck's measures against suttee and child marriage, our keeping the peace between Moslems and Hindus, our co-operation with the enlightened Princes and our surveillance of the less enlightened.

'Kipling's "poor little street-bred people" ', he adds, 'were led astray by the more cunning of their kind; and India went, to the great detriment of both parties.' Squire praises the fact that 'all this kind of question' is 'surveyed in Mr. Chaudhuri's book'.[70] In a similar vein, the *Sunday Times* reviewer describes Chaudhuri as exasperated by just those Indian qualities which so 'regrettably antagonised the British in India'.[71] Employing Chaudhuri's views to support a fading British imperialist ideology, Squire cites his claim that: 'as long as the English remained strong they had nothing to fear from Indian nationalism, but everything as soon as they grew weak . . .' He makes use of Chaudhuri's argument to warn against any weakening of British imperial resolve: 'the same thing . . . might be said about Burmese . . . Malayan . . . Persian . . . Egyptian . . . and even Russian nationalism.'[72] Squire's review was written in the context of the Persian crisis in 1951, when Teheran wanted to nationalise the Anglo-Iranian oil company and gave Britain fifteen days to leave. The degree to which Chaudhuri's position echoed the right-wing views of the Conservative Party can be seen from Winston Churchill's observation that: 'if a strong Conservative government had been in power the Persian crisis would never have arisen in this way. It is only when the British Government is known to be weak and hesitant that these outrages are inflicted upon us.'[73]

At the same time, however, some English reviewers of the *Autobiography* wished to balance Chaudhuri's criticisms of India by emphasising his censure of colonial rulers, citing this as evidence of his 'objectivity'. In 1951 Mortimer in the *Sunday Times* commented: 'If Mr Chaudhuri sees nothing good in his country do not imagine that he is indulgent to the English. He speaks with loathing of our superciliousness, cruelty and

---

[70] J. C. Squire, 'A Bridge between England and India', *Illustrated London News* (3 Nov. 1951), 706.

[71] Raymond Mortimer, 'The Square Peg' *Sunday Times* (9 Sept. 1951), 3.

[72] Squire, 'A Bridge', 706.

[73] Cited in 'Editorial', *Sunday Times* (7 Oct. 1951), 1.

despotism in the days of the Raj; he is equally severe upon those English who now—always from the lowest motive—express sympathy with India.[74] Similarly Squire wrote that 'Chaudhuri, a realist, is certainly no indiscriminate belauder of British rule; he has some damning things to say about the attitude of the British communities . . . towards the native inhabitants of India.'[75] In the same vein, several decades later, William Walsh attempted to refute charges of Chaudhuri's Anglophilia by drawing attention to his attacks on the colonial insolence of the local British Raj.[76]

Yet Chaudhuri's censure needs to be viewed in the context of his explanations. Like E. M. Forster, he avers that this colonial 'insolence' was the result of the enervating extremes of the climate on the English. Back in England, by contrast, their 'proper environment seemed to have reclaimed them, and restored their natural self' (*Passage* 118). Moreover, he never questions the legitimacy of British imperialism. Instead he insists to the last that 'there was never any time from the very beginning of British rule in India down to Lord Curzon's vice-royalty when the higher direction of the Indian Empire did not think that British rule existed primarily for the good of the Indian people'.[77] His only criticism of the English is that they educated the Bengalis to be like themselves and yet refused to treat them as equals. Nor does he ever dispute the basis of the British sense of superiority. Instead he seems to resent that he is not accepted as exceptionally similar to them. Chaudhuri objected to the 'apartheid' practised in colonial India and the hostility the colonisers felt towards Anglicised Indians who appeared to move beyond the required affiliation. Revealingly, Chaudhuri feels hurt that, in contrast to the cultural proselytization practised by French and Spanish colonisers, the British responded to Indians interested in European culture with 'unmeasured rancour . . . as if we were running off with their daughters' and 'resented our devotion to English literature as a sort of illicit attention to their wives' (*Passage* 21). His 'criticism' of the British amounts to the fact that, in his view, their arrogance led to the incomplete Anglicisation of India. Nor can Chaudhuri's later comments on the decadence of English people in *Three Horsemen*

[74] Mortimer, 'The Square Peg', 3.     [75] Squire, 'A Bridge', 706.

[76] William Walsh, 'The Meeting of Language and Literature and the Indian Example', in Guy Amirthanayagam (ed.), *Writers in the East–West Encounter* (Basingstoke: Macmillan, 1982), 119.

[77] Nirad C. Chaudhuri, 'The Wolf without a Pack', *Times Literary Supplement* (6 Oct. 1978), 1121.

*of the New Apocalypse* (1997) be taken as evidence of his objectivity. Such disapproval stems from any evidence of contemporary Britain attempting to abandon its racist, imperialist policies. The extent to which Chaudhuri was culturally colonised can be demonstrated by his insistence upon Britain's current state of 'deterioration', rather than offering any criticism of its former imperialism.

In Chaudhuri's subsequent book *The Continent of Circe* (1965) where Western influence is the subject of attack, it is the Indians themselves who are critiqued for false assimilation and imitation.[78] *Circe* delineates the 'degeneration' of the Aryans and contains particularly derogatory representations of Indians.[79] Here Chaudhuri expands his pet theory that the Hindus (by which he means the inhabitants of the Gangetic plain and Indus valley) were originally Europeans from 'somewhere between the Danube and the Volga'. Originally fair, the North Indian climate made them brown, unlike the original inhabitants the 'darks' or aboriginals, the 'children of Circe'. The book revolves around the thesis that the presiding spirit of India is a Circe who turns her inhabitants into swine. To escape their swinish plight, Chaudhuri writes, the Hindus resorted to religious asceticism, occultism, and a fatalistic acceptance of filth, misery, and disorder. Their addiction to sex became an anodyne destroying the possibility of genuine love between men and women. Chaudhuri concludes by arguing that 'there is no future for us Hindus [except] by recovering our original European character, and conquering so far as we can the Indian environment' (*Circe* 373–4). The only hope for India's economic future is 'a re-imposed foreign domination, accompanied by a loss of political as well as economic freedom' (*Circe* 373). He ends with his now characteristic self-separation and self-construction as an unheeded prophet: 'but why should I concern myself with them? I have rescued my European soul from Circe' and 'recovered my Ariel's body from Sycorax. So I can and should ignore the Yahoos. But I would save the fellow beasts. They do not, however, listen to me. They honk, neigh, bellow, bleat or grunt, and scamper away to their scrub, stable, byre, pen and sty' (*Circe* 376). Chaudhuri's dehumanisation of Indians approaches Swiftian proportions. At the same time, Chaudhuri was shrewdly and mischievously aware of the publicity value of his 'Anglomania' and extreme opinions on a range

[78] Nirad C. Chaudhuri, *The Continent of Circe* [1965] (Bombay: Jaico Publishing House, 1996). Hereafter *Circe* pagination will appear in the text.

[79] Although the Hindus (which constitute Indian for Chaudhuri) are his main target, his portrayals of India's Parsi and Eurasian communities are particularly racist.

of issues. Writing a chauvinistic article where he voiced opposition to the emergence of 'bourgeois, working women' in India and instead recommended early marriage, he aroused the anticipated flurry of debate in *The Statesman* of Calcutta and Delhi, just before the publication of *Circe*.[80] In a letter narrating the controversy to Chatto, Chaudhuri writes: 'My future articles too, I hope, will create interest in my writings. As I have told you, I am doing my best to prepare the ground or market for the book.'[81] Clearly this self-consciousness means his perspectives and pronouncements cannot be taken at face value. He is as adept as Tambimuttu in manipulating his readerships.

*Circe* won the prestigious Duff Cooper Memorial Prize for non-fiction in 1966. Nevertheless, Macmillan's initial acceptance of this text and Chaudhuri's ultimate break with the company over its publication, marks the first indication that Chaudhuri's views were becoming contentious and marginal in a Britain that was already transformed by the 'winds of change'.[82] The Chatto and Windus reader's report on *Circe* reveals the recognition that from the mid-1960s, the tide of popular British opinion was turning against Chaudhuri, who was increasingly becoming something of an anomaly. At the same time, the report dismisses such popular opinion as a form of 'political correctness'. The reader, Guy Wint, implicitly endorses Chaudhuri's ideas: 'It will be odd if a book on India does not get published because it takes a too favourable view about the British record. Publishers who desire to be more with it are likely to take a dim view of it for this reason.'[83] American attitudes to India differed from British ones. When Chatto and Windus tried to encourage Viking Press in New York in an American publication, Viking declined on the grounds:

I feel sure it will do well in England, aided by a lively controversy.

The trouble here is that we have no *sociological* interest in India. There is some rather dispirited, political interest, but the traditional center of our attention has been in the esoteric aspects of Hindu thought and practice. The soundness of Chaudhuri's views on these matters would hardly endear him to this audience.[84]

---

[80] Chaudhuri, Letters to the Editor, *The Statesman* (20 Mar. 1965), File Chaudhuri 1964–7.

[81] Nirad C. Chaudhuri, letter to Peter Calvocoressi, 22 Mar. 1965, File Chaudhuri 1964–7.

[82] I refer to Harold Macmillan's famous speech on decolonisation in 1960.

[83] Guy Wint, letter to Ian Parsons, 10 June 1964, File Chaudhuri 1964–7.

[84] Denver Lindley, letter to Peter Calvocoressi, 5 May 1965, File Chaudhuri 1964–7.

As we will see, America's 'traditional' interest in 'esoteric aspects' of Hinduism had important implications for Tambimuttu's reception in New York. What is significant here is the discrepancy between what the publisher really thinks of 'Hindu thought', and his sense of what would be marketable. It further demonstrates that in certain circles, private, residual endorsement of Chaudhuri's judgements persisted alongside a simultaneous awareness that his ideas did not fulfil the current demands of writings by a native informant.

The covert approval of Chaudhuri's opinions, masked behind seeming dissension, in Paul Scott's review of *Circe* in the *Times Literary Supplement* supports this contention. Notice the way a string of qualifications repeatedly undermines any ostensible opposition to Chaudhuri's beliefs, so that the review ultimately endorses his assertions, while attempting to appear impartial:

That India turns all her people into swine is too absurd a notion to call for detailed refutation (the existence of Mr. Chaudhuri is refutation enough). Nevertheless, a country that can set an urbane and gentle man like Mr V. S. Naipaul screaming and despairing within a few hours of arriving clearly performs miracles of character-transformation. . . . Most visitors to India may be able to offer particular evidence in support of one or more of Mr. Chaudhuri's generalizations, but his book can hardly be expected to win him friends in Delhi. Nevertheless, one may think, they needed to be made sweeping though they are. Tender natures are an expensive luxury for a nation. Mr. Chaudhuri's book brings into the open what for several years has been relegated to the darkest recesses of the minds of pro-India sympathizers: the suspicion that the Indians have begun to trade on the fund of admiration and sympathy they earned by their struggles and have grown to think of themselves as a people who ought not to be subjected to the law of diminishing moral returns, and therefore free from the restraints imposed in a civilized nation by criticism from outside.

Scott concludes rhetorically that 'It is up to [Indians] to answer Mr. Chaudhuri, not for us to say whether he is right or wrong.' However, it is clear what he thinks and that he is both pleased and relieved, as he puts it, 'that this time the criticism comes from one of their own most notable men of letters' which 'is all to the good'.[85] The privileging of preferred native informants allows the dominant community to refrain from criticising the other culture, because the function of providing a critical perspective has been assigned to the 'authentic' insider. This is confirmed by the Macmillan reader's report on *Circe*: 'As a reader I must

---

[85] Paul Scott, 'Bitter Potion for Circe's Swine', *Times Literary Supplement* (2 Dec. 1965), 1093.

admit that I would react badly to much of what he says if it came from a Western writer, and I should in that case advise against publication.'[86]

This disclosure reveals that Macmillan balked at publishing *Circe* because of its assessment of the reception of Chaudhuri's conservative views. With characteristic frankness, Chaudhuri explained his reasons for his break with Macmillan in a letter to his new publisher Chatto and Windus in 1964: 'Macmillan's suggestions amounted to a demand to write a new book to the publisher's reader's specifications.' Macmillan's wish to respond to revised readings of imperialism and Kipling, and to present Chaudhuri as uninfluenced by colonial ideology, can be inferred from Chaudhuri's objection to the editorial cuts Macmillan proposed. He writes:

A dozen appreciative references to Kipling were either removed or made colourless, on the grounds that the impression was not to be created that I was in any way inspired by Kipling. This coming to me from the publishers of Kipling, seemed indecently opportunistic. I, Kipling's bête noire, as a typical Bengali Babu was to be prevented from expressing my admiration for Kipling.

Chaudhuri's insight and self-description is revealing, as is his steadfast adherence to his views. His letter further suggests that Macmillan's reticence was selective. What is especially illuminating is Chaudhuri's recognition of the way some of his opinions were considered more acceptable than others. He insists that 'one reason I withdrew the book from Macmillan was that they removed from it all criticisms of Nehru'. Contesting Macmillan's claim that their editing was 'expositional', he commented: 'I could easily see that it was a suppression of certain of my views and conclusions, and that it was highly selective.' He goes on to support his accusation by arguing:

If my criticism was intemperate and my conclusions extreme, the intemperance and extremism should have been pruned all over the book evenly. *But there was no tampering with even the most severe criticism of the traditional Hindu life.* The editing was directed only towards those features of the book over which an Indophile Englishman of today has susceptibilities: namely Western writers who are writing on India today, Nehru, Anglicised Indians, Eurasians etc.[87]

This alleged selectivity suggests in the mid 1960s an appreciation of 'modern' Westernised Indians like Nehru with whom the British had

---

[86] Francis Watson, Second Reader's Report on *Circe*, 15 May 1963, Macmillan Archive.

[87] Nirad C. Chaudhuri, letter to Gabrielle Smith, 20 June 1964, File Chaudhuri 1964–7, emphasis mine, Chatto and Windus Archive.

negotiated, whilst more 'traditional' aspects of Indian society could be critiqued without controversy.

Whilst we need to allow for Chaudhuri's partiality here, Wint's suggestion that some publishers would take 'a dim view' of Chaudhuri's favourable view of the British record in India in his reader's report for Chatto seems to confirm the veracity of his assessment. The Macmillan archive does not house any documents explaining why they did not publish *Circe*. However, a letter to Chaudhuri from his friend Sir Roy Harrod, who investigated the matter on hearing Chaudhuri's story, exists in the British Library. Harrod confirms that Macmillan recommended changes *specifically* in relation to Chaudhuri's references to Nehru and Kipling. He reports to Chaudhuri that while Rex Allen from Macmillan 'absolutely denied that any conditions were imposed about your references either to Nehru or Kipling', Allen admitted to Harrod, 'some well meant advice might have been tendered in this regard. For instance, some sort of warning about your language making things difficult for you in India.' Allen insisted that 'anything that was said about Nehru or Kipling was intended only as kindly advice and in no sense as a condition of publication'.[88] While it is impossible to know for certain, Chaudhuri's conclusion seems persuasive, particularly because there is no other explanation as to why he would go to the trouble of placing his book with another publisher. Chaudhuri's letter reveals his paradoxical essence: his overt prejudices should not blind us to his perspicacious observation. Equally, the correspondence underscores the discrepancy between official and public pronouncements and privately nurtured prejudices.

As Wint's report on *Circe* implies, views such as Chaudhuri's were beginning to be challenged. Revisionary accounts in the 1960s and 1970s of Britain's imperial history led Chaudhuri to criticise 'certain English circles' for their 'violent rancour against . . . the greatest phenomenon ever known to history [the British Empire]'. He interprets criticism of the Empire and of 'English greatness' as a disavowal of their 'heritage'. Announcing that he rejects 'England totally as it is *active*', Chaudhuri explains that he wants 'to get back to Timeless England' which he paradoxically claims exists 'side by side' with contemporary England 'as another dimension'.[89] His dislocation from the Britain he chose to make his home in 1970 becomes evident in his later diatribes against abortion

---

[88] Sir Roy Harrod, letter to Nirad C. Chaudhuri, 21 May 1968, Add. 71620f.11 British Library.
[89] Nirad C. Chaudhuri, interview with D. Barlow.

and mini-skirts in *The Horsemen of the New Apocalypse*. Despite his self-Westernisation and emphasis on immersion into the host society, beyond a tiny circle of loyal publishers and friends, Chaudhuri never really assimilated in Britain because he sought to transform himself into outdated ideas of 'Englishness', remaining at odds with the host culture of 1970s Britain.

The style and quality of his later work reflects Chaudhuri's refusal to engage with contemporary debates and acknowledge or read revised historical accounts: 'I am old, and I cannot spend the few years that are left to me tilting at theories which I have taken a lifetime to outgrow.'[90] His subsequent texts are increasingly uneven, characterised by dense prose, repetition, the rehearsal of old arguments, sweeping generalisations, denunciations, and a hectoring tone of self-justification. There is something double-voiced in his later texts. He seems to address both 'his' specific readerships in Britain (identified by Macmillan as those 'friendly but not sentimental' towards India), and his critics in India.[91] This is particularly evident in his first book published in India and pitched to Indian readers, *The Intellectual in India* (1967), an account of Hindu, Muslim, and Western intellectual traditions in India, in which Chaudhuri expresses his perception of contemporary India as an 'anti-intellectual' country. In contrast to his early *Autobiography*, in these later texts his passionate outbursts, exaggerations, and subjective distortions are largely unrelieved by lyrical descriptions of growing up or his acute, particularised observations of the natural world and insight into social phenomena.[92] *Hinduism: A Religion to Live by* (1979), a discussion of religious beliefs, myths, and taboos, and a sustained critique of Hinduism as a 'worldly . . . social contract between two acquisitive communities' in contrast to Christian spirituality which enriches the mind is one example.[93] Certain critical responses to *Hinduism* also betray the sense of relief over the privileged native informant's endorsement of privately held received ideas. The Chatto and Windus archive contains an anonymous review of *Hinduism* which suggests that 'in overhauling the subject, Chaudhuri brings to it not only whimsy and illumination but also the feeling that

[90] Nirad C. Chaudhuri, interview with the author.
[91] Watson, First Reader's Report on *Circe*.
[92] The best examples of these descriptions are found in his *Autobiography* and early depictions of English countryside: 'Beyond the foamy patch the sea was shot with purple and heliotrope like the throat of a pigeon.' Chaudhuri, 'Indian England', 73.
[93] Nirad C. Chaudhuri, *Hinduism: A Religion to Live By* (Delhi: Oxford UP, 1997), 72. Hereafter *Hinduism* pagination will appear in the text.

Hinduism is every bit as peculiar as he says it is'.[94] The role of the native informant is clearly circumscribed to inform by *conforming*. His book is not a general, introductory or scholarly exposition of Hinduism. Clearly it is Chaudhuri's idiosyncratic views not his ability to 'inform' that makes him a privileged 'insider', as a reader's report for Macmillan confirms: 'Chaudhuri's outbursts, digressions . . . whimsicalities [were] among the things that commended him to us in the first place.'[95]

At the same time, as the publishers of *Hinduism* (Chatto and Windus and OUP) realised, Chaudhuri's observations were becoming increasingly inflammatory in the racially sensitive early 1980s. The Voice of India Society (London) and the International Society for Krishna Consciousness protested against what they saw as *Hinduism's* distortion, 'invective', and 'bigotry', especially in what was 'advertised as . . . an accurate picture of Hinduism'.[96] In an extreme letter to Chatto and Windus, Chaudhuri insists that such protests and 'threats . . . have a political significance for you [English people]. You notice its insolence. This is typical of the Indian immigrants . . . a movement of counter-imperialism—an attempt to establish Indian rule over you. The folly of admitting coloured immigrants into this country is becoming self-evident every day.' (Chaudhuri later returns to this argument in *Thy Hand*.) He links the objections to *Hinduism* to the contemporary protests against the controversial Nationality Act of 1981 that was about to be passed: 'The clamour against the nationality bill is all of a piece with the general attitude. The Indians try to do in Britain what they never attempt in America, Canada and Australia.' The similarities with right-wing views, such as those of Ray Honeyford and Norman Tebbit, on Britain's supposedly excessive liberality towards its ethnic minorities are striking. Chaudhuri concludes his letter to Chatto: 'In fact I think this letter should be sent to the Home Office . . . so that they may ponder over its significance.'[97] In a manner that makes this an interesting precursor to the Rushdie Affair, the publishers summarily dismissed the Indian protests against *Hinduism* as 'hysterical criticisms' and their

[94] Anonymous, undated review, File Chaudhuri 1979–83.

[95] Watson, First Reader's Report on *Circe*.

[96] Voice of India, letter to David Attwooll, 27 May 1981. See also the International Society for Krishna Consciousness, letter to David Attwooll, 23 May 1981, File Chaudhuri 1979–83.

[97] Nirad C. Chaudhuri, letter to Hugo Brunner, 4 June 1981, File Chaudhuri 1979–83.

'particular brand of censorship'. Nevertheless, realising that Chaudhuri was becoming a liability, they decided that a meeting between Voice of India and Chaudhuri 'would be a bad idea'.[98]

During the Thatcherite 1980s, which marked a shift to the right, and when national belonging was an especially fraught issue, it is easy to see why the *Daily Telegraph* chose to publish Chaudhuri's reactionary perspectives. Voiced through a 'native', now resident in Britain, they reinforced the newspaper's right-wing stance, whilst protecting it from accusations of racism. (*The Times* published Dom Moraes' similar observations on the perils of immigration.) In 1988 the newspaper published an article in which Chaudhuri bemoans the fact that the days when the former colonies' claim to share English 'greatness' through participation in her intellectual culture 'are gone forever' because of the influx of Bangladeshi immigrants who arrive in England 'ignorant of English'.[99] While this may stem from anti-Muslim sentiment, it is overdetermined by classism. Chaudhuri dismisses those immigrants who cannot speak English as uneducated: 'In the minds of the Bengalis, at least, education and English were inseparable.'[100] This, however, dissimulates the classed (and caste) access to English: the fact that fluency in English in the subcontinent has very little to do with education per se.[101] Chaudhuri interprets the arrival of 'these Bengalis from . . . East Bengal to turn England into a multi-racial, multi-lingual and multi-cultural country' as an illustration of the 'public *decline* of English greatness'.[102] In this suggestion that non-Anglophone immigrants are undesirable, and should be excluded wherever possible, once again Chaudhuri ratifies local British racist attitudes towards immigration. His argument that it results in a loss of identity and the erosion of a supposed common core of 'Englishness', similarly reinforces ideas disseminated by right-wing opinion: 'A vocal and influential minority are saying that the immigration of coloured people will enrich English life by making it multilingual and multicultural. Today, apparently, *the distinction between the words adulteration and enrichment has ceased to be recognized.*'[103] The imagery of pollution and contamination threatening cultural homogeneity is

---

[98] David Attwooll, letter to Hugo Brunner, 24 June 1981, File Chaudhuri 1979–83.
[99] Chaudhuri, 'Why I Mourn for England', 1.
[100] Chaudhuri, 'Opening Address', 11–12.
[101] See Partha Chatterjee, *The Present History of West Bengal*, 70.
[102] Chaudhuri, 'Why I Mourn for England', 1.
[103] Nirad C. Chaudhuri, *Three Horsemen of the New Apocalypse* (Delhi: Oxford UP, 1997), 98, emphasis mine.

significant. Chaudhuri acknowledged the impact of Spengler's *Decline of the West* (1928) on his ideas (*Autobiography* 473). (*Thy Hand* is modelled as a similar account of the pervasive decline of India.) In attributing the influx of outsiders as a factor in England's decline, Chaudhuri shares another key determinant of Spengler's ideology: Spengler's anti-semitism is transferred to Chaudhuri's rejection of Bangladeshi immigrants. This is in keeping with the way, as Richard Thurlow identifies, the non-white immigrant replaced the Jew as the main scapegoat in the demonology of such groups. Just as Spengler distinguished between 'good' Jews who assimilated into a national culture and 'bad' Jews who did not, Chaudhuri criticised immigrants who do not assimilate into the dominant culture.[104] The extremity of his views explains why Chaudhuri remained till his death fundamentally at odds with, and opposed to a post-imperial multicultural Britain. It is for these reasons that his reputation dwindled, and why he remained a marginal figure in Britain, despite honorary degrees from the Universities of Stirling (1978) and Oxford (1990), and the award of a CBE (1992). Occasionally cited to reinforce resurgent conservative ideologies, Chaudhuri became a historical witness who had outlived his era. He was a rather unsettling reminder to those who would rather forget imperialism's cultural denigration. Some minority groups in England (like some Indians in India) may have been embarrassed by the existence of those of his generation who adopted such an extreme form of motivated Anglicisation. As Ian Jack wryly observed on Chaudhuri's ninetieth birthday: 'Labour-controlled local authorities may rename streets after Nelson Mandela and libraries after C. L. R. James, but it is safe to assume that there will never be a Nirad C. Chaudhuri Drop-in Centre for Bengali adolescents in the London borough of Tower Hamlets. (He would be horrified by the honour.)'[105] As we will see in the second part of this chapter, while Chaudhuri became increasingly out of place in multicultural Britain, Tambimuttu continually translated himself into the demands of his immediate contexts.

[104] Richard C. Thurlow, 'Satan and Sambo: The Image of the Immigrant in English Racial Populist Thought since the First World War', in Kenneth Lum (ed.), *Hosts, Immigrants and Minorities* (Folkestone: Dawson and Sons, 1980), 55, 47.
[105] Ian Jack, 'The World's Last Englishman' in Swapan Dasgupta (ed.), *Nirad C. Chaudhuri: The First Hundred Years: A Celebration* (Delhi: HarperCollins, 1997), 42.

# Self-translation as Self-promotion:

## *II: M. J. Tambimuttu*

## ACCULTURATION IN COLONIAL SRI LANKA
## (1915–38)

Unlike Chaudhuri's active, studied process of self-Westernisation and self-education while he lived in India, Tambimuttu's acculturation to the colonial culture while growing up in colonial Sri Lanka (then Ceylon) was less self-conscious.[1] His middle-class, English-speaking, Roman Catholic, Tamil[2] family was more Westernised than Chaudhuri's. While Chaudhuri did not wear Western clothes till he was in his forties, early family photographs show Tambimuttu and his father in European suits.[3] In colonial Sri Lanka, as in India, education cut across caste and ethnic divisions at an elite level. Consequently at the beginning of the twentieth century, many members of this elite thought of themselves as Ceylonese, and not as Tamil, Sinhalese, or Muslim. The designation Ceylonese was itself a colonial construct.

---

[1] Sri Lanka was known as Ceylon until 1972. However I refer to the country as Sri Lanka throughout except where the word Ceylon appears in quotations.

[2] Although he was sometimes inaccurately referred to as an Indian writer, Tambimuttu belongs to the Sri Lankan Tamil community, which comprised about 11% of the population of colonial Sri Lanka. Tamils are predominantly Saivite Hindus, speakers of the Tamil tongue of the Dravidian family widely spoken in south India and largely based in the dry northern and eastern provinces of the island. Catholic Tamils were converted by the Portuguese (1505–1638), Christian Tamils by the Dutch (1638–1796) and the British (1796–1948). Although the Dutch persecuted the Sri Lankan Roman Catholics converted by the Portuguese, the British largely tolerated these Roman Catholics who would have seemed closer to the colonising power than the Buddhists and Hindus.

[3] For a discussion of the complex affiliations signified by dress, see Emma Tarlo, *Clothing Matters: Dress and Identity in India* (Chicago: University of Chicago Press, 1996).

This contrasts with Chaudhuri's strong sense of his Bengali identity. Knowledge of English was a barometer of social prestige, though the cost was that the processes of socialisation experienced by members of the Ceylonese elite separated them from their native culture and the majority population.[4] Unlike Chaudhuri, well versed in classical Bengali poetry and music, Tambimuttu was barely fluent in his native Tamil. His colonial education ensured that his first language was English and his second was Latin. Pupils were fined for speaking Tamil at his school. Tambimuttu's education at a Catholic convent in Trincomalee in the northern Jaffna peninsula, continued at St Joseph's College in the capital Colombo. In his poem *My Country, My Village*, he suggests that Colombo's metropolitan influence reinforced the process of Westernisation: it was Colombo as 'a home, a mould / That shaped me in the Western swirl and rush'.[5] In this way, Tambimuttu's alienation from native cultural forms was much more marked than Chaudhuri's.

Chaudhuri has been described as an Edwardian modernist of India; Tambimuttu can be located in the contexts of indigenous configurations of inter-war modernism articulated in, for instance, Sri Lankan George Keyt's (1901–93) hybrid paintings inspired by Sri Lankan temple paintings and Picasso, and verse influenced by surrealism and French poets Eluard and Mallarmé. Tambimuttu's early poems published in Colombo suggest he had absorbed modernist influences from such contexts before arriving in Britain. His use of lower case letters and poems with titles in French, such as 'L'Envoi' and 'Chanson', give a hint of his cosmopolitanism, itself a modernist trope. He acknowledges his friend Justin Pieris who 'first introduced me to the work of e.e. cummings'.[6] Tambimuttu's private correspondence indicates his friendship with the leading Lankan creative artists of the era, particularly photographer and musician Lionel Wendt, as well as his appreciation of Keyt's 'excellent verse' and David Peynter's art.[7] Tambimuttu published his first volume of poems, *Songs of Youth*, in 1932, setting the type himself on his grandfather's printing press. Related to Ananda Coomaraswamy, his family's

---

[4] Nira Wickremasinghe, *Ethnic Politics in Colonial Sri Lanka 1927–1947* (Delhi: Vikas, 1995), 25.

[5] *My Country, My Village* was first published in Jane Williams's festschrift to Tambimuttu. Jane Williams (ed.), *Tambimuttu: Bridge Between Two Worlds* (London: Peter Owen, 1989), 26.

[6] Tambimuttu, letter to Ralph Pieris, Apr. 22, 1947, Tambimuttu Papers, British Library, Dept. of Manuscripts, Add. 10028.

[7] Tambimuttu, letter to Fredoon Kabraji, Mar. 14, 1946, Tambimuttu Papers, British Library, Dept. of Manuscripts, Add. 10028.

literary and publishing background had encouraged Tambimuttu's literary and cultural interests. His grandfather was a famous poet and publisher, whose birthday poems inspired Tambimuttu's later penchant for festschrifts.[8] His grandfather owned and edited one of the first newspapers published in Tamil and English. Tambimuttu's father was also an editor and set up his own press. In 1936, Tambimuttu published another two volumes of poetry, *Tone Patterns* and *Och*. *Tone Patterns*, dedicated to his lover Miriam, contains several sensuous love poems such as 'Remembrance' and 'Woman'. 'Mutability' and 'Abstraction' are more general meditations. Although there is no evidence of his later interest in surrealism and the subconscious in this juvenilia, his preface articulates the makings of an aestheticist credo: 'I have attempted in most of these poems to capture beauty of sound, and ingenuity of texture, in graceful, symmetrical sound-patterns, animated with thought. I believe I have created the right atmosphere and obtained a correct relation of light and shade, in thought and sound and thus truth of effect.' The poem 'Monsoon' illustrates these ideas:

> zooms the monsoon
> zeppelins
> palm leaves
> whipt to splinters
> seething boisterous hordes tee- hee- E
> shells dropping in no man's-land
> crikey
> the sea is laughing
> catamaran clutter of crudity.[9]

The use of colloquial 'crikey' is a sign of Tambimuttu's familiarity with schoolboy English and the imported British boys' magazines he devoured as a child. It is a marker of fluency as well as class, since it establishes frequent use of English at an informal level.[10] At the same time, the discordant juxtaposition of aesthetic sensibility with such boyish slang recalls the techniques of Joyce's *Portrait of the Artist as a Young Man*.

Tambimuttu's family's privileged position in class and caste hierarchies, as landowning *vellalar* caste and colonial bourgeoisie, impinged on

---

[8] For instance Tambimuttu's festschrifts to T. S. Eliot and Marianne Moore
[9] M. J. Tambimuttu, *Tone Patterns* (Colombo: Slave Island Printing Works, 1936), 7.
[10] Arjuna Parakrama, *De-Hegemonizing Language Standards: Learning from (Post)-Colonial Englishes about 'English'* (Basingstoke: Macmillan, 1995), 96.

his affiliation with the ruling power. The legitimacy of British rule was sustained by an ideology where inequality was accepted and hierarchies determined by birth. British colonial policy reinforced categories of race and class, and also devised new patterns of stratification. Status, which is primarily concerned with social esteem and prestige, was at the centre of a clearly defined racial taxonomy and a hierarchy maintained in order to know and control the indigenous population.[11] The way this strategy worked can be seen in Tambimuttu's own recollection of his motivated affiliation to the colonising culture and the attendant sense of superiority towards less Westernised Ceylonese in his retrospective autobiographical essay 'Swami Rock, Raga Rock'.[12]

The boys from families who had to traffic with or work for the British . . . dressed like the British in shirt, shorts and tie. These woollen-socked and heavy-booted boys considered themselves the 'in' people, a feeling that I myself have experienced, which accentuated the split nature of my personality oscillating between the European and non-European. (*Tambimuttu* 37)

Tambimuttu recalls this ambivalence of affiliations signified by dress in a memorable passage from 'Swami Rock, Raga Rock' that suggests his neglected prose was often more vivid and impressive than his poetry:

In Ceylon or India, the dress and the way it is worn indicates race, religion, sect, profession, caste and marital state. People wore Hindu or non-Hindu clothes in public and these too were apt to be changed abruptly. The most dramatic exhibition of the phenomenon happens daily on the Colombo–Talaimanaar Express. The passengers who board the night train *en masse* in Colombo, and are tightly packed in the compartments, are Tamils, mostly in European dress, on their way to . . . Jaffna.

By daybreak the jungle has given way to the coral plains and the salt estuaries of the North with groves of coconut and palmyra, and the passengers have been transmogrified overnight, effecting a sartorial and personality change. The starched, constricting suits and shoes have disappeared in an avalanche of silk vertis, kurtaus, and sandals. . . . Cigarettes have been routed by the concerted assault of the northern-grown Jaffna cheroot. . . . The former bilingualism drowned with the sole use of Tamil . . . deliberately raised to . . . present . . . a sense of nationalism, with others trying to steer a sheepish middle course. (*Tambimuttu* 38)

The humorous use of 'routed' and 'concerted assault' reinforces the way these markers were seen as forms of resistance to the colonising

---

11 Wickremasinghe, *Ethnic Politics*, 11.
12 'Swami Rock, Raga Rock' was first published in Williams, *Tambimuttu*, 28–45.

culture. At the same time the ambivalence of these gestures is made clear. This performative aspect of identity and its inherent fluidity relates to Tambimuttu's self-transformation on migration: it was something he had seen enacted many times before.

In contrast to Chaudhuri's autobiography, Tambimuttu's retrospective account of his childhood self-consciously foregrounds the dislocating effects of colonial rule. However, Tambimuttu's recollections of his formative years are not straightforward. Although the exact date of the composition of 'Swami Rock, Raga Rock' is not known, it was written towards the end of his life, years after he first migrated to Britain, by which time his conscious self-representation as 'anti-colonial' had been long under way. His criticisms concerning the imposition of English culture and history, and the corresponding neglect of indigenous history and denigration of the native cultures, need to be seen in relation to this self-construction:

Ceylonese history was not taught at school . . . and what history I was taught by my family, or learnt from the gossip and folk-tales of our own people, was scoffed at. Ours was only myth and legend, uncorroborated by scholarship and the archaeological finesse of Europe. . . . Whatever our historians had gathered from Ceylon and Indian records was not history, since we claimed for ours an impossible antiquity. (*Tambimuttu* 28)

This passage is reminiscent of R. K. Narayan's description of such indoctrination in his novel *Swami and Friends*.[13] Tambimuttu writes: 'we were taught the falsity of Hinduism and the distrust of things Hindu at school' (*Tambimuttu* 31). Tambimuttu claims to have felt 'hesitant, embarrassed and even apologetic for our customs, manners, ceremonies, beliefs, . . . our lack of history, the feeling stretching back to the years before I was seven, the creeping mist over the bright film of childhood' (*Tambimuttu* 30). He recalls that his obsession with the mystery of Swami Rock and search for clues of the 'legendary' Thirukonarmarlai Temple was motivated by a desire to prove it was not a 'figment of our anti-colonial, defensive or aggressive minds' (*Tambimuttu* 35). This reinforces Tambimuttu's retrospective desire to present himself as 'anti-colonial', even though his early writings (in colonial Sri Lanka and during his first phase in Britain from 1938 to 1949) are far removed from the protest against colonialism articulated by his contemporaries in Sri Lanka, or indeed in Britain. (See for

---

[13] R. K. Narayan, *Swami and Friends* [1935] (London: Mandarin, 1990), 3–5.

instance, the progressive, anti-colonial monthly *Young Ceylon* published in Colombo during the 1930s.[14]) However, although not an outspoken opponent of colonialism like his contemporary Anand, Tambimuttu privately criticises his colonial education in a letter written in 1947: 'I cannot read Tamil very well (O education in Ceylon where I was taught all about King Alfred and his burnt cakes and Parakrama Bahu or Asoka were myths).'[15]

Chaudhuri's alienation made him anxious to mark a division between self and others, and his own separation from his native culture, maintaining that the Westernised Bengali intellectual tradition was all that was worth saving from his heritage. In contrast, Tambimuttu avers that his childhood was characterised by his experience of divisions within himself. He claims his perception of the 'stress and strain' between his multiple cultural inheritances created a fragmented 'split personality . . . characteristic of Ceylonese . . . in colonial times' (*Tambimuttu* 38, 29). In keeping with his self-conscious self-representation as 'utterly and essentially Hindu' *after* arriving in Britain, Tambimuttu portrays and perhaps exaggerates a conflictual account of his identity formation (*Tambimuttu* 21). Although he was born into a Roman Catholic family, in his autobiographical essay he foregrounds his Hindu roots as an important part of this duality. He repeatedly refers to the 'impenetrable . . . dualism' of his family by which he remained 'perplexed' (*Tambimuttu* 42). For on the one hand, Tambimuttu asserts that he was 'brought up to be proud of [his] family's Hindu heritage, which had been besieged in 1505'. His ancestors were captured by the Portuguese and converted in Goa before their return to Sri Lanka. On the other hand, he suggests that 'Hindu subjects were *verboten*' amongst his brothers, implying the fraught position that in practice they inhabited (*Tambimuttu* 31). Tambimuttu recalls how his parents '*smiled indulgently*' at his proud display of his newly acquired Ganesha statue. While he maintains that he was particularly struck by the dualism at home 'Christianity . . . counter pointed with our Hindu mode of life, Hindu customs and close affinity with our Hindu relatives', he also insists on 'the *irrelevancy* of Christianity to my own life, and that of my family' during his early years (*Tambimuttu* 31, 35, emphasis mine). This is difficult to reconcile with his family's strong Catholic

[14] Dunstan de Silva, 'A Myth that sustains an Empire', *Young Ceylon* 4.1 (May 1935), Colombo Municipal Library Archives, Sri Lanka.

[15] Tambimuttu, letter to Ralph Pieris, 22 Apr. 1947, Tambimuttu Papers, British Library, Dept. of Manuscripts, Add. 10028.

background and the fact that his elder brother Francis became a Catholic priest. Moreover, even the Hindu relations he speaks of were Hindu *two* generations before.[16] It is significant that Tambimuttu foregrounds his Hindu background with stories of his paternal grandfather who had Hinduised the Catholic Church in Atchuvely by introducing Hindu drummers.[17] Given the distance in time that his family was Hindu (1505), he seems to have invented a tradition of a Hindu heritage after he arrived in Britain and gravitated towards the bohemian artists and poets of London's Soho and Fitzrovia.

## ASSIMILATION AND SELF-TRANSLATION
## IN BRITAIN (1938–49)

The terms on which the Fitzrovian set, including Dylan Thomas (1914–53), George Barker (1913–91), William Empson (1906–84), and Gavin Ewart (1916–95) accepted Tambimuttu on his arrival in 1938 are complex. His assimilation was facilitated in part by his classed *similarity* to his elite, literary circle: his class background, English education, and appreciation of Western literature. As his contemporary Mulk Raj Anand suggests, 'the middle section took him up' because 'Tambi was already . . . a brown Englishman'.[18] Anand further suggests Tambimuttu's privileged class background explains why he failed to identify with or show any interest in the independence struggles of his own 'disinherited society', when they were at their height in the 1930s (*Tambimuttu* 195–6).[19] Anand's own urgent novels on the plight of the oppressed in India, and his play about the famine in India staged at London's Unity Theatre in 1943, contrast with the elitist preoccupations of both Chaudhuri and Tambimuttu. Like Chaudhuri,

[16] I am grateful to Tambimuttu's first cousin Joe Aloysius for this information. Joe Aloysius, interview with the author, 2 Jan. 2001.

[17] This may be to suggest that his ancestors were part of the indigenous religions' revivalist movements, which were, as Nira Wickremasinghe has shown, more than religious crusades against Christianity. They formed a way in which the new middle class could challenge the social values of a foreign Christian and British rule as a whole. Wickremasinghe, *Ethnic Politics*, 33.

[18] However he did not isolate himself from other South Asians, as is often assumed: he remained close to his friend and fellow writer Alagu Subramaniam. He frequented Ceylon House and helped to organise an exhibition of Jamini Roy's paintings in 1946.

[19] For a discussion of the role of the colonial bourgeoisie in Sri Lanka, see Kumari Jayawardena, *'Nobodies to Somebodies': The Rise of the Colonial Bourgeoisie in Sri Lanka* (Colombo: Social Scientists' Association and Sanjiva Books, 2000).

Tambimuttu appears to have seen very little outside the class 'broadly resembling' his own while in England (*Passage* 123).[20] Tambimuttu even fabricated a royal ancestry that was accepted by his new milieu.[21] The BBC addressed its correspondence to Prince Tambimuttu.[22] Perhaps he claimed to be a Prince in order to 'compensate' for his race, as a means of gaining acceptance. This gives us an insight into the conditions or terms on which foreigners were accepted in Britain at that time. As his former secretary, Betty Relle, recalls 'I did notice Tambi's underlying loneliness'. She remembers 'how he used to remind me he was a prince, and I used to wonder why he became conscious of this . . . coming from Sri Lanka at such a time to literary London, which was full of snobbery', a snobbery that would have included racism (*Tambimuttu* 77).

Tambimuttu seems to have accurately anticipated the response to such a self-representation, an early indication of his ability to judge his host community. Many of the contributors to the festschrift *Tambimuttu* speak approvingly of his class origins, 'that of a highly placed Tamil family in Ceylon' or 'Descended from the kings in Jaffna in Ceylon' (*Tambimuttu* 48, 21). A contemporary poet, Tom Scott, confirms the degree to which Tambimuttu's class background overrode racial distinctions, making Tambimuttu's assimilation into the privileged *Poetry London* circle easier than his own:

> But Tambi, and I had many things in common,
> not least that we were both aliens here,
> he a Ceylonese Tamil, I a Scot
> and I was the more alien of the two,
> class-conscious, proletarian Scot.
> He was upper caste and cosmopolitan,

[20] A contemporary, Julian Maclaren-Ross, mocks the classed nature of Tambimuttu's cosmopolitanism in his claim that 'Tambi for some reason loathed and despised Lascars [Indians] who, though all mankind was his country, did not to him belong to mankind.' J. Maclaren-Ross, *Memoirs of the Forties* (London: Alan Ross Ltd., 1965), 145. However Maclaren-Ross's account appears one-sided. Tambimuttu's personal correspondence reveals his efforts to assist fellow Sri Lankans (from a range of social backgrounds) with letters of introduction. Tambimuttu Papers, British Library, Dept. of Manuscripts, Add. 10028.

[21] Tambimuttu's family tree makes an unsubstantiated claim for his being descended from the last king of Jaffna, baptised Don Constantino. See Joe Aloysius, private papers. Tambimuttu's claims were mocked in the Sri Lankan English press. At the same time, the Sri Lankan press followed Tambimuttu's activities in England with interest and a degree of pride. Anonymous, 'Of Cabbages and Kings', *Ceylon Daily News*, 20 July 1955, 31, Lake House Newspaper Archives, Sri Lanka.

[22] K. F. Lowe, letter to Prince Tambimuttu, 17 May 1944, BBC WAC, Contributors Talks File 1 (1941–62).

educated, socially self-confident
where I was ill at ease.

(*Tambimuttu* 103–5)

G. S. Fraser's interpretation of Tambimuttu's projected aura reveals the particular combination of aristocratic pedigree and native innocence that appealed to this circle: 'one felt the background of Tamil grandees, the atmosphere of a childhood spent in a mixture of rustic simplicity and feudal state'.[23]

In this way Tambimuttu managed to mirror the specific nature of the demand for *difference* of his immediate circle. His assimilation in Britain equally depended on his ability to adapt and respond to the desire for certain forms of cultural difference, particularly his capacity to appear to represent the exoticism and wisdom of the Other world. This self-translation was partly self-created in Tambimuttu's poetry and editorials for *Poetry London*. Although his early poem 'Out of this War' broadly imitates Britain's poetic culture rather than inscribes difference on to it, it constructs the author-narrator as embodying the essence of the exotic East's warmth, plenitude, and fertility; here he is the sensuous rather than spiritual Easterner:

> I ROLL the suns of twenty-five summers in my fist
> Their bellies filled with fruit and corn and thunder.
> The many-flavoured waters of the East slide in my veins,
> And I am ripe for plunder.

As Sukhdev Sandhu suggests, the poem reinforces clichéd contrasts between the capital's sophistication and the simplicity of the poet's own background:

> . . . Neatly brewed and bottled, the heady liquor,
> Lies different on the tongue, to our simple wines.
>
> Tapes and setsquares, cones and tangents,
> The formal property of the cupboard brain;
> Are projected into further lines, cones and tangents,
> A nut too well precisioned for my head.[24]

This serves both to underline his difference and flatter British readers.

---

[23] G. S. Fraser, *A Stranger and Afraid: The Autobiography of an Intellectual* (Manchester: Carcanet Press, 1983), 176.

[24] M. J. Tambimuttu, *Out of this War* (London: The Fortune Press, 1941), 9. Sukhdev Sandhu, *London Calling: How Black and Asian Writers Imagined a City* (London: HarperCollins, 2003), 193.

Over the years Tambimuttu became increasingly keen to assert his ethnicity. As if to symbolise this embracing of his origins he dropped his baptismal names 'Meary/Mary James' employing only Tambimuttu and later the name 'Thurairajah'. 'T. Tambimuttu' first appeared in *Poetry London* in June–July 1948, a few months after Sri Lanka won independence. In this issue, instead of an editorial he reprints Gandhi's favourite *bhajan* in homage to 'the leader' who had been assassinated in January of the same year. We are told that Tambimuttu and H. G. Pandey translated the *bhajan* from Gujarati, although it is not clear the extent to which Tambimuttu himself knew Gujarati.[25] This marks the beginning of his self-construction as a native informant.

In 1948, Tambimuttu published his poem *Natarajah* in honour of T. S. Eliot's sixtieth birthday, the first of his festschrifts. Though self-consciously imitative of his mentor's poetry, in this case the mimicry is the converse of Anglicisation. In the dedication to Eliot, Tambimuttu refers to 'bits of your sentences, and maybe, some of the moods and weathers that have been your concern'. He writes that 'this is the fate of all important artists who have succeeded in transmitting something, however much or little, to other artists'. Ironically *Natarajah* incorporates not only the fragments of T. S. Eliot's 'Four Quartets' such as 'Whisper of running streams, and winter lightning. The wild thyme unseen and the wild strawberry', but also imitates Eliot's use of 'oriental' content and form.[26] It employs the stanza form, the use of 'The Yawn of inbetween' as a mantra and invokes the term 'Shantih' that Eliot employs in *The Waste Land*.[27] The line 'Acting or Not acting' echoes Eliot's allusions to Buddhism, 'At the moment which is not of action or inaction', in 'Four Quartets'.[28]

Tambimuttu's poems of this period reproduce orientalist portrayals of the East, providing further instances of the ways his assertion of cultural difference conforms to prevailing expectations. In 'Four Ceylonese Love Poems' the lover is likened to 'a pink cowrie', 'a heap of pomegranate seeds' and described as 'golden like tea-blossom':

[25] T. Tambimuttu, 'Preface' *Poetry London* 4.13 (1948), 3.

[26] Unable to place *Natarajah* with John Lane, *New Directions* or J. M. Dent Ltd., Tambimuttu published his poem in his own press. Tambimuttu, *Natarajah: A Poem for Mr. T. S. Eliot's Sixtieth Birthday* (London: Editions Poetry London, 1948), 2. T. S. Eliot, 'Four Quartets', *Collected Poems, 1909–1962* (London: Faber and Faber, 1963), 201.

[27] Tambimuttu, *Natarajah*, 8. Eliot repeats Shantih as in a formal ending to an Upanishad. T. S. Eliot, 'The Waste Land' *Collected Poems, 1909–1962* (London: Faber and Faber, 1963), 79.

[28] Tambimuttu, *Natarajah*, 1. Eliot, 'Four Quartets', 211.

For I want to have you Naya, delicately in my blood, like the spices
    that breathe impalpably in the Moorman's muscat and his
    sherbet wine.
And I want to breathe and throb and live and die with you in a
    loneliness
For you are the dark oil within the bowl and I the wick
And how shall I ever burn without you?[29]

In his poem 'My Country, My Village', he constructs orientalist images
of colonial Sri Lanka as feminised, passive, exotic, and tempting:

But, this is my island, this my native earth
That bore me gently from a woman's sigh.

Her eye a blackbird among the tumbling bushes,
Her lashes, the black silk of a deep night,
Her body the pure long scarf of Laxapana.

(*Tambimuttu* 27)

His introductory essay to a collection, *India Love Poems* (1954), is
replete with similar objectifications of Eastern women.[30] Reproducing
orientalist representations of the East, he participates in mutually
supportive discourses of patriarchy and colonialism, which produce
Eastern women in stereotyped, essentialised, and eroticised terms.

Tambimuttu's criticism of poetry that replaced natural impulses and
emotions with objects forms a recurrent motif in his editorials. At
one level, this was a transparent attack on the poetry magazines *New
Verse* and *Twentieth Century Verse*, and a response to the poetry of
political commitment of the 1930s, such as John Lehmann's left-
wing *New Writing*. The latter set out to showcase 'reporting' verse
and prose that had 'a vivid meaning for the men and women who
have lived and died among the wars and rumours of wars'. Home
to Auden, Isherwood, and Spender, it was concerned with 'topical
disturbances' and forms of war reportage and documentary realism.[31]
Articulating his opposition to such 'objective reporting' of the external
world of objects and events, Tambimuttu aligns himself instead with
the New Romanticism of the 1940s that succeeded the New Apocalypse
movement founded by Henry Treece and J. F. Hendry. Tambimuttu

[29] M. J. Tambimuttu, 'Four Ceylonese Love poems', *Poetry London* 1.2 (1939), n.p.
[30] T. Tambimuttu, 'Woman in India', in T. Tambimuttu (ed.), *India Love Poems*
(New York: Peter Pauper Press, 1954), 7–30.
[31] John Lehmann (ed.), *Poems from New Writing, 1936–1946* (London: John
Lehmann, 1946), 6.

advocated sensuous, impromptu, incantatory, and unrestrained poetry 'that stirs the unconscious',[32] qualities epitomised by the poets he published and later called 'The New Moderns': Kathleen Raine, George Barker, Dylan Thomas, and David Gascoyne (the poet most associated with surrealism).[33] His partiality partly explains why anti-intellectualism repeatedly surfaces in his editorials: 'How much "learning" can lead people astray is evidenced by certain bi-monthly periodicals of verse, which neglect the simplicity of life.'[34] However, a closer perusal suggests that Tambimuttu's anti-rationalist stance and preference for 'mystical, mantric' poems, because the appeal of 'definite rhythms and rhymes in poetry is primitive and spontaneous', cohere with the stereotype of the untamed oriental that he had begun to embrace.[35] In this way, his 'specular' reflection of contemporary literary debates and his role in publicising historically local movements such as neo-romanticism, feed into his mirroring of sections of the host society's perceptions of the Orient. Therefore Tambimuttu contrasts rationalism, which has been 'the deeper current in European philosophy', with 'Oriental culture . . . founded on a tradition . . . of spontaneity',[36] which makes 'Oriental life . . . more perfect [than Occidental culture]'.[37] Parallel to his positioning of emotion and intellect as antithetical, were his repeated references to irreconcilable cultural differences between the East and the West, reproducing notions of the essential simplicity of the former versus the complexity of the latter.

Tambimuttu's Eastern self was not only self-created, but partly constructed for him. The degree to which some perceived him as a source of regeneration is clear from a letter from Kathleen Raine to Tambimuttu. She writes: 'I see you as a sort of prodigal sage of Ceylon and India, where God knows, I would dearly love to go sometime before I die.' She draws a comparison between the East where 'there are beginnings, new things happening' and the 'already deadened' West.[38] Elsewhere Raine writes:

[32] M. J. Tambimuttu, 'Third Letter', *Poetry London* 1.3 (1940) 65.
[33] T. Tambimuttu, 'Editorial', *Poetry London-New York*, 1.4 (1960) 3.
[34] Tambimuttu, 'Second Letter', n.p.      [35] Tambimuttu, 'Third Letter', 65–6.
[36] M. J. Tambimuttu, 'Sixth Letter', *Poetry London* 1.6 (1941) 162.
[37] Tambimuttu, 'Third Letter', 66.
[38] Kathleen Raine, letter to Tambimuttu, 22 Nov. no year, MS Coll. Poetry London-New York Records, 1943–68, Columbia University Rare Book and Manuscript Library. Tambimuttu's close friend and co-founder of *Poetry London*, Anthony Dickins, similarly suggests that in contrast to 'wise' men in the East, 'this Western so-called "civilisation" is collapsing, it is the end of an epoch'. Anthony Dickins, letter to

Tambimuttu discerned in my work some quality India looks for and recognizes *whereas England, since the war . . . does not. All is cerebral and political and mundane* whereas Tambi heard in my verses some music of the soul; the music of the goddess Sarasvati who was the form in which he himself worshipped the Goddess.[39]

This is symptomatic of the general attempt to identify Tambimuttu, like Tagore before him, as the embodiment of Eastern spirituality, and points to the way his reception was mediated by essentially spiritual representations of the subcontinent set up in opposition to Western rationality.[40] Robin Waterfield's observations provide a further example: 'Tambi in all essentials was to the Western, logical and rational, analytical mind, incomprehensible—he had just to be accepted, lived with, argued with, rejected in exasperation for a while . . .' (*Tambimuttu* 23). While these Western representations of Eastern spiritualism cannot escape the taints of orientalism, most of Tambimuttu's circle saw Eastern ideas as a force for the expansion and enrichment of traditional Western outlooks. Geoffrey Ellborn writes: 'it was pointless to attempt to impose a Western pattern of behaviour on Tambi, for his whole being was rooted in a civilisation much wiser than ours' (*Tambimuttu* 163). This points to the changing conceptions of cultural difference that date back to the 1890s: an inversion of the colonial denigration of the passive, primitive subject peoples, albeit in equally stereotyped terms. The stress is on irreconcilable, absolute difference rather than our contemporary emphasis on cultural hybridity. At the same time, these orientalist constructs were also invoked as a means of criticism. With regard to Tambimuttu's well-documented pursuit of women, Maclaren-Ross claimed that Tambimuttu's 'attitude, to most things Europeanized, was

Tambimuttu, 18 Dec. 1949, Tambimuttu Archive, Northwestern University, Box 35 folder 6.

[39] Kathleen Raine, *India Seen Afar* (Devon: Green Books, 1990), 12, emphasis mine. This book is dedicated to Tambimuttu.

[40] It is possible that Tambimuttu modelled himself on Tagore (1861–1941). Descriptions of Tagore's reception are similar to accounts of Tambimuttu's reception, although Tagore was more firmly based in Bengali culture. See Hugh I'Anson Fausset, 'Rabindranath Tagore: Mediator Between East and West: Divine Visionary', *Times Literary Supplement* (16 Aug. 1941), 394–5. Significantly, Tambimuttu's self-fashioning represented what Chaudhuri abhorred in both Asians like Tagore (who similarly participated in such constructions) and in white British people who seek versions of Indian spirituality which Chaudhuri describes as figments of the Western imagination. Nirad C. Chaudhuri, 'The Wolf without a Pack', *Times Literary Supplement* (6 Oct. 1978), 1029–31.

to girls exclusively Oriental' in his partial account of Tambimuttu.[41]
Similarly Derek Stanford suggested 'his nature was not a deep one
and his mind was uninhibited and uncomplicated'.[42] Tambimuttu
exploited some of these constructions and would allegedly excuse delays
in editorial procedures stating that 'I haven't a European conception
of time'.[43]

Tambimuttu's self-translation was a necessary strategy, not simply
to gain acceptance socially, but ironically, to be taken seriously profes-
sionally. Tambimuttu's career ultimately depended upon his assertion
of difference and self-reinvention. Nicholas Moore, one of the few
contributors to Tambimuttu's festschrift who did not accept his self-
construction at face value, suggests the image of ' "mystic guru" and
"intuitive editor" were gambits to persuade backers that he was a
genius' (*Tambimuttu* 64). Tambimuttu seems to have been successful
in this. His talents are always equated with, and perceived as inher-
ently deriving from the exoticism of his formative environment. A
contemporary, Diana Gardener writes: 'Tambi's view was inspired and
original, also exotic because of his background' (*Tambimuttu* 48). Jean
MacVean enthuses: 'With Tambi I was aware of a deep inner current
flowing like some great Indian river towards distant, yet-to-be explored
territory' (*Tambimuttu* 179). Francis Scarfe describes Tambimuttu's
poems as 'less sophisticated and more natural than Louis MacNeice's'.
Scarfe admires those 'parts of the poems in which the rhythms are
completely spontaneous and uncontrolled. Here are the rhythms of an
unspoiled poetic talent.'[44] The desire for primitivism and the emphasis
on 'unspoiled' and 'natural' is reminiscent of colonial and primitiv-
ist rhetoric describing the native as uncontaminated by processes of
Westernisation. Raine observes that Tambimuttu wrote his best poetry
when he expressed himself as an Indian, rather than when he tried
to be English; a recurrent trope in the reception of Asian writers by
their Western interpreters.[45] These comments echo the advice received

---

[41] Maclaren-Ross, *Memoirs*, 142. Gavin Ewart suggests that Tambimuttu cultivated
a role of the great lover in order to cope with internalised feelings of racial inferiority.
Gavin Ewart, 'Tambi the Great', *London Magazine* 5.9 (1965), 60.

[42] Derek Stanford, *Inside the Forties: Literary Memoirs, 1937–1957* (London: Sidgwick and Jackson, 1977), 155.

[43] Maclaren-Ross, *Memoirs*, 147.

[44] Francis Scarfe, 'Poles of Poetry', *Poetry London* 1.6 (1941), 202.

[45] Raine claims 'Gita Sarasvati' is Tambimuttu's 'one impressive poem' because it
'speaks with the voice of India'. She prefers this poem to what she describes as his
unsuccessful attempts to write Western poetry in the 1940s. Raine, *India Seen Afar*, 12.

by Tambimuttu's predecessors, Malabari and Bengali poet and patriot Sarojini Naidu (1876–1949).[46]

His assertion of difference paradoxically contributed to Tambimuttu's assimilation in Britain's world of letters. Where Chaudhuri is categorised as Indian, despite his ardent desire to be British, Tambimuttu was included in British literary encyclopaedias of the period. Anthony Dickins discusses the importance of this:

It is significant that Tambimuttu's name is found in the Cambridge History [of English Literature] in the mainstream section, 'Poetry since Hopkins', where he exerted his influence, and not *relegated* with Tagore and Sarojini Naidu to the chapters on Anglo-Indian or Dominion Literature. His, indeed, is the only name in the mainstream section that is not of native British origin; and it must have been disconcerting to some of the editors of the Thirties, limited as they were to the narrow horizons of local politics, to find this *swarthy genius bursting out on them from Ceylon's bamboo jungle* with his message about the noumenal function of poetry.[47]

In this instance this very 'inclusion' is framed within an assertion of 'difference'. Dickins' own stereotyping of Tambimuttu in his attempts to praise him is typical of this particular circle at this juncture. Nevertheless, George Orwell's letter to Alex Comfort (editor of *Lyra*) confirms that Tambimuttu's place in London's literary scene was exceptional in comparison to the marginal position occupied by other Asian writers (such as Bhuphen Mukherjee, B. Rajan) of that era in Britain:

I saw you had a poem by Tambimuttu. If you are bringing out other numbers you ought to get some of the other Indians to write for you. There are several quite talented ones and they are very embittered because they think people snub them and won't print their stuff. It is tremendously important from several points of view to try and promote decent cultural relations between Europe and Asia.[48]

---

[46] Max Müller advised Malabari that 'It is in the verses where you feel and speak like a true Indian that you seem to me to speak most like a true poet.' Cited in C. L. Innes, *A History of Black and Asian Writing in Britain, 1700–2000* (Cambridge: Cambridge UP, 2002), 139. Similarly, Edmund Gosse advised Sarojini Naidu to concentrate on becoming 'a genuine Indian poet of the Deccan' rather than writing English Romantic poetry. Cited in Elleke Boehmer (ed.), *Empire Writing: An Anthology of Colonial Literature 1870–1918* (Oxford: Oxford UP, 1998), 489.

[47] Anthony Dickins, 'Tambimuttu and *Poetry London*', *London Magazine* 5.8 (1965), 53, emphasis mine. Dickins refers to George Sampson and R. Churchill, *The Concise Cambridge History of English Literature* (Cambridge: Cambridge UP, 1961), 973.

[48] George Orwell, letter to Alex Comfort, 11 July 1943, in Peter Davison (ed.), *The Complete Works of George Orwell: Two Wasted Years* (London: Secker and Warburg, 2001), 166.

Tambimuttu's poems appeared in several contemporary anthologies of verse and magazines bearing out Orwell's point.[49] The *Times Literary Supplement* reviewed *Out of this War* 'as powerful, penetrating' but 'too rhetorical'.[50] The dominant society's privileging of 'preferred' authors overshadows the work of other minority writers, a trend that recurs across the generations.

Ultimately, Tambimuttu was more important and influential as an editor and publisher than as a poet. I want now to consider the extent to which he modified his cultural space, and to what degree he reflected uncritically the literary and political concerns of wartime London, by examining the contexts he entered on arrival. During the early years of the war the public demand for verse increased with leisure to read during the curfews.[51] According to Fraser, 'The war had provoked a great many people into writing sincere, occasional verse.'[52] Tambimuttu's *Poetry London* was also an example of the little magazine phenomenon that from the beginning of the twentieth century was characterised by a vital sense of cultural re-examination. As Ian Hamilton observes, in contrast to the commercial or established press, the little magazine existed outside the usual business structure of magazine production and distribution. It was characteristically independent, amateur, and idealistic.[53]

What was Tambimuttu's line when he began? Did *Poetry London* represent a different orientation from other contemporary little magazines? How did *Poetry London* become one of the more significant little magazines, exerting a decisive influence? Tambimuttu's editorials and inclusive editorial policy emphasise his democratising stance against the 'pre-war poetry world . . . built on snobbery and pride'. His first editorial famously pronounced that 'Every man has poetry within him. . . . No man is small enough to be neglected as a poet.'[54] *Poetry London* was designed 'for poets who required more freedom than that

---

[49] M. J. Tambimuttu, 'From *Out of this War*', *Kingdom Come* (Spring 1941), 70–1. His work is featured in Norman Nicholson (ed.), *The Penguin Anthology of Religious Verse* (London: Penguin, 1942). However, he does not appear in any major or subsequent anthologies of verse. For instance, John Heath-Stubbs and David Wright (eds.), *Faber Book of Twentieth Century Verse* (London: Faber and Faber, 1953) and D. J. Enright (ed.), *The Oxford Book of Contemporary Verse, 1945–1988* (Oxford: Oxford UP 1988).

[50] Hugh I'Anson Fausset, 'Three Poets', *Times Literary Supplement* (13 Sept. 1941), 457.

[51] Maclaren-Ross, *Memoirs*, 58.          [52] Fraser, *A Stranger*, 177.

[53] Ian Hamilton, *The Little Magazines: A Study of Six Editors* (London: Weidenfeld and Nicolson, 1976), 7–8.

[54] Tambimuttu, 'First Letter', n.p.

afforded them in the papers of little hen-coops and cliques'. In marked contrast to the literary coteries of the day, *Poetry London* was to be characterised by a 'catholicity which is not a party and therefore has no policy and is important as a principle, in life and art'.[55] From the first number, *Poetry London* represented all schools of contemporary English poetry the Imagists, a Stephen Spender and MacNeice group, a Dylan Thomas group. Although Tambimuttu published many of the Oxbridge poets, such as Julian Symons (editor of *Twentieth Century Verse*), he tried to reach beyond this circle. One issue was devoted to poets who had not appeared before in print or in *Poetry London*.[56] Significantly his rivals dismissed Tambimuttu's magazine's catholicity as his 'vast junk shop or *oriental bazaar*'.[57] Yet the number of rejection letters in Tambimuttu's personal correspondence contests Geoffrey Grigson's claim that for Tambimuttu 'all poems are poems equally worth printing'.[58]

Tambimuttu is considered variously by rival camps as an inspired poet, intuitive editor or fake charlatan as subversive or naive and stupid, a shaper of wartime literary tastes, or a mirror and disseminator of contemporary preferences. Stanford suggests Tambimuttu 'was not an original thinker' and simply proved 'a useful publicist for some of the opinions then in circulation'.[59] As we have seen, there is some truth in this statement. At the same time, Tambimuttu published most of the important English and international writers of his day such as Walter de la Mare, Stephen Spender, Louis MacNeice, and Dylan Thomas. He was among the first to recognise then emerging talents such as Keith Douglas, Lawrence Durrell, Michael Hamburger, Elizabeth Smart, and Kathleen Raine. He published some of their first books or volumes of poetry. His imprint Editions Poetry London also published the first London editions of novels by Anaïs Nin and Vladimir Nabokov. He had a dynamic influence on the content and format of British books, commissioning artists such as Henry Moore, Lucian Freud, Mervyn Peake, Graham Sutherland, and Barbara Hepworth to design covers for his publishing imprint and for his illustrated texts (*Tambimuttu*

---

[55] M. J. Tambimuttu, 'Second Letter', *Poetry London* 1.2 (1939), n.p.

[56] M. J. Tambimuttu (ed.), *Poetry London* 2.10 (1945).

[57] Anonymous citation in Ian Hamilton (ed.), *Oxford Companion to Twentieth Century Poetry in English* (Oxford: Oxford UP, 1994), 554, emphasis mine.

[58] Geoffrey Grigson, letter to Tambimuttu, 11 Dec. 1947, Tambimuttu Papers, British Library, Dept. of Manuscripts, Add. 10028.

[59] Stanford, *Inside*, 155.

50). These lithographs and illustrations were considerable achievements given the constraints on paper and publishing during the war.

Explanations of Tambimuttu's success fall into two extremes. As we have seen, Jane Williams' festschrift *Tambimuttu* voices a host of appreciative fans, who tend to equate Tambimuttu's talent with his Asian background, suggesting it makes him innately intuitive and subversive. On the other hand, commentators such as Ian Hamilton belittle Tambimuttu's distinctive taste, talent, and achievement by claiming that 'simply by being there in London, with a magazine, Tambimuttu also got some fine poems from Alun Lewis and Keith Douglas'. Hamilton ignores the fact that, in spite of wartime conditions, numerous financial difficulties, and irregular publication Tambimuttu built up *Poetry London*'s circulation to 10,000, a remarkable achievement for a poetry magazine. It was the main poetry magazine of the war and for a long time afterwards retained its position as a leading vehicle for modern poetry, and as a proving ground for promising younger poets, surviving *New Verse* (1933–9), *New Writing* (1936–46), *Twentieth Century Verse* (1937–9), *Kingdom Come* (1939–42), and *Horizon* (1940–9). *Poetry London* (1939–50) folded a year after Tambimuttu departed for Sri Lanka in 1949. Hamilton goes on to argue that, for Douglas and Lewis, Tambimuttu 'might have been a bit of a joke, but they were grateful for his presence . . . for . . . Lewis in India and Douglas in North Africa, it mattered a lot that they were getting recognition in the capital'.[60] Keith Douglas' letters support Hamilton's hunch over the discrepancy between Tambimuttu's utility value, and this poet's private opinion of Tambimuttu. In a letter to Tambimuttu Douglas writes: 'Thank you for your letter, and for publishing my poems—I had given up all idea of writing in the Army until your efforts and John Hall's nerved me to try again.'[61] Compare this with Douglas' letter to his mother written only a month before, which refers to ' . . . Tambimuttu—who, it appears is Senegalese and a complete shit'.[62] While for some Tambimuttu is beyond reproach and innately gifted simply because he is foreign, for others the opposite applies. While we can infer from other correspondence that Douglas' negative opinion of Tambimuttu derives partly

[60] Ian Hamilton, 'Bonny Prince Charlatan', *Times Literary Supplement* (1 Dec. 1989), 1335.

[61] Keith Douglas, letter to Tambimuttu, 11 July 1943, in Douglas Graham (ed.), *Keith Douglas: The Letters* (Manchester: Carcanet Press, 2000), 291.

[62] Keith Douglas, letter to Marie J. Douglas, 9 June 1943, in Graham (ed.), *Keith Douglas*, 285.

from the publisher's delay in commissioning (and later producing) a collected edition of his poems and his war narrative, *Alamein to Zem Zem*, it is also problematically linked to his mistaken assumptions about Tambimuttu's race. Such contrary responses illuminate two extremes of the spectrum of attitudes to black and Asians at this time.

## TALKING TO INDIA

As a participant in the BBC radio series aimed at India's English speakers, *Talking to India*, broadcast during the Second World War, Tambimuttu's cultural translation was not directed exclusively to his new home. In translating and refracting particular versions or aspects of British culture to the subcontinental audiences, his contributions were incorporated into British (and later North American) political agendas. The Indian section of the Eastern service comprised news bulletins written by Orwell and read aloud by Asian speakers, and some cultural broadcasts written by the Asian contributors. A memorandum by the head of the Overseas Service reveals its agenda: 'the primary purpose of news commentaries to the subcontinent is propaganda. They make it possible to put across the British view of the news without sacrificing the reputation that has carefully been built up for veracity and objectivity.' The memo defines the role of 'Dominion speakers' as cultural mediators: 'The use of Dominion speakers increases the confidence felt by the audience; particularly in times of difficulty or strained relations, there is thought to be great merit in leaving *the right type of Dominion speaker* free to reflect criticism and in other ways to build up confidence in himself as much as a representative of the Dominion audience as a British spokesman.'[63]

These news bulletins were distinct from the educational, cultural broadcasts that served to disseminate propaganda in different ways. Orwell describes the purported aims of one such programme, entitled 'Through Eastern Eyes':

The general idea is to interpret the West, and in particular Great Britain, to India, through the eyes of people who are more or less strangers. An Indian, or a Chinese perhaps, comes to this country, and because everything is more or less

---

[63] R. A. Rendall, Memo, 9 Feb. 1942, in Peter Davison (ed.), *The Complete Works of George Orwell: All Propaganda is Lies* (London: Secker and Warburg, 2001), 88–9, emphasis mine.

new to him he notices a great deal which an Englishmen or even an American would take for granted.[64]

Some of Tambimuttu's contributions invoke such a stranger's defamiliarising perspective. In 'Mind the Traffic' he describes the 'red buses and black taxicabs . . . [that] weave smooth patterns round the circle [Piccadilly Circus] with the precision of mechanical toys'.[65] Keeping in mind his instruction that his talks should 'have a direct bearing' on his subcontinental audience, he likens the 'immense London bus' 'to a Ceylon tea-factory on wheels'. As anticipated, his cultural mediation connects distant, distinct cultures and populations (and implicitly their political destinies) through simple, visual images.

The cultural broadcasts were clearly intended to offer more than fresh perspectives on aspects of everyday British life and culture. Orwell implicitly encouraged one contributor to make observations that would incite Indian listeners' sympathy for Britain's war effort. Orwell suggested to Damyanthi Sahni that in her talk about London theatre she 'might mention the damage that London theatres have suffered in the air raids, the courageous struggle by which the dramatic profession have carried on. These are only suggestions.'[66] Tambimuttu needed less prompting. In his talk 'The Man in the Street' broadcast in 1941 he describes London's wartime pub culture during the blackouts and air raids, where London streets were rendered 'unreal and intangible' by the 'dim blue lighting'. Situating the pub as a site of social transformation where the 'BBC news, newspapers, and personal opinions' were 'digested to form British public opinion', Tambimuttu presents a sympathetic portrait of the Englishmen who feel this war 'keenly' and discuss it with 'judicial patience'. He describes the few French pubs where one meets 'free French . . . in pubs adorned with photos from the Paris that was'.[67]

[64] Orwell, Memo, 1 Feb. 1942, in Davison (ed.), *All Propaganda*, 163. *Through Eastern Eye's* format of a series of talks addressed to a group unfamiliar with British culture, may owe something to Mohamed Ali Duse's articles published between 1909 and 1911 in the *New Age* edited by Orage and supported by Shaw and Pound. As Innes has argued, Ali adopts the persona of an un-Anglicised Egyptian for whom all things British are something new and strange that may in turn have been influenced by Malabari's criticisms of English culture in his 'An Indian Eye of English Life' (1893). Innes, *A History*, 185–6.

[65] Tambimuttu, 'Mind the Traffic', 2 Dec. 1941, BBC WAC, Contributors Talks File 1 (1941–62), 1.

[66] Orwell, letter to Sahni, 3 Oct. 1942, in Davison (ed.), *All Propaganda*, 53.

[67] Tambimuttu, 'The Man in the Street', 17 Oct. 1941, BBC WAC, Contributors Talks File 1 (1941–62), 4.

These cultural broadcasts concerning symptomatic aspects of British culture (particularly the series 'How British Institutions Work' and 'Books that Changed the World') feed into the overarching promotion of a critical liberal humanist tradition in opposition to political orthodoxy. This belief is endorsed in Tambimuttu's talk 'How it works—The British Press' where he posits a 'free' press, in contrast to a controlled Marxist press: 'English journalism is, in my view, of a higher standard than the journalism in America and the continent. . . . English journalism is generally sober and pries into other people's lives as little as possible. English journalists are mostly chosen for their ability to write well and accurately about facts and events.'[68] Similarly his 'Open Letter to a Marxist' gives a predictable critique of Marxism: 'the danger of Marxism, as I see it, lies in its ecclesiastical dogmatism, which is steadily growing on its disciples. Many who have accepted the doctrines of Marxism . . . have transformed the economic interpretation of history into a metaphysical dogma of deterministic materialism . . . [it is a] theory that ignores the individual element in history and reduces it to an automatic repetition of abstract formulae.'[69]

Orwell suggested to Tambimuttu that the purpose of the 'Open Letters' series was 'to discuss the origins and meaning of the war and to put this in a simple popular form of open letters to imaginary people representing the most important trends of modern thought'.[70] In his invitation to his friend Anand (who fought alongside Orwell against Franco in the Spanish Civil War) to participate in the same series, Orwell was more straightforward about the programme's real purpose: 'an opportunity to do a bit of anti-Fascist propaganda'.[71] This suggests that Tambimuttu was not identified with politics to the same degree as Anand or at least that Orwell did not feel that he could be so candid with him. In *George Orwell: The War Broadcasts*, W. J. West argues that Tambimuttu was not used as much as Anand because he had 'never been to India and his voice was not easily understood there'.[72] However, it is more likely that Tambimuttu was seen to have assimilated, and was not known for his nationalism. In this context, Anand rather than

[68] Tambimuttu, 'How it works: The British Press', 21 Dec. 1941, BBC WAC, Contributors Talks File 1 (1941–62), 5.

[69] Tambimuttu, 'Open Letter to a Marxist', 20 Sept. 1942, ibid. 4.

[70] Orwell, letter to Tambimuttu, 23 June 1942 in Davison (ed.), *All Propaganda*, 369.

[71] Orwell, letter to Mulk Raj Anand, 27 Feb. 1942 in ibid. 193.

[72] W. J. West (ed.), *George Orwell: The War Broadcasts* (London: Penguin, 1987), 44 n. 86.

Tambimuttu would have been considered 'the right type of Dominion speaker'.

## NATIONALISM, COSMOPOLITANISM, AND UNIVERSALISM (1949–52)

In the wake of independence, while Chaudhuri penned his infamous preface to the British Empire that seemed calculated to affront post-Independence Indian nationalist feelings in Delhi,[73] Tambimuttu visited newly independent Sri Lanka from 1949 to 1952 for personal rather than political reasons. After a decade in Britain, his ejection from *Poetry London*, after falling out with his business partner Richard Marsh, precipitated this extended sojourn that preceded his move to the US. Accounts of the events leading to Tambimuttu's departure from *Poetry London* are conflicting.[74] The poet's neglected, unpublished radio play in verse, *Return Journey to Ceylon*,[75] written during this visit reveals some of the specific discursive pressures operating on the expatriate writers of newly independent nations. The play engages with interrelated issues of national and cosmopolitan identity, location, belonging, and allegiance.

Taking the form of a dialogue between the protagonist John (clearly modelled on Tambimuttu) who visits his homeland after an absence of several years and his interlocutor Paul, the play debates whether John should remain in his newly independent country. The characters articulate conflicting aspirations and perceptions that the poet experienced and externalised while in his native land. It may reflect his responses to questions posed to him during his visit to his country of origin, shortly after it gained independence in 1948. Like Chaudhuri, Tambimuttu (via

---

[73] 'To the memory of the British empire in India which conferred subjecthood on us but withheld citizenship; to which yet every one of us threw out the challenge: "Civis Britannicus Sum" because all that was good and living within us was made, shaped and quickened by the same British rule.' Nirad. C. Chaudhuri, *The Autobiography of an Unknown Indian* [1951], Bombay: Jaico Publishing House, 1997, preface.

[74] Correspondence between Tambimuttu and his contributors testify to his inefficiency and chaotic approach. However the termination of Tambimuttu's role as editor met with protest from his friends and contributors, organised by Anthony Dickins who alleges that Tambimuttu's business partner Richard March 'took *Poetry London* out of Tambi's hands by a deft legal stroke' as he had 51% of the shares. Dickins,'Tambimuttu and *Poetry London*', 53. Conversely, Ronald Bottrall defends March, asserting that he faced bankruptcy and 'acted in a most honourable and generous way'. Ronald Bottrall, 'Letter to the Editor', *London Magazine* 5.8 (1965), 102.

[75] Tambimuttu, *Return Journey to Ceylon*, Tambimuttu Archive, Northwestern University, Box 2 folder 6. Hereafter *Return* pagination will appear in the text.

his closely autobiographical John) constructs himself as a cosmopolitan citizen of the world, contesting nativism and the models of identity that conflate identity and location, articulated by Paul. As in Chaudhuri, intellectual ties are privileged over those of place.

JOHN: And tell me what is country, but in the mind?
  The net result of those things one holds precious?
  The world has contracted, I think to a billiard ball,
  And one's roots are in England, Africa or elsewhere,
  You cannot change yourself.
  . . . and how can it [Independence] concern me
  Who am the inheritor of the world's noise,
  Except I was born here, which was an accident? (*Return* 7)

The text explicitly articulates the perception of 'unbelonging' and contests notions of one's birthplace as defining one's identity.

As in Chaudhuri, the nature of cosmopolitanism articulated is pro-affiliation and anti-national. Although both Chaudhuri and Tambimuttu present themselves as citizens of the world, their stance is typical of early definitions of cosmopolitanism of the elite variety that derives from assumptions of the universality of Western culture. Chaudhuri says 'just as I am both Bengali and *universal* I write in both Bengali and English' (emphasis mine).[76] Promoting assimilation into the host culture, Chaudhuri defines 'true cosmopolitans as those with a high capacity to assimilate themselves into any environment and move naturally in it'. At the same time, he betrays a defensive anxiety in his reiteration that his assimilation (or what he refers to as cosmopolitanism) does not involve any loss of 'particularity': 'I remain a Bengali, an Indian, an Englishman, while being a citizen of the world. I have not had to give up anything in order to become cosmopolitan. My cosmopolitanism is deeply rooted in all the particular soils—material or mental—in which I have grown.'[77]

In Tambimuttu's poem, cosmopolitanism is particularly expressive of disaffiliation from the country of origin, portrayed as too wearisome, stifling, and 'local'. John's motivated affiliation is linked to his sense of internal exile within the home country, which has increased after his sojourn in Britain. A key scene is set during the annual Independence Day celebrations:

---

[76] Nirad C. Chaudhuri, interview with D. Barlow, 3 Oct. 1974, BBC 'Profile', BBC WAC, emphasis mine.

[77] Nirad C. Chaudhuri, *Thy Hand, Great Anarch! India, 1921–52* (London: Hogarth Press, 1987), 534.

JOHN: Independence day! What can it mean
   When in Ceylon, I do not feel independent?
   The world's hungry itch for knowledge
   Has made me independent. I am no longer
   My mother's boy, what I was;
   Each must to his task for discovery,
   Or failing, become a stuffed bird in the museum. (*Return* 7)

For Tambimuttu, it seems, to remain is to become stultified and
fossilised.

John debates this with Paul whose stance clearly, if clumsily, 'represents' the nationalist fervour of a newly liberated former colony. Paul
insists 'Every man must do his bit / For his country. We must see / That
the cannas bloom again for us!' (*Return* 20). In response John constructs
the country as a fool's paradise, an enticing but cloying prison, 'a cage
of flowers' (*Return* 20). The text implies that in contrast to the simpler
locals (who are denied the status of being human, but are a less extreme
version of Chaudhuri's description of Indians as 'Yahoos' in his *Circe*),
it is now no longer possible for the recently returned protagonist to be
content with such 'simple' duties. He has 'evolved' beyond his country
and outgrown it.

JOHN: If I were a bee, I will be drunk all day
   In this cage of flowers. . . .
   My duty will be simple, and straightforward,
   Making merry among the rainbow colours
   Of a bee's kingdom's
   But I am human. (*Return* 20)

Hence the text concludes with John's decision 'not yet, not yet, for me
my own country' / 'I must away, away to the work that I must / Do.
And Home is where one's work / And interest lie' (*Return* 23).

Although Tambimuttu's text does not privilege the migrant as 'objective', the expatriate is portrayed as brave to leave, and this courage is
defined in opposition to the easier option of staying:

PAUL: the expatriate is always pathetic . . .
JOHN: he must pluck at courage
   To chase the swallow of his dreams:
   To forgo the enchanting and lyrical island,
   The quiet hermitage, the refuge for toil,
   Is not easy. I will serve my country
   But in my own time, and way, not squabbling
   In the market place. (*Return* 23)

This argument forms part of the rationalisation of expatriation and anticipates a key theme that surfaces in the work of later migrant writers. In contrast to his earlier poems and editorials, Tambimuttu's text engages in a dialogue with the debates and concerns of his country of origin. As we saw, such a dual readership can also be identified in Chaudhuri's later work, which challenges perceptions that the work of both writers was exclusively directed to a Western audience. While I do not want to overstate the identification between Tambimuttu and his narrator John, correspondence indicates that Tambimuttu felt dissatisfied during this visit. Kathleen Raine's letter addressed to Tambimuttu in Colombo in 1951 reads: 'Your letter was sad. I am glad you are writing for the papers and writing poems, but sorry that you hate it all so much.'[78] To a greater degree than in Tambimuttu's other work, this narrator's subject-position as a migrant evinces the political and cultural pressures on such an individual. Here Tambimuttu, on return from Britain and contemplating migration to North America, dramatises the question of whether to move on:

Anyway, who can tell me my duty,
To my country, to myself?
How may one serve one's country best,
Buried in her or fruiting in foreign soil?
I must find out. (*Return* 7)

Chaudhuri's private correspondence reveals a similar rationalisation, self-consciousness, and anxiety about being perceived as disloyal for choosing to live abroad.[79]

However, where Chaudhuri opposes nationalism largely because he sees it as blind to the benefits of imperialism, in Tambimuttu's text, scepticism of nationalism is situated in relation to the post-Independence assertions of Sinhala Buddhist dominance in the nation state. The misgivings partly stem from an apprehension of the causal

[78] Kathleen Raine, letter to Tambimuttu, 15 Apr. 1951, MS. Coll. Poetry London-New York Records, 1943–68, Columbia University Rare Book and Manuscript Library.

[79] Chaudhuri's private correspondence calls for a reappraisal of his construction as an 'India-hater'. He expresses unease over the idea of permanently residing in England: 'I have been very unwilling to settle in England even if I had the money. I thought that I ought to be in India to be of use to my country and people.' Chaudhuri, letter to Laurens Van der Post, 10 June 1974, Chatto and Windus Archive, University of Reading, File Chaudhuri 1971–4. Of course the possibility that Chaudhuri is rationalising his decision to stay cannot be excluded. Nevertheless, this is a significant statement for an alleged 'India-hater'.

connection between nationalism and communalism. Given that these erupted manifestly only in 1956, Tambimuttu was prescient on the dangers of such assertions.

MOTHER: Give us time . . .
　There is a Buddhist revival, and of arts
　We shall usher in another Golden Age!
JOHN: Revivals are clever playthings
　Of politicians. Frankly mother,
　I am Buddhist, Hindu, Christian and Mussalman,
　And life too short for me to waste my time
　Awaiting revival. We are the fusion of a culture
　That is world wide now. (*Return* 22)

In contrast to Chaudhuri, the nature of cosmopolitanism expressed here goes beyond an identification with Britain, and gestures towards an embracing of a plural, multi-ethnic, and religious identity. Tambimuttu's emphasis on plural identities (in contrast to Chaudhuri's Hindu majoritarian outlook) may stem from his growing recognition of the minority and marginalised status of Tamils in post-Independence Sri Lanka. This underscores the impact and influence of the context of the country of origin in relation to evolving migrant identities. However, it was his subsequent move to New York in 1952 that produced a shift in Tambimuttu's residual adherence to universalist criteria, in response to the demand for cultural difference that he encountered in his new milieu.

## SELF-TRANSLATION IN THE US (1952–68)

Although his self-transformation began in England, Tambimuttu's move to New York seems to have been the catalyst for an even more heightened projection of his ethnicity. The most immediately striking aspect of his metamorphosis is evinced in his choice of dress. Photographs of his first phase in England show him in both Western suits and sherwanis. Later photographs in the US show him in exclusively in sherwanis. *Time* magazine features a photograph of Thurairajah Tambimuttu and his second wife, 'pretty Bombay-born' Safia Tyabjee in traditional Eastern clothes.[80] Tyabjee comments on the impact of their dress: ' . . . I found

---

[80] Anonymous, 'New Magazine in Manhattan', *Time* (14 May 1956), 64.

being an Indian was an advantage, as everybody made so much of Indians. My saris and Tambi's *sherwanis*, which he habitually wore in preference to Western clothes, were everywhere commented on and admired' (*Tambimuttu* 132).

Tambimuttu's intensified self-translation was his response to the expectations of his new host country: North America's traditional interest in esoteric aspects of Hinduism illuminates Tambimuttu's reception, metamorphosis, and heightened Hinduism in New York. (Tambimuttu's reinvention is in part echoed in Narayan's mystic turn, which paid off particularly in relation to the US. Narayan's *Mahabharata* was written at the instigation of his publisher.) As J. J. Clarke observes:

The work of both Huxley and Hesse, like Edwin Arnold's *The Light of Asia* in an earlier period, had a powerful impact on the imagination of a readership, which, from the 1950s onwards, shared their desire to reach out to new artistic and spiritual horizons. This period witnessed a rapid growth of interest in Eastern ideas amongst both intellectuals and the educated public in general, and orientalism as a conspicuous socio-cultural phenomenon can conveniently be dated from the emergence of the so-called 'beat' movement in this period. This movement, which centred on bohemian artist communities in the USA . . . played a crucial role in propagating an interest in the Eastern way to personal authenticity and heightened states of consciousness.[81]

Beatnik, bohemian, and esoteric interests help produce a more 'Indian' version of Tambimuttu as cosmopolitan poet: his reputation as a bohemian poet plus his Asian background positioned him at the confluence of the 'beat' movement *and* the heightened interest in Eastern ideas. Such interests drew on Zen Buddhism, Hinduism, and Taoism and anticipated the hippie movement of the 1960s. During this era, beat poetry was seen as a way of defying conformity: Allen Ginsberg's mantras and chants are examples of orientalist trends in the American literary scene. Exchanging Fitzrovia for Greenwich Village, Tambimuttu was quick to respond to the beat movement, carrying the work of vogue beatniks Ginsberg and Jack Kerouac in his later issues of his new venture, the short-lived *Poetry London–New York* (1956–60). (Many leading Anglo-American poets including Robert Graves, Marianne Moore, William Empson, Walter de la Mare, W. H. Auden, and e.e. cummings donated poems for his first issues. This suggests that Tambimuttu was as well connected in New York, as he had been in London. The initial

---

[81] J. J. Clarke, *Oriental Enlightenment: The Encounter between Asian and Western Thought* (London: Routledge, 1997), 103.

printing of 4,000 copies of the first issue was quickly sold out.) The way he conformed to the craze for Eastern spirituality and its offer of heightened consciousness can be seen in the manner in which he emphasised his 'Hindu' roots. He experimented with meditation, yoga, and LSD at Timothy Leary's League for Spiritual Discovery Centre at Millbrook. Tambimuttu was even voted Vice President of the centre or 'ashram' as the members called it. The league's mission statement describes it as an 'incorporated religion dedicated to the ancient sacred sequence of turning-on, tuning-in, and dropping-out. Our aim is to help recreate every man as God and every woman as Goddess.'[82] The affiliations of 1960s' counterculture with 'ancient' religions such as Hinduism is clear. Tambimuttu's internalisation of this pastiche surfaces in 'Swami Rock': 'It is impossible for me to describe the perfect high that a Hindu temple with its site, its rituals and atmosphere gives me' (*Tambimuttu* 35). Williams suggests the role he played at the centre 'as their "guru" conducting meditations, was one he took seriously and with which the Hindu in him closely identified' (*Tambimuttu* p. ix). However, Tambimuttu's participation appears to have been a relatively token one, and is best understood as a pragmatic career opportunity. In the records the only motion proposed by Tambimuttu was for 'the League to publish a magazine under the auspices of the publications committee'.[83]

His desire to affirm his spiritual, visionary credentials in his own writing is equally evident. During the late 1960s he left New York for Cambridge, Massachusetts, where he wrote a long poem, 'Gita Sarasvati. A Theology for Modern Science, the Creation and the Dissolution of *Kosmos*'. Williams' claim that this 'exquisite poem . . . contains the core of his philosophy' is somewhat inflated. The 'philosophy' remains obscure. The poem touches on Tambimuttu's critical ideas: the third verse begins 'The poetic word should contain large, agglutinative masses of Meaning. / . . . The Word, the Word, Veda, Veda . . . the immense word / In which are telescoped all sounds, meanings, forms'. The poem makes the point that unlike in Christianity, '*Dharma*, the Word / is not incarnated in / One historical person, but in all matter and men' (*Tambimuttu* 265). Apart from odes to the Hindu goddess of the arts, 'Sarasvati, the female energy who is the Word: O Divine

[82] Timothy Leary, *How to Start Your Own Religion,* Tambimuttu Archive, North-western University, unpublished pamphlet, Box 2 folder 3, 2.
[83] Ibid. 23.

Essence, *Hamsa*, free wanderer between celestial and earthly spheres' (*Tambimuttu* 266–7), the poem centres on an explanation of what appears to be a key term, *sat-cit-ananda*. *Sat*—the substratum of space is existence, *cit*—the substratum of thought is consciousness or intuition of laws, *ananda*—the substratum of time is experience or enjoyment or supreme Consciousness and Supreme Bliss and reality (*Tambimuttu* 269). But do these barely connected strands of thought amount to a 'philosophy'? The poem is an incoherent jumble, heavily inflected with italicised, transliterated Sanskrit terms such as '*sanantana dharma*', '*prasarati*', '*nama*', and '*rupa*' and repeated invocations of 'OM'. It is intended for recital like a mantra. The emphasis is always on how the poem sounds, as opposed to what it means.

Williams' emphasis on Tambimuttu's Hindu philosophy needs to be seen in relation to her, and other commentators', concomitant neglect of his humorous treatment of Indian 'yogis' in his unpublished musical comedy *The Wayward Yogi*, and his sending up of American tastes for 'Eastern thought' and 'Boodist meditashun'.[84] He writes: 'At a party for Americans it is the right form to talk with conviction about the rope trick, vanspati, vedanta.'[85] Williams does not refer to these writings although they would certainly have been familiar to her as his literary executor. Perhaps they were ignored because they are incompatible with her constructions of Tambimuttu. Such completely alternative perspectives in Tambimuttu establish his distance from the ideologies his other texts reproduce, and distinguish his calculated self-reinvention from some unconscious desire to please.

A further change discernible during his stay in the US is apparent in Tambimuttu's more pronounced (self-)construction as a native informant on Sri Lankan social and cultural structures. He first published creative writing with specifically Sri Lankan content after moving to New York. Tambimuttu's short stories give us an insight into the relationship between exotic subjects and their metropolitan consumers. His semi-autobiographical stories, laden with details of rituals and customs, depict the privileged existence of the Tamil leisured, landed class. This use of autobiographical experience as a form of reportage is far removed from any attempt to tell the story of the collectivity through that of

[84] Tambimuttu, *The Wayward Yogi: A Musical Comedy*, Tambimuttu Archive, Northwestern University, Box 21 folder 9, 2.
[85] Tambimuttu, *Americans* (1951), Tambimuttu Archive, Northwestern University, Box 21 folder 9, n.p.

the individual or explore 'embattled public Third World culture'.[86] Tambimuttu's short stories perform the task of the native informant giving the reader an insight into a feudal landowning background where caste hierarchies were strictly observed. 'The Tree Climber' depicts the servants performing traditional rituals of respect to their higher caste masters.[87] Characteristically, Tambimuttu was aware of the impact of this kind of representation on his assimilation in his new home. As children, he and his siblings spent most of their time in Colombo and only their holidays in Jaffna. However, all his autobiographical short stories are set in his grandparents' home in Jaffna. This may be because Tambimuttu's immediate family's fortunes declined and they were forced to live in humbler circumstances in Colombo:[88] by setting the stories in Jaffna, Tambimuttu could emphasise a background of feudal wealth and privilege. In view of the marketability of the native voice for Western consumers, Tambimuttu's choice of the Jaffna setting may also have been determined by its more exotic aura in relation to the more urban and Westernised Colombo setting, where caste hierarchies were somewhat modified. These stories offer a glimpse into the 'backward' practices of these 'Other communities'. Their enthusiastic reception stems from more than the strengths of Tambimuttu's prose style.[89]

However, Tambimuttu may also have sensed that while a patrician background would have appealed to his broadly upper-middle-class circle in London, some of his American readers may have found such an *uncritical* flaunting of inherited privilege less to their taste. Hence 'Elizam: a Reminiscence of Childhood in Ceylon' opens with the author-narrator criticising the fact that while he had a 'freedom of choice' of career and partner, the servant girl Elizam had not. The narrator claims this 'made me furious'.[90] Revealingly, the narrative cannot sustain this critique, which appears crudely rhetorical. The denouement of Tambimuttu's short story is interesting: what begins as a critique of the disparity between his privileged existence and that of the servants

[86] Fredric Jameson, 'Third-World Literature in the Era of Multinational Capitalism', *Social Text* 15 (1986), 69.

[87] T. Tambimuttu, 'The Tree Climber: A Short Story Set in Ceylon', *The Reporter* 13.4 (1955), 38–42.

[88] P. Poologasingham, *Poet Tambimuttu: A Profile* (Colombo: P. Tambimuttu, 1993), 5.

[89] Tambimuttu received an offer to publish a collection of short stories from publisher Bobs-Merril Co.

[90] T. Tambimuttu, 'Elizam: A Reminiscence of a Childhood in Ceylon', *The Reporter* 11.12 (1954), 38.

dissolves into an endorsement of the continuity of this social structure. After elaborate descriptions of Elizam's arranged wedding festival, the rituals observed and the Tamil delicacies served, the story ends with the narrator enthusiastically describing Elizam's younger sister's wedding, the earlier misgivings forgotten. This pattern is repeated in the story entitled 'The Tree Climber'. When Velu who plucked coconuts for Tambimuttu's family dies from a fall, he is immediately 'replaced' by his son Gundu: 'When Gundu is up in the trees with the breeze ripping through the trees and the nuts dropping around him, we almost imagine[d] it is Velu.'[91] The blurring of the father's and son's identities suggests the way one family member is simply exchanged for another. The short stories are not centrally concerned with the 'servants' as their titles suggest. The emphasis is ultimately on the way their labour is essential for sustaining the privileged way of life of the upper-middle classes.

At the same time a broader Asian identity as opposed to a specifically Sri Lankan one remained essential for Tambimuttu's enhanced role publicising Asian writers in the West. From its inception *Poetry London–New York* carried the translated work of Indian poets Buddhadeva Bose, Jibananda Das, Amrita Pritam, and Amiya Chakravarty, alongside foremost Anglo-American poets. Tambimuttu was guest editor of *Poetry Chicago*'s number devoted to Indian poetry. He edited a book of ancient *India Love Poems* (1954) translated from Sanskrit, Gujarati, Assamese, and Tamil. Tambimuttu acknowledges the contribution of translators in each language, but the extent to which he knew these languages is deliberately obscured. Evidently this publication served to enhance his reputation as a South Asian expert. His Tamil heritage possibly influenced and facilitated this broader perspective and identification with India. The geographical proximity as well as common culture of South India to the Jaffna Peninsula created strong ties between the regions. The host country's homogenising tendencies and ignorance of the diversity of the subcontinent would have further aided this self-construction. Clearly being non-Western was more important than coming from any specific location. In reviews Tambimuttu's native Sri Lanka continued to be subsumed as a part of India. This regional identity is one that, as we shall see, he continued to develop on his return to the UK.

In North America as in Britain, his self-translation was the key factor in his assimilation to his bohemian circles. However, the role of native

---

[91] Tambimuttu, 'The Tree Climber', 42.

informant appears to have been necessary for his assimilation at levels beyond social integration. It is invoked in an appeal on Tambimuttu's behalf for Permanent Residence in the US. In a letter supporting his application, James Laughlin (editor of *New Directions*) writes: 'I have known Mr. Tambimuttu for a number of years and consider him to be a competent editor and writer and a qualified authority on Indian and Ceylonese culture. Mr. Tambimuttu's publications have made a valuable contribution to American understanding of Asia.'[92] This not only raises questions over who is empowered to confer such authority, but also underlines how such expectations and constructions were not confined to literary discourse and the popular imagination. They had permeated political and public discourse, giving us an insight into North American political culture and decision-making in the late 1950s.

## FURTHER SELF-TRANSLATION IN BRITAIN (1968–83)

After failing to obtain a post teaching creative writing at Harvard University came a sojourn in Paris at the Shakespeare & Co. bookshop on the Rive Gauche, before Tambimuttu returned to London in 1968, and founded the short-lived Lyrebird Press in 1972 in what was to be his final phase in Britain. Returning to a country that had seen a major influx of South Asian, African, and Caribbean immigration during the 1950s and early 1960s, Tambimuttu carved a new niche for himself, and became involved with Asian cultural activities in three ways. First, he adopted a more politicised role as spokesperson for the people of the newly created Bangladesh. Tambimuttu's continual metamorphosis becomes clear when the activities and writings of this second phase in England are compared with the first. Most marked is the new politically charged focus and polemical tone self-consciously asserted in his introduction to his selection of *Poems from Bangla Desh: The Voice of a New Nation*. His explicit critique of imperialist 'looting' contrasts sharply with the purely aesthetic concerns of *Poetry London* and the earlier absence of any interest in or commitment to Indian or Sri Lankan anti-colonial resistance:

[92] James Laughlin, letter to the US Immigration Department, 22 Apr. 1959, James Laughlin correspondence, 1942–72, Harvard University, BMS Am 2077 (1635), Folder 2.

A more tragic disaster than the one in 1939, when most of us were united in our course [has overtaken the people of Bangla Desh]. A worse Khan than all the bloodthirsty Khans Europe or Asia had ever seen, struck at civilisation. Neither democratic America nor brilliant 'Common-Wealth' Britain, which owes so much to Bengal (the looting of a single province is said to have made possible the industrialization of England), has made a single move to stop the . . . utter degradation of humanity and civilisation.[93]

From a marketing perspective, Tambimuttu was clearly aware that political crisis fuels interest and book sales, and that India would be motivated to promote the book given its role in arming Bangladeshi refugees, the Mukti Bahini guerrillas, in the war against Pakistan. He writes: 'I hope the Indian Ministry of External Affairs will favourably consider ordering a special edition of the book for their own use', adding: 'We were sure where we stood in 1939 when I managed my publishing house here. I am just as sure in this present world crisis against the Victorian gunboat diplomacy launched by the US and China.'[94] Interestingly, the publishers of *New Directions* in the US rejected Tambimuttu's offer to produce an American edition of *Poems from Bangla Desh,* ignoring the declaration of independence and still referring to 'East Pakistan':

I fear we had better bow out on the idea of publishing your proposed Poems from Bangla Desh: The Voice of a New Nation. How bright of you to get this going at such a time. However, we have to get to work now with our Fall 1972 list, and we hope that long before that the whole business of East Pakistan will have been settled, and happily. Good luck with it.[95]

Their reluctance may be due to the absence of American readerships and interest in *political* events in the subcontinent and because of Tambimuttu's criticism of American foreign policy in his preface.

Secondly, Tambimuttu maintained his role of promoting writers from the subcontinent. He was 'anxious to have a couple of poems from India for the first number' of *Poetry London-Apple Magazine* in 1979.[96] Under

[93] T. Tambimuttu (ed.), *Poems from Bangla Desh: The Voice of a New Nation* (London: The Lyrebird Press, 1972), 1.

[94] Tambimuttu, letter to Indian Ministry of External Affairs, 15 Nov. 1971, Tambimuttu Archive, Northwestern University, Box 7 folder 1.

[95] Robert M. MacGregor, letter to Tambimuttu, 13 Dec. 1971, BMS Am 2077 (1635), James Laughlin correspondence 1942–72, Harvard University, Folder 2. A violent overthrow of the Awami League Government in a CIA aided military *coup d'état* occurred in 1975.

[96] Tambimuttu, letter to Safia Tyabjee, 27 July 1978, Tambimuttu Archive, Northwestern University, Box 3 folder 1.

Alan Ross's editorship from 1961, *The London Magazine* had also begun to publish notable modern American and Commonwealth writers along with English ones. Tambimuttu continued to respond to the interest in India, simultaneously including the songs of contemporary counter-culture songwriters such as Bob Dylan and Leonard Cohen. Responding to the vogue for yoga and meditation, his Lyrebird Press published Ranmurti Mishra's *The Textbook of Yoga Psychology* and commissioned Mishra's *Fundamentals of Yoga*. The interest in South Asia notwithstanding, Joan Bakewell's interview with Tambimuttu on TV sheds light on the kind of representation of Asians that passed as 'acceptable' in British media in the 1970s. The interview was preceded by an actor reading from Maclaren-Ross's memoirs, supposedly citing Tambimuttu's famous sayings, in an *extreme* caricature of an 'Indian' accent. Bakewell appears unaware that this accent is offensive. However, immediately after the reading Tambimuttu asks Bakewell: 'Do you think this sounds like my voice?' and reminds her about his talks for the BBC, again a bid for affiliation.[97]

Tambimuttu evidently sensed the need to reposition himself in relation to the new cultural mix of multicultural Britain. In a retrospective account of his days in Fitzrovia during the 1940s, Tambimuttu expresses an enhanced awareness and appreciation of 'the eternal migration and intermingling of cultures [in London]'.[98] He reinvents himself as 'the pioneer of all this hustle and bustle, this little Indian colony' (*Tambimuttu* 227–8). On his return in 1968, he cultivated the role of mentor and patron of Asian cultural activities in Britain, attending Bengali poetry readings at the Poetry Society in London.[99] He became increasingly involved with the subcontinent after a successful trip to India and Sri Lanka in 1982 when he met the leaders of both countries. He founded the Indian Arts Council (IAC) in London in May 1983 with a grant of £20,000 from Indira Gandhi. He conceived the IAC, a 'secular and aesthetic body', as a permanent arts and cultural centre for countries in the Indian subcontinent. It would foster 'fusion between the art traditions of India and those of the West' and 'greater cross-cultural understanding between the majority community and the

97 Tambimuttu, interview with Joan Bakewell, *Line Up*, BBC 2, 26 Feb. 1971.
98 'Fitzrovia' was first published in *Harpers and Queens* in 1974.
99 V. West, letter to Tambimuttu, 24 June 1973, Tambimuttu Archive, Northwestern University, Box 3 folder 1.

British Asian community'.[100] However, years of alcoholism, diabetes, and continual financial stress (as Tambimuttu's various financial backers tired of his chaotic ways) took their toll and, precipitated by a fall, he died on 22 June 1983 before he could see his project actualised.[101] Yet his talent to situate himself where the future was poised is clear.[102]

## CHAUDHURI AND TAMBIMUTTU: MIMICRY AND AMBIVALENCE

What then, is the impact of these two writers on South Asian writing in Britain? Their writings lend expression to the extreme particularity of the cultural and linguistic crises of their historical position, and to the multiplicity of constraints of race, class, and target audience expectations that they wrote within. At the same time, such themes of cultural dislocation and the rationalisation of expatriation recur in later authors. At times, their writings address a dual readership, which challenges the idea that this generation of Anglophone writers were solely writing for a Western audience.

Chaudhuri's perspectives find closest resonance in Naipaul who shares his perception of India's 'lack of knowledge' and as an area of darkness. Naipaul's reviews of Chaudhuri's work reveal his close engagement with Chaudhuri's oeuvre. Both writers from reformist Hindu backgrounds, they were drawn to the civic, conservative culture of England where they

[100] IAC, letter to the GLC, 24 July 1982, Tambimuttu Archive, Northwestern University Box 42 folder 17.

[101] Despite his unreliable behaviour his stalwart friends Jane Williams and Kathleen Raine supported Tambimuttu. He also received regular grants from the Royal Literary Fund. (Chaudhuri also received grants from this fund, as well as personal loans from his publisher Hugo Brunner at Chatto and Windus.) The publishers' and the Royal Literary Fund's letters of obvious concern for both these writers necessitate a reappraisal of notions of metropolitan exploitation of minority artists. See Anthony Mackenzie, letter to Tambimuttu, 14 Jan. 1983, Tambimuttu Archive, Northwestern University Box 34 folder 2. Towards the end of his life Tambimuttu writes 'I personally believe that I owe a lot to Great Britain, where I have been a resident for many years.' Tambimuttu, letter to President J. R. Jayewardene, 2 Feb. 1982, Tambimuttu Archive, Northwestern University, Box 42 folder 17.

[102] The IAC held several events and made great efforts to develop Tambimuttu's plans. The IAC later supported the influential Horizon Gallery. Correspondence suggests internal fighting undermined the now dormant IAC.

lived as émigrés. Both sought after the English countryside and timeless, unchanging England, interpreting even democratic changes in Britain as decline. However, while on arrival Chaudhuri is delighted to find his imagined England, it is the younger writer's fiction that thematises the illusory nature of the London he sanctified in his imagination. Naipaul's semi-autobiographical narrators, particularly Ralph Singh, clearly articulate this disappointment with London, which failed to live up to the romantic expectations he had held since he was a colonial schoolboy. Naipaul's *The Mimic Men* identifies one of the central disillusionments of the colonial experience, a defining moment in postcolonial migrant literature, rediscovered again and again by the Caribbean and Indian writers who followed in his footsteps. Mumbai-born critic Homi K. Bhabha regards this perplexing revelation as the most important lesson he had to learn in England: 'what one expects to find at the very *centre* of life or literature may only be the dream of the deprived and the powerless; the centre may be most interesting in its elusiveness, as the enigma of authority.'[103] Neither Chaudhuri nor Naipaul embraced the position of a minority writer. Both yearned to be seen as cosmopolitan and removed from blackness, though unlike Chaudhuri, some of Naipaul's novels do describe life within a constantly shifting immigrant society. In different ways, both writers, concerned with the enduring tensions of uneven and unequal world development, self-consciously foreground their independence of judgement in the teeth of opposition. The trope of the 'true' vision of the alienated, displaced observer that resonated in both writers' work has had lasting impact on the construction of South Asian writing in the West, as we shall see in the chapters on Rushdie and Kureishi.

Exile, displacement, and migrancy have become synonymous with objectivity in postcolonial studies. Yet all three writers force a re-consideration of this construction of intellectuals on cultural borders. Chaudhuri's attitudes particularly disturb Said's theory that the exile's 'contrapuntal juxtapositions . . . diminish orthodox judgements and elevate appreciative sympathy'.[104] It is difficult to see how Chaudhuri offers fresh perspectives on either England or India. When he visits England for the first time he looks for 'Timeless England', 'the fiction told to the colonized by the colonizer in the very process of fabricating

---

[103] Homi K. Bhabha, 'The Vernacular Cosmopolitan', in Ferdinand Dennis and Naseem Khan (eds.), *Voices of the Crossing* (London: Serpent's Tale, 2000), 137.

[104] Edward Said, 'Reflections on Exile', *Granta* 13 (1984), 172.

colonial domination'.[105] Many of his views of India are equally conditioned and diagnostic of alienation. Similarly, Tambimuttu's work reproduces images of England that largely correspond to the expectations of a dominant group in England, and pictures of colonial Sri Lanka recognisable only to the indigenous elite.

Articles by both writers published in the US further underline the way migrant writers are co-opted to reinforce the shifting, ascendant ideologies of the dominant metropolitan countries; in this instance fears of the dangers of communism in suitably alarmist tones. During the 1950s Chaudhuri published an article in the American journal the *Atlantic Monthly*. Reading this we can see that US editors had a different agenda to British ones in publishing the work of certain South Asian intellectuals in the context of the military, political, and ideological rivalry between communist and capitalist systems during the Cold War. In accordance with the dominant political consensus of the time, the *Atlantic Monthly*, like *Encounter*, aimed to produce a counter-intellectual movement to communism.[106] In this vein, Chaudhuri warns:

Indians with Western leanings are prone to overlook the danger from Communism, because from their standpoint Communism is as Western as the liberal civilization of Western Europe, and also because they feel that the spread of Communism will . . . promote the sole form of Westernization they are now capable of understanding—namely, Westernization in material things. Thus many upper class Indians are flirting with Communistic ideas in the same manner as the French nobility, blissfully unconscious of their march towards guillotine, flirted with the ideas of Voltaire and Rousseau.

Chaudhuri's cautiously optimistic conclusion clearly invites and justifies Western interference and intervention:

The only . . . rival for retrograde Hinduism [Hindu nationalism] . . . is Communism. . . . there is bound to be a conflict for power between Hindu nationalism and Communism.

It is my personal belief that in this struggle, unless there is active intervention by the Soviet Union, combined with complete inaction on the part of the West, Communism will *not* win. . . . It may make a world of difference if the true West shows itself capable of revivifying and renovating its faith and values,

[105] Dipesh Chakrabarty, 'Postcoloniality and the Artifice of History: Who Speaks for "Indian" Pasts?', in Padmini Mongia (ed.), *Contemporary Postcolonial Literary Theory* (London: Arnold, 1996), 230.

[106] *Encounter* was an anti-communist literary and political monthly initially secretly funded by the US Central Intelligence Agency. See Hamilton (ed.), *Oxford Companion*, 512.

and preaching them to Asia . . . something can still be done to create a militant Western faith which will be an adequate substitute for Communism and a dissolvent of retrograde Hinduism.[107]

Writing for the *Atlantic Monthly* in the 1950s, Tambimuttu's article on 'Indian Poetry' appeared alongside essays and stories by Narayan, Anand, Rao, Sahgal, and Vijaya Lakshmi Pandit in a supplement entitled 'Perspectives of India' in October 1953, published shortly after the end of the Korean War, when the US was particularly paranoid about communist propaganda. The supplement purported to showcase the writing and 'contemporary culture of countries whose achievements are little known in the US, and to further a sense of intellectual community with these countries'. But like *Encounter*, the magazine's real agenda was to maintain contact with Indian intellectuals to pre-empt 'leanings' to communism, as the editorial by Harvey Breit makes clear:

While in many instances the [Indian] writer is oriented towards the West, especially if he has had a British education, he may also be one who feels a magnetic pull toward Moscow or Mao. He is often an Indian democrat who, like some of his political leaders, identifies the West with imperialism and therefore views it with distrust.

Who can blame him? . . . In India . . . where illiteracy is a basic problem, the intellectual plays a weighty role in his country's life. Far more than we can imagine, he helps create the climate of opinion. We ought not to neglect him. It remains for us to exchange our ideas with those of the Indian reader, and to show him that we are not indifferent to the creative process wherever we find it.[108]

The US presented its anti-communism movement as anti-imperialistic: according to Gayatri Chakravorty Spivak, native informants from formerly colonised countries 'gave support to the American self-representation as the custodian of decolonization' during the Cold War years.[109]

North American critiques of British colonialism may explain why the tone of Tambimuttu's writing in the US marked a new anti-colonial thrust. In contrast to his earlier silence on such topics, Tambimuttu's

---

[107] Nirad C. Chaudhuri, 'The Western Influence in India', *Atlantic Monthly* 193.3 (1954), 73–4.

[108] Harvey Breit, 'Editorial', *Atlantic Monthly* 192.4 (1953), 3. Later Breit wrote a preface for Tamil writer M. Anantarayanan's (1907–63) *The Silver Pilgrimage* originally published by Criterion Press in New York in 1961.

[109] Gayatri Chakravorty Spivak, *A Critique of Postcolonial Reason: Towards a History of the Vanishing Present* (Cambridge, Mass.: Harvard UP, 1999), 360.

short story 'Uncle Gamini and the British' mocks the Anglomania of some Westernised Sri Lankans. Tambimuttu satirises Uncle Gamini for wanting the 'resident English men and Scotsmen' to patronise 'him in a make-believe that he was near English himself'.[110] As with Chaudhuri's unselfconscious criticisms of 'imitation' Englishmen, Tambimuttu appears not to be aware of the ways in which he could exemplify the very type he satirises. Like Chaudhuri's *Circe*, Tambimuttu critiques the formerly colonised's internalisation of the coloniser's superiority. This new ideological direction in relation to colonialism also surfaces in his article on poetry in India where he criticises Indian writers' capacity to be influenced by Western poets:

The modern period in Indian poetry, which may be said to have begun about one hundred years ago, witnessed first a phase of extreme Westernization, then one slow recovery from it. By 1850 many Indian poets were writing in English; . . . Vernacular poetry did not get the attention it deserved. . . . the excesses of Victorian poetry in England awoke in Indian readers a very strong native feeling for the extravagant and the unreal. Unable to distinguish between the basically sound and merely pretty in English verse, Indians imported a great fund of the vague, sentimental and facile. Now that Indian independence has at last been accomplished, poets are turning with ever-greater enthusiasm to the native and colourful life of India.[111]

Again, this is ironic given that Tambimuttu's early poetry derives all too easily from the poetry of his fellow poets in London, even if the mimicry is the converse of received forms of Anglicisation. Tambimuttu's comments suggest his identification with the modernist critique of aestheticism.

The ideological thrust underpinning Tambimuttu's and Chaudhuri's cultural translation demonstrates the maintenance, rather than the subversion, of the dominant discursive frameworks of the period. Neither modifies the centre nor mirrors it critically. This may explain why both have received relatively little attention from postcolonial perspectives that seek to foreground a continuity of radical resistance. However, these writers need to be located as modernists, rather than simply as assimilationists. In this way their reception contrasts to that of Jean Rhys who has been retrospectively inserted into the modernist tradition, without the prevarication that attends these writers' positioning.

[110] T. Tambimuttu, 'Uncle Gamini and the British', *The Reporter* 10.3 (1954), 44.
[111] T. Tambimuttu, 'Poetry in India: Its Heritage and New Directions', *Atlantic Monthly* 192.4 (1953), 148.

While Tambimuttu's role in mid century literary London can be excavated from recent neglect, largely because of his involvement with the major white literary figures of his day, he is barely traceable in Sri Lanka today.[112] In contrast, Chaudhuri's decreasing popularity in Britain has been matched by the recent resurgence of interest in his work in India that suggests the long-standing hostility is gradually abating. Although still regarded by some as India's senile Anglophile, in a post-nationalist India the earlier hostility to Chaudhuri seems to have been replaced by a desire to rediscover him. Towards the end of his life a range of mostly Indian academics and journalists honoured him with a collection of essays entitled *Nirad C. Chaudhuri: The First Hundred Years: A Celebration*. Many contributions focus on his talents as a writer and argue for a re-evaluation of some of the criticisms of Chaudhuri, although he is taken to task for his derogatory comments on India's minority communities in *Circe*. Several contributors demonstrate an increasing interest in his writings in Bengali.[113]

Nevertheless his reception in India remains characterised by ambivalence as the *Times of India* obituary, 'Bengal's Love-Hate for Niradbabu', makes clear: 'The intelligentsia here [in Calcutta] is divided in its assessment of Chaudhuri as a writer.'[114] Some of the criticism was and is symptomatic of the resentment against Chaudhuri's admiration of England and hostility to India. Yet it has also served to dismiss him as an eccentric who does not have to be considered seriously as an intellectual personality. Just as metropolitan critics make the awkward equation between exile and objectivity, some subcontinental critics perceive all of Chaudhuri's criticisms of India solely as evidence of dislocation. The reactionary nature of some of his views overshadows certain pertinent points: for example, his acute analysis of the role of class and wealth in contemporary Indian society in *Three Horsemen of the New Apocalypse*. Similarly while Chaudhuri's patrician contempt for the Gandhi-led mass movement is classed, his fears concerning the xenophobia and jingoism of Hindu nationalism expressed in his autobiographies need

---

[112] See for instance Michael Bakewell, *Fitzrovia: London's Bohemia* (London: National Portrait Gallery Publications, 1999) and Ian Hamilton, 'Sohoitis', *Granta* 65 (1999), 291–303.

[113] Swapan Dasgupta (ed.), *Nirad C. Chaudhuri: The First Hundred Years: A Celebration* (Delhi: HarperCollins, 1997).

[114] Shika Mukherjee, 'Bengal's Love-Hate for Niradbabu', *Times of India* (3 Aug. 1999), 8. See also M. K. Naik on the contradictory perceptions of Chaudhuri in India. M. K. Naik, 'Tributes', *Journal of Commonwealth Literature* 35.1 (2000), 179.

to be re-evaluated in the light of the excesses of contemporary Hindu nationalism. On the other hand, Chaudhuri betrays an overtly majoritarian stance regarding the position of Muslims in India.[115] In the context of the rise of Hindutva in India, Chaudhuri's recent recuperation by right-wing Hindus is not surprising. In his introduction to *Nirad C. Chaudhuri: The First Hundred Years: A Celebration*, the editor Swapan Dasgupta attempts to present Chaudhuri as sharing his own Bharatiya Janata Party (BJP) affiliations. Analogously, Naipaul stands accused of colluding with Hindu communalists by critics such as Suman Gupta who argue that his beliefs have shaped his travel writing on Islamic countries as well as his fiction.[116]

On the whole, Tambimuttu's perpetual self-reinvention underlines the fluidity of his ideological orientations and political affiliations, as well as the performance of cultural identities. While Chaudhuri reveals a subjectivity indelibly shaped by certain strains of colonial ideology and remains rooted in internalisations of Indian inferiority, Tambimuttu goes on to repeat and reinforce different aspects of Western orientalist ideology. Although, as Bhabha suggests, mimicry can be perceived as subversive because it threatens constructions of difference, Chaudhuri's extreme Anglicisation appears disempowering.[117] However, the subtle irony with which Chaudhuri enacts the ambivalence of the colonial subject, his 'impish, colonial intelligence's urge to be seen as enfant terrible', and his delight in what his friends see as his 'chronic Anglomania' indicate a self-consciousness, which tilts against this condition of powerlessness.[118] Tambimuttu's shift from imitation is ambivalent in a different way. On the one hand, the simulation of cultural identity suggests a degree of agency on the part of the performer: Tambimuttu is in control of his self-construction rather than being defined. It is adopted for his own purposes. However, Tambimuttu's reception outlines the limited nature of the 'subversive' potential of such performance. Tambimuttu's 'false' self-translation in response to metropolitan demands simultaneously serves to reinforce dominant expectations that such a spiritual essence exists and contributes to a form of ethnic absolutism. The insistent focus on his colour and physicality often in terms

[115] See for example, Nirad C. Chaudhuri, 'The Vicious Spiral of Hindu–Muslim Hatred', *The Times*, 21 Dec. 1971, 10.

[116] Suman Gupta, *V. S. Naipaul: Writers and their Works* (Plymouth: Northcote House Publishers, 1999).

[117] Homi Bhabha, *The Location of Culture* (London: Routledge, 1994), 85–92.

[118] Salman Rushdie, *The Satanic Verses* (London: Viking, 1989), 398.

of animal imagery—'swarthy genius', 'wild impresario',[119] 'with face mantled by a puma-black mane', and 'lemur-like fingers'[120]—suggests he cannot escape 'the fact of blackness'. Tambimuttu, to expand Fanon's words, remains 'overdetermined from without' and is *both* 'the slave of the "idea" that others have of [him]' and 'of [his] own appearance'.[121] The insight these writers offer us into shifting conceptions of cultural difference in the adopted land, and the erasure of fixed boundaries between assimilation and abrogation, enable us to develop a genealogy of the construction of migrant identities. In terms of a dialogue across generations, as we will see, Kamala Markandaya is not only comparable to Tambimuttu in class affiliation but similarly plays to exoticised versions of the East in order to assimilate. This form of cultural translation *as a method of acculturation* will be pitilessly mocked in Kureishi's *The Buddha of Suburbia*. At the same time, there are parallels between the self-fashioning undertaken by Tambimuttu and the ways in which Kureishi both exploits and resists his ethnic identity in his writing.

119 Dickins, 'Tambimuttu and Poetry London', 53.
120 MacClaren-Ross, *Memoirs*, 145.
121 Frantz Fanon, *Black Skin, White Masks* [1952], trans. Charles Lam Markmann (London: Pluto Press, 1986), 109, 116, emphasis mine.

# 3

# Assimilation and Resistance: Kamala Markandaya and A. Sivanandan

Chaudhuri and Tambimuttu gravitated towards different historically localised movements in Britain. This chapter focuses on two younger South Asian writers: biographical contemporaries, who impacted on different strands of Britain's public consciousness in strikingly dissimilar ways. Indian author Kamala (Purnaiya) Markandaya (1924–2004) arrived in Britain in 1948. Her writing career can be seen in terms of the emergence of a liberal university interest in Commonwealth Literature. The radical Sri Lankan left-wing ideologue Ambalavener Sivanandan (1923– ) came as an exile in 1958, and soon emerged at the forefront of the rise of black socialist politics in Britain. In the context of such different and concurrent phenomena, simple notions of formerly colonised writers responding to a monolithic 'centre' do not survive scrutiny. Can these contemporaries be understood in conjunction? They remained unaffected by each other's politics and projects. Their divergence makes clear the diversity of South Asian Anglophone writing, if not the limits of the label 'South Asian'.

Sivanandan and Markandaya were not exact contemporaries as writers. In the literary climate during the 1960s and 1970s, Markandaya's Anglo-American publishers constructed her reputation as 'the best Indo-Anglian writer now writing'.[1] By contrast Indian responses, particularly those of locally based critics, have tended to be more critical of Markandaya's fiction than their Western counterparts. Many would endorse Tapan Kumar Basu's description of 'Nectar in a Sieve as the most over-prescribed text for study at the University of Delhi . . . at best, a mediocre production by an Indo-Anglian author'.[2] Markandaya stopped

---

[1] Orville Prescott, *New York Times* and John Masters cited in blurb, *A Handful of Rice* (London: Putnam, 1966). Hereafter *Handful* pagination will appear in the text.

[2] Tapan Kumar Basu, 'Class in the Classroom: Pedagogical Encounters with *Nectar in a Sieve*', in Rajeswari Sunder Rajan (ed.), *The Lie of the Land: English Literary Studies*

writing in 1982, and disappeared from public view, when literary conditions in Britain were no longer auspicious for her rarefied, leisurely novels on Indo-British relations. In contrast, Sivanandan, consumed by activism for many decades, turned to fiction late in life. Recalling fragments of his native country's history for over fifteen years, he published his first compelling, disturbing part novel, part memoir *When Memory Dies* in 1997, in a cultural environment at that time more receptive to his record of a still little-known island's turbulent post-Independence history, than in previous years. This somewhat atypical first novel won the Commonwealth Writers First Book Award in the same year.

Melissa Benn rightly observes that Sivanandan's socialist politics, more than his colour, contributed to his neglect in Britain.[3] While his work is beginning to receive the wider recognition it deserves, the now virtually ignored Markandaya deserves re-evaluation for different reasons. Markandaya's novels and their publishing history (1954–82) shed new light on our understanding of the reception of South Asian Anglophone writing during this period.[4] This material demonstrates the degree to which this author sought approval from the mainstream literary establishment. Referring to an article on her novels featured in the *Journal of Commonwealth Literature*, she comments: 'I would trade these mentions in exotic media . . . for one serious, good review in *The Times* (of which I've not had a single one).'[5] Her fiction and its reception trace the accommodations she was expected and prepared to make, in

*in India* (Delhi: Oxford UP, 1992), 105. Of course, there is no monolithic Indian reader response to South Asian Anglophone texts, as the range of local critical responses to her work shows. See P. Geetha, 'The Novels of Kamala Markandaya: Reassessing Feminine Identity', in Kamini Dinesh (ed.), *Between Spaces of Silence: Women Creative Writers* (Delhi: Sterling, 1994). Sharad Srivastava, *The New Woman in Indian English Fiction: A Study of Kamala Markandaya, Anita Desai, Namita Gokhale and Shoba De* (Delhi: Creative Books, 1996).

[3] Melissa Benn, 'Island in the Stream of History', *Independent* (11 Jan. 1997), online edition.

[4] Markandaya published her first four novels *Nectar in a Sieve* (1954), *Some Inner Fury* (1955), *A Silence of Desire* (1960), *Possession* (1963) with Putnam (now Bodley Head), *A Handful of Rice* (1966) and *The Coffer Dams* (1969) with Hamish Hamilton, and *The Nowhere Man* (1972) with Allen Lane (Penguin Press/Longman). She shared Chaudhuri's agent Innes Rose and similarly published her last three novels *Two Virgins* (1974), *The Golden Honeycomb* (1977), and *Pleasure City* (1982) with Chatto and Windus. All her novels were published in the USA with John Day Company and Jaico and Orient in India.

[5] Markandaya, letter to John Guest at Longman, 21 Jan. 1972, 'The Nowhere Man' File, Allen Lane: Penguin Press, 7139.0467.4 [DM 1852], University of Bristol Special Collections.

contrast to the more confident rejection of such prescriptions particularly by subsequent writers such as Rushdie. Moreover, examining over time the processes of cultural translation at work in her texts, alongside their contexts of literary production, offers insights into changing responses to cultural difference. Her publishers' intervention in shaping this issue of difference, as mediators between the author and her reading public during this period, is particularly significant.

Both Markandaya and Sivanandan arrived in Britain during the high period of post-war migration, a process recorded in Sam Selvon's and George Lamming's well-known accounts of post-war Caribbean settlement.[6] Given the background of heightened racial intolerance exacerbated by immigration, it is no surprise that the representation of racial tension in Britain emerges in both Sivanandan and Markandaya's work, although to differing degrees and ideological ends. Sivanandan is first and foremost a political activist and an organic intellectual immersed in practical politics. This sets him apart from the other writers selected for discussion in this book, and from most of the black and Asian writers who emerged in the 1950s with no direct personal involvement in political movements. Sivanandan belongs to the first generation of the Tamil minority displaced from Sri Lanka after the anti-Tamil riots of 1958. While Markandaya chose to settle in Britain after her marriage to an Englishman, Sivanandan made Britain his home as a political exile, and threw himself into the cause of the marginalised. In interviews he emphasises the shock of leaving Sri Lanka and having to start life anew at the age of 35.[7] He left the violence against the Tamils in Sri Lanka to arrive in a Britain ablaze with the anti-black hostility of Notting Hill, London. He describes it as a 'double baptism of fire—Sinhalese–Tamil riots there, white–black riots here' (*Communities* 9). Sivanandan's minority background helps explain his articulate critiques of racism, and his interest in the difficulties that postcolonial societies like Sri Lanka, and multicultural societies like Britain, have faced in the evolution of pluralistic social formations. He is more sensitive to the hegemonic, repressive aspects of nationalism than Markandaya.[8] His politicisation

---

[6] Sam Selvon, *The Lonely Londoners* (1954) and George Lamming, *The Emigrants* (1956).

[7] A. Sivanandan, *Refugee Tales*, Channel 4, 24 May 2000.

[8] Sivanandan was marginalised as a Hindu in a Catholic school; in retrospect he suggests that his experiences gave him a hatred of injustice caused by all forms of oppression. Sivanandan, interview with the author, 12 Apr. 1999.

in Sri Lanka coincided with the rise of the revolutionary Left and then its decline as it was fragmented by communal tensions. These intersections of race and class politics inflect his polemical and creative analyses of his adopted and home countries, conditioning his cultural translation. Sivanandan's experiences of a Sri Lankan political crisis where issues of race undermined class solidarity provide some explanation for his emphasis on the dangers of privileging race over class. His involvement with the Trotskyite Lanka Sama Samaja Party (LSSP) as a student in Sri Lanka clarifies his affinity with International Socialism on his arrival in Britain. It provided a natural context for him to join.[9] Since 1972 he has been the director of the Institute of Race Relations in London, remoulding the institution into Britain's first anti-racist, anti-imperialist think-tank, and providing a venue for radical often-marginalised Third World scholars. He has written extensively on black British politics and Marxist internationalism. His polemics, collected in two volumes of essays, *A Different Hunger: Writings on Black Resistance* (1982) and *Communities of Resistance* (1990), provide definitive histories of this era. After four decades of anti-racist activism in Britain, Sivanandan then wrote his first novel, to 'make a contribution to my own country'.[10] A collection of short stories, *Where the Dance is: Stories from Two Worlds and Three* (2000) followed.

In sharp contrast to Sivanandan's numerous radical, politicised essays on race and racism, only one of Markandaya's ten novels, *The Nowhere Man* (1972), examines race relations in Britain, articulating a diffident, apologetic critique through the passive protagonist Srinivas.[11] Over her

[9] Many of Sivanandan's Sri Lankan lecturers were members of the LSSP. As a result he observes, 'politics was not just what we learnt as part of our degree syllabus but also those activities we took part in outside university hours when we went to public meetings, or attended various LSSP study groups and societies.' A. Sivanandan, *Communities of Resistance: Writings on Black Struggles for Socialism* (London: Verso, 1990), 6. Hereafter, *Communities* pagination will appear in the text. The LSSP was one of the three most successful Trotskyite or Internationalist Socialist movements in the world. From its foundation in 1935 until its expulsion from the Fourth International (because it joined a coalition government led by the Sri Lanka Freedom Party) in 1964, it played a decisive role in Sri Lankan politics. It mobilised militant trade unions, strikes, and anti-colonial demonstrations and at first fought the contentious Sinhala Only state language issue. It constituted the main opposition to the post-Independence governments. See Al Richardson (ed.), *Blows Against the Empire: Trotskyism in Ceylon: The Lanka Sama Samaja Party, 1935–1964* (London: Revolutionary History Porcupine Press, 1997).

[10] Sivanandan, interview with the author.

[11] Kamala Markandaya, *The Nowhere Man* (London: Allen Lane, 1972). Hereafter, *Nowhere* pagination will appear in the text.

long career, from *Nectar in a Sieve* (1954) to *Pleasure City* (1982), Markandaya continued to write a similar kind of novel: she mirrors the fervour of India's nationalist struggle, changing Indo-British relations, the problems of decolonisation and unequal gender relations in India. Before she settled in England, Markandaya, who was educated at Madras University, was a journalist for *The Hindu*. After her arrival in England, she moved from journalism to fiction and strongly resisted a 'representative' role in her novels: '*in everything I say I speak for myself.* I am not, and never have been, a spokeswoman . . . for India . . . although I do find myself, from time to time, shoved into this heady, but frightful position.'[12] Her self-effacing stance is gender-inflected and in keeping with a rhetoric of feminine self-devaluation. Perhaps Markandaya is also distancing herself from the privileged and representative status accorded to her as one of the few Indian women writing in English and publishing in England. She and her contemporaries Nayantara Sahgal (1927– ) and Attia Hosain (1913–98) began writing when both Indian writing in English and migrant writing were seen as male-dominated genres, monopolised by the older male writers Rao, Anand, Chaudhuri, and Naipaul. This heightened their burden of representation. Markandaya's stance contrasts with Sivanandan's assertive and combative Third-Worldist self-representation as a spokesperson for oppressed minorities in Britain, Sri Lanka, and elsewhere, a position naturalised by the (male) sex of the writer. His first foray into fiction is a self-consciously *collective* history of Sri Lanka.

## MARKANDAYA: CONTEXTS OF LITERARY PRODUCTION AND CONSUMPTION 1954–82

'India sells abroad' is now a truism in many metropolitan publishing houses. It is easy to forget that this was not always the case. Launching her literary career in the mid 1950s, in an environment inhospitable to South Asian writing in English and cultural difference except on specific terms, Markandaya translates the East to the West in ways that closely conform to the expectations of her adopted home, particularly those of her publishers. At the same time, as we will see, the views of

---

[12] Kamala Markandaya, 'One Pair of Eyes: Some Random Reflections', in Alastair Niven (ed.), *The Commonwealth Writer Overseas: Themes of Exile and Expatriation* (Brussels: Didier, 1976), 27 (emphasis in original). Hereafter 'One Pair'.

the host country are themselves complex, calling into question simple notions of dominant expectations. For Markandaya's self-construction as an 'anti-colonialist' writer is in part a response to the liberal humanist critiques of colonialism within Britain in the 1960s and 1970s.[13] Her writing always remained contained within the limits of this liberal questioning. It would be wrong, however, to suggest that Markandaya's representations remain static throughout her long career. Her work reflects her engagement with the shifting, specific, historicised, cultural expectations that emerged across the decades.

Correspondence between Markandaya and her British and American publishers throughout her career disclose the extent to which they were concerned about the commercial appeal of her work. Readers' reports typically comment that 'her books should attract some good notices but not I fear much in the way of sales'.[14] Apart from her first bestseller *Nectar in a Sieve*, sales of Markandaya's novels, including *Silence of Desire* (1960) and *Possession* (1963), were below half of the print run.[15] The publishers' communications reveal that the Indian subject matter was a key factor in their commercial concerns. Markandaya's publisher at Putnam describes to his American counterpart how they have to keep any suggestion of India 'carefully concealed for the British market'.[16] Like Narayan and other South Asian Anglophone writers, Markandaya sold more books in the US than in Britain. However, her North American publisher went as far as to omit the tilak marks on the foreheads of the two Hindu girls on the cover of her novel *Two Virgins* (1974). He explained to Markandaya that this was in order 'to play down the Indian background and to foreground the timeless, universal aspects of the story . . . [and] to prevent the Indian locale from adversely affecting sales'.[17] This suggests that whereas cultural texts of hegemonic cultures were perceived as intrinsically interesting to a broad reading public, works such as Markandaya's describing dominated cultures were

---

[13] Markandaya, cited in John Wakeman, *World Authors, 1950–1970: A Companion Volume to Twentieth Century Authors* (New York: Wilson, 1975), 948.

[14] Elizabeth Rosenburg to John Guest, Reader's Report on *Nowhere Man*, 17 Sept. 1973, 'The Nowhere Man' File, Allen Lane: Penguin Press, 7139.0467.4 [DM 1852], University of Bristol Special Collections.

[15] Correspondence relating to her contemporary Attia Hosain's work reveals similar concerns, alongside her editor Cecil Day Lewis's difficulties over getting an 'unknown' Pakistani writer reviewed.

[16] Roger Lubbock, letters to Richard Walsh, 15 Oct. 1954 and 1 Feb. 60, File Markandaya 1954–60, Chatto and Windus Archive.

[17] Richard Walsh, letter to Kamala Markandaya, 24 Aug. 1973, File Markandaya 1970–6.

received as strange, alien, difficult, and esoteric, of interest only to specialist audiences. Over her long career, Markandaya's readership remained confined to a small number of predominantly white people who enjoyed reading about India.

The difficulty of publishing fiction about India in the West at this time helps to explain why Markandaya's novels appear to be written with an eye to getting read and accepted by British and American critics. As we shall see, it is not simply the format, but also the content and language of Markandaya's texts that manifest evidence of assimilation. Her novels embody the 'domesticating' forms of cultural translation for the benefit of an implied Western reader. Notwithstanding her critique of imperialism, Markandaya's ideological position, her aesthetic, and her language suggest that cultural translation for her has an ambivalent relationship to orientalist discourse, and evince her willingness to assimilate her representations of India to prevailing Western expectations, norms, and genres.

In her first novel *Nectar in a Sieve* (1954), Markandaya emphasises India's *inherent* inability to live in the 'modern' world. At times, her analysis comes close to Naipaul's impatience with India, a view confirmed in *Nectar*'s English doctor Kenny's exasperation with the dispossessed villagers '. . . meek suffering fools. Why do you keep this ghastly silence? Why do you not demand—cry out for help—do something?'[18] Markandaya's criticisms may be more tempered with compassion than Naipaul's, but in Kenny's conversations with the protagonist and narratorial persona Rukmani, he expresses bafflement at the passive native's irrationality. While Markandaya's novels present convincing depictions of admirable women's deprived lives, they define the capacity for fatalistic resignation and endurance of pain as a feminine quality, embodied by Rukmani in *Nectar*. She is described in the blurb of the Signet edition as a 'simple peasant women in a primitive village in India whose whole life is a gallant and persistent battle to care for those she loves'. Pearl Buck's (1892–1973) story about Chinese peasants, *Good Earth* (Methuen, 1931, later translated into Hindi, Kannada, and Oriya and widely read in India), haunts Markandaya's characters, descriptions, and situations. Produced a few years before the hit film *Mother India* (1957), the novel's and film's popularity suggest the appeal of epics of female endurance and toil at this juncture.

---

[18] Kamala Markandaya, *Nectar in a Sieve* [1954] (New York: Signet, 1982), 47–8. Hereafter *Nectar* pagination will appear in the text.

Similarly, in *A Handful of Rice* (1966) Nalini endures domestic violence, difficult pregnancies, and overwork without protest. Only English observers, or Indian men like Nalini's husband Ravi or Rukmani's sons, express anger and rebel against conditions of poverty and suffering. Ravi's outbursts against a cruel fate prove futile, which could suggest that Nalini's tolerance is a sign of her pragmatism and strength, rather than weakness; to varying degrees, Rukmani and Nalini's endurance enable them to regenerate or transform the corruption around them. Yet the overall impression is one of a disturbing acceptance of these conditions. Chandra Talpade Mohanty initiated the debate over the particular problems in associating Third World women with images of underdevelopment and as victims of patriarchy, as Markandaya does in *Nectar*. Mohanty draws attention to the production of reified representations of Third World women within Western discourse in terms of a covert orientalism. The Third World woman's comparatively greater oppression renders her society as backward in relation to the First World.[19] *Nectar*'s endorsement of these hegemonic, received ideas of Third World poverty and 'Indian womanhood' may explain in part *Nectar*'s curious afterlife as Markandaya's only commercially successful novel, and her only text still in print. It sold over 250,000 copies and was translated into seventeen languages. Despite several Indian commentators' criticisms of the writer's portrayals of the underprivileged, and observations on the incongruity of the English realist novel set in Indian rural situations, a Penguin teacher's guide to *Nectar in a Sieve* claims that the text ably 'introduces Western students to life in rural pre-independence India'.[20] *Nectar*'s status persists, though not in literature courses, where if her work is discussed at all, feminist and postcolonial literary critics tend to analyse it in terms of its tendency to reinforce existing domestic hierarchy.[21] However, the book is, tellingly,

[19] Chandra Talpade Mohanty, 'Under Western Eyes: Feminist Scholarship and Colonial Discourses,' *Boundary* 2 (1984), 333–58.

[20] <http://www.penguinclassics.com/CAN . . . rs_guides/t_markandaya_nectar. html>. Adil Jussawalla, Paranjape Markand among others.

[21] This is in contrast to the recent appeal of the Muslim writer Hosain's single novel *Sunlight on a Broken Column* (1961) after Virago republished it in 1988. A text at A Level and in undergraduate courses in Britain, it is especially popular amongst young British Asian women who identify with the young Muslim protagonist in pre-war India who overcomes family conservatism to choose her own husband. See Ranjana Ash, 'Remembering India: Homeland, Heritage or Hindrance in the Writings by Women of the Indian Diaspora' in Kathleen Firth and Felicity Hand (eds.), *India: Fifty Years after Independence* (Leeds: Peepal Tree Press, 2001), 93.

a set text in courses titled Women and International Development in the US.[22]

Nevertheless, Markandaya's second novel *Some Inner Fury* (1955), set during the tumultuous period of the Quit India movement of 1942, was one of the first texts by an Indian Anglophone female writer to foreground a feminine and feminist viewpoint against the backdrop of anti-colonialist nationalist projects. Markandaya invests her female narrator and protagonist Mira with an evolving political consciousness.[23] In this way, her text both shapes and documents the investment of gender in the 'often contradictory configuration of the nation in process'.[24] Inspired by the nationalist Roshan, Mira leaves her 'home, with its peaceful ordered living'. Like Markandaya, Mira becomes a journalist and discovers 'at last the gateway to the freedoms of the mind' (*Fury* 71).[25] At the same time, the remaining central characters are engulfed by the independence struggles and meet tragic ends. Mira's choice of participating in the nationalist movement rather than staying with her English lover Richard is also symptomatic of the conservative nature of Indian nationalism, notably Gandhi's gendered subordination of the private to a larger public good.[26] The novel closes with Mira's observation: 'I knew I would go, even as I knew Richard must stay. For us there was no other way, the forces that pulled us apart were too strong' (*Fury* 285). In this way, Mira's characterisation embodies the ambivalence of nationalist ideology towards women's rights: the conflictual relations between feminist and anti-colonial emancipation. Markandaya's work mirrors the ways in which issues of nationalism and gender were intertwined during this era. Writers such as Bapsi Sidhwa, Hosain, and Rushdie have by contrast tended to be much more direct in

---

[22] San Diego State University <http://www.inform.umd.edu/EdRes/Global/international-development>.

[23] Kamala Markandaya, *Some Inner Fury* (London: Putnam, 1955). Hereafter *Fury* pagination will appear in the main text.

[24] K. Lalitha and Susie Tharu (eds.), *Women Writing in India: 600 B.C. to the Present*, 2 vols. (London: Pandora, 1993), 44

[25] The Dewan's daughters in *The Golden Honeycomb* follow a similar trajectory moving from the private, gendered space of 'home' to participation in the 'world'. These parameters are set up in Rabindranath Tagore, *The Home and the World* (Leipzig: Bernhard Tauchnitz, 1921).

[26] For discussions of Gandhi's ambiguous mobilisation of women for national liberation, see Geraldine Forbes, *Indian Women and the Freedom Movement: A Historian's Perspective* (Bombay: Research Centre for Women's Studies, 1997). Ketu Katrak, 'Indian Nationalism, Gandhian Satyagraha and Representations of Female Sexuality', in Andrew Parker et al. (eds.), *Nationalisms and Sexualities* (London: Routledge, 1992), 395–406.

the scepticism they show towards nationalism and women's exclusions from definitions of the people.

The first British critical assessments of *Fury* did not focus on Markandaya's portrayal of urban and middle-class female participation in the independence struggles. Instead the *Times Literary Supplement*'s review perpetuates the discursive projects of cultural hegemony in its emphasis on, and sympathy with, Anglicised Indians 'understandably' dislocated from their own culture. Mira's dilemma, torn between her English lover and her country is 'particularly... moving... when, as here, education and background give the Hindu girl more in common with the Europeans at the club than with the *loin-clothed mob* of her fellow countrymen'. In the same vein, the reviewer singles out Mira's brother Kit 'who returns from Oxford disorientated and more British than the British' as the 'most successful and *significant* character'.[27] Given the difficulty of publishing material on India at this time, alongside the elements of the text that her British reviewer foregrounds, it is hard to resist the sense that the reviewer's interest in this book resides in seeing the legacy and continuing pull of Britain's cultural hegemony, represented in a novel by an Indian woman. Analogously, Markandaya's British publisher summarises 'the fine and fascinating subject' of her next book *Silence of Desire* (1960) as 'India still resenting and yet still dependent on the British influence'.[28]

It was not until the 1960s that India began to make a comeback in terms of interest in the public sphere with a re-emerging fascination with forms of Indian spirituality. That Markandaya, like Tambimuttu, wrote about an India of the Western imagination for specific Anglo-American tastes is evident in her subsequent decision to mine the opposition between a cerebral, rational Western habit of mind, and a more ancient ritualistic Indian sensibility, a polarity that resurfaced with renewed intensity during this period. *Silence of Desire* (1960) manifests this kind of representation in the novel's central argument between Sarojini and her Anglicised husband Dandekar, who opposes his wife receiving faith healing from a swami. Sarojini argues: '... you with your Western notions, your superior talk of ignorance and superstition... you don't know what lies beyond reason and you

---

[27] Marigold Johnson, 'Unhappy Love Affairs' *Times Literary Supplement* (23 Dec. 1955), 773, emphasis mine.

[28] Roger Lubbock, letter to Richard Walsh, 1 Feb. 1960, File Markandaya 1954–60, Chatto and Windus Archive.

prefer not to find out.'[29] Markandaya pits narrow Western ideas against more inclusive Eastern ones. Yet the novel rehearses, without unsettling, ancient conflicts of science against superstition. It reinforces occidental representations of India as irredeemably 'different', defined against the progressive West. Western materialism in conflict with Indian spiritualism forms the subject of her next novel *Possession* (1963).[30] The schematic portrayal of wealthy, white Caroline, who lures artist Valmiki from his mentor, the contemplative, passive swami, confirms the extent to which Markandaya's work remains within the parameters of orientalist discourse.

Markandaya responds to the rise of neo-imperialism and racism in Britain during the late 1960s, in her subsequent novel *The Nowhere Man* (1972), a moving examination of immigration and exile. The superior publicity machinery of publisher Allen Lane/Longman meant the novel was widely reviewed in the national media. However, once again, it earned poor sales and was remaindered five years later (by 1976, the rate of sale was only 21 copies per annum).[31] Compared to her engagement with feminist politics, *Nowhere* reveals an even more ambivalent stance on agency and resistance in relation to racism. Markandaya's critique of racism is made somewhat apologetically, and here the contrast with Sivanandan is particularly instructive. This novel reveals the difficulty of Markandaya's ideological position. Her own internalisation of certain dominant paradigms undermines her efforts to mirror these structures critically. The narrative flits between the post-imperial present of 1968 and the colonial past to show how the latter affects immigrants in Britain. The nowhere man of the title is the protagonist Srinivas, an elderly, impoverished Brahmin trader in spices who has lived in south London for over thirty years. Gentle, sensitive, and mystically minded, he rather improbably idealises British justice and decency, even though it was the British Raj that ruined his family's timber business, destroyed his wife Vasantha's family, abridged his own promising university career when he contested his subservient status, and prompted him to emigrate in despair to Britain. These events in colonial India (1910–40), strategically placed in the middle of the book, manifest as a flashback, prompted by the rising tide of Enoch

---

[29] Kamala Markandaya, *A Silence of Desire* (London: Putnam, 1960), 87. Hereafter *Silence* pagination will appear in the text.

[30] Kamala Markandaya, *Possession* (London: Putnam), 1963.

[31] Penguin, letter to Innes Rose, 6 Aug. 1977, 'The Nowhere Man' File, Allen Lane: Penguin Press, 7139.0467.4 [DM 1852], University of Bristol Special Collections.

Powell-incited racism Srinivas encounters after living peacefully and quietly in Britain for many decades. The recollection not only presents a more balanced historical record, but also underscores the cruelty of racism against those who have been 'sinned against rather than sinning' (*Nowhere* 177). Srinivas ponders:

What wrongs had been done, what crimes committed that called for such punishment? . . . Instead, creeping up on him, came truths not to be denied strange barbed thoughts. That this bland country owed debts it had not paid, rather than scores that it had to settle . . . crimes that had not been atoned for, nor even acknowledged save by the honourable few. (*Nowhere* 177)

Markandaya connects past and present imperialism when the Suez Crisis of 1956 prompts Srinivas to recollect his experiences as a colonial subject in India. The Suez Crisis is often used as a literary trope for looking back at what typified Britishness at that time, as in Kazuo Ishiguro's *The Remains of the Day* (1989), namely Britain's and France's attempts to reassert their imperial role.[32] The crisis was central to the remaking of British post-imperial identity. For Srinivas, the Suez Crisis suggests a continuing imperialism, and the different value of white and black lives. In the bombing of Egypt, Srinivas 'discerned the old pattern: a ratio of forty to one, forty Oriental lives for each European, the familiar equation with its bitter inflections. Life is cheap in the East' (*Nowhere* 99–100). Srinivas recalls the Amritsar massacre with deliberate echoes: 'A hundred Indians for each Briton. That is their scale, the scale by which they value themselves and against which we are measured' (*Nowhere* 122). Srinivas is disillusioned that Britain has reverted 'to peremptory imperial ways' (*Nowhere* 98).

At the same time, Srinivas' reluctance to censure injustices, for fear of being ungrateful, renders the critique somewhat ambivalent. He feels guilty about his anti-British feeling when housed by that host country: 'Where then was his own honour, he asked himself, when he harboured these rancorous thoughts of a country that had taken him in, given him shelter, restored his manhood and his self-respect, and become in the end his own?' (*Nowhere* 177). In a rare personal address elsewhere, Markandaya describes her own experience of this very conflict. She feels the 'fearful struggle between . . . a desire to point up past injustice, and a deep sense of obligation to the country from which one has received so much courtesy and kindness, and the chance to follow one's chosen career, as I have done'.[33] Her correspondence underscores her diffidence in criticising British colonialism. Markandaya thanks her next publisher Chatto and Windus, for the enthusiasm with which they received her novel *The Golden Honeycomb*, which is, she adds, 'after all, critical of the Raj'. She attributes their response to 'a quixotic characteristic' she deems 'unique to the British'.[34] Her anxiety manifests itself in her desire not to antagonise the British reader, explicitly giving this, for example, as the reason she wants to change her earlier use of British 'overseer' to the politer term British 'adviser' in her blurb.[35]

Markandaya's articulation of a gratitude that inhibits criticism reflects perhaps certain right-wing expectations of minorities who choose to settle in England. Such an outlook was openly voiced some years later in an extreme book entitled *Anti-Racism: A Mania Exposed*, with a foreword written, significantly, by Enoch Powell. Singling out Sivanandan for criticism concerning his indictment of racism in Britain, the book accuses him of publishing anti-racist educational books that give 'such a grotesquely distorted picture of the British among whom he has made his home'.[36] Markandaya's delineation of immigrants' reactions to racism contrasts sharply with Sivanandan's combative stance. His insistent emphasis on the connection between imperialism and contemporary racism differs from Markandaya's reluctance to speak out over past injustices in view of her 'sense of obligation' to Britain. Linking the exploitation of minorities to the global economy, and interpreting immigration as a result of the former colonisers' depredations of Third World economies, Sivanandan emphasises the interdependency between immigration and Third World poverty: 'The West must either put money into these countries or let their people come to it. It can't go round the world robbing people blind without the world arriving at its doorstep.'[37] Sivanandan's response forms the subtext of some second-generation minority communities' defiant rejoinder to racists who question their presence in Britain: the slogan, 'We are here because you were there.'

[33] Markandaya, 'One Pair', 30.
[34] Markandaya, letter to Norah Smallwood, 17 Oct. 1976, File Markandaya 1976–82, Chatto and Windus Archive.
[35] Markandaya, letter to D. J. Enright, 26 May 1975, File Markandaya 1970–6, Chatto and Windus Archive.
[36] Russell Lewis, *Anti-Racism: A Mania Exposed* (London: Quartet Books, 1988), 99.
[37] A. Sivanandan, 'European Commentary: Racism, the Road from Germany', *Race and Class* 34.3 (1993), 72.

Markandaya's Srinivas feels pain but is unable to express anger against the white racism inflicted on him. Significantly the *Listener* warms to the portrayal of Srinivas' response to racism, which is not one 'of reproach but of distressed love'.[38] Srinivas develops leprosy, an archaic, stereotypically Asian disease associated with the colonies. He has no place in 1960s Britain and it seems almost inevitable that he will die. Markandaya portrays with sympathy Srinivas' bewilderment at the aggressive treatment he receives from the offspring of his suburban neighbours of thirty years. Yet this quietist, passive acceptance is the very image that Sivanandan's sociological work on race relations attempts to counter. His essays and pamphlet *Afro-Asian Struggles in Britain* specifically show how African, Caribbean, and Asian people resisted and fought back against racism.[39]

In this context, the *Times Literary Supplement*'s favourable review of *Nowhere* when it first appeared, praising Markandaya for her exposure of 'the hideous suppurating threat of racialism' and for not being 'afraid to be a Cassandra on racialism', is noteworthy. The review indicates Markandaya's literary, liberal readership's complex responses to her novel in the early 1970s. On the one hand, like several other reviews, it evinces white liberal guilt: 'She deserves and will surely receive, the guilty ear of us all.' Another reviewer feels similarly 'chastened by the delineation of the blind spots of the English'.[40] Simultaneously, an element of denial, and a desire for a more 'balanced' portrait emerges: one critic recoils from Markandaya's portrait of the racists, suggesting it is too crude and that she 'spoils the balance of compassion' in the novel with 'these brutally caricatured ignorant thugs'.[41] *The Daily Telegraph* similarly finds Markandaya's English instrument of prejudice, Fred, 'barely believable'.[42]

For the early British reviewers of *Nowhere*, the favourable portrayal of Mrs Pickering assuages Markandaya's condemnation of British racism. The elderly divorcee befriends the melancholic Srinivas, who becomes increasingly isolated after his wife Vasantha dies. (Where Vasantha resisted cultural assimilation, Mrs Pickering helps Srinivas adapt to England: a parable of assimilation emerges.) Several reviews emphasise

---

[38] Ronald Bryden, 'Kinship', *The Listener* (12 Apr. 1973).
[39] A. Sivanandan, *Asian and Afro-Caribbean Struggles in Britain* (London: Institute of Race Relations, 1986).
[40] Anonymous, 'rev. of Nowhere Man', *Yorkshire Post* (20 Apr. 1973).
[41] Marigold Johnson, 'Long Race', *Times Literary Supplement* (20 Apr. 1973), 437.
[42] Michael Maxwell Scott, 'rev. of Nowhere Man', *Daily Telegraph* (19 Apr. 1973).

Markandaya's admiration of the 'English' values Mrs Pickering is supposed to embody. *The Yorkshire Post* suggests 'The practical English lady who becomes the Brahmin's mainstay represents those qualities which this writer would be the last to deny.'[43] *The Guardian* writes 'Mrs Pickering is one of the successes of the book, English in a way we all hope we are English.' The author's appreciation and 'understanding for our British virtues' seem to validate her criticisms, particularly as they are articulated 'without bitterness', making her 'sad book important' to these readers: 'Because as well as being written by an Indian, it is Indian in spirit . . . written with imaginative sympathy about us. We need a bit of kindness and understanding at this moment, we also need to understand others and ourselves better.'[44] The initial, short-lived interest in finding out more about 'our Srinivases' shifts to a concern for the native community in crisis, and in need of compassion. In this way Markandaya's reception offers insights into even the liberal press's ambivalence towards dark-skinned immigrants. *The Listener* praises the novel's affectionate recollection of 'the England, which found foreigners odd but acceptable, where Indian and native could share a bomb-shelter [Srinivas' basement] in the Blitz'.[45] This underlines the reviewers (and author's) nostalgia for a time before mass immigration, when Asians were 'odd but acceptable': singular, exceptional and, most importantly, in small numbers. Analysing *Nowhere*'s reception in the early 1970s reveals how little known Markandaya was, even at this stage of her career when she had already published six novels in Britain. One review of *Nowhere* suggests this is because 'oriental names are notoriously difficult for occidental memories to retain', but argues 'a niche should be found for Miss Markandaya, who has been described with some justice as "the ablest Indian novelist now writing in English" '.[46]

Praise for Markandaya's universalist qualities characterises the critical reception of *Nowhere* (and Markandaya's fiction in general) in Britain and North America during the 1970s. What becomes clear is the way hegemonic notions of universalism that transcend the local subcontinental contexts form the criteria for acceptance at this time. John Wakeman insists that the author 'is not *merely* a regional novelist [read Indian]; in her *best* work she achieves perceptions which are relevant

[43] Anonymous, 'Review of Nowhere Man', *Yorkshire Post* (20 Apr. 1973).
[44] P. J. Kavanagh, 'Enoch's England', *Guardian* (19 Apr. 1973).
[45] Bryden, 'Kinship'.
[46] Alan Hunter, 'Fate of an Indian in London', *Eastern Daily Press* (18 May 1973).

to the whole human condition', adding 'And in *The Nowhere Man,* indeed, she switches her scene to the London suburb.'[47] Incredible as it may seem in retrospect, Markandaya's American publisher suggests that the universality of Markandaya's themes, alongside her role in promoting a wider understanding of the people of India, merit consideration for her to be nominated for the Nobel Prize.[48] While her British publishers Chatto and Windus remained circumspect, partly because they did not want to nominate her against their other Indian author Narayan, this very suggestion conveys the political and cultural investment in prescribed notions of universality at this juncture. It is precisely this quality that US-based critic Emmanuel Nelson objects to, two decades later, in his criticism of Markandaya's 'reduction of the Indian immigrant experience to a metaphor for the universal human conditions of alienation and dislocation' in *Nowhere*. He suggests that the text presents the 'loneliness' and 'frustration' of the white characters Mrs Pickering and Dr Radcliffe as not unlike the dilemmas of the Indian characters, and that 'this shift towards the symbolic . . . does violence to the *uniqueness* of our post-colonial and immigrant inheritances'.[49] Nelson's desire to see assertions of cultural difference and specificity rather than universalism indicates the impact of academics from the former colonies in the US and Britain, and of academic postcolonialism on the critical reception of postcolonial texts in the 1990s. Nelson comments on the absence of engagement with contemporary race politics in *Nowhere*. His response points to a similar kind of reader expectation with regard to feminist politics, albeit in the different area of race relations: the desire to see a model of activist resistance rather than simply a critique of existing inequalities. Nelson challenges the 'practical value' of *Nowhere* 'to the immigrant communities she writes about'. He critiques the 'disconcertingly superficial' analysis of racism and Markandaya's 'resolutely apolitical stance', claiming she recreates the pain of immigrant experiences without any 'redemptive transcendent vision' (though Nelson's own anticipated vision itself sounds rather ethereal.) He writes 'what we need from our artists who give voice and

---

[47] Wakeman, *World Authors,* 948, emphasis mine.

[48] Richard Walsh, letter to Norah Smallwood, 17 Jan. 1974, File Markandaya 1970–6, Chatto and Windus Archive.

[49] Emmanuel S. Nelson, 'Troubled Journeys: Indian Immigrant Experience in Kamala Markandaya's *Nowhere Man* and Bharati Mukherjee's *Darkness*', in Anna Rutherford (ed.), *From Commonwealth to Post-Colonial* (Sydney: Dangaroo Press, 1992), 59, emphasis mine.

form to our immigrant experience is an activist consciousness, not just helpless angst.'[50]

The way Markandaya embraces a universalist metaphysic and subsumes the 'Indian' aspects of her work, suggests an affinity between her perspectives and the first (particularly) Western critics of Commonwealth literature's preoccupation with universal, abstract concerns above specific national contexts. Markandaya emphasises the abstract and rarefied nature of her interests: 'Literature brings out the elementary truths of a human commonality.' She maintains that 'one's ethos and one's roots are . . . fundamental' yet become 'purely external . . . when set beside that luminous and extraordinary cortex that exists in all of us . . . that roving and imaginative entity that reaches into and extracts the truth of such universals *whether experienced or not*'. Insisting that '. . . we are involved in universals', she adds '. . . I say this despite the fact that I think of myself as an Indian writer'.[51] As John McLeod observes, while 'Commonwealth Literature may well have been created in an attempt to bring together writings from around the world on an equal footing . . . the assumption remained that these texts were addressed primarily to a Western English-speaking readership. The "Commonwealth" in "Commonwealth Literature" was never fully free from the older, more imperious connotations of the term.'[52] Markandaya's universalist metaphysic and implied Western reader were key to determining her favourable reception by British and American critics when she first began to publish. More recently, as Chinua Achebe notes, universalism has been criticised as a loaded term fraught with colonialist and Eurocentric undertones.[53] Markandaya's texts foreground a falsely inclusive Eurocentric universalism and efface cultural difference. By contrast Sivanandan locates his novel within a more locally situated and politically radical universalist framework.

Commonwealth Literature tended to privilege the impact of British rule in the former colonies, and foreground the legacy of the colonial encounter. This paradigm shaped and continues to shape what constitutes the subject of postcolonial literature in English, particularly Indian writing in English. As Meenakshi Mukherjee argues, 'vernacular authors who write about local social tensions putting the British experience in

---

[50] Ibid. 54, 57–8, 59.

[51] Markandaya, 'One Pair', 25.

[52] John McLeod, *Beginning Postcolonialism* (Manchester: Manchester UP, 2000), 12–13.

[53] Chinua Achebe, *Hopes and Impediments* (London: Doubleday, 1988), 3.

the background tend not to reach a global audience.'[54] Markandaya's novels often focus on the interracial, intercultural relations between the former colonisers and the colonised. Her emphasis suggests a degree of cultural colonisation in her inability to think outside dominant paradigms where the Indian characters need to be defined in relation to English ones. Unlike Sivanandan's experience of Sinhalese racism, it is only in colonial encounters under the British Raj and in white Britain that Markandaya is displaced from her privileged position in the racial hierarchy.

The relative success of Markandaya's next book, *The Golden Honeycomb* (1977)—a semi-historical recreation of colonial Indo-British relations, depicting three generations of royalty in the princely state of Devapur—reflects the revived interest in the Raj identified in the introductory chapter.[55] As Mohanty observes, 'texts are not produced in a vacuum . . . [they] owe their existence as much to the exigencies of the political and commercial marketplace as to the knowledge, skills, motivation, and location of individual writers.'[56] Markandaya's Anglo-American publishers' correspondence confirms this point. In 1976 Markandaya's American publisher suggests to her English counterpart that they should encourage Markandaya's next book to be historical rather than contemporary. She emphasises that interest in the historical context of the Raj was an important element in *Honeycomb*'s initially enthusiastic reception and its nomination for Book Club of the Month in the USA.[57] Then, as later, literature that highlights the colonial experience is received in a publishing context defined by metropolitan parameters, agendas, and the selective criteria of the recipient culture. This context confers authenticity on the preferred native informant: Markanadya's 'own Indian background is in any case sufficient guarantee of authenticity'.[58]

Yet paradoxically we also find in *Honeycomb* a desire to cater to the liberal, university interest in Commonwealth writing arising from the

[54] Meenakshi Mukherjee, *The Perishable Empire: Essays on Indian Writing in English* (Delhi: Oxford UP, 2000), 179.

[55] Kamala Markandaya, *The Golden Honeycomb* (London: Chatto and Windus, 1977). Hereafter *Honeycomb* pagination will appear in text.

[56] Chandra Talpade Mohanty, 'Cartographies of Struggle', in Ann Russo,Torres Lourdes, and Chandra Talpade Mohanty (eds.), *Third World Women and the Politics of Feminism* (Bloomington: Indiana UP, 1991), 33.

[57] Cynthia Varten, letter to Norah Smallwood, 20 Sept. 1976, File Markandaya 1976–82, Chatto and Windus Archive.

[58] Eric Stokes, 'Generally Ravishing', *Times Literary Supplement* (29 Apr. 1977), 507.

collapse of imperial ideologies outlined earlier. Markandaya reflects this impulse to interrogate the Raj in Britain in the 1960s and 1970s. Her critique of colonialism is more pronounced in this text than in her earlier texts published in the 1950s. In *Honeycomb,* Markandaya also seeks to respond to the revisionist readings of colonialism. In 1975, she explained that colonial history 'seeps through' her recent work because she encountered attitudes in Britain either of 'profound indifference' to the Commonwealth, or of interlocutors 'ready to tell you of the benefits that accrued to empire and colony'. She observes: 'nothing drives one back to the history books more quickly than this.'[59] Clearly responding to 'dominant' expectations can be complex: there is no straightforward opposition between the centre and a 'revolutionary' margin. My symptomatic reading of *Honeycomb* situates Markandaya's critique of colonialism within the limits of the liberal discourse of this historical era. This text manifests the contradictory interplay of the reconfiguration and reaffirmation of monolithic notions of the imperial 'motherland'.

Markandaya strips imperialist rhetoric of its claim to altruism, acknowledging instead the heterogeneity of the imperial experience, and the inextricability of the supposed benefits, from a history of exploitation. However, her text undermines the indictment of colonial rule with certain rationalisations, making her criticisms more palatable. At first sight, the narrative emphasises the 'rapacious' British efforts at manipulating the Indian Princes: 'The British have early understood the importance of the Native Princes, the one class in the country bound to them by every tie of self-interest, in the Imperial scheme, (*Honeycomb* 33). The novel highlights the colonials' manipulative skills. The Dewan describes the British as 'superlative potters . . . who could shape and manipulate the most recalcitrant clay to their requirements' (*Honeycomb* 294). Similarly, 'The British refer to the Maharajahs as partners in the solemn act of governing the country.' This is ironised and exposed as a convenient fiction: 'In franker moments they see them as handy tools with which to subdue the nation' (*Honeycomb* 64). The lightness of Markandaya's touch should not blind us to her caustic undertones. An important theme is the discrepancy between the rhetoric of Empire and its material purpose. The Dewan's Brahmin intellectual elite 'agreed that above all it would be fatal to underestimate the adversary, or to dismiss the co-existence of a bluff exterior and classical tenets with the enterprise

<hr>

[59] Markandaya, 'One Pair', 29–30.

and sharp practice of the marketplace', making clear such tenets serve to rationalise material exploitation. The novel suggests that while the British (such as the Resident Arthur Copeland) may have been self-deceived about their altruistic purpose and role in India, the Indian nationalists were not: 'However credulous the British might be about themselves, the whimsical notion that the Empire had been acquired in a fit of absentmindedness—an idea to which Sir Arthur was devoted—raised the thinnest of smiles in these circles' (*Honeycomb* 216). Nonetheless, the issue of self-deception is problematic. Even today the argument that the British *thought* they were aiding India is sometimes offered as a justification for imperialism. Copeland is repulsed by the idea of running any country on the 'thumbscrew and rack'. It is 'too jarring for his *English sensibility*' (*Honeycomb* 217, emphasis mine). Does this equating of Copeland's distaste for violence with his '*English sensibility*' reinforce the implicit suggestion that 'Englishness' cannot be defined by its imperialist violence, and infer (as Chaudhuri does) that such aggression is an aberration from true 'Englishness'? Is there a sense of mitigation because the imperialist administrators *thought* they were being altruistic?

The fullest portrayal of any English person is that of the Resident Sir Arthur Copeland. We tend to see most of the characters through his eyes. In this way, *Honeycomb* rehearses a range of colonial stereotypes of the colonised, underscoring Markandaya's internalisation of colonial discourse. The Maharajah's spirited mistress Mohini is the exotic seductress, and even the Dewan is a canny, unknowable Brahmin. The Maharajah, Bawajiraj III, yearns for a closer acquaintance and intimacy with the British Resident. He is 'dreadfully afraid of appearing uncivilised in British eyes'. When invited to the Resident's home he shakes Lady Copeland's hand with his 'fervid and podgy paw' (*Honeycomb* 171). Defined against his wife's neurotic fears of racial massacre, the British resident is represented as a flawed but basically decent man who has internalised the idea of the 'civilising mission' and sees himself as a willing sacrifice to this cause. Markandaya ironises his self-deception: ' . . . Sir Arthur felt most acutely the burden he bore, dwelt on the sacrifices he made, and speculated querulously whether the country was even aware, let alone grateful' (*Honeycomb* 193–4). This qualification aside, the overriding impression of Copeland is that of integrity personified. At the novel's close it is Copeland's 'infernal fairness' (not the Maharajah's rebellious son or lover) that persuades the Maharajah to make financial concessions to his own people (*Honeycomb*

464). Markandaya emphasises the good intentions of the British, again making her comparable to Chaudhuri. At times, her portrayals of British colonisers suggest a residual sense of the elemental rightness of the imperial order. Despite the element of critique, the novel projects the imperial presence as benign, restraining, and paternal. It is easy to see the appeal of portrayals of kind English colonials who meant well and thought they were doing their duty in the context of the nostalgia for Empire of the 1970s. This is especially so when such observations are authored by a member of the former colony. Paul Scott's positive review of *Honeycomb* in *The Times* confirms this: 'For once in a novel by an Indian, the British presence is illuminated in a way that commands admiration as well as recognition.'[60]

For many generations, Markandaya's own family has been closely connected to the Dewans of Mysore.[61] Her overriding characterisation of British imperialism is symptomatic of the elite's transactions with imperial structures and powers during the Raj, interactions that were not the norm or experience of most of the colonised. Furthermore, the relationship between the British and the ministers of the Princely States was very different from their relationship with anti-colonialist members of the elite, as Nayantara Sahgal's contrasting childhood experiences of political struggle, ideological debate, and imprisonment at the heart of India's fight for independence, in her autobiographical *Prison and Chocolate Cake* (1954) and *From Fear Set Free* (1962), suggest.[62] In a letter to her British publisher, Markandaya describes the relationship between her ancestor, the first Dewan of modern Mysore, and the British Resident, Colonel Hill, as based on friendship and suggests that 'they apparently administered the state together amicably'.[63] Markandaya characterises British governance in both colonial India and Britain in terms of what she sees as 'quintessentially British qualities of compromise

[60] Paul Scott, 'Fiction', *The Times* (28 Apr. 1977), 22.

[61] Markandaya, letter to Smallwood, 8 Nov. 1976, File Markandaya 1970–6, Chatto and Windus Archive.

[62] Nayantara Saghal's self-representation is more self-consciously politicised. She observes: 'At home I was nourished on revolt.' While she 'did not set out to write "political fiction"' she adds that 'Politics for me was an environment in which every issue was a political issue, and personal and political fates were inextricably bound . . . politics was for so long dictated by other people's view of us that I have found it satisfying to give it Indian expression and interpretation'. Nayantara Sahgal, 'The Schizophrenic Imagination', in Rutherford (ed.), *From Commonwealth to Post-Colonial* (Sydney: Dangaroo Press, 1992), 32, 33, 34.

[63] Markandaya, letter to Smallwood, 8 Nov. 1976, File Markandaya 1970–6, Chatto and Windus Archive.

and working together'.[64] Again such representations contrast sharply with Sivanandan's mapping of a working-class history, as I shall show in the second part of this chapter.

Markandaya's efforts to translate the Indian context into an idiom recognisable to the host culture are particularly evident in her use of language. *Nectar* and *Two Virgins*, both set in rural India and narrated by villagers, are peppered with colloquialisms such as 'trollope' (*Nectar* 31), 'ninnies', 'codswallop', and 'narked' (*Two Virgins* 16, 113, 23) that would be considered dated even in the English context. Markandaya's villagers use the terms 'Mother-in-law' and 'Old Granny' instead of the vernacular kinship terms that are common in contemporary postcolonial writing (*Nectar* 54, 66). Krishna Rao suggests that the dated language of *Honeycomb* conveys the late Victorian era of the novel.[65] This may explain the utterances of the Anglicised Indian Royal family, although even here some of the slang is anachronistic. However, why should the Indian workers (whom the Maharajah's son Rabi encounters when he tours the insalubrious world of the mill workers) speak in a rather forced representation of British working-class slang?

The lewd imprecation draws a frown from the woman walking alongside, a mill hand in her middle years, her sari respectably swathed about her head and person.
   'Keep it clean, will you? There're some of us as aren't used to your filth, can't you see? Nor care for it either.' (*Honeycomb* 267–8)[66]

Similarly, the worker that Rabi encounters describes herself as a 'mill lass' (*Honeycomb* 265). This kind of language seems jarringly incongruous with the Indian setting. The real purpose seems to be an attempt to transpose English class markers onto the Indian cultural locality to denote the working-class status of Indian characters, so as to render it accessible to the target English audience and naturalise the 'foreign' context.[67] The assumption is that English can mirror and transcend the

---

[64] Markandaya, letter to Smallwood, 11 Aug. 1976, File Markandaya 1970–6, Chatto and Windus Archive.

[65] A.V. Krishna Rao, 'The Golden Honeycomb: a Brief Study' in G. S. Balarama Gupta (ed.), *Studies in Indian Fiction in English* (Gulbarga: JIWE Publications, 1987), 82.

[66] This last construction should be a double negative.

[67] Tabish Khair observes: 'The case of the odd Indian English novel based in a village is even more complicated. Here we have to assume a complete translation of the local language into English. [Markandaya's *Nectar in a Sieve* does this] by taking recourse to a correct but slightly dated style and language.... [This] creates some interesting situations, such as making an Englishman speak a vernacular dialect which is then reported in English by an Indian woman who does not know any English.' Khair

complexities of the local Indian contexts in which the novel is set. In general this kind of domesticating of language and content favourably conditioned Markandaya's early reception in Britain.[68] According to one review the 'most significant feature of *A Handful of Rice* is that its central character Ravi might almost have been filched from a modern English novel about working-class life north of the Trent'.[69] Like Chaudhuri before her, Markandaya was praised for her ability to write 'with a fresh and precise understanding of *our* language'.[70]

As we can see, Markandaya's work confirms postcolonial theorising on writing *for* translation. However, as the previous discussion of Tambimuttu showed, while forms of cultural translation assimilate to the target language and culture by domesticating or minimising the foreign content, they can also assimilate by emphasising the foreign, albeit in an idiom recognisable to the target culture. In this way, Markandaya's texts elude the polarities set up between foreignising and domesticating translation, as well as those that underpin the abrogation versus assimilation paradigm. For instance, sections of *Honeycomb* emphasise the 'foreign', reinscribing notions of India as exotic, alluring, and unknowable, but in orientalist terms familiar to the target audience. Markandaya's aestheticised descriptions of the Durbar of 1903 are elaborate and evocative of imperial splendour. (Markandaya here draws on the fact that her granduncle attended the Durbar and 'passed down vivid memories of the event'.[71]) Similarly, the Palace is described as a 'place of unfolding delight for child and grown-up alike . . . exquisite marble traceries and the delicate gold-leaf gilding . . . the hand of distant artists—Persian, Mughal, Venetian—can also be traced in elegant inlays and timework and mosaic, and in the little garden pavilions set among brilliant lawns and pools' (*Honeycomb* 45). What is

identifies 'a (hidden and unconscious) seepage of English into the vernacular spoken by a character which is supposed to have been *reported* in English. This may or may not be a flaw, but it ostensibly reverses the direction in which this seepage is supposed (and claimed by critics) to take place.' Tabish Khair, *Babu Fictions: Alienation in Contemporary Indian English Novels* (Delhi: Oxford UP, 2001), 104–5.

[68] Although some reviewers point out Markandaya's lack of familiarity with working-class and suburban British idioms which lead 'her Brixton housewives to talk in the tones of housekeepers out of Henry James' in *Nowhere*. Anonymous, 'Review of *Nowhere Man*', *The Times* (26 Apr. 1973).

[69] Frank McGuinness, 'Rev. of *A Handful of Rice*', *London Magazine* (May 1966), 106.

[70] Marigold Johnson, 'Living by Faith', *Times Literary Supplement* (2 Dec. 1960), 783, emphasis mine.

[71] Markandaya, letter to Smallwood, 17 Oct. 1976, File Markandaya 1976–82, Chatto and Windus Archive.

at work in this text is what Richard Jacquemond refers to as the subtle game of 'complementary–contradictory exoticization and naturalization'.[72] Cultural or ethnic difference is simultaneously universalised and essentialised.

The complex, discursive pressures operating on writers publishing fiction on India in an inhospitable climate clearly inflect Markandaya's work. This context changed in the 1980s when Indian material began to be marketable, in the wake of the success of Rushdie's novel *Midnight's Children* (1981).[73] The year 1982 saw the Festival of India in Britain and one of the first conferences on Asian writing in English, 'The Eye of the Beholder'. As Susheila Nasta observes, the conference ignored the work of Asian women writers living in Britain (as well as those in India) such as Markandaya and Hosain. It focused on the elder statesmen of Indian letters and the young Salman Rushdie, heralded as the new voice of Indian writing in English.[74] (Asian women's writing in Britain came to the fore only in the late 1980s, and then by a later generation of Asian women writers who articulated very different concerns to those of Markandaya, as we will see in the discussion of Meera Syal.) This oversight clearly raises questions of gendered exclusion, but also questions of form. For by the time the publishing contexts became more favourable in the 1980s, Markandaya was supplanted by subsequent writers, notably Rushdie: his *Midnight's Children* (1981) in part created (and was therefore better able to feed) the demands of this new interest in fiction from India. Granada Publishers rejected the paperback rights to Markandaya's last novel *Pleasure City* (1982) a year after the publication of *Midnight's Children*. Acknowledging the novel's sensitivity and imagination and the current marketability of Indian writing in English, *Pleasure City* was deemed as too slow and low-key, especially in relation to the other novels on India available at

[72] Richard Jacquemond, 'Translation and Cultural Hegemony', in Lawrence Venuti (ed.), *Re-thinking Translation: Discourse, Subjectivity and Ideology* (London: Routledge, 1992), 153.

[73] As Meenakshi Mukherjee cautions, it is important not to attribute too much to the influence of one book. Rushdie's culturally hybrid text is a product of the globalised economy and culture that has become increasingly integrated, since the rise of economic liberalism and mass migration to the West. Meenakshi Mukherjee, introduction, in Meenakshi Mukherjee (ed.), *Midnight's Children: A Book of Readings* (Delhi: Pencraft International, 1999), 12.

[74] Susheila Nasta, 'Homes Without Walls: South Asian Writing in Britain', in Ralph J. Crane and Radhika Mohanram (eds.), *Shifting Continents/Colliding Cultures: Diaspora Writing of the Indian Subcontinent* (Amsterdam: Rodopi, 2000), 87–8.

the time.[75] Markandaya's slow-moving, broadly linear narratives lost their appeal, appearing stagnant in content and form, in relation to the manic energy of Rushdie's quirky, jumpy, more ambitious and experimental narratives. The dynamics of the genre of Indian writing in English began to be set by writers like Rushdie. This is not to suggest that postmodernism is necessarily more progressive than realism, rather to comment on the changing perceptions and trends that influenced *in part* the decline of interest in writers such as Markandaya, who then stopped writing. In the 1980s the imbrication of the term 'Commonwealth Literature' with imperialism became increasingly problematic, and this body of writing began to be called postcolonial literature. The decline of interest in Markandaya's work also needs to be seen in relation to this shift, as well as the interdisciplinary, cultural, and literary theory that emerged during this same period to influence textual reading practices.

Perceived limitations of the genre of realism and the shift to meta-fictional works, largely initiated in Indian writing in English by Rushdie, eclipsed writings like Markandaya's: postmodern, meta-fictional, non-mimetic narratives that problematise notions of reality were viewed as possessing more radical potential. Marakand Paranjape suggests that 'Kamala Markandaya's clumsy and unconvincing naturalism . . . do[es] not show any political commitment' and that with this generation 'the post-independence Indian novel remains pretty bourgeois in both form and content, liberal in outlook, but implicitly accepting the social and political status-quo. In all cases, the form [is] placid, more or less in the realistic mode . . .'[76] Paranjape summarises Rushdie's contrasting impact: 'Realism, consistent characters, linearity, order are "out", non-linearity, fantasy and disorder are "in".'[77] Rushdie's fictionalising of history and break with realism would also impinge on Sivanandan's later novel. While Sivanandan's broadly realist novel *Memory*—published much later than Markandaya's fiction—shows a similar commitment to naturalism, post-structuralist, and postmodern impulses that undermine the monolithic singular 'History' inform the narrative. The novel thematises unverifiability and the role of the imagined in writing history, and presents history as an arena of contestation in a manner akin to

[75] File Markandaya 1976–82, Chatto and Windus Archive.
[76] Marakand R. Paranjape, 'Inside and Outside the Whale: Politics and the New Indian English Novel', in Viney Kirpal (ed.), *The New Indian Novel in English: A Study of the 1980s* (Delhi: Allied Publishers, 1990), 215.
[77] Ibid. 220.

Rushdie's, which suggests that he and Sivanandan can be productively examined in dialogue with each other.


## SIVANANDAN: RACE AND CLASS

Sivanandan's mature novel embodies tensions between orthodox and new postcolonial forms of Marxism, a split he both exemplifies and straddles. Where his work has received critical attention, it tends to be considered either in terms of his political writing or his fiction. My discussion examines both his polemical journalism and his tightly structured, symmetrical novel of genealogy *When Memory Dies* (1997), focusing on the interrelationship between the two, and by extension, the relationship between his engagement with Sri Lankan and British politics. *When Memory Dies* dramatises the story of three generations of a Jaffna Tamil family in the three sections of the novel: the story of Sahadevan (the second son of a postal worker from a 'bone-dry village in the north of Ceylon', who, like Sivanandan, was sent at a young age to Colombo, to live with a relative and attend a Catholic school), his son Rajan, the narrator, and Rajan's adopted Sinhalese son, Vijay.[78]

The novel's title and the dialogue between the generations signal the novel's project of historical retrieval, dramatised through the contrasting perspectives of a range of characters. Sahadevan's anti-colonial education begins with meeting Sinhalese railwayman and union militant S.W. and his wife Prema. S.W. foregrounds the importance of recovering, and of reclaiming histories to counter British versions: 'There were rebellions going on all the time. . . . But your history books wouldn't tell you that, would they? After all, they are written by the English. Soon no one will know the history of our country' (*Memory* 40). Where Markandaya locates anti-colonial resistance solely in the upper class, in *Fury* Sivanandan foregrounds native politics and organised working-class resistance to British rule in the 1920s in the form of revolts, uprisings, and mutinies, rather than the elite's contribution to the nationalist struggle.[79] S.W. reminds Sahadevan of the sacrifices made by

---

[78] A. Sivanandan, *When Memory Dies* (London: Arcadia Books, 1997), 3. Hereafter, *Memory* pagination will appear in the text.

[79] As we saw, Markandaya's novel reflects Ranajit Guha's argument that 'the historiography of Indian nationalism has for a long time been dominated by elitism—colonialist

the strike leaders and the ordinary people 'who suffered a lot of hardship in helping the strikers. It is their sacrifices that made things better for the rest of us' (*Memory* 56).

If Markandaya intends to counter colonial versions of the imperial past, this is only one strand of Sivanandan's purpose, as is to be expected in a book written so many years later. Sivanandan's main concerns include the continued re-writing of the nation's past by Sinhala and Tamil nationalists, and charting the Left's various forms of resistance to colonialism and its failures. First, the novel delineates Labour Party member A. E. Goonesinha's move towards parliament and co-option by the British Labour Party. Secondly, the narrative delineates the Lanka Sama Samaja Party's failure to combat the rise of communalism, the extreme racism of the Sri Lankan Freedom Party and its institutionalisation of Sinhala Buddhist nationalism, and finally the novel portrays the LSSP's own capitulation to communalism and the beginning of separatist violence in the early 1980s. *Memory* has an essentially political character and appears to be offered as a summing up of the contemporary history and class politics of a country. The generational structure delineates how the fraught politics of Sri Lanka's civil war are imbricated in stories of the past. *Memory* counters dominant Sinhala accounts of the causes of this conflict and puts forward alternative views emphasising the oppressions faced by Sri Lanka's Tamil minority, giving his work a comparatively greater contemporary relevance and urgency.

In contrast to Markandaya, Sivanandan more directly and provocatively disturbs hegemonic representations in his writings on race relations in Britain and Sri Lanka. He is not 'defining the identity and homogeneity' of the dominant group.[80] In Homi Bhabha's formulation, he occupies and uses a liminal space to question, and instructively and radically problematise, prevailing representations of the dominant majority in both countries, tracing trends shared by

---

elitism and bourgeois nationalist elitism . . . Both varieties share the prejudice that the making of the Indian nation and the development of the consciousness—nationalism— . . . were exclusively or predominantly elite achievements.' Ranajit Guha (ed.), *Subaltern Studies I: Writings on South Asian History and Society* (Delhi: Oxford UP, 1982), 1. In contrast, Sivanandan's re-writing of the historiography of nationalism can be located in relation to the Subaltern Studies project, although he uses a different method.

[80] Abdul JanMohamed, 'Worldliness-Without-World, Homelessness-as-Home: Towards a Definition of the Specular Border Intellectual', in Michael Sprinker (ed.), *Edward Said: A Critical Reader* (Cambridge, Mass.: Blackwell, 1992), 103.

racism in Britain and communalism in Sri Lanka.[81] His engagement
and political involvement with Sri Lanka's debates and conflicts after
forty years in Britain disrupts the boundaries between home and
metropolitan country. Sivanandan is an intellectual engaged at home
and in the metropolis. His negotiation of his identity plays out in
terms of an international socialism not aligned to any particular racial
identity or geographical location. He situates himself within a larger social struggle, and draws on Marxism as a way of interpreting
the world in order to change it. His self-representation is assert-
ively Third Worldist, rather than Sri Lankan. The full title of *Race
and Class* is *A Journal for Black and Third World Liberation*. This
announces his organisation's wider, sustained commitment to supporting Third World socialist struggles worldwide. His deconstruction
of given historiographies by introducing other genealogies that have
hitherto been precluded in the Sri Lankan context is paralleled by
his achievement in historicising black British communities and their
resistance.

## ANTI-RACISM IN BRITAIN

Sivanandan's polemical essays and activism emerged in the context of
the anti-racist socialist and Black Nationalist movements in Britain and
the USA in the 1960s and 1970s.[82] An unflinching and tireless determ-
ination to fight against the injustice, disempowerment, and racism
experienced by Britain's working-class black communities characterises
his long career. Under his leadership the Institute of Race Relations (IRR)
became identified as a radical black, political voice. Sivanandan initiated
a series of IRR research pamphlets and anti-racist educational publications, whilst supporting a range of black self-help movements such as
Black Unity and Freedom Party, as well as projects such as documenting
black deaths in police custody. From the start he demanded equality,
seeking neither acceptance nor approval from the host community: 'I
don't care if you like me or not, I just want to be able to send my child to
the same school as yours.'[83] This marked an important deviation from

---

[81] Homi Bhabha, *The Location of Culture* (London: Routledge, 1994), 9.

[82] For further reference, see Kim Gordon, C. L. R. James, and Anthony Bogues,
*Black Nationalism and Socialism* (London: Socialists Unlimited for Socialist Workers
Party, 1979).

[83] Sivanandan, interview with the author.

the cultural cringe of the culturally colonised as expressed by someone like Chaudhuri. Sivanandan's outspoken personality and commitment inspired generations of anti-racist socialists, as the many contributions to the *Race and Class* issue in his honour bear testimony.[84]

He has long maintained that racial oppression cannot be dissociated from class exploitation, forging a link already emphasised by C. L. R. James and W. E. Du Bois. As his analysis of the race and class dynamics in both Britain and Sri Lanka illustrate, this relationship is not always mutually reinforcing or beneficial. The very nature of the intimate association between race and class means that if one category is prioritised, it will be at the expense of the other. Over the last forty years he has attempted to redress any overemphasis on one that subsumes the other. The title change of the IRR's journal (from *Race* to *Race and Class*) points to a commitment to pose a counter view to the Left in the West that sees race as subordinate to class: 'White radicals continue to maintain that colour oppression is no more than an aspect of class oppression. Hence they require that the colour line be subsumed to the class line and are satisfied that the strategies worked out for the proletariats serve equally the interests of the black.'[85] Sivanandan asserts that in contrast to the Left in the West: '*Race and Class* never subsumes race under class. It looks at race in terms of class, while at the same time bringing to an understanding of the class struggle the racial dimension' (*Communities* 14).

His emphasis on the connection between race and class constituted a major step towards a revision of Left politics. However, his articulation of the relation between race and class never adequately theorised or accounted for gendered and cultural difference. This is symptomatic of what effectively divided anti-racist Marxist movements in the UK in the 1970s. Post-structuralism tried to break up monolithic concepts of Marxism by introducing concepts of alterity; this divided the old and new Left.[86] Sivanandan did not move theoretically beyond a common black identity, which explains why (as we will see) he had no sympathy for the emergence of identity politics, or for Marxists like Stuart Hall

[84] Colin Prescod and Hazel Waters (eds.), *A World to Win: Essays in Honour of Sivanandan, Race and Class* 41.1/2 (1999).

[85] A. Sivanandan, 'The Liberation of the Black Intellectual', *Race and Class* 18.2 (1977), 339.

[86] For an account of the mutually modifying influences of French post-structuralist theory and British 'native' Marxist traditions, see Antony Easthope, *British Post-Structuralism Since 1968* (London: Routledge, 1988).

who saw potential in the 'new' theory to define difference within black culture. Just as Sivanandan criticised traditional Left white radicals for prioritising class over race, he censures the primacy of 'race' and 'ethnicity' in identity politics, arguing that it deflects attention from class injustice. He refers to 'the tyranny of identity politics' where 'one remains fixed in his or her subjectivity', and insists that 'one should fight in terms of principles' not in terms of 'primordial affiliations'.[87] Wanting to see both concepts operating at the same time, he maintains the 'flight from class' has meant that 'the fight against racism has become a fight for culture, masking institutionalised racism, the racism that kills and the material conditions of the blacks of the 'slum city' whose only ' "identity" is their poverty'.[88]

In an article, 'New Times', written in 1990, Sivanandan identified what he referred to as the gradual taming of the British Left, criticising Stuart Hall and his colleagues' *Marxism Today* as 'a mirror image of Thatcherism passing for socialism. New Times is Thatcherism in drag' (*Communities* 19).[89] Aijaz Ahmad suggests this essay is proleptically 'a devastating critique of what we now know as post-colonial theory. Most of the thematics of that theory, and most of what has been wrong with it, are all here.'[90] In another essay, Sivanandan critiques postmodern intellectuals 'who have fled into discourse, deconstruction and representation, as though to interpret the world is more important than changing it . . . as though changing the interpretation is all we could do in a changing world'.[91] Sivanandan's attitude towards literature and politics, in relation to postmodern writers and theorists appears to parallel a key division within postcolonial studies: notably, the criticisms of post-structuralists Homi K. Bhabha and Gayatri Spivak, or postmodern writers such as Salman Rushdie, made by commentators such as Benita Parry.[92] While Parry claims that Bhabha's early work downplays the idea of anti-colonial struggle and agency and that his emphasis on ambivalence suggests that no discourse is resistant,

[87] Sivanandan, interview with author.        [88] Ibid.

[89] 'All that Melts into Air is Solid: The Hokum of New Times' was first published in *Race and Class* 31.3 (1990). My citations are from its reprint in Sivanandan, *Communities*, 19–59.

[90] Aijaz Ahmad, 'Out of the Dust of Idols', *Race and Class* 41.1/2 (1999), 3.

[91] A. Sivanandan, 'La trahison des clercs', *New Statesman and Society* (14 July 1995), 20–1.

[92] Parry criticises Spivak for her over-concentration on colonial discourse analysis, which she claims eradicates oppositional agency. Benita Parry, 'Problems in Current Theories of Colonial Discourse', *Oxford Literary Review* 9.1/2 (1987), 39.

Sivanandan's own novel foregrounds the native's role as historical subject and reinstates the importance of decolonising narratives and anti-imperial liberation movements.[93]

At one level, Sivanandan and a writer such as Rushdie are products of a generational divide in British intellectual culture. Marxist critics Ahmad and Timothy Brennan's critique of postmodern writers such as Rushdie is a product of the split within Marxism identified above. At the same time, Sivanandan's concern with the writing of history and the fictionalising of history suggests an engagement with post-structural conceptions of history, which may seem surprising in terms of his pronouncements cited above. As suggested earlier, this shows he can be productively read in dialogue with Rushdie and underlines the ways in which generational influences are not uni-directional.

## *WHEN MEMORY DIES*

*Memory*'s treatment of history comes closer to Rushdie than may be initially apparent. It appears to be a historical novel; socially realist in form and narrative style, charting the trajectory of a group of predominantly working-class characters, it conforms to the method of socialist realism. However, although the novel proceeds in a straightforwardly realist fashion, the opening paragraph suggests that the novel emerges as the product of Rajan's memory from exile in London.

My memory begins, as always, with the rain—crouched as a small boy against the great wall of the old colonial building that once housed the post office. It frightened me, the great monsoon downpour, and saddened me too, threw me back on my little boy self and its lonelinesses . . . the first feel of the sadness of a world that kept Sanji from school because he had no shoes. Other seasons I would come to know . . . . But the things that crowded in on me that other day in the rain, and in many rains after, and made me an exile for the better part of my life, were, also the things that connected me to my country and made me want to tell its story. (*Memory* 5)

The opening suggests that, akin to Rushdie, although a story of a country is offered in the following pages, it will not be the whole story:

---

[93] Parry cautions that increased concern with the textual obscures necessary attention to socio-historical events. She argues: 'By subsuming the social to textual representation, Bhabha represents colonialism as transactional rather than conflictual.' Benita Parry, 'Signs of Our Times: Discussion of Homi Bhabha's *The Location of Culture*', *Third Text* 28/29 (1994), 2, 16.

But there is no story to tell, no one story anyway, not since that day in 1505 when the fidalgo Don Laurenco de Almeida resplendent in gold braid . . . landed on our shores and broke us from our history. No one story, with a beginning and an end, no story that picks up from where the past left off—only bits and shards of stories, and those of the people I knew, and that only in passing, my own parents and son, or heard tell of, for there was no staying in a place or in a time to gather a story whole, only an imagined time and place. (*Memory* 5)

The whole story is impossible to narrate, in part because of the effects of colonial dislocation. Furthermore, as in Rushdie's *Midnight's Children*, a subtext for the unverifiability and the role of the imagination is the migrant's own distance in time and space. While this novel's style is certainly not Rushdie's magic realism, *Memory* thematises the recuperation of history as a method of fictionalising experience, subject to the selective truth and inevitable distortions of personal memory, analogous to the pickling process that pervades *Midnight's Children*: 'To pickle is to give immortality . . . a certain alteration, a slight intensification of taste. . . . The art is to change the flavour in degree but not in kind; one day perhaps the world may taste the pickles of history.'[94] *Midnight's Children* self-consciously foregrounds the idea that we make our own history. The focus on Parvati's child Aadam Sinai, who symbolises the future, and the empty pickle jar figured at the close of the novel in relation to the 'chutnification' of history, signifies the future left for successive generations to determine. Sivanandan similarly represents individuals functioning as active agents in the construction of history, and emphasises the political machinations behind Sri Lanka's political crises. In a personal interview he contextualises his utopian conclusion by suggesting that 'the resolution is not for me, the resolution is in the hands of the generations to come'.[95] *Memory* can be read as manifesting the tensions between fiction and history, between orthodox Marxist and post-structuralist conceptions of history. The novel's hopeful close embodies and underscores these tensions.

For Sri Lankan commentators such as Regi Siriwardene (poet and critic and Sivanandan's contemporary), the broadly realist novel's ending marks a glaring departure from the grim actuality of much of the book. In the novel, the separatist Commander Ravi is likened in physical appearance to the actual leader of the Liberation Tamil Tigers of Eelam (LTTE) Prabhakaran, 'a portly figure in battle fatigues' (*Memory* 410).

---

[94] Salman Rushdie, *Midnight's Children* (London: Picador, 1981), 444.
[95] Sivanandan, interview with the author.

Ravi's brutal, ruthless approach is contrasted with that of the moderate Yogi. In the final episode of the novel, Commander Ravi kills Kugan, whom he mistakenly takes for an informer, and then shoots Vijay who attempts to rescue Kugan. The novel ends with this incident, provoking Yogi to assert his command over Ravi, knocking the pistol out of Ravi's hands with the words: 'That's enough . . . I am taking over' (*Memory* 411). Sri Lanka-based Siriwardene argues that the implicit suggestion that Yogi's more 'humane' influence will now direct the movement is at odds with the actual years of violence that followed:

> What does this conclusion mean? . . . Does Yogi's knocking the gun out of [Ravi's] hand signal the end of that ruthlessness? Is this another alternative history we are expected to credit, although we already know the appalling reality of the next twelve years? Or is the conclusion just an escape from the author's own uncertainties and dilemmas: does the novel stop where it does because he can't resolve them?[96]

In a personal interview Sivanandan suggests that he created this ending in order to reflect a positive path that the separatists *might have followed* at the time during which the ending of the book is set: 'The upbeat ending is not contradictory if you follow Yogi. Yogi is the socialist and his taking over from violent Ravi is the moment of socialism. It is not a factual ending, I only wanted to suggest that there are moments of socialism and we have to seize the time. Socialism doesn't come after liberation.'[97] In contrast to Siriwardene, other younger Sri Lankan critics like Suvendrini Perera endorse this utopian ending. Perera writes that the novel's achievement is that it 'registers the possibility of other choices, the directions not taken which have added to the making of the present. In doing so, it also builds a case for a future politics of co-existence. . . . The possibility of asserting Tamil rights and aspirations, while rejecting ethno-nationalism . . . is fleetingly imagined at the close of *When Memory Dies.*'[98]

Just as Sivanandan attempts to subvert dominant perceptions of colonialism and race relations, in this broadly realist novel on Sri Lanka he resists producing an exoticised spectacle of Otherness for a Western

[96] The 'appalling reality' Siriwardene refers to includes the brutality of the actions of both the Sri Lankan governments and the LTTE.

[97] Sivanandan, interview with the author.

[98] Suvendrini Perera, 'Unmaking the Present, Remaking Memory: Sri Lankan Stories and a Politics of Co-existence', *Race and Class* 41.1/2 (1999), 195. See also Qadri Ismail, *Abiding by Sri Lanka: On Peace, Place and Postcoloniality* (Minneapolis: University of Minnesota Press, 2005).

readership. This contrasts with Markandaya's fiction, written earlier. Sivanandan roots his novel in its physical contexts of Colombo, Sandipalay, and Jaffna, without exoticising or orientalising the landscapes, unlike some recent Sri Lankan writing in English such as Romesh Gunesekera's *Reef* (1994). Significantly, Sivanandan had difficulty publishing this novel, with several publishers asking him for 'more local colour'.[99] By emphasising the political machinations that triggered the crisis, he tries to resist colonial and neo-colonial readings of Sri Lanka's innate violence, although this attempt is fraught with ambivalence. Delineating close, middle-class inter-community friendships and marriages, the text emphasises that the two communities are not inevitably mutually incompatible, antagonistic, and hostile. This position is articulated in Rajan's reflections from exile in England: he left Sri Lanka after his wife Lali was raped and killed by Sinhalese thugs who thought she was Tamil during the anti-Tamil pogrom. The expression of past amity is poignantly juxtaposed with present violent atrocities:

I thought I lived in a world where there was no communal hatred or conflict, where we didn't kill each other just because we spoke different languages. It is not even that we had so much in common, Sinhalese and Tamils, Buddhists and Hindus, or that we derived from the same racial branch of the tree of man. We were one people. We sang each other's songs as our own, ate each other's food, talked each other's talk, worshipped each other's Gods. Even when we lived our particular lives, they always touched on those around us, and theirs on ours. (*Memory* 283)

This recreation of a past peaceful coexistence is an important part of the book's argument, just as Rajan's loving marriage to Sinhalese Lali, and up-country Tamil Meena's understanding of Vijay signify the possibility of another future. These relationships counter representations (especially in the Western press) of the current crisis as endemic or as an 'ethnic' or 'religious' war between Hindus and Buddhists. It shifts the debate from intrinsic differences to wider questions of power sharing and social relations.

Sivanandan's work shows the difficulty of rationalising the violence that is destroying a once peaceful island. In *Memory*, after the brutal murder and rape of his sister Lali, Lal imagines her 'leaping like a mist across the mountains, chanting over and over again . . . the terrible lines

---

[99] Sivanandan, interview with the author.

of that ill-begotten hymn she had learnt at convent school: "Where every prospect pleases and only man is vile". He writhed in *discomfort* (*Memory* 259, emphasis mine). Lal's unease at the memory of Bishop Heber's words perhaps reflects Sivanandan's own position.[100] It is as if Sivanandan has deliberately resisted colonial accounts like Heber's, and yet at the same time finds it difficult to reject them totally in view of the appalling atrocities witnessed. Sivanandan's novel discovers its own postcolonial heart of darkness in sectarian rape and ethnic violence. This ambivalence suggests how hard it is to deal with 'communal' violence outside these dominant paradigms.

Although *Memory*'s contestation of certain orientalist tropes contrasts with Markandaya's more pronounced efforts to conform to Western expectations, Sivanandan chiefly addresses a wider, international audience. This address has significant political implications, as we shall see. As Paul Gilroy argues, Sivanandan brings to his analysis of UK race relations 'the political traditions, which the blacks who arrived here since the Second World War brought with them'. Gilroy refers to 'the forms of struggle, political philosophy, and revolutionary perspectives of non-European radical traditions' in which Sivanandan's 'now transplanted political consciousness was forged'.[101] At the same time, it is Sivanandan's experiences in Britain that provide him with analogies for analysing the stratification of power in his novel on Sri Lanka. His perceptions of the race and class dynamics in Sri Lanka both feed into and are reinforced by his immersion in black British socialist politics over the last forty years.[102] Given that he did not visit Sri Lanka between 1982 and 2003, his experience of Britain becomes an even

---

[100] This juxtaposition between Sri Lanka's idyllic environment and her barbarous people has remained a commonplace in writings about Sri Lanka from Bishop Heber's orientalist statement on Sri Lanka, 'Though every prospect pleases / And only man is vile', in R. Heber, *Hymns, Ancient and Modern* (London: William Clowes, 1924), to William McGowan, *Only Man is Vile: The Tragedy of Sri Lanka* (London: Picador, 1992).

[101] Paul Gilroy, 'Steppin' Out of Babylon—Race, Class and Autonomy', in Centre for Contemporary Cultural Studies (ed.), *The Empire Strikes Back: Race and Racism in 70s Britain* (Birmingham: Hutchinson in association with the Centre for Contemporary Cultural Studies, University of Birmingham, 1982), 286.

[102] This is not to suggest that Sivanandan's articulations of race and class dynamics derive exclusively from his involvement with black British anti-racist socialism. The novel must be read in the context of the work of Sri Lankan Marxist social historians, notably Kumari Jayawardena and Ranjith Amarasinghe, who have theorised the 'Sinhala Only' Act in terms of the Left's capitulation to communal politics. Kumari Jayawardena, *The Origins of the Left Movement in Sri Lanka* (Colombo: Sanjiva Books, 1988). Y. Ranjith Amarasinghe, *Revolutionary Idealism and Parliamentary Politics* (Colombo: Social Scientists' Association, 1998).

more important factor in understanding Sri Lanka's past. This suggests the primacy of the host country in his reflections: the 'real' ground of comparison is Britain.

This becomes apparent in the way Sivanandan's theoretical articulations of the relations between race and class in Britain are embodied in his fictional treatment of their dynamics in Sri Lanka in *Memory*. The two interrelated parallels between race and class in Britain and Sri Lanka are anachronistic rather than contemporary. *Memory* portrays inter-communal amity forged in the beliefs of the Left and the Labour movement united by 'a fight . . . not just against the bosses but against the British' (*Memory* 67). This echoes Sivanandan's work on African-Caribbeans' and Asians' common fight against British state racism. Similarities also surface in his depiction of the way Sri Lanka's revolutionary Left became fissured by communal interests, like the black communities in Britain who 'were a community and a class' (*Communities* 65) but allowed themselves to be 'broken down into their cultural or ethnic constituents'.[103] The failures of Sri Lanka's Left are voiced through the critical perspective of Dr Lal. On the Sri Lanka Freedom Party's 'Sinhala Only' Language Act of 1956, he comments that 'socialism is dead . . . we'll no longer be fighting injustice but each other' (*Memory* 204). He observes that his old party's talk of 'working class unity is sullied with communalism'. He goes on to prophesy that 'this combination of religion and race will finish class politics forever' (*Memory* 230). The emphasis is on horizontal class divisions, riven vertically by communal cleavages in both the Sri Lankan and British contexts.

Sivanandan also maintains that social change can only be achieved by a collective struggle focusing on the common denominators of racial oppression and class exploitation. He insists that if you fight for one and not the other you only 'end up exchanging one oppression for another' (*Communities* 13). *Memory* foregrounds the way the 'Sinhala Only' policy secured class mobility for one group (the Sinhala-educated majority) by displacing the elite English-educated class, but simultaneously instituted another form of oppression against a linguistic minority, the Tamil-educated. Through the fictional figures of Ramaswamy and Meena, *Memory* also narrativises the experiences of the most exploited, ignored sector of Sri Lankan labour, the up-country Tamils. Just as Sivanandan insists that in Britain racial and class exploitation cannot be dissociated, he draws attention to the class and race dynamics in

---

[103] A. Sivanandan, 'Race Against Time', *New Statesman and Society* (15 Oct. 1993), 16.

some of the interconnected areas of dispute in the Sri Lankan conflict, namely economic factors, language rights, employment, and university admissions policy. He argues that the 'Sinhala Only' policy substantially reduced chances of education and employment for the Tamil minority. If, as Sivanandan defines it, racism stems from the state's power to discriminate on the basis of race, then the communalist policies of the Sinhala-dominated state with its power to discriminate against the minority communities can better be described as a form of state racism. Communalism implies hostility between two not necessarily, but usually unequal groups. Sivanandan emphasises the structural inequality between the Sinhala-dominated government and the Tamil minority. This echoes his work in the British context where he contests the 'liberal fallacy' which gives white and black racism 'equal weight' despite the unequal power relations between the two groups.[104]

Although Sivanandan's analysis of his countries of origin and destination in terms of each other contrasts with Markandaya's more uni-directional mode of cultural translation, he translates the conflicts in Sri Lanka into a British political idiom, accessible to his implied readers in Britain.[105] This can be seen in the way his depictions of Sinhala scapegoating of the Tamil are mediated through the idiom of white British racism: 'they've got our jobs, our land, our everything' (*Memory* 295). If you substitute 'land' for 'houses', you have the voice of the British National Party and the National Front. Similar echoes surface in Sivanandan's attempt to represent the way the Tamils are presented as 'outsiders' in populist Sinhala ideology, as if Sri Lanka was not their home: 'Why don't they go back to where they came from?' (*Memory* 295). (Compare this with an actual translated example of this kind of rhetoric: 'Aliens you have danced too much; your destruction is at hand. This is the country of us, the Sinhala.'[106]) Sivanandan's novel does not confine itself to the way communalism was institutionalised in the state, but also depicts the way it combined with hegemonic Sinhala–Buddhist ideology, and became reproduced and widely accepted in popular culture among the majority community. In his insights and portrayals of populist ideologies, further similarities between aspects of

---

[104] A. Sivanandan, 'White Racism and Black', *Encounter* 31.1 (1968), 96.

[105] In contrast, for Spivak translation, or the analogous task of postcolonial reading, should attend to cultural difference, specificity, and the 'limits of translation', and disrupt the effect of social realism. Gayatri Chakravorty Spivak, *Outside in the Teaching Machine* (London: Routledge, 1993), 193, 197.

[106] Cited in Mohan Ram, *Sri Lanka: The Fractured Island* (Delhi: Penguin, 1989), 52.

white British and Sinhala racism become pronounced. Sections of both 'majorities' have a 'minority' complex. The drive to present Sinhala–Buddhist culture as the 'national' culture and the perceived threats to it are not dissimilar to Thatcher and other right-wing conservatives' claim that the 'real' white Anglo-Saxon Protestant culture of Britain was endangered and being swamped by the influx of immigrants.

This is not to say that Sivanandan refuses the specifics of the problems of racism in Britain and communalism in Sri Lanka, or that he attempts 'to make everything identical to the problem at home'.[107] His reading of one through the lens of the other extrapolates common features. Yet it is important to remember that the similarities are pronounced because Sivanandan's own perceptions are mediated and influenced by his immersion in black British politics, and that he is translating the conflicts in Sri Lanka into a British context. A fascinating paradox of Sivanandan's work is the slippage between present and past experience: his experience of the changing social structure in Britain consolidates his understanding not of Sri Lanka's present, but of its past.

## MARKANDAYA AND SIVANANDAN

Their ideological differences notwithstanding, certain thematic and formal correspondences between Markandaya's fiction and Sivanandan's mature first novel may be symptomatic of the specific realities of their particular generation of colonised subcontinentals, and the influence of their formative colonial contexts on their work. In contrast to the autobiographical mode of the authors of the previous generation, these writers are concerned with wider, more public forms of history. Both foreground thematically, metaphorically, and structurally, the clash between tradition and modernity in postcolonial states, the erosion of historical memory during colonial times, and the re-writing of the nation's past from the view of the colonised. Like *Memory,* many of Markandaya's novels are grounded in a multi-generational narrative structure.

Both writers' stories about living under colonial rule describe the conflict between nationalist and collaborationist impulses experienced by a certain class during this era. Markandaya's *Nowhere* dramatises the

---

[107] Sneja Gnew and Gayatri Chakravorty Spivak, 'Questions of Multiculturalism', in Mary Broe and Angela Ingram (eds.), *Women's Writing in Exile* (Chapel Hill, NC: University of North Carolina Press, 1989), 418.

young Srinivas, torn between co-operating in 'India's own humiliation' by working for the colonial government and fear of sacrificing 'home . . . family . . . career and ambition' as he came of age during the anti-colonial struggles in India (*Nowhere* 110). The protagonist Rajan experiences this same conflict in a Sri Lankan context in Sivanandan's novel (*Memory* 67). Sivanandan describes his early adulthood in Sri Lanka as marked by this very dilemma between 'becoming a nationalist and becoming a comprador' (*Communities* 4).

Both writers question assumptions of the benefits of colonial rule and address the dislocations for the colonised that derive from the imposition of colonialism, whilst acknowledging the importance of industry and modernisation. In Markandaya's rural tragedy *Nectar in a Sieve*, this questioning is articulated through the deprived female protagonist Rukmani's ambivalence towards the tannery, which is set up in her village. Its economic impact and the social improvement it produces are juxtaposed with the threat of urbanisation for the landless. It causes the death of her son. The comments of Srinivas' grandfather as he watches the imperialists' destruction of his teakwood plantation in her later novel *Nowhere* need to be read in this context:

What compensation can they give us for purloining what has taken a hundred years to grow? . . . They will tell you with pride . . . how they have built roads and railways in our country. Well, no doubt they have. The devil must be given his due. But remember too—you must never forget—how it was done and why. (*Nowhere* 111–12)

In strikingly similar terms Dr S. W. in *Memory* comments on the disruption of capitalist modes of production:

'They say they are bringing civilization to us, with railways and roads, when what they are really doing is transporting the wealth out of the country' . . . I am not saying that everything [the British] did is bad. I am not saying that the railways are a bad thing; after all I am a railwayman myself, but we would have come to it in our own time, at our own speed . . . it wasn't the right time . . . the rhythm was all wrong, they were no longer in tune with themselves. (*Memory* 38)

In comparison to Chaudhuri and Tambimuttu, albeit to differing degrees, Markandaya's and Sivanandan's work marks, in Ngugi's phrase, a further stage of 'decolonising the mind'.[108]

---

[108] Ngugi Wa Thiong'o, *Decolonising the Mind: The Politics of Language in African Literature* (London: James Currey, 1986).

However, the overriding differences in their fictional recreations of their countries of origin and destination signal different perceptions on history, class, gender, ethnicity, that underscore the distinct approaches to agency, and the contrasting politics which underpin their writings. Markandaya's *Fury* shows the effects of patriarchy and suggests how women functioned centrally in the nationalist struggles, but were not empowered or treated as equal partners. Her novels *Fury* and *A Silence of Desire* critique the patriarchal expectations of the Anglicised male protagonists, Kit and Dandekar, despite their secular and modern outlook.[109] Sivanandan's *Memory* raises gender issues, such as Lali's sectarian rape, as part of his political project. However, his emphasis is less on the fact that communal violence is fought on the site of women's bodies, and more on the impact of the rape on the deceased rape-victim's husband. Lali fulfils her function and then cannot be accommodated in the narrative. Sivanandan's concern is not female interiority, subjectivity, agency or the questioning of prescribed gender roles. Even his assertive, independent female characters such as Meena, Mrs Bandara, and Manel are not the subjects of his novel, but constitute its background, functioning as an exotic backdrop. The novel's masculinised perspective describes the women in exoticised and eroticised terms. On the other hand, Sivanandan's inclusive portrait of twentieth-century Sri Lanka, with its genealogy of cultural hybridity and blurring of ethnic boundaries, emphasising inter-ethnic friendship, class solidarity, and intermarriage, contrast with the hegemonic representations of ethnic and caste difference that mark Markandaya's writing, which valorises the dominant caste community of Hindu Brahmins.[110]

The two writers have different views on the relation between literature and politics. Sivanandan privileges activism above literature and discourse more generally. He wrote his first novel perhaps to renegotiate the

---

[109] Markandaya ridicules Kit's disappointment with Premala for not fulfilling the role of a society wife (*Fury* 147) and Dandekar's disbelief when his wife does not provide him with his usual hot meal (*Silence* 60).

[110] In *The Golden Honeycomb* the wily, intellectual Brahmin Dewan is contrasted with the foolish Maharajah, of Kshatriya caste. There is a recurrent emphasis on the contrast between Rabi's love of blood sports (as a member of the warrior Kshatriya caste) and his gentle Brahmin tutor's distaste. 'The squeamish Pandit, his flesh holed by the spears with blood channels, reduced to a quivering silence' at Rabi's account of the 'gratuitously vicious act of pig-sticking' (*Honeycomb* 229). In Markandaya's work, there is also a positing of Hindu spirituality versus Muslim barbarity. In *Two Virgins*, even when sending up Amma's pet hate 'that Muslims actually ate cow's flesh', the emphasis is on Hindu distaste and by implication greater sensitivity. Kamala Markandaya, *Two Virgins* (London: Chatto and Windus, 1974), 23.

relationship between aesthetics and politics, and to reinstate the importance of decolonising narratives, contesting colonialist, neo-colonial, and
dominant Sinhala extremist historiographies. For Sivanandan, literature
must engage with, challenge or contribute to politics, and stem from
an aesthetic that brings to light marginality and oppression. Unlike
Markandaya, he uses all genres for political purposes. She seems to set
up a division between her writing and politics, which stems from views
of literary texts as hermetic and self-referential: Markandaya observes
that the 'didactic novelist is a poor novelist'.[111]

   While Sivanandan's text, written subsequently, shows his response to
Rushdie and postcolonial theory, Markandaya's adherence to Standard
English and dominant forms of the Western novel appears conformist
when juxtaposed with Rushdie's methods of cultural translation and
his use of Angrezi. However, as we have seen, in garnering mainstream
recognition and acclaim for her command of the criteria for the
Western novel, she and others writers of her generation, paved the
way for later writers like Rushdie, as the following review of her novel
*Possession* in 1963 implies.[112] It contrasts Markandaya's mastery of
Standard English with what is patronisingly described as the 'curiously
amateurish' efforts of earlier Indian writers in English such as Anand
and Rao. Significantly, their politicised attempts to 'Indianise' Standard
English are misinterpreted as 'errors' and as their 'writing against the
grain': 'There was the feeling that some part of their minds was still
thinking merrily in Hindi, Urdu or Tamil. All this is now changed.'[113]
Markandaya's and others' expertise in the dominant form and style of
the English novel, enabled later writers to kick against these forms,
paving the way for their contestations to be seen as subversions, rather
than as 'errors' and 'mistakes'.

[111] Cited in Rama Jha, 'Kamala Markandaya: The Woman's World' in Robert L.
Ross (ed.), *International Literature in English: Essays on the Major Writers* (London: St.
James, 1991), 251.
   [112] This point is discussed more fully in Ruvani Ranasinha, 'Constructions of identity
and cultural translation: A generational comparison of South Asian migrant and minority
writers in Britain', D.Phil. University of Oxford (2001). See also Shyamala A. Narayan
and Jon Mee, 'Novelists of the 1950s and 1960s', in Arvind Krishna Mehrotra (ed.), *A
History of Indian Literature in English* (London: Hurst and Co., 2003), 231.
   [113] Robert Payne, 'rev. of *Possession*', *Saturday Review* (25 May 1963), 34.

# 4

# Writing Back, Re-writing Britain: Farrukh Dhondy and Salman Rushdie

In this chapter I compare Indian writer Salman Rushdie (1947– ) and his contemporary, Indian novelist and playwright Farrukh Dhondy (1944– ). Coming from broadly similar formative contexts—both migrated to Britain in their teens during the 1960s—they differ from the British-born generation that came after them in significant ways. They are unlike their successors who have little first-hand knowledge of the country of 'origin', and to differing degrees their stories display their transplanted subjectivities and evoke the country of their childhood. Rushdie's original impulse behind *Midnight's Children* was to recapture memories of growing up in Mumbai: his heightened evocation of Mumbai's linguistic verve, vitality, and metropolitan excitement in several novels suggests that it is the memories of the place of one's childhood that haunt the exile.[1] Unlike earlier generations, these writers grew up in a newly independent India. Both have a greater distance from the colonial era and reconstruct this history differently to their precursors in this book. Rushdie locates himself in the 'generation . . . too young to remember the Empire or the liberation struggle . . . yet a generation that had been sold the ideal of secularism' (*Imaginary* 26). Rushdie's indictment of post-Independence India and Pakistan differs from the decolonising narratives of previous Indian writers in English such as Raja Rao (1909–2006) whose *Kanthapura* (1938) foregrounds the Gandhian struggle for national independence.[2] However, Rushdie's scepticism about nationalism is not directed at the ideal of secular national unity, but at nationalism's totalising and essentialist claims, especially in the

---

[1] Salman Rushdie, *Imaginary Homelands, 1981–1991* (London: Granta, 1991), 10. Hereafter *Imaginary* pagination will appear in the text. In this regard see also Romesh Gunesekera's *Reef* (1994) and Ardashir Vakil's *Beach Boy* (1997).
[2] Rumina Sethi, *Myths of the Nation: National Identity and Literary Representation* (Oxford: Clarendon Press, 1999), 196.

nationalism of the Emergency and, in *The Moor's Last Sigh*, recent Hindu nationalism. *Midnight's Children*'s Saleem Sinai produces a detotalising fragment of his 'memory's truth'.[3] While Rushdie may be too young to remember the liberation struggle, he positions himself as 'the child of a successful revolt against a great power', and his consciousness as 'the product of the triumph of the Indian revolution'.[4] For Dhondy, originally from Poona, 'Growing up in India during the first two or three decades of independence meant being part of the debate on [the] place of the language of the former coloniser . . . which had a literary adjunct, should Indian writers write in English?' alongside a self-distancing from 'India's blinding nationalism'.[5]

With their respective Muslim and Parsi family backgrounds, Rushdie and Dhondy come from Anglicised minority environments within India. What kind of difference does this make to their construction of South Asian identity, and to their relationship to ethnic communities in Britain? Rushdie suggests that even before coming to Britain: 'I've been in a minority group all my life—a member of an Indian Muslim family in Bombay, then of a "mohajir" —migrant—family in Pakistan and now as a British Asian' (*Imaginary* 4). Rushdie's role as an influential commentator and his high-profile interventions in debates on race in the press, particularly in the 1980s, alongside some race-relations work in Camden, led to his coming to be regarded as a representative of ethnic minorities in Britain. The subsequent furore over *The Satanic Verses* in 1989, however, marked sections of the British Muslim population's self-separation from the intellectual constructed as their representative.[6] Dhondy's efforts to broaden ethnic minority representation in Britain can be seen in a similar context. While displacement can make one anti-nationalist, as we saw with Sivanandan, coming from a minority community conditions one's perspectives of the new home, heightening one's investment in positive

---

[3] Salman Rushdie, *Midnight's Children* (London: Picador, 1982), 253. Hereafter *Midnight* pagination will appear in the text.

[4] Salman Rushdie, *The Jaguar Smile: A Nicaraguan Journey* (London: Picador, 1987), 12.

[5] Farrukh Dhondy, 'Speaking in Tongues' in Ferdinand Dennis and Naseem Khan (eds.), *Voices of the Crossing* (London: Serpent's Tale, 2000), 165. Hereafter 'Speaking' pagination will appear in the text. In this context, Dhondy, one of the few Asian writers to admire Naipaul, views *An Area of Darkness* as a book written by 'a brown man, albeit from abroad, trying to see India without nationalistic spectacles, without guilt, almost without ideology' ('Speaking'168).

[6] David Bowen (ed.), *The Satanic Verses: Bradford Responds* (Bradford: Bradford and Ilkley Community College, 1992).

race relations. The younger Sri Lankan writer Romesh Gunesekera (1954– ) who also moved to Britain in 1972 for higher education at the age of 18, comes from a majority Sinhala background: he suggests he does not feel part of any group in Britain; nor is he searching for affiliations.[7]

Enacting the Anglicised aspirations of their parents, both writers came to Britain for their education. Within this broadly speaking Anglicised Indian elite, Rushdie's family was more privileged than Dhondy's, perhaps influencing their differing politics and trajectories. Rushdie arrived in Britain in 1961, at the age of 14. Privately educated at Rugby School, he read History at King's College, Cambridge. He adopted British nationality in 1974 and lived in London until he moved to New York in 2000. The son of an army officer, Dhondy moved from Poona to Mumbai to study chemical engineering. Reading Lawrence Durrell's *Alexandria Quartet* while travelling on the trams, first intimated to Dhondy the political possibilities of fiction: 'If Arabs could be written into the narrative web of what I prematurely thought was a masterpiece, then so could Indians' ('Speaking' 165). Dhondy obtained a British higher education by winning a scholarship to read Physics at Cambridge, where he later read English Literature (1964–7), shortly before the slightly younger Rushdie arrived at King's College. Their paths diverged after leaving Cambridge. Moving away from the elitist environment of Pembroke College, Dhondy wrote a thesis on Kipling at Leicester University (1967–9), which later formed the basis of his play, *Kipling Sahib* (1982), an enquiry into the imperialist mind. He embraced a more overtly activist Left politics than Rushdie, who after Cambridge started out working as a copywriter for an advertising company. Dhondy embraced his move from India finding the 'anonymity and freedom from social bonds in India . . . exhilarating'. At the same time, his migrant position seemed 'a condition of total powerlessness. You didn't exist as a social entity in the fabric of social Britain. You were nobody. Politics is the pursuit of dignity. I signed up' ('Speaking' 169). Dhondy worked with the Indian Workers' Association in Leicester, before joining the Black Panthers, a movement he describes as predominantly African Caribbean 'with a smattering of smart Asians' ('Speaking' 170). He became a member of the Race Today Collective, an activist organisation which produced a key journal for the dissemination of black and Asian culture within Britain, and taught in inner city London secondary schools before becoming a full-time writer in 1982. During this

[7] Romesh Gunesekera, Lecture, University of London, 1 Dec. 1998.

time, he wrote *East End at your Feet* (1976), *Come to Mecca* (1978), *Siege of Babylon* (1978), *Poona Company* (1980), *Trip Trap* (1982). After writing plays and a sitcom for television as a freelance writer, Dhondy became Channel 4's commissioning editor for multicultural programming from 1984 to 1997. He is now an independent producer and columnist for the *Asian Age*, and most recently the author of the novel *Bombay Duck* (1990), *C. L. R. James: A Life* (2002), and *Run* (2002).

In this chapter, I compare these writers' influence, cultural perspectives, and constructions of South Asian identity, within British cultural production and Indian writing in English: cultural strands that this generation, particularly Rushdie bestrides. Rushdie's increasingly keen sense of his multiple audiences can be read as his response to the discursive pressures on the expatriate writer straddling these groupings, particularly his delicate subject position as an Indian Muslim writing about the Indian subcontinent, from Britain.[8] The key question in relation to Rushdie is, what kind of break did his novel *Midnight's Children* produce for both British literary culture and Indian writing in English? Alongside the formally experimental works of his broadly left, anti-Thatcherite contemporaries Ian McEwan, Martin Amis, and Julian Barnes, Rushdie's anarchic, inventive novel gave new impetus to the literary novel. This group challenged the realist novel of the 1950s, 1960s, and early 1970s, in the context of a new market for the literary novel, and the hype generated by the Booker Prize. (That *Midnight's Children* remains widely read over twenty years after it was published, and was awarded the Booker of Bookers—the best of the previous winners—in 1993 underscores Rushdie's continued dominance of contemporary British fiction.) With Rushdie's Booker Prize success and the spate of critical writings that followed in the wake of *Midnight's Children*, postcolonial literature (which began to supersede the term Commonwealth Literature with its liberal humanist bias, partly as a result of the growth of postcolonial theory in the 1980s), particularly Indian writing in English, gained wider currency. While there had been numerous British university and Inner London Education Authority (ILEA) courses on African, Caribbean, and Indian Literature from the 1970s, the success of *Midnight's Children*

    [8] Compare Rushdie's attitude towards his local Indian readers in *Imaginary Homelands* with his later stance in his edited volume of *Indian Writing* (1947–97) where he created a furore with his claim that 'Indian writing in English represents perhaps the most valuable contribution India has yet to make to the world of books'. Salman Rushdie and Elizabeth West (eds.), *The Vintage Book of Indian Writing in English, 1947–1997* (London: Vintage, 1997), p. x.

marks a shift from the study of such texts to broader readerships. Tracing the transformations and changes that the 'postcolonial' introduces, shows how belated full-blown 'postcolonialism' actually was in cultural studies, beginning in the literary sphere with Rushdie in the 1980s. There always was much politics of a polemical variety; but the new sophistication of postcolonial theory arrived with the articles of Rushdie's friend Homi K. Bhabha, whose work complements Rushdie's in the writing scene. The conjunction of Rushdie's influence and the impact of South Asian academics such as Bhabha and Gayatri Chakravorty Spivak in the West, and of academic postcolonialism more generally, marked the rise of South Asian Anglophone writing. Rushdie's influence on the field of postcolonial studies is evinced by the title and ethos of an early postcolonial theoretical text about postcolonial writers in the former British Empire writing back against the literary dominance of their former imperial masters, inspired by his influential phrase 'The Empire Writes Back', itself a play on the title of the first major book that emerged from the Birmingham Centre for Cultural Studies, *The Empire Strikes Back* of 1982.[9] In contrast, Dhondy shaped a different sphere. As a novelist, playwright, and Channel 4's first minority commissioning editor, Dhondy not only pioneered black and Asian cultural representation in the media, but also supported the independent black sector. He was instrumental in setting up production companies such as the well-known Bandung Productions. According to JanMohamed's formulation for the intellectual, both Dhondy and Rushdie, syncretic in intellectual formation, perform a specular function by reflecting and intervening in wider theoretical and political debates.[10]

In different ways both writers also straddle the politics of 'writing back' and 're-writing Britain'. As we have seen, questions of authenticity,

---

[9] Birmingham Centre for Cultural Studies, *The Empire Strikes Back: Race and Racism in 70s Britain* (London: Hutchinson, 1982). The use of the term postcolonial itself dates from Bill Ashcroft, Helen Tiffin, and Gareth Griffiths, *The Empire Writes Back* (London: Methuen, 1989).

[10] Abdul JanMohamed's two typologies syncretic and specular border intellectuals can often be expressed within the same writer so it is preferable to speak of the two positions as a dialectical continuum, rather than (as Mohamed does) polarised and mutually exclusive entities: 'the specular intellectual subjects the cultures to analytic scrutiny rather than combining them.' Abdul JanMohamed, 'Worldliness-Without-World, Homelessness-as-Home: Towards a Definition of the Specular Border Intellectual' in Michael Sprinker (ed.), *Edward Said: A Critical Reader* (Cambridge, Mass.: Blackwell, 1992), 97. This constitutes a major difference from Homi Bhabha's conceptualisation of the migrant's hybridity as an integral part of his or her potential to contest the dominant culture from a borderline position.

exoticism, East–West relations, and colonialism recur in the work of the early, 'minor', migrant writers. By the 1980s and early 1990s—as the work of Dhondy and Rushdie among others reflects—it becomes a question of a multicultural Britain with a greater emphasis on questions of identity, sexuality, interracial romance, and race. These questions have different meanings and resonances in this later context partly because of demographic changes, and consequent anxieties about racial mixing from both majority and minority perspectives. Broadly speaking, for the minority Asian community, generational divides are heightened by the different formative contexts of British-born Asian children, and those of their first-generation migrant parents. Sexuality, particularly female sexuality, features prominently in the work of both writers, as also in that of Hanif Kureishi. Their portrayals contest stereotypes of Asian women as desexualised and passive, and subvert the divisions imposed by both minority and majority communities, whilst highlighting the way that female sexuality is seen as particularly threatening to racial boundaries. Both Rushdie (in *Shame*) and Kureishi (in his essay 'Bradford') focus on some British Muslim fathers' fear of and attempt to control their British-born daughter's sexuality.

Rushdie's fiction in particular forms a transformative bridge between the two broad configurations of 'writing back' and 're-writing Britain', identified above. For as I have argued, in earlier decades, forms of 'authentic' cultural difference were welcomed on prescribed, specific terms as we saw in the way Tambimuttu and Markandaya played to exoticised versions of the East. At the same time, critics' emphasis on the primarily universal content of Markandaya's work, and the effacing of forms of cultural difference from her and other writers' texts, show the extent of pressure on the previous generations of writers to conform to a West-centric universalism that transcended local cultural contexts. In contrast, Rushdie came to the fore in the wake of an intensified demand for Otherness and in part even created this taste through the inventiveness of his work. As Graham Huggan observes, this desire 'is tied up with . . . an exoticist perception of India filtered through the familiar topoi of Raj nostalgia, and a metropolitan desire through this reified "India", to rejuvenate a humdrum domestic culture'.[11] Rushdie bridges the gap between generations partly because his early texts are produced in the context of this renewed interest in India and exoticism,

---

[11] Graham Huggan, *The Post-Colonial Exotic: Marketing the Margins* (London: Routledge, 2001), 74.

and also because he moves from concerns of colonialism and post-Independence subcontinental politics and 'writing back' in *Midnight's Children* (1981), towards re-writing multicultural Britain in *The Satanic Verses* (1989). Although in *Midnight's Children* Rushdie's position as migrant intellectual is suppressed within the text, the migrant's distance is thematised as the unreliability of memory. In *Shame* (1983), he explicitly discusses the issue of migrancy. In a more overt manner than in Sivanandan, *Shame* analyses both countries, Britain and Pakistan, in terms of each other, using analogies from the British present to analyse Pakistani politics of the past.[12] Exploring the relationship between shame and violence, Rushdie forges a connection between second-generation black British youth's anger and alienation at the extent of white racism that erupted in the black urban uprisings in 1981, and Sufiya's 'violence which had been born out of shame' (*Shame* 268). This parallel is made explicit within the novel. The author-narrator describes the 'ghosts' that entered his protagonist Sufiya Zinobia: 'Looking at the smoking cities on my television screen, I see groups of young people running through the streets, the shame burning on their brows and setting fire to shops, police shields and cars. They remind me of my anonymous girl. Humiliate people for long enough and a wildness bursts out of them' (*Shame* 117). *The Satanic Verses* is more obviously a migrant novel, arising from Rushdie's desire 'to give voice and fictional flesh to the immigrant culture', but Rushdie also contests the amnesiac, exclusive constructions of British heritage and identity and draws attention to the marginalisation of black contributions to history. He writes: 'See, here is Mary Seacole, who did as much in the Crimea as another magic-lamping lady, but, being dark, could scarce be seen for the flame of Florence's candle.'[13]

Dhondy's literary career traces the opposite trajectory. He first explored 'multiracial' Britain (as it was then referred to) from the perspective of second-generation black and Asian children in his early fiction, *East End at Your Feet* (1976), *Siege of Babylon* (1977), and *Come to Mecca* (1978), and plays, before depicting a boyhood in urban Poona in a series of loosely linked short stories, *Poona Company* (1980),[14]

---

[12] Salman Rushdie, *Shame* [1983] (London: Vintage, 1995). Hereafter *Shame* pagination will appear in text.

[13] Salman Rushdie, *The Satanic Verses* (London: Viking, 1988), 292. Hereafter *Satanic* pagination will appear in the text.

[14] Farrukh Dhondy, *Poona Company* (London: Gollancz, 1980). While *Poona Company* was not concerned with minorities in Britain it was still received in terms of this

and engaging with questions of migrancy, nationalism, and religious fundamentalism in his novel *Bombay Duck* (1990), shortlisted for the Whitbread first novel award. This lively, ambitious, and experimental book moves between London, Delhi, and Bombay, and forms a contrast to his earlier realist narratives. *Bombay Duck* shares Rushdie's self-reflexivity about the status of the migrant writer to a much greater degree than the examples from previous generations, as well as Rushdie's and Kureishi's preoccupation with syncretism, eclecticism, and the politics of representation. Dhondy's early stories and plays, notably *Mama Dragon* (1980), form a transformative bridge between writing back and re-writing Britain by mapping out themes of generational conflict, class tensions within Asian communities, alongside the topical, vexed debates on the appropriate response to racism, and the role of violence in the anti-racist struggles, that Kureishi began to explore in his early plays such as *Borderline* (1981) from the perspective of a second-generation 'Anglo-Asian' writer.

## FARRUKH DHONDY: PIONEER OF CONTEMPORARY BLACK AND ASIAN CULTURE IN BRITAIN

Like Sivanandan, Dhondy began his career in Britain as an activist at the forefront of the political and cultural alliances between African-Caribbean and Asian groups during the 1970s and 1980s. Though far less well known as a writer, he was in fact the first to broach many of the issues and themes that became identified with the work of Rushdie and later writers such as Hanif Kureishi. Dhondy was the first writer to fictionalise British Asians in London's East End, and to write about their relations to African-Caribbean and white communities. In his different roles as writer and producer, he contributed to several collaborative projects that supported this association. With Mustapha Matura of the Black Theatre Co-operative (1979), Dhondy wrote

agenda. As Dervla Murphy's review suggests: '*Poona Company* serves to aid integration in another way . . . a writer of Dhondy's quality can do . . . much to increase not only an inter-racial understanding, but also an understanding by British-born Indians of their own civilisation. The second-generation cannot be expected to integrate successfully if he is only vaguely aware of his own traditions.' Dervla Murphy, 'In the Chowk Tea-house', *Times Literary Supplement* (21 Nov. 1980), 1322.

the first black British TV sitcom *No Problem!* (1983–4) about the adolescent Powells, whose parents have returned to Jamaica, leaving their offspring to fend for themselves in Willesden Green. He produced the Channel 4 TV programme *Bandung File* that sought to embody the connection between African-Caribbean and Asian people across the world. Dhondy's writings straddle African Caribbean, Asian, and British cultures to a greater extent than either Rushdie's or Kureishi's. Tracing his literary career from the late 1970s, we can see that he often presents African-Caribbean protagonists in his early short stories, and in the first plays he wrote for the Black Theatre Co-operative such as *Mama Dragon* (1980) (about a disaffected African-Caribbean soldier returning from Northern Ireland, which drew on 'black' British culture with a reggae commentary), and in *Shapesters* (1982) (an ironic look at *Othello* through the eyes of black teenagers), before moving towards an increasing engagement with British Asian culture. He began to concentrate on portraying British Asians when he wrote the first British Asian TV plays in 1983, followed by the first British Asian soap opera *Tandoori Nights* (1985), about two rival Indian restaurants, and the controversial *King of the Ghetto* (1986), a cynical drama series about East London Bangladeshis exploited by their own community. The shift in Dhondy's focus both mirrors and contributes to the destabilising of dominant notions of blackness and common black identity, and the emergence of cultural representations of British Asian (sometimes referred to as Anglo-Indian in reviews) identity during this period.

Dhondy's first short stories for adolescents sprang out of a specific context of race politics and education in the late 1970s: the debates that appeared in the *New Statesman* between the Children's Rights Workshop and the Society of Authors on racist portrayals in children's books is one example. The publisher Collins created a prize 'for reflecting the variety and complexity of living in multi-ethnic Britain' which Dhondy went on to win. After reading his story about a tough multiracial school in London in the Black Panther Movement's paper *Freedom News*, Macmillan's editor Martin Pick sought out Dhondy and commissioned his first collection of short stories *East End at Your Feet* (1976). As Dhondy comments, 'Britain was ready for "multicultural" writing before it existed.' As a result, as he observes in retrospect, his early fiction carried a rationale of an 'unbearably ponderous' burden of representation: 'If young black and brown people could see themselves in stories it would build confidence in their identity' ('Speaking' 171). At the time Dhondy commented that he was 'not interested in making up stories about rabbits'; instead he was concerned with 'people struggling in Great Britain today', alluding to the more fanciful children's stories by writers like Quentin Blake. *The Times* dismissed Dhondy's comment as 'tireless patronising didacticism' symptomatic of the 'joyless orthodoxy of our new children's book therapists'.[15] In contrast reviewer Dervla Murphy commended Dhondy's talent and fictional insights.

One such story 'Salt on Snake's Tail' (from the award-winning collection *Come to Mecca*, 1978) explores, from the perspective of young Jolil, the different ways his Bangladeshi Muslim tailoring family in Brick Lane have adapted to life in Britain in the context of escalating racist violence in the East End. At first the story sets up an opposition between Jolil's father and his two sons. The former 'swallowed insults' and avoided the problem by delivering homilies to the family on the 'truths of life'.[16] Like Monica Ali's Chanu in *Brick Lane*, 'The more trouble there was the more philosophical he became.' Jolil's older brother Khalil adopts a more defiant, combative response to racism; 'this is jehad, a holy war. If we want to stay in this country we have to fight' (*Come* 90). One evening, ashamed of his father's retreat from racist taunts, Jolil seeks to learn Bruce Lee inspired self-defence strategies. Dhondy uses the dilemmas of individual black or Asian children to explore the challenges they face in urban Britain. For Jolil's father their English neighbours are 'creatures with whom one had to share the planet', 'rubbish people' who 'signified nothing' (*Come* 95). This self-protective rejection is not possible for Jolil who has mixed with white children for six years at school and 'knew every twist of the language they spoke . . . their reason and unreason' (*Come* 94–5). The story ends with a reversal of expectations: the suggestion that Jolil's father was involved in a reported attack on their tormentors.

With acutely observed insights, Dhondy explores the way immigrant experience is inflected by class, generation, and gender. In his short stories his sympathies lie broadly with the younger generation, and their open or clandestine rejection of the first generation's conservatism, resistance to change, policing of their daughters, and racism towards black people. Jolil's father admonishes his son for his friendship with an African-Caribbean schoolmate: 'it's time you stopped running around with the darkies. You should be down in the basement learning to

---

[15] Brian Alderson, 'Children's Fiction', *The Times* (7 Jan. 1981), 7.
[16] Dhondy, *Come to Mecca* (London: Macmillan, 1978), 90. Hereafter *Come* pagination will appear in the text.

read Arabic' (*Come* 85–6). Dhondy's trenchant, vivid, terse, penetrative writing historicises an era of doubt and anxiety about the future of multicultural Britain, and appears in marked contrast to the feel-good optimism and sunny multiculturalism of more recent productions such as the film *Bend it like Beckham* (2002). However, although sardonic and sharply insightful, these early stories broadly served to contest negative stereotypes of ethnic minorities circulating in the media. They underscore the working-class Asians' lack of access to dominant modes of representation, as in 'Iqbal Café'. Similarly, *Siege of Babylon* (1978), loosely based on the London Spaghetti House siege, concentrates on the media's distortion of the event. It was this burden of representation that Kureishi kicked against, and which Dhondy himself—given his own predilection for irreverence, and opposition to the idea that art 'should be dedicated to the propagandist objectives of good race relations'—soon himself came to reject.[17] Dhondy explains the marked shift in tone between his early short stories, and his later more critical, caustic, and provocative representations:

Finding a voice is inseparable from finding an audience. And yet once I had found a particular audience through four or five books whose stories came from the new ghettos, the frightened communities, I wanted to put a distance between the sympathy of this audience and myself. The sympathy has turned sour, become perverse. It was making its own demands and there were other writers expanding into the vacuum with autobiographical hard luck stories. Winning sympathy for oneself through writing defeats the ironical object of writing, it's braver and riskier to sympathise with the nasty and turn away from the easy target. ('Speaking' 172–3)

In 1981 Dhondy formed the Asian Theatre Company with H. O. Nazareth and Harmaje Kalirai. In 1983 five of Dhondy's plays were shown on BBC 1, including *The Bride* and *Romance, Romance*. Of these two, *The Bride* is the less successful, with its condensed dialogue, and reliance on clichéd representations of white, working-class masculinity and Asian patriarchy. The play is narrated in a flashback by a white skinhead from Southall who falls in love with his Sikh schoolmate Jasminder who kills herself alongside her Muslim lover, rather than marry the man chosen for her by her father. Its contemporary reception suggests the play served to reinforce preconceptions of 'India's shockingly inhumane marriage customs'.[18] It was this kind of creative engagement

---

[17] Farrukh Dhondy, Comment, *The Times* (21 June 1995), online edition.
[18] Michael Church, 'Nein Danke', *The Times* (12 Nov. 1983), 6.

with this trope and its reception that Kureishi responded to and complicated in his subplot in *The Buddha of Suburbia*.

Dhondy's deft comedy *Romance, Romance* won the Samuel Beckett Award for Best First TV Play screened in 1983. The play featured many of the actors, such as Rita Wolf and Derrick Branche, who Kureishi is usually credited with bringing to the fore in his screenplay *My Beautiful Laundrette* in 1985. Set in a close-knit Asian community in Birmingham, *Romance, Romance* revolves around feisty Satinder (played by Rita Wolf) and her affectionate yet combative relationship with her prosperous father Chadda (played by Saeed Jaffrey) who at times regrets 'treating her like an equal'.[19] Jaffrey's and Wolf's performances lend a great deal to their characters and one can see the resonances of these roles when they subsequently play father and daughter in Kureishi's *Laundrette*. *Romance, Romance* concludes with a tentative 'exploratory reconciliation' between father and daughter in sharp contrast to the bitterness of Tania's and Nasser's relationship in *Laundrette*. Satinder eludes her parents' unsubtle attempts to fix her up with the eligible entrepreneur Bunny Singh of the Anglo-Asian Conservative Association, preferring instead to pursue a career as a dramatist. Singh's patriarchal pomposity is well captured when he assures Chadda that he is 'not put off by [the] rebellious fibre' of Satinder's nature, and claims that to 'tame a wild stallion . . . makes the best mount' (*Romance* 19). In the conversations of this Thatcherite, Anglicised Asian middle class, we see the same classed self-separation of the postcolonial elite from the working-class and peasant populations who 'give us such a bad name' that Kureishi explores in his *Birds of Passage* (1983), *Laundrette* (1985), and *Sammy and Rosie Get Laid* (1987) (*Romance* 16). To a greater extent than in Dhondy's short stories, both generations are sent up in this play with warmth and subtle humour. Chadda shares the cultural confusion of his Anglicised daughter, trying to instil in her a respect for 'ancient' Eastern traditions whilst he himself chases Western values and social status. Chadda mocks his daughter's espousal of 'feministic' trends and her plays preaching to converted 'multi-cultural wallahs' about 'Punjabi peasants although she has never been to India' (*Romance* 14). Debates over the politics of representation are more fully explored in Dhondy's subsequent play, *Vigilantes*, performed in 1985 by his Asian Theatre

---

[19] Farrukh Dhondy, *Romance, Romance and The Bride* (London: Faber and Faber, 1985). Hereafter *Romance* pagination will appear in the text.

Company, and firmly rooted in its immediate socio-political context. A group of young Asian actors quarrel about their subject. Some want to do a play about the war of Bangladesh and the Mukti Bahini guerrillas, to encourage young Asians to find out more about their 'history and culture'. For others like Gita, there's 'no harm in a bit of history, but now we've arrived here'. The play thematises the agenda of the white-dominated media: 'what they really want to do is a film about you the new British'. Others protest they 'Make us out to be victims . . . it's like we're not seen until whites put us under a microscope'. Hasna claims the 'educated British only want to know blacks who are crying out about the injustices of the whites'.[20]

Significantly the arguments over representation are not confined to the depiction of British Asian communities, as in Kureishi's work, but extend to the manner in which the subcontinental country of origin is portrayed. The group condemn Hasna's involvement in a documentary on Bangladesh concerning the scandal of adulterated powdered milk given to young children causing the death of fifty children. Gita calls the documentary 'political pornography' insisting it serves to reinforce conceptions that 'These people can't look after themselves'. (This argument may allude to an actual incident when Pakistani groups were enraged at Channel 4's documentary critical of the Pakistani military regime, entitled *The Blood of Hussein*.) Yet Hasna's opposing view is made even more forcefully:

GITA: But your film . . . it just confirms stereotypes.
HASNA: There's no such things as stereotypes.
GITA: What do you mean? People are seen as . . .
HASNA: Seen, seen, seen. You . . . all of you, you're just bothered about how we're seen, instead of being bothered about how we are. 'Stereotypes'—everybody talks about stereotypes as though we only exist when a camera is focused on us. . . . Put a frame around it and it becomes true. (*Vigilantes* 50)

Hasna argues that any resistance to this kind of documentary stems from a generational divide: 'Everyone who comes from India or Pakistan or Bangladesh knows what it is like. It is just our generation . . . who don't like Asians telling the truth.' Gita disagrees: 'Every time a politician makes a speech, some racist junk, we get the fallout' (*Vigilantes* 48–9). This kind of dialogue prefigures the similar debates between Tracey and

[20] Farrukh Dhondy, *Vigilantes* (London: Hobo, 1988). Hereafter *Vigilantes* pagination will appear in the text.

Karim in Kureishi's *The Buddha of Suburbia* (1990). Dhondy engages with the politics of race and representation by dramatising the minority actor-protagonist's interaction with the arts scene of the mid 1980s. In doing so, he also foreshadows Saladin Chamcha's encounters with the theatrical and advertising world in Rushdie's *The Satanic Verses* (1989).

In Dhondy's novel *Bombay Duck* (1990), minority penetration of mainstream theatre is viewed mercilessly through the ironic perspective of the voluble narrator of the first part of the novel: an actor of African-Caribbean origin, Gerald Blossom who adopts a Muslim moniker Ali Abdul Rahman. Ali plays Lord Rama in David Stream's enactment of the epic *Ramayana*. Here Dhondy parodies Peter Brook's production of *The Mahabharata*. (Kureishi recalls Peter Brook's disappointment with British Asians like himself who were not exotic enough and the lack of knowledge of Hindu culture. This is satirised in Karim's encounter with theatre in Kureishi's *The Buddha of Suburbia*.) David Stream, a 'twentieth-century trans-oceanic cultural trader', aims to dramatise 'the trans-cultural, the human beneath the skin, the conflagration of nationalities' by cross-casting the various ethnicities of his international cast of the *Ramayana*.[21] As we will see with Kureishi, the narrator takes the opportunity to make caustic swipes at all shades of political opinion and cultures. No political standpoint is privileged; all are undermined. For the cosmopolitan lead actress Anjali who plays Sita, Stream's version is 'what Indians really believe, the sort of belief they give their lives for, fanatically, and through David it becomes mainstream, a direction in European theatre'. Stream's version is simultaneously revealed as transcultural hype and a 'cynical parading of people . . . an extension of tourism . . . some trendy white director thinks he can capture Indian culture?' (*Bombay* 80), or is he just another white director 'so fucking keen to tell you they know how black people feel'? (*Bombay* 30).

Dhondy ironises white liberal condescension in his portrayal of Sara Fraser Stuart, a white journalist and 'chronicler' of the show whose diary entries intercut Ali's narrative, and for whom race relations in Britain is 'reading the newspaper reviews that sympathise with shit plays because they've got some blacks doing them or some Asian writing or dancing' (*Bombay* 94). Without simplifying questions of unequal access to media representation (a theme he explores in 'Iqbal Cafe'), Dhondy

[21] Farrukh Dhondy, *Bombay Duck* (London: Cape, 1990), 64. Herafter *Bombay* pagination will appear in the text.

consistently subscribes to the critical position that one creative text is 'demonstrably better than another and that the demonstration consists of a critical dialogue with the text in hand' ('Speaking' 168). This is an integral part of Dhondy's argument that 'too much substandard work by black writers appears on our screens which has been put there only to assuage the guilt of liberal commissioning editors'.[22] He represents sexual desire as the interest that really animates Sara's (and most of the other characters') motives and 'ideologies': 'Sara . . . despite a certain air of upper-middle-class cynicism which comes from being in the papers and all, was really soft on multiculturalism and next to blacks bedding down with whites like herself she was in favour of them bedding down with Asians' (*Bombay* 78). Similarly, the white liberal media interprets a fight between African-American George and black British Tawanda as 'fight over divergent ideologies', when it was in fact a fight over Sara.

In the same vein we learn how white liberals build up playwright Jam Jamal and 'encourage him to write shit about Indians and Asians'. Maureen, Ali's former partner and mother of his daughter, preferred Ali when he was a struggling actor doing 'bum plays in bum theatres' and 'didn't like blacks being organised and famous' (*Bombay* 15). Duped by a Pakistani gunrunner, Maureen accuses Ali of being 'bought off by British imperialism', and the police of 'racism' rather than confront her boyfriend's actions. In a zany twist Ali finds his association with Maureen makes him a suspected arms dealer and this threatens to put the show in jeopardy.

Through Ali's commentary we also witness the divisions between Asian and black communities. Ali's African-Caribbean friends 'don't care shit about Indian culture, and some of them rude racist too' (*Bombay* 56). Asian racism particularly towards black men is satirised when Ali's African-Caribbean friend Scobee signs up to a dating agency for Asian women: 'Saree-clad angel slam door in his face. Guess who's coming to dinner? Ooo Scobie boy, she thought he was the minicab man' (*Bombay* 115). The text alludes to the ethnicised rivalry for minority arts funding when Ali is criticised by fellow Caribbean actors for his involvement in the *Ramayana* production in the context of 'the refusal epidemic' to fund Caribbean cultural plays because of the rise of the 'Hasian cultural ting' (*Bombay* 57). All notions of authenticity are exposed as myths: 'Caribbean cultural plays. What the fuck is that? Cricket, Calypso, Reggae, slavery, KFC? Give us a break' (*Bombay* 57).

---

[22] Dhondy, Comment, *The Times* (21 June 1995).

Through Dhondy's African-Caribbean narrator, the text enacts a self-reflexive, defamiliarising perspective on British Asians: comically highlighting ways in which during this period British Asian cultural identity was overshadowed by 'cooler' black African-Caribbean British culture, and hinting provocatively at its derivative nature that was partly a result of repressive formative conditions:

I always thought Asian guys were soft. Sharp at some things but soft when it came to chatting up or impressing a woman or anything. No style. Nice guys, but wear anything, nylon shirts and flares. Then just as I was finishing drama school they started to get smart. Two gangs. One copied the white kids and one copied the black kids.

See, them Asian guys had to construct themselves from scratch. Zilch. Zero. No reggae, skank, no black power, just plenty rules—eat this, eat that, can't go here, can't marry this, can't fuck that—tradition and some get push into heavy education. (*Bombay* 51)

Equally, Ali's commentary satirises Indian classed acculturation when he visits Anjali's Anglicised middle-class circle in Delhi 'dressed in sarees and suits. They pass the nuts around. It could be Hampstead' (*Bombay* 129).

Rather than solely focusing on black Britain, like *The Satanic Verses* (and unlike the British-born generation's texts), *Bombay Duck* explores the themes of migrancy, zealotry, as well as sexuality that connect Delhi and London. While David Stream's interpretation of the Hindu epic and its casting, and staging is enthusiastically received in London, when the production moves to Delhi, its audience in India have a different history and response. There are objections to the play's interpretation, casting, and to its liberal mode of hybrid plagiarism:

What kind of genius has mixed up verses from the Koran and the Guru Granth Sahib with the holiest of Hindu holy books? Is it mischief and total disregard or deliberate insult? Those who want to break up our country are given their religious plantation right inside the heart of our holy of holy legends and stories on which every patriotic family brings up its newborn generations. (*Bombay* 148)

Members of the Hindu right see the interpretation as an 'affront and civilisational insult' to Hinduism, particularly furious that a black 'Muslim' 'has dared to play Ram. The hussy has dared to portray Sita' (*Bombay* 148). In the ensuing riot Anjali is murdered and Ali attacked and the play abandoned: Ali grimly observes 'All the world's no fucking stage' (*Bombay* 149). Written in the aftermath of the *fatwa* on Rushdie, *Bombay Duck* needs to be seen in dialogue with this context. Although the play ends in violent tragedy, as Dhondy later made clear, his serio-comic 'novel was never intended as a warning. It was an attempt to examine the cross-cultural incest of ideas and traditions that sometimes in our liberal globalised culture turns into its opposite.'[23]

The second part of the novel is the interrelated story of narrator Xerses, a Parsi historian who smuggles Indian children into Britain. A master of cross-cultural transference on many levels, he translates for the BBC. In contrast to the emphasis on empowering notions of translation explored in Rushdie's writings, for Xerses 'Translating is pimping for the inter-cultural voyeur' (*Bombay* 159). *Bombay Duck* foregrounds the various forms of translation (self-reinvention, translation between the different codes in the novel) as open to misconstruction and inevitable ambivalence. Xerses performs a series of odd jobs before becoming a supply teacher. This account of the aspiring author and teacher draws on some of Dhondy's own experiences of that world. Like Dhondy, a publisher spots Xerxes' writing when it appears in an amateur newspaper. The conversation between publisher Mr De Freitas and Xerxes satirises the habit of some mainstream publishers' to try to set the agenda, and encourage minority authors to confine their work to what the majority white readerships can relate to. Here the real source of the publisher's interest is the familiar British character and settings, rather than the 'inaccessible' Parsi customs:

Mr de Freitas: 'Shouldn't the stories be about your experience in Britain or a cross between the two settings?'
   Xerxes: 'Why should they?'
   'I never tell writers what to write, but it really depends on what kind of readership your imagination demands and commands?'
   'Sure.'
   'There are touches of the West in your story—the Associated Board of the Royal Schools of Music, the British examiner, but then you lose that thread and take up another with the honeymoon and the lover and very sort of unexplained, well inaccessible customs and mentalities of Parsees. I love the ending, though, the Oxford Street and Marks or wherever it is.'
   '. . . But the point of the story was the relationship and the song he writes.'
   'That works marvellously, but I just wanted to know a bit more about the English examiner.' (*Bombay* 205)

As well as showing the way publishing houses attempt to influence marg-inal voices, this dialogue in fact also works as a self-reflexive comment

---

[23] Dhondy, 'Different Strokes', 13 Mar. 2004, www.mid-day.com, online edition.

on Dhondy's text where Xerses' digressions on Zoroastrian culture, in his quest to explore his heritage, do appear rather unassimilated and extraneous to the narrative. Though Dhondy's novel is less successful as a novel, it nevertheless shows him at his best in providing the most searching and far-reaching analysis of the politics of black and Asian participation in British culture of the 1980s. At the other end of the spectrum from an assimilationist writer such as Chaudhuri, Dhondy was the first writer and TV/film-maker to stage representations of contemporary black and Asian urban culture in Britain, the pioneer of a field that later writers such as Rushdie, Kureishi, and Meera Syal would make their own. It was Dhondy and then Kureishi who first delineated the diversity of the British Asian community in his plays in the early 1980s. While Rushdie offers satirical representations of the minority communities themselves, especially the British Asian bourgeoisie that exploits the underclass (in *The Satanic Verses,* the lack of 'public housing' enables Hind to *'make fortunes of the misery of your own race'* (*Satanic* 264, 290, emphasis in original), it was Dhondy who first showed the possibilities of moving from the politics of the positive image to the development of a specular, self-reflexive critique of British black and Asian culture which took it out of the area of the 'minority report' and allowed it to develop its own inherent cultural dynamics.

## SALMAN RUSHDIE: HOW DOES NEWNESS ENTER THE WORLD?

If Dhondy's early work grew out of, and was perhaps constrained by, black British politics and the need for representations of blacks and Asians in Britain, as I have suggested earlier, Salman Rushdie came to the fore during a resurgence of interest in British India. Over the decade prior to the publication of *Midnight's Children*, three Booker prizes were awarded to novels about India, all written by Europeans. South Asian Anglophone writers were textually anticipated in two ways. They wrote for audiences in Britain and North America already 'informed' by a Eurocentric orientalist discourse assimilated by writers such as Chaudhuri and Markandaya. In this context, Rushdie was not alone in seeking to break with a series of traditional, monolithic tropes about the Indian subcontinent, and present a newer and fresher picture.

Pakistani writer Bapsi Sidwha's *The Crow Eaters* (self-published in Lahore in 1978, by Orient Longman in India in 1979, and subsequently by Jonathan Cape in 1980) was widely praised in Britain, the US, and India particularly for its irreverence and its uninhibited bawdy humour. The impact of this boisterous, darkly comic tale of the rise of the Parsi Junglewalla family in pre-partition Lahore (1900–47) signals an important shift in mainstream reception of South Asian Anglophone texts, as Judy Cooke's review in the *New Statesman* suggests, '*The Crow Eaters* is an excellent novel, a book about India which one can whole-heartedly enjoy, rather than respectfully admire.'[24] Gita Mehta's satirical essays *Karma Cola: Marketing the Mystic East* (1980), also published by Cape, provides a further example. Nevertheless, although their works pre-dated *Midnight's Children*, Mehta and Sidwa gained wider attention, retrospectively, in the aftermath of *Midnight's Children*, which appeared to usher in a new wave of South Asian writing in English.

A reader's report in the Jonathan Cape Archive on Rushdie's unpublished manuscript *Madame Rama* (a political novel about India, which Rushdie subsequently 'plundered' for *Midnight's Children*) identifies a particular interest in literary explorations of India hitherto unexplored by colonial perspectives that predates the publication of *Midnight's Children*. Although reader Judy Cooke (also the reviewer of *The Crow Eaters*) concluded that *Madame Rama* should not be published, she comments that it is a 'pity, because, India seems to be a good ground for novelists these days and when I began the book I was interested and hoped I'd learn about the areas of the continent which Forster *et al* hadn't got down in print'.[25] Subsequently, Rushdie's own description of *Midnight's* achievement echoes this idea. This kind of comment may have influenced his own concern to explore aspects of India (rather than British India) either ignored or distorted by European perspectives and a colonial sensibility. On winning the Booker Prize in 1981, Rushdie expressed his unease over the problematic aspects of the recent appeal of novels on India. He commented that he hoped 'it's not entirely

---

[24] Judy Cooke, 'Review of *The Crow Eaters*', *New Statesman* (19 Sept. 1980), 23. Sidhwa suggests that her descriptions of 'the parents in *The Crow Eaters* influenced Rushdie's presentation of the parents in *Midnight's Children*, its bawdy humour perhaps, providing a sort of subliminal permission to express his own brand of humour. We shared the same editor [Liz Calder] at Cape, and I know Rushdie had read the manuscript. It was also the first major novel about Parsis. After *The Crow Eaters*, other authors like Rushdie and Chandra were able to introduce Parsi characters more naturally; and it influenced not only a new crop of Parsi writers, but many Indian and Pakistani writers.' Sidhwa, interview with Julie Rajan, *Monsoon* magazine, online edition.

[25] Judy Cooke, Reader's Report on *Madame Rama*, undated, Jonathan Cape Archive, Reading University Archives, Reading.

because it's a novel about India that it has won the prize. After all novels not about India have won. I like to think of it as Indo-Anglian not Anglo-Indian, and not writing from the colonial point of view.'[26] Elsewhere Rushdie expands on the limitations of writers like Forster: 'The Indian subcontinent is more extreme in more ways than anywhere else. But the English fiction set in India—Kipling, Forster, Jhabvala or Paul Scott—has only been about what happened to the West when it went East; either delicate or exotic. The language, contents and tone have never reflected how Indians experience India.'[27]

Rushdie suggests that he wrote *Midnight* partly because he felt that 'not much of really high quality had been written in English about India. I'm not a great admirer, for instance, of Paul Scott. It was almost virgin territory.' He observes that in Forster's *A Passage to India*: 'The Indian characters are condescendingly treated. The way they speak is wrong. You won't find many Indians who like it.'[28]

Rushdie was not alone in his commitment to the explicit revision and deconstruction of the orientalist's India, as he implies. His statements above tend to exclude his Indo-Anglian predecessors such as Raja Rao, R. K. Narayan, and Mulk Raj Anand, and other creative genres. Although poets occupy a very different position in this literary landscape, earlier Indo-Anglian poets Nissim Ezekiel and Adil Jussawalla shared his endeavour, and like Rushdie had moved away from exclusively English poetic precursors, drawing on writers such as Albert Camus, Pablo Neruda, and Günter Grass. This raises the question of whether any literature can be truly inaugural. To what extent did *Midnight's Children* create a rupture with the past? Its appearance during a fallow period in Indian writing in English heightened its impact: the older Indian Anglophone writers like Mulk Raj Anand had by this time written their best work and were now spent forces. Timing and contextual factors aside, Rushdie's re-writing of history, integration of acute historical insight and fabulist narratives, inter-related to his Joycean attempt to abrogate Standard English, produced linguistic, formal, and aesthetic innovations that shaped the new literature of the metropolitan centre, and helped to internationalise the parochial British novel, thus opening up mainstream readerships for younger South Asian Anglophone writers.

---

[26] Rushdie, *The Booker Prize*, BBC 2, 20 Oct. 1981.

[27] Cited in Ho Nazareth, 'Handcuffed to History', *Time Out* (May 8–14 1981), 20.

[28] Anne Chisholm, 'Changing the Anglo-Indian Literary Landscape', *National Times* (4 Oct. 1981), 13. N. Chaudhuri comments on Forster's 'insultingly condescending delineations of Indians' in *Circe*, 101.

Rushdie's contestation of a normative concept of 'correct' or Standard English constitutes his most immediately striking intervention. His revisionary impulse to inscribe difference into Standard English and formalise the cross-cultural character of the linguistic medium contrasts with many first-generation migrant writers' motivated assimilation into a mono-cultural literary tradition. Rushdie makes self-conscious efforts to signify the use of Indian English colloquialisms and transpose Urdu linguistic patterns, rhythms, and intonations.[29] He presents his abrogation of Standard English as a form of reverse colonisation. He suggests: 'people who were given the English language are now in the process of taking over the language of the erstwhile rulers.'[30] Penetrating cloistered publishing houses in the West, he is largely responsible for making Indian English a literary style.[31] Many Anglophone and bilingual writers of South Asian origin describe Rushdie's subversion of English as inspirational: Rukhsana Ahmad observes: 'For a very long time I had believed that it would not be possible for me to write a novel because I could never capture my characters in English. I might not have attempted a novel in English had I not read Salman Rushdie's *Midnight's Children*. Rushdie had managed to subvert English for his own purpose.'[32] His ear for spoken dialects and language blazed a trail for a range of writers including Zadie Smith and Monica Ali.

Of course Rushdie's hybridised non-Standard English remoulded to bear other cultures and tongues has many predecessors, such as the work of Chinua Achebe. As we have seen, Mulk Raj Anand and Raja Rao had already begun to rework English idioms in an Indian mode. The Caribbean Creole of the Trinidadian Sam Selvon (1924–94) marked a similar endeavour. Rushdie's acknowledged debt to migrant writer G. V. Desani's (1909–2000) subversion of Standard English suggests the ways in which earlier anti-colonialist writers had made his oppositional rhetoric possible, and point to the generational dynamics

[29] Indian languages inflect his Angrezi in less obvious ways. The impetus behind his literalisation of standard metaphors, or indistinguishability of the metaphorical and the literal, may be the highly figurative content of Indian languages.

[30] Rushdie, *The Booker Prize*.

[31] While Indian English has become more marketable, this is not necessarily the case for African-Caribbean patois. Diran Abedayo's editor advised him to reduce the patois in the first half of his second novel so as not to put off potential readers. Diran Abedayo, interview, *Newsnight*, BBC 2, 2 Dec. 1999.

[32] Rukhsana Ahmad, 'In Search of a Talisman', in Ferdinand Dennis and Naseem Khan (eds.), *Voices of the Crossing* (London: Serpents Tale, 2000), 113.

in the reception of migrant writers.[33] Desani's 'rigmarole English' did not have the same subversive impact as Rushdie's Angrezi. Although enthusiastically received by T. S. Eliot, E. M. Forster, and later Anthony Burgess,[34] a dismissive review of Desani's *All About H. Hatterr*, when first published in 1948, indicates other responses to the subversion of Standard English in the socio-political climate in which Desani wrote, only a year after Indian Independence. In 1948 the *Times Literary Supplement* suggested that Desani's novel is 'strictly speaking' not in the 'realm of fiction'. It describes Desani's 'largely colloquial style' as one which 'allows him to take all kinds of liberties with common English usage, and a fresh if somewhat blustering approach to everything that comes within his scope'. At best, Desani's writing 'never loses a certain jejune verve'. The novel is summed up as 'a morass of verbiage'.[35]

As in Desani and Joyce before him, the coexistence of Standard English and non-Standard varieties of spoken Englishes in Rushdie marks a postcolonial syncretism that defies earlier demands that writing must be in 'unadulterated' Standard English. Emphasis on this coexistence should not overlook the hierarchy of Englishes, particularly in *Midnight's Children*. In this text, the standard form is usually the preserve of the first-person narrator. The most pronounced use of stigmatised non-Standard forms of Indian English are spoken by 'low brow' characters in the social hierarchy, Padma, Mary, and Alice Pereira: 'What type of answer is blue, Father, how to believe such a thing?' (*Midnight* 104), and 'What are you talking?' (*Midnight* 194, 203). In contrast, *Shame* incorporates the syntactic characteristics of Indian English into both the narrator's speech and the dialogue, partly to convey the sense of a spoken narrative: the narrator's 'longlong ago' and 'thenagain' (*Shame* 13). Non-Standard varieties are not only used by the 'servants' but incorporated into Omar Khayyam-Shakil's speech: ' "God knows what you'll change with all this shifting shifting" ' (*Shame* 71) and Bilquis ' "Stop, darling, what a dirtyfilthy mind!" ' (*Shame* 73). However, the 'incorrect' use of the second language provides humour for the enjoyment of the English-educated subcontinental or Western reader. (In striking

[33] Salman Rushdie and Elizabeth West (eds.), *The Vintage Book of Indian Writing in English*, p. xviii.

[34] Burgess' introduction to the 1970 reprint of Desani's text calls for a re-evaluation of Desani's 'gloriously impure English'. G. V. Desani, *All About H. Hatterr* (London: Bodley Head, 1970), 10–11.

[35] Neville Braybrook, 'rev. of *All About H. Hatterr*', *Times Literary Supplement* (15 May 1948), 273.

contrast, the pidgin English spoken by the Asian immigrants recreated in Dhondy's early short stories serves to underscore these characters' disempowerment rather than generate humour: for instance, Langda in 'Iqbal Cafe': 'it is good to talk with intelligence people' (*Come* 49.) Such uses of the parodic forms of 'Other' Englishes embedded within a context of Rushdie's own evident mastery of Standard English compromises the extent to which the hegemony of Standard English is destabilised. There is, however, a distinction between Rushdie's representation of the way people speak and the more potentially subversive inter-lingual punning in language that is not representational: for example, his use of insaan/insanity/human to signify that to be insane is to be human.[36] A comparable linguistic shift is evident regarding the question of untranslated words and the privileging of the subcontinental, indigenous reader, and the challenges this implies for the subversion of centre–periphery relations.[37] Rushdie's efforts to address subcontinental readers differ from Markandaya's and others writers' attempts to solicit an implied Western reader, where the degree of explanation of culturally specific items and practices posits an implied reader who has minimal knowledge of the region.

While the linguistic content was an integral part of *Midnight's* impact, Rushdie's anti-realist, non-linear narrative appeared particularly path breaking. Although writers such as Wole Soyinka, Wilson Harris, and R. K. Narayan[38] had previously published work with a non-realist dimension, and of course the work of Rushdie's major source in this regard, the novels of Gabriel Garcia Marquez, was already well known, Rushdie recalls his fears that *Midnight's Children* would not be published because his magic realist, digressive, disruptive narrative was not still 'acceptable in style or form'.[39] In retrospect this is ironic given that its seminal impact has spawned a school of writers of this style. However, at the time of publication, although hailed as a masterpiece in the US, his novel was received in Britain as 'different and therefore difficult'. As

---

[36] Salman Rushdie, *The Moor's Last Sigh* (London: Vintage, 1996), 350. Hereafter *Moor* pagination will appear in the text.

[37] See, however, Harish Trivedi's questioning of the alleged subversiveness of Rushdie's language. Harish Trivedi, 'Salman the Funtoosh: Magic Bilingualism in *Midnight's Children*' in Meenakshi Mukherjee (ed.), *Midnight's Children: A Book of Readings* (Delhi: Pencraft International, 1999), 69–95.

[38] See for example the popularity of Narayan's novel *The Man-Eater of Malgudi*.

[39] Chisholm, 'Changing the Anglo-Indian Literary Landscape', 13.

his editor Liz Calder privately observed, in contrast to the reception in the US, the reviews in Britain 'while admiring, come with government health warnings'.[40] She refers to Victoria Glendinning's review in the *Sunday Times*. It begins: 'Bear with me for a moment. *Midnight's Children* . . . is not the sort of novel we are used to.' This 'long, prolix, eccentric, brilliant piece of writing' makes 'a fantastic book—and, I think, an important one for Europeans to read. But special pleading may be necessary. It's hard to face the at first uncertain pleasures of the unfamiliar in fiction, so easy to go for the safe and proven tastes of the homegrown.'[41] This reception underscores the nature and extent of Rushdie's intervention, and the difficulties he faced in penetrating 'mainstream' or 'home-grown' literature, which are easy to forget in view of the book's later acclaim. Although Rushdie's publishers at Jonathan Cape made great efforts to get his book reviewed in Britain, *Midnight's Children* received very little attention in Britain until it won the Booker Prize. Liz Calder wrote to several potential reviewers, including Claire Tomalin at the *Sunday Times,* asking her: 'to consider doing a profile of this very gifted young Indian writer, hailed as the new Marquez or Grass in the US, patted on the head in England, his adopted country . . . and [to] ask why it is like this—so often.' She ends 'Surely we can find some space for [Rushdie] in our tight little circles?'[42]

In shifting from realism, and applying a version of magic realism to South Asian subjects, Rushdie defined a certain new form of novel. He had a major impact on the way that future novels of this sort would be read, setting the criteria for the genre. His kind of writing has become a landmark for subsequent writers to engage with. A younger group of South Asian Anglophone writers (such as Arundhati Roy and Vikram Chandra) has been dubbed 'Rushdie's children' in reviews.[43] Rushdie seems to be also writing against the earlier studies of 'real' Indian villages in the works of Mulk Raj Anand and R. K. Narayan, even though as Rushdie points out 'there were elements of the fabulous . . . even in the work of the committed realists' (*Moor* 173). Rao's *Kanthapura* braided myth and legend with political realism. Yet Rushdie was perhaps the

---

[40] Liz Calder, letter to Claire Tomalin, 30 Apr. 1981, Jonathan Cape Archive, Reading University Archives, Reading.
[41] Victoria Glendinning, 'The Naked and the not so Naked', *Sunday Times* (26 Apr. 1981), 42.
[42] Calder, letter to Claire Tomalin, 30 Apr. 1981.
[43] Anthony Spaeth, 'Rushdie's Children', *Time* (16 Dec. 1991), 98–100.

first Indian writer in English to combine such a high level of fantasy with social and political critique in fabulist historiography, or what Linda Hutcheon has called 'historiographic metafiction', an intensely self-reflexive, theoretical awareness of history and fiction.[44] Rushdie emphasises the limitations of realism and the creative potential of non-naturalistic images in *Shame*:

By condensing the naturalistic connection between shame and violence into a non-naturalistic image like the girl, it seems to me that you said more than you would by describing it sociologically or within the rules of realism in the novel, and I think all those non-fictional passages were condensed and intensified in that way.[45]

In *Midnight's Children* Rushdie attempts a definition of his brand of magic realism: 'matter of fact descriptions of the outré and the bizarre, and their reverse, namely heightened, stylized versions of the everyday...' (*Midnight* 218). This is inextricably entwined with his satirical purposes. For example, the internalised racism and elitism of post-Independence Indian businessmen that turns them into Europeans who become literally white and insist: 'All the best people are white under the skin' (*Midnight* 176). The literalisation of metaphors is a source of much of the comic-fantastical atmosphere of the book. His use of formal devices (such as metafiction and an unreliable narrator who provides a variety of versions of events) demystifies history and provides 'a counter-narrative to the official history of Indira Gandhi and the nostalgic histories of the apologists for British imperialism'.[46] In this way, as an intellectual on cultural borders, Rushdie provides a doubly specular role providing a distorting mirror to critique the dominant ideologies of both countries. Homi Bhabha endorses Rushdie's paradoxical equation of the migrants' 'stereoscopic' vision with increased clarity: 'as Salman Rushdie reminds us the truest eye may now belong to the migrant's double vision.'[47] In his literary criticism Rushdie suggests the disjunction between image and substance is heightened in the migrant writer's perspective. Rushdie emphasises 'the migrant intellect roots itself in itself, in its own capacity for imagining and re-imagining the world...A writer who understands

[44] Linda Hutcheon, *A Poetics of Postmodernism* (London: Routledge, 1988), 6.
[45] Interview with Ronald Hayman in *Books and Bookmen* (Sept. 1983).
[46] David Price, 'Salman Rushdie's Use and Abuse of History in *Midnight's Children*', *Ariel* 25.2 (1994), 93.
[47] Homi Bhabha, *The Location of Culture* (London: Routledge, 1994), 5.

the artificial nature of reality is more or less obliged to enter the process of making it' (*Imaginary* 280–1).

Rushdie rejects realism as a suitable mode for representations of India, where he makes a somewhat dubious claim that fantasy is normative because of the everyday interpenetration of the divine and the ordinary. He comments that 'mystical and surreal . . . useful techniques . . . can't really be avoided—your daily experience of the India media is that strange things happen.'[48] He explains his own use of fantasy as an 'attempt honestly to describe reality as it is experienced by religious people, for whom God is no symbol but an everyday fact' (*Imaginary* 376). Hence we are told in *Midnight*: 'reality can have a metaphorical content that does not make it less true' (*Midnight* 200). Rushdie emphasises a specifically Indian source for his non-realism, in order to establish himself as an *Indian* English writer and his text as emblematic of a non-Western discourse. In other contexts, Rushdie has commented that his sense of the limitations of realism stems from an awareness of its inadequacy as a creative medium in a post-1960s context with the advent of structuralism and post-structuralism:

For realism to convince, there must be fairly broad agreement between the author and the reader about the nature of the world that is being described. I think that for Dickens,[49] George Eliot and others, that would by and large be true. But now we don't have that kind of consensus about the world. . . . the 1960s represented a kind of shift in people's perceptions. The simplest of these was the perception that reality was no longer something on which everyone could agree.[50]

His adoption of strands of radical European thought suggests that, as a South Asian migrant writer domiciled in the West, responding to changes at the 'centre' is complex and can be progressive. Clearly Rushdie's non-mimetic mode cannot be located solely in India's supernatural dimension, his exposure to Mumbai's 'cinema of the fantastic' and his interest in oral narratives, as he emphasises in many interviews and critical essays.[51] Locating Rushdie in these wider intellectual contexts also explains his deep engagement with European film aesthetics, not

[48] Ho Nazareth, 'Handcuffed to History' *Time Out* (8–14 May 1981), 20.
[49] Dickens' use of the grotesque disturbs a neat labelling of his work as realist. Rushdie also employs the grotesque in his depictions of Saladin Chamcha's physical transformations in *The Satanic Verses*.
[50] David Brooks, 'Interview with Salman Rushdie', *Helix* 19/20 (1984/5), 55.
[51] Salman Rushdie, *The Wizard of Oz* (London: British Film Institute, 1992), 11.

simply the much emphasised and obvious influence of Indian film and Bollywood.

Rushdie's works are symptomatic of a generational shift in British intellectual culture and a change in literary tastes. For example, Rushdie's interest in Lawrence Sterne needs to be contextualised in relation to the re-evaluation of writers like Sterne during the 1970s and 1980s that was the result of a new interest in the ideological significance of language and the possibilities of self-conscious, self-parodic narration. Rushdie began to write in an intellectual climate influenced by the challenge of the French theorists Julia Kristeva and Roland Barthes (and others associated with the journal *Tel Quel*) to traditional Marxist views on realism versus modernism. The split between traditional Marxism and post-structuralism was further developed by the intervention of *Screen* theory in the early 1970s that set out to theorise 'the encounter of Marxism and psychoanalysis on the terrain of semiotics'. Launched in 1972 by Rushdie's contemporaries at Cambridge, Stephen Heath and Colin McCabe, the journal *Screen* provided an important focus for theoretical debates about film and the relations between culture and signification. *Screen* film theory criticised the realist tradition and followed Brecht's emphasis on the subversive potential of modernist techniques.[52] As Antony Easthope suggests, '*Screen* theory' radically affected theoretical accounts of film, television, cultural studies, and literary theory.[53] These changes had wide theoretical implications for Rushdie's work and the way it was read, particularly by critics such as Homi Bhabha, whose first major essay appeared in *Screen* in 1983.[54]

---

[52] MacCabe argues that realist narratives were not critical of current political ideologies. This was because realism was a set of representational codes, which offer the viewer a comfortable position from which to see the representation even of bitter political struggles as inevitable. Hence, it defuses any potential for a critical or 'progressive' reading. Colin MacCabe, 'Realism and the Cinema: Notes on some Brechtian themes' *Screen*, 15.2 (1974), 7–27. It is possible to argue that Ahmad et al.'s critiques of Rushdie are another version of the debates on aesthetics and politics between Georg Lukács and Brecht in 1938. See Robert Young, *White Mythologies: Writing History and the West* (London: Routledge, 1990), 23.

[53] Antony Easthope, *British Post-Structuralism Since 1968* (London: Routledge, 1988), 34.

[54] Homi K. Bhabha, 'The Other Question', *Screen* (1983), 18–35. Rushdie's and MacCabe's arguments are very closely positioned. While Rushdie has emphasised the influence of Joyce on his work, MacCabe's Cambridge Ph.D. thesis on Joyce was later published as Colin MacCabe, *James Joyce and the Revolution of the Word* (Basingstoke: Macmillan, 1978). Here MacCabe makes a Brechtian argument for the revolutionary implications of Joyce's modernism for theorising the dialectical relation between reader and text, and for challenging a representational theory of language.

There are, in particular, close similarities between Colin McCabe's critiques of realism in *Screen*, published from 1972 onwards, and some of the ideas that Rushdie explores, particularly in *Midnight's Children*, such as his emphasis on the 'writtenness' of the text, the notion of the author as ideological construct, the lack of transparency of language, and the positing of problems of representation. For example McCabe writes:

For anti-realists no discourse can ever be adequate to the multifarious nature of the real. . . . The classic realist text attempts to present itself as transparent denying its own status as writing. . . . In the claim that the narrative prose has direct access to a final reality we can find the claim of the classic realist novel to present us with the truths of human nature.[55]

These ideas are enacted as a debate in *Midnight*, where truths are turned into unverifiable facts: 'What's real and what's true aren't necessarily the same' (*Midnight* 79). The text abounds with the conflicting, alternative perspectives of different characters, which seem real to each of them. MacCabe observes: 'The classic realist text cannot deal with the real as contradictory because of the unquestioned status of the representation at the level of dominant discourse. The real is not articulated—it is.'[56] In *The Satanic Verses* we are told that: 'The world is incompatible, just never forget it: gaga, Ghosts, saints, Nazis, all alive at the same time; in one spot, blissful happiness, while down the road, the inferno' (*Satanic* 201). At the suggestion of Colin McCabe when he later became Director of the British Film Institute, Rushdie wrote an appreciation of the proto-magic realist film *The Wizard of Oz* for the BFI classics series, arguing that the MGM classic speaks powerfully to the migrant exile's perceptions of reality: in *The Wizard of Oz* 'the imagined world became the actual world as it does for all of us . . . not that "there's no such place like home", but rather that there is no longer any such place *as* home: except, of course, for homes we make, or the homes that are made for us'.[57]

MacCabe characterises the intellectual context of his era at Cambridge (1968–81) as the 'union of post-structuralism and leftism but which at the time was experienced more simply as a belief that the development of crucial categories in the humanities could be understood as a fundamental political task'. He suggests that it was a product of the

[55] MacCabe, 'Realism and the Cinema', 8, 9, 10.
[56] Ibid. 12.    [57] Rushdie, *The Wizard of Oz*, 57.

way 'art and politics were interwoven in the student movements of the late 60s'.[58] Rushdie's early work can be clearly situated in this intense theoretical milieu of Cambridge in the 1970s and London of the 1980s. During this time, both McCabe and Rushdie participated as influential figures in London's Institute of Contemporary Arts, the foremost forum of the time for discussions on the 'new' theory, organised by the then Director of Talks at the ICA, Lisa Appignanesi.

Homi Bhabha and Stuart Hall were equally visible at the ICA during this period (Hall's influential 'Minimal Selves' essay, for example, was first given at an ICA symposium on identity, 'The Real Me'). The position of these figures at the core of these reciprocal intellectual, theoretical debates supports my earlier argument that the difference between Sivanandan's and Rushdie's works is symptomatic of the split in Marxism identified in the previous chapter, in which orthodox Marxism was challenged and redefined by the inclusion of concepts of alterity and difference. Post-structuralism, though criticised for deviating from Marxist orthodoxies, was instrumental in creating the theoretical space where issues of gender and ethnicity could be considered alongside those of class. Although Rushdie describes his own politics as broadly Marxist, he has been criticised by Marxist critics subscribing to the thought of an earlier generation, including Timothy Brennan and Aijaz Ahmad.[59] Brennan is sceptical of what he calls Rushdie's 'Third World Postmodernism' and cosmopolitanism. He compares Rushdie unfavourably with Sivanandan and, more surprisingly, Paul Gilroy whom he sees as much closer to the decolonising nationalist purposes of the first wave of anti-colonialists Cabral and Fanon and to 'the crucible of British expulsion/acculturation'.[60] In contrast to the impulse of the earlier liberation movements, Ahmad and Brennan argue that Rushdie's representations of the postcolonial world leave no space for resistance.[61] Moreover, Ahmad argues that Rushdie is too dismissive of the complexity of lived experiences in Pakistan. His exclusion of 'the dailiness of lives

[58] Colin MacCabe, *The Eloquence of the Vulgar* (London: British Film Institute, 1999), p. v.

[59] Aijaz Ahmad, *In Theory* (London: Verso, 1992), 332 n. 6.

[60] Timothy Brennan, *Salman Rushdie and the Third World* (Basingstoke: Macmillan, 1989), 51, 166.

[61] Ahmad observes that Rushdie creates in *Shame* 'an image of the public sphere of politics so replete with violence and corruption that any representation of resistance becomes impossible'. Ahmad, *In Theory*, 127. Brennan argues that in *The Satanic Verses* Rushdie ignores the fact that 'black British cultures can affirm and protest'. Brennan, *Salman Rushdie*, 165.

lived under oppression . . . human bonding . . . resistance . . . decency'
is symptomatic of what Ahmad identifies as Rushdie's 'aesthetic of
despair'.[62] What is noticeable here is that Ahmad and Brennan's critique of Rushdie on Marxist grounds is made in terms of older Left
traditions of social realism. Ahmad's objections to Rushdie's partial and
selective representation of Pakistan in terms of 'slices' (and his praise
of Sivanandan's broadly realist novel) suggest that Ahmad's critique is
fundamentally predicated on a Lukácsian realist aesthetic, evident in
his comment that: 'The confessed fragmentariness of the experience
precludes, for example the realist option, because realism presumes, at
the very least, an integral experience which includes more than mere
"slices".'[63]

The 'old' Left was not concerned with issues of gender and ethnicity, or with the related questions of representation or the ideological
significance of language. As part of the 'new' Left, Rushdie is interested in the way language is used to help construct ideology, and
in the disjunction between language and the world, the process of
art and the constructedness of the text. As we saw in the previous
chapter, although his text is influenced by postmodern conceptions
of history, Sivanandan has expressed criticism of postmodern writers
who like Rushdie suggest that 'description is a political act' and that
're-describing a world is the necessary first step towards changing
it' (*Imaginary* 13–14).[64] Sivanandan suggests that such oppositional
rhetoric is just that—rhetoric.[65] Ahmad is similarly impatient with
'metropolitan theory's inflationary rhetoric'. He refers to what he sees
as Bhabha's 'exorbitant praise of Rushdie's magic realism as the "literary
language of the emergent postcolonial world" '.[66] Ahmad's critiques of
Rushdie are closely linked with his opposition to Bhabha, whose work
is challenged on the same grounds. In short, Ahmad et al.'s dismissal
of Rushdie and Bhabha is exactly related to the broader phenomenon
of mainstream Marxist attacks on what they see as postmodernists'
excessive concern with semiotics and language, rather than material and

---

[62] Ahmad, *In Theory*, 139, 155.     [63] Ibid. 138.

[64] For Sivanandan's critique, see A. Sivanandan, 'La trahison des clercs', *New Statesman and Society* (14 July 1995), 20–1.

[65] Although Rushdie cannot be dismissed as a playful, weightless postmodernist, some of his utterances leave him vulnerable to these criticisms. Rushdie does have a tendency to inflate the powers of metropolitan authors: 'to dream is to have power', and the dream world of the artist has 'the power . . . to oppose this dark reality' (*Imaginary* 122).

[66] Ahmad, *In Theory*, 69.

social realities.[67] This divide within Marxist theory remains very much in evidence in Marxist critiques of postcolonial studies today.

The previous chapter sketched the decline of traditional Left assumptions and strategies in relation to their failure to deal with cultural and gendered difference. The postmodern attempts to create new formulations of ethnicity, identity, and culture developed relationally by Rushdie and Bhabha need to be seen in relation to this decline. Rushdie's fictional insights into hybridity and mixture, developed theoretically by Bhabha, have shown how the processes of cultural hybridisation that accompany the increasingly integrated world economy and mass migration to the West challenge traditional notions of nationhood, metropolitan discourses of inter-cultural relations, and essentialist conceptions of cultural, class, and national identity.[68]


## CULTURAL TRANSLATION AND HYBRIDITY

In part as a result of Salman Rushdie's fiction and the impact of his work on Bhabha, translation and hybridity have become the favoured metaphors for the condition that postcolonial migrants inhabit.[69] Rushdie's definition of himself as a translated man could be said to have been the defining moment. The narrator of *Shame* (who has many biographical similarities with the author) suggests: 'I, too, am a translated man. I have been *borne across*. It is generally believed that something is always lost in translation; I cling to the notion—and use, in evidence, the success of Fitzgerald-Khayyam—that something can also be gained' (*Shame* 29, emphasis in original). Rushdie conceives the processes of migrancy, linguistic and cultural translation, emphasis in original and hybridisation as analogous. In the process of being 'carried across' something new is created that is composed of elements both of origin and destination, but does not derive exclusively from either. Like Bhabha, Rushdie emphasises the subversive potential of migrancy and the act of translation, particularly the 'creation of radically new types

[67] See Terry Eagleton's critique of *Screen* theory, discussed in Easthope, *British Post-structuralism*, 61–2.

[68] Bhabha acknowledges his debt to Rushdie. Bhabha, *The Location of Culture*, p. ix.

[69] Stuart Hall also endorses Rushdie's celebration of hybridity as 'the authentic voice, the credo of the post-colonial, the diaspora imagination'. Stuart Hall, 'Review of *Imaginary Homelands*', *Sight and Sound* 1 (1991), 32.

of human beings': 'But the migrant is not simply transformed by his act; he also transforms his new world. Migrants may well become mutants, but it is out of such hybridization that newness can emerge' (*Imaginary* 210). This idea works for Rushdie partly because of his own contexts and trajectory. It is exemplified in his recreations of the pluralistic Mumbai of his childhood and in the British Asian context.[70] It does not work in *Shame* where the migration of the mohajirs first emerges. For Rushdie, Pakistan does not offer the same opportunities for minorities as Nehru's conception of a secular India or London's multiculturalism. In the author–narrator's imagined Pakistan, Islam cannot bear the weight of the nation: its monotheism and absolutism do not allow hybridity. Rushdie's formulations of cultural hybridity lend themselves to an uncritical endorsement of a liberal orthodoxy of multiculturalism. While mongrelisation is suited to postmodern cultures, it is also profoundly anti-Islamic. Rushdie writes '*The Satanic Verses* . . . rejoices in mongrelisation, and fears the absolutism of the Pure' (*Imaginary* 394). Rushdie's phrase the 'absolutism of the Pure' forges a link between his contestation of notions of purity (of origins) and his contestation of the absolutism of religious faith. For Rushdie, if hybrid identities contest or destabilise claims to mono-cultural identities, this is a parallel process to undermining the monologism of faith central to most understandings of Islam. Despite the trenchant critique of many forms of racism in *The Satanic Verses*, Rushdie cannot envisage a place in Britain for those who withstand his vision of multicultural hybridity, endorsed by a liberal minority. We will see this contradiction in a more pronounced form in the work of Hanif Kureishi.

For Rushdie there is no 'pure' Indian or English: the challenge he poses for multicultural societies is not how to learn to live together and 'tolerate' cultural differences, but to accept that we are all plural beings. Similarly, Bhabha distinguishes between a cultural diversity that assumes pre-given cultural forms—multiculturalism—and cultural difference. He describes his hybrid 'Third space' of enunciation as a site of potential counter-authority where cultural purity is contested, but also

---

[70] Although, as Kumkum Sangari observes, this is itself a rather distorted view: *Midnight's Children* 'appears at times to grasp Indianness as if it were a torrent of religious, class and regional diversity rather than a complex articulation of cultural difference, contradiction, and political use that can scarce be idealised'. See Kumkum Sangari, 'The Politics of the Possible', *Cultural Critique*, 7 (1987), 180.

as a location where cultural difference can be renegotiated towards new cultural forms and identities.[71] More recently, Bhabha has commented on the eclecticism of the Bangladeshi migrant and co-owner of the Shandahar Café in *The Satanic Verses*. Bhabha suggests Hind's 'gastronomic pluralism', inspired by her husband Mustafa Sufyan's 'pluralistic openness of mind', points to forms of vernacular cosmopolitanism that have a non-European origin. Bhabha argues that in this way the South Asian immigrant experience may be exemplary of a new global trend and that this vernacular cosmopolitanism of the postcolonial or minoritarian subject is not now in itself a Western characteristic.[72]

As a novel, *The Satanic Verses* can be seen to stage the very tensions of assimilation versus hybridity that we have shown to mark and condition the situation of all South Asian writers in the twentieth century. For Rushdie, the question of dealing with one's origins as a migrant involves an acceptance of hybridity. In *The Satanic Verses,* he deploys the palimpsest image (first used to depict the mohajirs' attempts to erase their Indian past in *Shame*) to describe the way migrants attempt to deal with their past and origins in London. Allie Cone's Polish father Otto's 'lust for integration' involved attempts to 'wipe the slate clean' in order to erase the horrors of the concentration camps (*Satanic* 298). He made every effort to eradicate his Jewishness, he changed his name from Cohen to Cone; he read no Polish literature because 'language was irredeemably polluted by history' (*Satanic* 297). This course of action does not save him: 'Otto Cone . . . jumped into an empty lift-shaft and died' (*Satanic* 298). Otto Cohn's 'lust for integration' differs (in motivation although not in practice) from Saladin Chamcha's attempt at assimilation. Chamcha's attempt to overwrite his past in the context of migration to a hegemonic culture is critiqued as a form of assimilation that stems from cultural denigration. Rushdie traces a genealogy for Chamcha's motivated assimilation and Anglophilia: he delineates the similarities between his character and the writer Nirad Chaudhuri, who as I have suggested supremely exemplifies the processes of self-translation and assimilation. Like Chamcha, Chaudhuri can equally be described as 'seeking to be transformed into the foreignness he admires' (*Satanic* 426). Chamcha's characterisation echoes Chaudhuri's personality, for whom 'the debasing of Englishness by the English was

71  Bhabha, *The Location of Culture*, 37–8.
72  Homi Bhabha, 'Paean for Pluralism', *India Today International* (29 Dec. 1997), 24k.

a thing too painful to contemplate' (*Satanic* 40). Chamcha's attempt to differentiate himself from 'riff-raff from villages in Sylhet or the bicycle-repair shops in Gujranwala', and his classed notions of what constitutes Britishness is also reminiscent of Chaudhuri: 'But they [Mishal and Anahita] weren't British, he wanted to tell them: not *really*, not in anyway he could recognise' (*Satanic* 159, 259, emphasis in original). Later in the text the parallel is made explicit: 'He had been striving, like the Bengali writer, Nirad Chaudhuri, before him . . . to be worthy of the challenge represented by the phrase *Civis Britannicus sum*' (*Satanic* 398). Rushdie's critique of assimilation underscores its intimate relation to the internalisation of inferiority. At the same time, a rejection of assimilation does not mean an advocacy of complete abrogation. Rushdie suggests that it is equally impossible to eradicate the imperial past and (in the case of Pakistan, Indian culture) and return to an untarnished nativist pre-colonial state. This is dramatised through the Methwold narrative and by revealing the English roots of Saleem's ancestry in *Midnight Children*. Again in *The Satanic Verses*, Rushdie derides both the impulse and attempt to expel the foreign: 'let us not pretend that Western culture is not present; after all these centuries, how could it not also be part of our heritage?' (*Satanic* 246). Rushdie's own intervention is to modify this assimilation versus abrogation binary through his emphasis on hybridity. In Chamcha's case, his assimilation contains the possibility of hybridity. Rushdie critiques assimilation but suggests that not all transmutations of the self are flawed or need to be according to dominant expectations. All such translations are how 'newness enters the world'.

In comparison to Dhondy, Rushdie is evidently a more complex, theoretically aware writer with a prophetic strain. While Rushdie's extraordinary talent and complex, incendiary novels inevitably overshadow Dhondy's achievements, it must be acknowledged that he too has played an important role in paving the way for younger writers. Dhondy's intervention in framing the debates over the politics of representation and in delineating South Asians, particularly working-class Bangladeshis growing up as Muslims in the East End of London, anticipates the writings of Kureishi and Monica Ali. Moreover, in the wake of the racialisation of Muslim identities in the context of the Rushdie Affair, 9/11, and the more recent global war on terror, Dhondy provides a more trenchant critique of liberal multiculturalism and the limits of representation than either Rushdie or Kureishi. It is Dhondy who makes the point that:

There are no mainstream editors who understand and empathise with the mindset of jehadis, killers of authors and burners of books, families which force marriage contracts or polygamists (or perhaps I am mistaken about this last). Neither should there be—but with such a prohibition, one ought to accept that multiculturalism in Britain is mono-ethical. Other frames of morality can be observed but not approved of. They must inevitably be reduced to polite or critical anthropology.[73]

---

[73] Dhondy, 'The Death of Multiculturalism', *Guardian* (8 Nov. 2002), online edition.

# 5

# Staging Cultural Difference: Cultural Translation and the Politics of Representation: Hanif Kureishi and Meera Syal

## SITUATING HANIF KUREISHI AND MEERA SYAL

In this chapter, I compare the work of British-born writers and film-makers Hanif Kureishi (1954– ) and Meera Syal (1963– ). Over ten years older, and the first to come to the fore, Kureishi paved the way for younger writers like Syal. Yet their work merits comparison for several reasons. First, they differ from their predecessors in distinct ways, particularly in their role as cultural mediators. Kureishi's and Syal's work charts the uneasy relationship between postcolonialism and multiculturalism, addressing in particular the legacy of colonialism, and its effects on immigrants and their descendants in contemporary Britain. What is distinctive about their generation is that they act as cultural translators, in their mediations between majority and minority communities, rather than between countries. The politics of first-generation migrant writers' reconstitution of the foreign country for the target Western audience contrasts with the later minority genre that juxtaposes, challenges and reinforces dominant notions of these communities. Kureishi recalls how he began his writing career as a cultural translator. He suggests his early work was materially produced in the 'politically conscious seventies, [when] there was, in TV and theatre, a liberal desire to encourage work from unmapped and emergent areas. They required stories about the new British communities, by cultural translators, as it were, to interpret one side to the other.'[1] He admits that at the time he was happy to assume the position assigned without unpacking its implications: 'I didn't think much about whether I was the sort of writer best-suited to this kind of work; I just knew I was being paid to write' (Introduction, *Outskirts* p. xviii). As I alluded to earlier, a hallmark of Kureishi's work is the way he, like Tambimuttu before him, both exploits and resists his ethnic identity. His early complicity with this role is ironic in that much of his later work questions some of the problematic implications of traditional conceptions of cultural translation, in particular the implicit assumption that the two cultures undergoing translation are discrete entities sealed off from one another, where the translator bridges separate cultures. Kureishi undoes this assumption, underlining the extent to which the histories of the subcontinent and Britain are ineluctably intertwined and continue to be so despite the separation of decolonisation. In 'Pakistan, Britain just wouldn't go away', writes Kureishi in his autobiographical essay, 'The two countries . . . have been part of each other for years, usually to the advantage of Britain. They cannot now be wrenched apart, even if that were desirable. Their futures will be intermixed.'[2] In the same way, Kureishi avers that notions of Asian and British cannot be defined separately. His protagonists live the potentials and experience the pitfalls of mixing and métissage, emphasising the precarious, ambivalent nature of all cultural translations. His work parodies the idea of homogenous, distinct, racially defined communities. For her part, Syal foregrounds syncretism in a different way. She traces her love of comedy to watching *It Ain't Half Hot Mum, Dad's Army, Steptoe and Son*, and *Morecambe and Wise* as a teenager. She notes the influence of *Monty Python* and *Harry Enfield* sketches on the fast-paced, trailblazing TV comedy *Goodness Gracious Me*.[3] In interviews she suggests these satiric influences blend with 'the fun-poking aspect of Punjabi culture . . . the cockneys of India'.[4] Such statements and, as we will see, thematising of hybridity in her work dovetail rather self-consciously with the work of theorists of hybridity such as Paul Gilroy and Homi Bhabha. This suggests the extent to which minority cultural representation is influenced and even mutually produced by writers, academics, and critics as well their readers.

[1] Hanif Kureishi, *Outskirts and Other Plays* (London: Faber and Faber, 1992), pp. xv–xvi. Hereafter *Outskirts* pagination will appear in the text.
[2] Hanif Kureishi, 'The Rainbow Sign' in *My Beautiful Laundrette and Other Writings* (London: Faber and Faber, 1996), 91, 102. Hereafter *Rainbow* pagination will appear in the text.
[3] Meera Syal, letter to the author, 12 Feb. 2000.
[4] Meera Syal, *The South Bank Show*, ITV, 3 Mar. 2002.

Both writers explore the paradoxes of their position as hybrid insiders/outsiders and as mediators between communities. Writers of this generation, however, are not in any simple sense 'outsiders'; nor have they been physically translated, although sometimes they are constructed in these terms by the dominant culture. The popular assumption, especially when Kureishi first emerged, was that his generation were still migrants in some sense: hence Kureishi's objection to the term 'second-generation' on the grounds that it ensures 'that there was no mistake about our not really belonging in Britain' (*Rainbow* 134–5). First-generation migrant narratives of acculturation describe transplanted subjectivities formed during different stages of the colonial and de-colonised history of the former colonies. As Anglicised Asians from the former colonies, Rushdie and Naipaul have described the shock on arrival of being perceived as alien in the 'mother' country.[5] However, as Rushdie suggests, 'At least I know that I really am a foreigner, and don't feel very English. I don't define myself by nationality—my passport doesn't tell me who I am.'[6] For the generation who were born or grew up in Britain, by contrast, the dominant culture's attempts to exclude them is felt more acutely and very differently. As Kureishi observes, 'for me and the others of my generation born here, Britain was always where we belonged, even when we were told—often in terms of racial abuse—that this was not so' (*Rainbow* 135). Kureishi and Syal differ from and enlarge the space created for them by their forerunners by articulating what it is like to feel British, grow up in Britain, and be regarded as foreign. This disjunction (between how Kureishi sees himself and how wider society perceives him) is a formative influence that animates his work. More than British, however, he sees himself as a Londoner. Postcolonial London is central to Kureishi's artistic and cultural representations: his exposure of its underbelly as well as his celebration of its potential for self-reinvention, its multicultural possibilities, freedoms, and energising creative potential are comparable with Rushdie's recreations of Mumbai and London. Syal's regional upbringing in the West Midlands, and contrasting relationship to her community and cultural background, on the other hand, results in a very different take on these issues.

While first-generation authors like Sam Selvon, V. S. Naipaul, and Rushdie narrate the experience of arrival in Britain from the former colonies, this story forms the experience of Kureishi's father (who

[5] Salman Rushdie, interview with Joan Bakewell, *Heart of the Matter*, BBC 2, 10 July 1988.
[6] Salman Rushdie, 'An Interview', *Literary Review* 63 (1983), 31.

migrated from Mumbai to study law in 1947) and Syal's parents (who arrived in Britain from Delhi in 1960). Kureishi's and Syal's semi-autobiographical first novels *The Buddha of Suburbia* (1990) and *Anita and Me* (1996) re-visit the first-generation immigrants' stories of the dislocation of partition, arrival in Britain, and the different ways they have adapted to life in Britain through the eyes of their offspring, providing a very different perspective to that of Dhondy's short stories. Their novels explore the different generations' relationship to the 'host' and 'home' countries, and the impact on identity-formation of their contrasting formative experiences. Their work articulates the gap between the first-generation immigrants from the former colonies in the subcontinent and their offspring who have little first-hand knowledge of South Asia, which is mediated through a variety of sources. In their formative years, until they are able to make 'independent' observations, this generation's knowledge of the culture of 'origin' tends to be filtered through their parents' perspectives. It is based on the eclectic *bricolage* of whatever elements of the culture exist within the parental home or British Asian household. As Ravinder Randhawa's protagonist observes, India was 'for those born here a patchwork land transmitted through parents' stories of places, people, happenings'.[7] The mass, differentiated appeal of diasporic forms of transportable culture, such as Bollywood films, increasingly marketed to diasporic rather than local audiences, further emphasises the *mediated* nature of the cultural input that informs some British Asian experiences of growing-up within a minority community. Syal observes that she had a 'rather mythological impression of India for years' until her first visit on her own at the age of 22. She suggests that the cultural resources from 'home' that first-generation immigrants attempt to impart to their children are frozen and fossilised in the 'usual immigrant bubble where Indians abroad are more traditional than their counterparts at "home"', over-anxious to preserve what they remember as the homeland'.[8] Any suggestion that the first generation represents an 'authentic' India is disrupted in her work: '. . . in actuality, the India they all knew had vanished around the time of black and white movies and enforced sterilization'.[9] This time lag is a recurrent preoccupation for Syal. In her screenplay *Bhaji on*

[7] Ravindher Randhawa, *A Wicked Old Woman* (London: The Women's Press, 1987), 31.

[8] Meera Syal, letter to the author.

[9] Meera Syal, *Life Isn't All Ha-Ha, Hee-Hee* (London: Doubleday, 1999), 192–3. Hereafter *Life* pagination will appear in the text.

*the Beach* (1993), Rekha, the glamorous Chanel-clad socialite visiting the UK from Mumbai, mocks Asha for wanting to teach her children values from 'home': 'Home? What home? When was the last time you went home? Look at you, your clothes, the way you think . . . You're all twenty years out of date.'[10]

The writings of Kureishi and Syal are centrally concerned with the differences between first-generation immigrants' and their children's values and beliefs. Rather than focus on conflicts between *cultures*, they portray discord between *generations* and *within* communities. This focus on generational difference forms the basis of their appeal to a new generation of readers, for whom these differences may be part of their own experience. This emphasis also makes them accessible to a mainstream audience familiar with this 'between two cultures' thesis from media and social science perspectives on Asian immigrant communities. Yet both writers' representations allow for a more complicated formulation of the ambivalent relations between the first and second generation, particularly through the portrayal of the close relationships between Meena and her parents, and Karim and his father in their first novels. These relationships articulate intersection and intra-generational dialogue rather than clear-cut generational divide, and disturb binary polarities that equate the first generation with tradition, and the second with modernity.[11] Furthermore, both writers examine the considerable diversity and debate about how best to 'make Britain habitable' and define one's British Asian identity *within* each generation (*Outskirts* 158).

Juxtaposing these two writers shows how the cultural contexts of the 1980s and 1990s outlined in the introductory chapter decisively shaped both. Kureishi's early play, *Borderline*, grew out of the black uprisings in 1979 in Southall where Asians opposed a provocative National Front pre-election rally, and in July 1981 where there were confrontations with both the National Front and the police. Syal appears to politicise her own work by positioning herself as one of 'the generation who had watched the footage from Southall and vowed that things must change'.[12] As we shall see, such an unambiguous identification was not

[10] Meera Syal, *Bhaji on the Beach*, dir. Gurinder Chadha, Films on Four, unpublished screenplay, 1993, 45–6. Hereafter *Bhaji* pagination will appear in the text.
[11] For a discussion of the way Kureishi subverts the potential cliché of the arranged marriage in the sub-plot of *The Buddha of Suburbia* see Ruvani Ranasinha, *Hanif Kureishi* (Plymouth: Northcote House Publishers, 2002), 66–8.
[12] Meera Syal, ' "PC: GLC" ', in Sarah Dunant (ed.), *The War of Words: The Political Correctness Debate* (London: Virago, 1994), 120. Hereafter *PC* pagination will appear in the text.

so easily available to bi-racial Kureishi. As noted earlier the financial support for minority art by the Greater London Council (GLC) and the British Film Institute led to the creation of several Black and Asian theatre and film collectives, and the Asian Women Writers' Workshop of which Syal was a founding member. With reference to right-wing vilification of the GLC's funding of 'loony left', politically correct groups, Syal recalls how she benefited from the promotion of the rights and sensibilities of racial and sexual minorities through education, positive discrimination, and culture. 'It was the first time that an elected council was making very public and legislative steps to tackle racism and inequality', Syal observes (*PC* 122).

The decisive moment in terms of institutional financial support, however, came with the creation of Channel 4 in 1982. Channel 4 funded both Kureishi's *My Beautiful Laundrette* and Syal's first feature films *A Nice Arrangement* and *Bhaji on the Beach*. Syal co-wrote two episodes for Dhondy's Channel 4 soap opera *Tandoori Nights* (1985). Subsequently promoted by the BBC in the early 1990s, Syal wrote and performed in BBC 2's *The Real McCoy*. A report from the BBC in 1976 suggests the corporation's earlier *laissez-faire* approach to the question of minority representation, underlining Channel 4's more interventionist role in the 1980s. At this juncture the BBC saw its role as either making programmes about the specific predicaments facing ethnic minorities (which tended to confine and define them as a problem) or reflecting 'coloured' immigrants' penetration of mainstream society *as it occurred*:

A contemporary series like 'Z Cars' is bound to include opportunities for coloured actors to play all kinds of parts and this process will advance, as society in Britain advances with the task of absorbing its immigrant communities.

The contemporary dramatist . . . will be reflecting the society in which we live. This means the writer will take explicit account of immigrants in writing stories that concern the problems of an immigrant community. He will also take implicit account of immigrants by including them naturally, wherever in society they are most likely to appear. Naturally is the key. It would be the worst form of condescension if the BBC Scripts Unit were to start inserting immigrant parts into scripts.[13]

With this emphasis on the reflection of a sociological 'reality', the BBC report significantly ignores and evades the media's concomitant role in shaping and defining social and cultural identities. Identity does not

[13] Naseem Khan, *The Art Britain Ignores: The Art of Ethnic Minorities in Britain* (London: Community Relations Commission, 1976), 154.

precede representation as the report implies, but rather, as Stuart Hall points out, is 'always in process, and always constituted within, not outside representation'. Hall suggests that 'the form of representation which is able to constitute us as new kinds of subjects . . . is the *vocation of modern black cinemas*.'[14] As we shall see, both Kureishi and Syal in distinct ways offer alternative 'black' subjectivities, although they conceive of 'black' politics and subjectivities in a very different way to Sivanandan.

These cultural contexts mean that in contrast to the first generation of immigrants, these artists achieved greater access to wider, more public forms of representation. BBC producer Anil Gupta identifies some of the reasons why penetration of the media was a specifically 'second-generation' phenomenon:

The ethos of first-generation immigrant culture is to work hard to get a profession or work in business. You don't think, 'I'll break into the mainstream media' when you've just arrived and you're building a community. The children of those immigrants who came in the 1960s are now finding confidence in their own identity and are saying, 'This is who we are.'[15]

Such widely circulated texts fuelled debates on the politics of representing a minority community to the dominant gaze of the majority community, as well as to the minority communities themselves. Some of these debates invoked the problem Kobena Mercer has characterised as the 'burden of representation': 'the assumption that minority artists speak *for* the entire community from which they come'. Mercer argues that this assumption both circumscribes the artist and reproduces the racist stereotype that 'every minority subject is, essentially, the same'.[16]

Their designation as cultural translators privilege such notions of the 'original', authentic insider, an integral part of the burden of representation. Both Kureishi and Syal, however, repudiate any claims to authentic or accurate portraits. Kureishi comments: 'But then I don't pretend to be a spokesman for the Asian community, and they shouldn't expect me to do PR for them, any more than you'd expect Neil Jordan

---

[14] Stuart Hall, 'Cultural Identity and Disapora', in Jonathan Rutherford (ed.), *Identity: Community, Culture, Difference* (London: Lawrence and Wishart, 1990), 222, 237, emphasis mine.

[15] Cited in James Rampton, 'A Message to Take Away', *Independent* (17 Jan. 1998), 68.

[16] Kobena Mercer, *Welcome to the Jungle: New Positions in Black Cultural Studies* (London: Routledge, 1994), 214.

to do PR for the Irish community.'[17] Similarly, Syal disavows this role: 'I don't claim to speak for anyone. It's crass to think you can speak for a whole community. The version of the truth I present can only be mine.'[18] The non-realist self-reflexive elements of their films are an important part of their contestation of this burden of representation, which privileges realism. In Syal's films, the characters' fantasies in the inflated style of Bollywood movies fracture notions of an unmediated reality and foreground the illusion of an authentic transcendental voice. In *My Sister-Wife*, the protagonist's daydreams that idealise relations between the mythical sister-wives become increasingly vivid, disturbing notions of the real.[19] Kureishi's and Stephen Frears' films also break the conventions of realism but not by using 'Asian' influences. These disclaimers notwithstanding, however, the question of privileged insiders or translators 'chosen' to mediate and interpret is inescapably raised. As Spivak has shown, it is impossible for the 'native informant' residing within the metropolis to avoid complicity with dominant structures. For her, the 'worst' option for such an individual is 'to play the native informant uncontaminated by disavowed involvement with the machinery of the production of knowledge'.[20] This chapter is centrally concerned, therefore, with whether or how Kureishi's and Syal's work critically reflects the majority and minority communities. How far does it question or challenge neo-colonial ideologies and perceptions and to what extent does it embody them? Although they are 'translating' minority communities for the majority, in their delineations of the majority community both also invert the dominant 'gaze'. As Coco Fusco suggests, 'to ignore white ethnicity is to redouble its hegemony by naturalising it. Without specifically addressing white ethnicity, there can be no critical evaluation of the construction of the Other.'[21] In this way Syal's portrayal of neglected, white, working-class Anita acts as a foil to Meena's protected upbringing in *Anita and Me*. Susan the white journalist in Kureishi's *Borderline* admits her parents 'do mind' about her career as a journalist and 'think it's time [she] married

---

[17] Jane Root, 'Scenes from a Marriage', *Monthly Film Bulletin* 52/622 (1985), 333.

[18] James Rampton, 'No More Mrs. Patel for Meera', *Independent* (12 Apr. 1997), 45.

[19] Meera Syal, 'My Sister-Wife', in Rukhsana Ahmed and Kadija George (eds.), *Six Plays by Black and Asian Women Writers* (London: Aurora Metro Press, 1993), 111–59. Hereafter *Sister-Wife* pagination will appear in the text.

[20] Gayatri Chakravorty Spivak, *A Critique of Postcolonial Reason: Towards a History of the Vanishing Present* (Cambridge, Mass.: Harvard University Press, 1999), 360.

[21] Coco Fusco, 'Fantasies of Oppositionality: Reflections on Recent Conferences in Boston and New York', *Screen* 29.4 (1988), 91.

an architect and had kids' (*Outskirts* 127). This points to the gender constraints and patriarchal expectations within white British culture and revises simplistic contrasts between a progressive, white Britain and its 'backward' minorities.

Kureishi's and Syal's work in TV, radio, theatre, and cinema as well as fiction, reflects the extent to which migrant (now minority) texts have diversified from their more narrowly literary origins. At the same time, both Kureishi and Syal made their names first as screen-writers before overcoming the greater hurdle of gaining acceptance as successful novelists. In regard to fiction writing, Kureishi recalls in his memoir *My Ear at his Heart* (2004) the support of Salman Rushdie, Philip Roth, Bill Burford of Granta, and later V. S. Naipaul. Kureishi's and Syal's narratives reflect their immersion in British pop-ular culture, evident particularly in the style of humour and sitcom aesthetic of their films and novels. This differs from earlier writers, who restricted their expression to high literary forms. For Kureishi, British and American pop was the 'first sort of common culture that [he] was ever aware of'.[22] His texts are permeated by transatlantic youth culture, not the Indian popular film culture informing Rushdie's novels or Syal and director Gurinder Chadha's *Bhaji on the Beach* (1993). The exuberance of *Bhaji on the Beach* is largely ascribable to its enthusiastic evocation of Indian popular culture, with its Punjabi version of Cliff Richard's 'We're All Going on a Summer Holiday', its aesthetic quality of bright colours, energy, and scenes reminiscent of Bollywood movies. It draws on Bollywood fantasy and popular morality tales painted in vivid strokes to provide an ironic frame to the action, notably in the frustrated shopkeeper Asha's daydreams, in which deities from the Hindu pantheon appear amid smoke-puffs and deafening cymbals. In Syal's novel *Anita and Me*, Meena's parents' Punjabi folk songs make her realise there is a corner of her that will be 'forever not England'.[23] In her novel *Life isn't all Ha Ha, Hee Hee* Syal rep-resents younger second- and third-generation British Asians' particular eclectic selection, recombination, and transformation of elements of the originary culture and mainstream youth culture in a description of a British Punjabi band whose music epitomises the mutual, cultural

---

[22] Hanif Kureishi, 'Interview with Colin MacCabe: Hanif Kureishi on London', *Critical Quarterly* 41.3 (1999), 46.
[23] Meera Syal, *Anita and Me* (London: Flamingo, 1996), 112. Hereafter *Anita* pagination will appear in the text.

inflections and fusion that characterise this new generation's cultural output:

> The drums they knew, their parents' heartbeat, folk songs sung in sitting rooms, the pulse of hundreds of family weddings; but then the guitarists, cold steel and concrete, the smell of the Bullring, the frustration bouncing off walls in terraced houses in Handsworth, hurried cigarettes out of bathroom windows, secret assignations in libraries, hurrying home with a mouthful of fear and desire. The lyrics parodied I Love You Love Me Hindi film croonings, but with subtle, bitter twists, voices coming from the area between what was expected of kids like them and what they were really up to. (*Life* 41)

Despite these broad similarities, analysis of the two writers' cultural contexts and writings makes clear the diverse spectrum that constitutes the condition of being of Asian origin in Britain. Born to a white mother and Pakistani father, Kureishi foregrounds his 'mixed race' protagonists in *My Beautiful Laundrette* and *The Buddha of Suburbia* as 'in-betweens'.[24] What emerges from his autobiographical essay, 'The Rainbow Sign' (1986) and semi-autobiographical novel *The Buddha of Suburbia* (1990) is that the racialising of identity is particularly problematic for the subject whose racial identity is not clear-cut: it underlines the instability and indeterminacy of race as a category. A mixed descent exacerbates the notion of choice, and of belonging in neither community, and is riven by ambivalence, labile and mutable identities. Syal's identity in turn is formed in relation to at least two contexts: mainstream culture and elements of the culture of origin, with the relationship between the two becoming increasingly porous. Like many British Asians she has access to the same cultural references as their white counterparts in class and education, with the added dimension of the parental culture. Syal, fluent in Punjabi, has more than a passing familiarity with and access to a cultural base, resources, vernaculars, information, and experiences.[25] This enables a dialogic relationship with the Punjabi community she describes, in contrast to Kureishi who was brought up in white suburban Kent, largely isolated from Pakistani communities. Kureishi never heard Urdu at home, because his father's first language was English; he describes his father's family as Anglophone,

---

[24] Hanif Kureishi, *My Beautiful Laundrette and Other Writings* (London: Faber and Faber, 1996), 134–5, 20. Hereafter *Laundrette* pagination will appear in the text.
[25] Her work is inflected with Punjabi words, but there is not a Rushdiesque reworking of language. Her incorporation of Punjabi words supplements English where there is no equivalent.

Anglophile, and like Chaudhuri 'alien even in India'.[26] For Kureishi, the 'Asian' dimension of his ethnic identity was a defining experience but not the only one or even *the* defining one. In an interview he describes his upbringing as mono-cultural: 'I was brought up really as an English child . . . my father was very Westernized—he wasn't a practising Muslim, for example, he didn't believe in arranged marriages or practices that would have conflicted with what was around us. I wasn't influenced by Asian culture at all.'[27] Kureishi characterised his childhood as one where there was no conflict between his Pakistani father's input and 'what was around us' and re-creates this in Karim's 'English' upbringing in *The Buddha of Suburbia*. This is one of the main differences between the two writers' *Bildungsromans*. Syal's semi-autobiographical coming of age narrative, on the other hand, traces a subjectivity and upbringing divided between home and the outside world, a generation gap heightened by the family's migration, although not without ambivalence. *Anita and Me* conveys both the claustrophobia and security of the close-knit Punjabi circle that influenced the protagonist's formative years. However, the overstatement in Kureishi's last line is perhaps a response to being repeatedly categorised in essentialist terms, and in relation to formulations of culture clash and generational divide that dominate popular and ethnographic accounts of British Asian communities. While Kureishi is not obviously syncretic either in intellectual formation or in literary practice, at the same time he is influenced by Asian culture. His exposure, for example, to his relatives in Pakistan and his British Asian relations provide him with an added dimension of ethnic and cultural experience. This becomes apparent in his portrayals of the culturally hybrid nature of Nasser's family dynamics in *My Beautiful Laundrette*. This perspective is both similar to but not the same as Edward Said's 'contrapuntal' awareness of intellectuals situated on cultural borders or Rushdie's 'stereoscopic' vision.[28] In fact Kureishi's intellectual formation is moulded by many cross-cultural, transnational influences. He is steeped in what might be regarded as English traditions of social criticism and political analysis through irony and satire, notably the Royal Court Theatre's tradition of dissent. He also draws on the intellectual cross-fertilisations of what Paul Gilroy defines as the 'black

[26] Frank Kermode, 'Voice of the Almost English', *Guardian* (10 Apr. 1990), 42.
[27] J. B. Miller, 'For His Film, Hanif Kureishi reaches for a "Beautiful Laundrette"', *New York Times* (2 Aug. 1992), 16.
[28] Edward Said, 'Reflections on Exile' *Granta*, 13 (1984), 172. Salman Rushdie, *Imaginary Homelands, 1981–1991* (London: Granta, 1991), 19.

Atlantic', and acknowledges the influence of James Baldwin and Richard Wright. Equally his work is shaped and permeated by white-authored American texts by Philip Roth, Norman Mailer, Saul Bellow, J. D. Salinger, and Jack Kerouac. Similarly Syal, another product of the Royal Court Theatre, cites multiple influences 'Dickens, Austen, Alan Bennett, Harper Lee, Woody Allen, Rushdie', alongside black American women writers Toni Morrison and Alice Walker, confirming the cross-cultural nature of models of cultural identity that cannot be located in relation to origin and destination alone.[29]

## THE EARLY RECEPTION OF HANIF KUREISHI

Nowadays the media describe Kureishi as a British writer. However, his early reception emphasized his outsider status. Some early reviews categorize Kureishi as an 'Asian playwright' and emphatically *not* British: one explicitly contrasts his work with that of his British (read white) counterparts. His play *The King and Me*—about a working-class woman's escapist obsession with Elvis Presley—is described in *The Times* as 'another first-hand report from the bottom of the social heap. The difference is that, where British specialists in the field are apt to give their characters up for lost, Mr. Kureishi ends by showing that there are other escapes from the social trap than dreams.'[30] Here the difficulty of being (part) Asian and British is apparent (Kureishi's mother's descent is frequently ignored). Kureishi's skill in not allowing his outlook to be influenced by his 'Asian-ness' is praised! The same reviewer also notes approvingly Kureishi's 'capacity to write about working class Britons (read white) without the least trace of ethnic bias' in *The King and Me*.[31]

It was in writing his early play *Borderline* (1981), that Kureishi discovered the dramatic potential and the complexity, fissures and 'diversity' of the Asian community, largely by exploring the differences of gender, generation, and class (*Outskirts* p. xix). Like Dhondy's early fiction and plays, *Borderline* deftly points to the various, complex factors that impinge upon immigrant experiences and the diverse responses

    [29] Meera Syal, letter to the author.
    [30] Irving Wardle, '*The King and Me* (review)', *The Times* (9 Jan. 1980), 11.
    [31] Irving Wardle, 'Collision of Cultures: *The Mother Country* (review)', *The Times* (23 July 1980), 13.

to immigration. The play similarly debates the appropriate response to racism and the politics of representation, identifying the reciprocal political agenda preoccupying minority writers at this juncture.

Kureishi's multigenerational focus delineates a community constantly evolving and redefining itself in response to changing cultural contexts, and so refutes static, reified representations. The protagonist Amina's family diverges in their response to their neighbours' racist attack on her father, Amjad. Despite having suffered the racial assault, Amjad insists that a 'few' English racists should not force them to leave. His wife Banoo's spirited response to the attackers contrasts with his denial. Yet living in fear of further racial hostility is unbearable; she wants to return to Pakistan, and does so after Amjad's death. For her daughter this is not an option: Amina says 'I belong here. There's work to be done. To make England habitable' (*Outskirts* 158).

*Borderline*'s feisty female activists Yasmin and Amina suggest a similar emergent defining of British Asian identity that we saw in Dhondy's narratives. Kureishi's characterisations contest the mainstream media's effacing of the agency of female activists and exclusive focus on the role of African-Caribbean British males.[32] Kureishi explodes stereotypes of young British Asians as quiescent, passive, depoliticised, family types often defined in contrast to the more 'difficult' British African-Caribbean youth.[33] His young Asian activists are endowed with a militant defiance that was considered the preserve of their African-Caribbean counterparts.

At the same time, Kureishi disrupts notions of a monolithic Asian community by depicting one fractured by competing class interests. He counterpoints the alliances of Amina's group of anti-racist activists with the way illegal immigrants are exploited as cheap labour by Haroon's father, a restaurateur who gives free meals to white policemen and displays notices condemning 'all those who plan any counter-demonstrations against neo-fascists' (*Outskirts* 113). His capitalist ethic is more effectively actualised in Omar's uncle Nasser and Salim in *My Beautiful Laundrette* (1985). Portraying these characters as 'too busy keeping this damn country in the black. Someone's got to do it',

---

[32] Avtar Brah, *Cartographies of Diaspora* (London: Routledge, 1996), 47, 44.

[33] An article in the *Sunday Telegraph* written in the aftermath of the Brixton riots in 1981 is an example of the way Asian youths were constructed as different from 'young blacks and some whites [who] have slipped completely from the control of their parents. Asians' culture has bound them tightly as both families and communities—in ways in which many white and black parents would envy'. Gordon Brook Shepherd, 'Where the Blame for Brixton Lies', *Sunday Telegraph* (19 Apr. 1981), 16.

Kureishi subverts racist stereotypes of Asian immigrants as a drain on the country's resources, 'sponging off' the state (*Laundrette* 14–15). The text self-consciously asserts psychological as well as material empowerment. Kureishi's early play, *Birds of Passage* (1983), features a similarly materially empowered Pakistani protagonist. *The Times* review observes that Kureishi's characterisation of the proud, wealthy Asif differs from usual representations of Pakistani immigrants: 'It is . . . a salutary shock to see a Pakistani character elevated from *corner shop subservience* into the moneyed arrogance of an old Etonian.'[34] The 'salutary' notwithstanding, his 'shock' reveals how deeply ingrained derogatory, narrow perceptions of Asian immigrants were and underlines the achievement of Kureishi's representations. The Pakistani characters have a robust assertiveness and confidence. As Kureishi observes, none of his Asian characters are '*victims*'.[35] He does not, however, simply exchange negative images for positive ones. His portrayals move beyond the dichotomy of positive or negative stereotypes. This is a political move in terms of the politics of representation in offering 'new' black subjectivities.

## NEW ETHNICITIES AND THE POLITICS OF REPRESENTATION

It was Kureishi's groundbreaking screenplay *My Beautiful Laundrette*—with its gay romance between Omar, a gauche, yet ambitious mixed-race British Asian and his former schoolmate, white, working-class and ex-National Front member Johnny—rather than Kureishi's early plays, that brought Kureishi and British Asian experiences into the wider public view. With a more far-reaching circulation than previous films about Asians in Britain, it was hugely successful, making the unexpected move into mainstream culture and commercial audiences.[36] In the screenplay, Kureishi creates contrary Asian characters like Nasser who have both shortcomings and strengths. In a manner suited to the immediacy of the film medium, he distils Nasser's character in a few memorable sentences. Nasser's advice to Omar to learn how to 'squeeze the tits of the system'

[34] See Irving Wardle, 'Us and Them . . . and Those: *Birds of Passage* (review)', *The Times* (17 Sept. 1983), 9, emphasis mine.
[35] Root, 'Scenes from a Marriage', 333.
[36] For example, in contrast to Ahmed Jamal's *Majdar* (Retake Film and Video Collective, 1984).

embodies both his ruthless capitalism and callous sexism (*Laundrette* 17). He is portrayed as an exploitative, venal, passionate man. Yet despite the critique of his pitiless ethos and patriarchal double standards, the high-living Nasser is an attractive character with an exuberant passion for his white mistress Rachel and a genuine desire to help his brother and nephew. Kureishi does not shy away from criticising Nasser's and Salim's merciless tactics as slum landlords: they embody the ruthlessness of the Thatcherite ethos of competitive individualism and the erosion of social responsibility.

Kureishi's portrayals provoked controversy amongst some minority critics in the late 1980s who, like Mahmood Jamal, felt that his text re-iterated dominant perceptions of Asians as 'money-grabbing, scheming, sex-crazed people'.[37] The realist assumptions taken for granted in Jamal's critical framework underlines the extent to which the burden of representation assumes and privileges realism. The realist aesthetic not only serves to reinforce 'the tokenist idea that a single film can be regarded as "representative" of every black person's perception of reality', it assumes that 'reality has an objective existence "out there" that the process of representation simply aims to correct'.[38] In this way Jamal's criticisms are caught up in what Robert Stam and Ella Shohat identify as 'the moralistic and essentialist traps embedded in a "negative-stereotypes" and "positive-images" analysis'.[39] This is precisely the trap that Kureishi wants to break from by articulating a range of diverse, conflicting perspectives of the community. He does not homogenise the experiences of first-generation migrants: they are not all 'money-grabbing'. Omar's left-wing father and the Asian poet whom Nasser evicts suggest that not all Asians have prospered from the enterprise culture, nor support it. A characteristic feature of Kureishi's work is its articulation of a range of conflicting voices. Omar's father wants him to leave the laundrette and return to college, insisting that education is power and that Omar 'must have knowledge. We all must, now. In order to see clearly what's being done and to whom in this country' (*Laundrette* 53). However, this voice

[37] Mahmood Jamal, 'Dirty Linen', in Kobena Mercer (ed.), *Black Film, British Cinema* (London: Institute of Contemporary Arts, 1988), 21–2.

[38] Kobena Mercer, 'Diaspora Culture and the Dialogic Imagination: The Aesthetics of Black Independent Film in Britain', in Mbye B. Cham and Claire Andrade-Watkins (eds.), *Black Frames: Critical Perspectives on Black Independent Cinema* (Cambridge, Mass.: MIT Press, 1988), 53.

[39] Robert Stam and Ella Shohat, *Unthinking Eurocentrism* (London: Routledge, 1994), 215.

is 'drowned out' by the narrative. Omar's father's decline into poverty enhances the appeal of his uncle Nasser's ethic that money is the source of power and mobility, rather than education. Nasser asserts his identity in relation to class and not race and negates the power of racism in the face of capitalist success. He insists 'I'm a professional businessman not a professional Pakistani. There's no such thing as race in the new enterprise culture' (*Laundrette* 41). Salim observes the converse aspect of this perspective, ruefully commenting on Omar's father's descent from Bhutto's close friend in Pakistan to bedridden, impoverished socialist in Britain: 'But we're nothing in England without money' (*Laundrette* 48). While certain stances are structurally privileged, all are subjected to scrutiny and interrogated. Kureishi maintains an ironic distance posing difficult questions and resolutely refuses to provide closure. He gestures towards a range of possibilities from which the reader or viewer can develop his or her opinion. His ambivalence and ironic distance also make his work more difficult to interpret politically. Kureishi's irony is itself a refusal to commit. The various genres he employs embody this validation of uncertainty, resistance to totalising narratives and concern with the relativity of perception in different ways.

At the same time, Jamal's suggestion that *My Beautiful Laundrette* was popular with European audiences because 'it says everything they thought about us but were afraid to say' cannot be dismissed as a knee-jerk reaction to unflattering portraits of his community. Jamal is concerned with the implications of the release of these representations into a context where they can be manipulated by racists. His objections to the film are specifically located in the context of years of minimal, overwhelmingly negative representation of ethnic minorities. He observes: 'being constantly misrepresented in the media can make one unbearably sensitive to issues of stereotyping and lead us into protecting and defending every stain that shows up when we wear our badly washed clothes.'[40] More recently Kureishi counters that being 'so diverse, so broad in terms of class, age and outlook . . . it doesn't make sense to talk about the so-called Asian community'. He observes that 'the importance of having a full range of writers writing about this community is precisely because of this rich disparity.'[41] However, the film appeared when there was not 'the range of writers' to represent the community's diversity. *The New York Times* suggests *Laundrette*

---

[40] Jamal, 'Dirty Linen', 21.
[41] Kureishi, address, Cheltenham Literary Festival, 17 Oct. 1997.

'opened the *surprising, hitherto obscure* world of London's Indian and Pakistani immigrant cultures to public scrutiny'.[42] Kureishi is also described as 'the lone spokesperson' for Asian communities.[43] Although the less well known works of Farrukh Dhondy and Tariq Mehmood are ignored in such white media constructions, this *perception* of Kureishi as the first and only writer to depict the British Pakistani community gives his work a representative status. While Kureishi's portrayals are not intended as representative, we need to distinguish this from their political *effect*. Consider Frears' comments on *My Beautiful Laundrette*: 'it was astonishing because [Kureishi] got it so right. That someone could be so right, so confident about it, make the jokes, be so on the inside.' How can Frears (or anyone else) confer this authenticity? [44] The negative stereotypes could provide a safe outlet (safe because articulated by Kureishi, one of 'them') for the fears and prejudices of some of the dominant community.

In contrast to Jamal's and other commentators' criticisms of Kureishi's films,[45] other minority critics, notably Stuart Hall, interpreted Kureishi's screenplays as evidence of an important shift in black cultural politics. For Hall, they mark the movement from black groups asserting their right to represent themselves and countering negative images with positive ones, to a more complex agenda of a new 'politics of representation' that eschews positive images and 'engages rather than suppresses *difference*'. In this way it entails 'the end of the essential black subject': the idea that a subject is constituted by 'authentic', fixed, pre-existent essences or characteristics. It registers instead 'the recognition of the extraordinary diversity of subjective positions, social experiences and cultural identities which compose the category "black"'.[46]

The formal disruptions, the parallel editing, voice-overs, swish pans, and elements of farce and spectacle, that fracture conventions of

[42] Glenn Collins, 'Screen Writer Turns to the Novel to Tell of Race and Class in London', *New York Times* (24 May 1990) 17, emphasis mine.

[43] Irving Wardle '*Borderline* (review)', *The Times* (6 Nov. 1981), 18, emphasis mine.

[44] Stephen Frears, 'Keeping His Own Voice: An Interview with Lester Friedman and Scott Stewart', in Wheeler Winston Dixon (ed.), *Re-Viewing British Cinema, 1900–1992* (Albany, NY: State University of New York Press, 1994), 233.

[45] See also Perminder Dhillon-Kashyap, 'Locating the Asian Experience', *Screen* 29.4 (1988), 120–6. Pratibha Parma, '*Sammy and Rosie Get Laid*' (review), *Marxism Today* 32 (1988), 39. bell hooks, *Yearning: Race, Gender and Class Politics* (Boston: South End Press, 1991).

[46] Stuart Hall, 'New Ethnicities', in Mercer (ed.), *Black Film, British Cinema*, 28.

naturalism in Kureishi/Frears' films are an integral part of this 'new' politics of representation. As suggested earlier, these elements formally foreground issues of representation, alongside the impossibility of representing a stable, external reality and fixed, coherent identities. Kureishi's novels are similarly characterised by a mixture of realism and comic exaggeration. With his complex, contradictory characters including gay Asian heroes, and Asian and African-Caribbean feminists and lesbians, Kureishi not only explores a range of 'black' identities, his intersections of ethnicity, gender, sexual orientation, and class examine identity in terms of these multiple, overlapping, and colliding categories. This marks a divergence from 'a great deal of black politics, constructed . . . directly in relation to questions of race and ethnicity, [which] has been predicated on the assumption that the categories of gender and sexuality would stay the same and remain fixed and secured'.[47] I would add, as I have argued elsewhere, that Kureishi's intervention in *My Beautiful Laundrette* lies in its articulation of the way sexual pleasure is imbricated in wider societal conflicts and racialised hierachies in the compelling, contradictory relationship between Johnny and Omar, and its redefinition of masculinity in relation to race, class, and queer desire.[48]

Finally, although Jamal et al. raise legitimate questions concerning the political impact of Kureishi's portrayals, to follow their arguments to their logical conclusion would be to constrain the minority artist into replacing negative portrayals with positive ones and to 'be kept captive by the racist prejudices of the majority'.[49] This would result in images of minorities remaining circumscribed by a few narrow stereotypes, without any degree of heterogeneity and complexity. Kureishi's artistic response to the diversity and complexity of British Asian experiences is a progressive deconstruction of received, conventional assumptions of minority communities and leads to a broader self-definition. However, the controversy his films provoked illustrate the difficulty of this move. It is not without risks: his ironising and subversion of certain stereotypes makes him vulnerable to accusations of reinscribing others and underlines the precariousness of his position in trying to move beyond

[47] Hall, 'New Ethnicities', 29.

[48] See Ruvani Ranasinha, *Hanif Kureishi: Writers and their Work* (Plymouth: Northcote House Publishers, 2002), 43–50.

[49] Salman Rushdie, 'Minority Literatures in a Multi-cultural Society', in Kirsten Holst Peterson and Anna Rutherford (eds.), *Displaced Persons* (Sydney: Dangaroo Press, 1992), 41.

the positive/negative binary. The contradictory reception suggests the difficulty of reading Kureishi politically: his characterisations are read as path-breaking or retrograde, even neo-orientalist. His later represent-ations of British Muslims would in turn appear in the context of the racialisation of British Muslim identities.

## KUREISHI'S REPRESENTATION OF BRITISH MUSLIM IDENTITY

Kureishi's engagement with British Muslim identity in his fictional responses to the issues raised by the Rushdie affair in his novel *The Black Album* (1995) and screenplay *My Son the Fanatic* (1997), now appears prescient in view of the scrutiny of this community in the context of 9/11, global warfare, and 7/7. In fact Kureishi's anxieties about radical orthodox Islam and separatism date back to his early essays 'The Rain-bow Sign' (1986) and 'Bradford' (1986). In 'The Rainbow Sign', he explains the revival of Islam in its diasporic forms in loaded terms: as a 'symptom of extreme alienation', but also as an '*aberration*' (*Rainbow* 79).[50] He describes separatism though 'spawned by racism' as a '*pathetic elevation* of an imaginary homeland' (*Rainbow* 94, emphasis mine).

Despite his sympathy regarding the conditions that heighten radical orthodox Islam, in his later novel *The Black Album*, and screenplay *My Son the Fanatic*, monolithic portraits of Islamic believers remain circumscribed within narrow polarities. In marked contrast to his earlier absorbing narratives that diversify representations of ethnic minorities, to differing degrees these texts crudely and uncritically reflect and embody rather than question predominant fears, prejudices, and per-ceptions of practising British Muslims as 'fundamentalists', a group already constructed as particularly threatening in the West. His carica-tures further objectify this already objectified group, whilst reinscribing dominant liberalism as the norm. Unlike *Laundrette*, where mainstream media representations are challenged and unsettled, this recent work,

---

[50] In *The Black Album* Kureishi describes the heightened Islamic fervour amongst the younger generation in Pakistan as a reaction against their parents' 'English accents, foreign degrees and British snobbery'. Kureishi, *The Black Album* (London: Faber, 1995), 91–2. Hereafter *Album* pagination will appear in text. As this suggests, fundamentalism is also a class issue. Although Kureishi presents the differences between Riaz and Shahid as ideological, they are also classed: the text implicitly contrasts the working-class 'fundamentalist' Muslims with Shahid's Anglicised middle-class background.

implicitly directed at the dominant majority, reaffirms its values and is consistently constructed in terms that it will find sympathetic.

Five years on from his first novel *The Buddha of Suburbia*, in *The Black Album* (1995), Kureishi creates another young British Asian, Shahid Hassan, who escapes suburban Kent for a life in London as a student in 1989. Shahid, the third-person narrator, is eager to learn, to experience the pleasures of his new, amorphous city, and to 'slough' off his former life and self (*Album* 190). His coming of age is dramatised within a loose picaresque form in which he is confronted with different choices to those of his precursors. The novel explores the conflict between fundamentalism and a form of liberal individualism that is bound up with sensual gratification. The choice is personified somewhat schematically between Shahid's Asian neighbour, Riaz, a mature student, and stern leader of the young Muslims at Shahid's derelict North London college, and his white, liberal ex-hippie tutor Deedee Osgood who offers him sex, raves, Ecstasy and postmodern uncertainties. She is a somewhat caricatured figure of white feminised sexual hedonism. The insistent juxtapositions of Shahid's sexual life with Deedee and his encounter with the 'rave' scene of 1989, and the Islamic group 'forbidden to kiss or touch' are overdone (*Album* 126). Shahid wavers between intimacy and sexual experimentation with Deedee, and helping in anti-racist vigils and typing Riaz's religious tracts. Finally the Muslim students burn a copy of Salman Rushdie's *The Satanic Verses* on campus, which precipitates his decision to leave the group. Deedee speaks out against the book-burning and calls the police. The group plan to teach her a 'lesson', when they discover Shahid's own act of blasphemy in re-writing Riaz's religious writings as an erotic epic. Chad and Sadiq assault Shahid for having 'deceived and spat on his own people' (*Album* 266). At the last moment Shahid's wastrel brother Chilli (a familiar Kureishi creation of a brash, materialistic arch-Thatcherite) saves Shahid and ejects the posse. The group moves on to 'other business', and Chad, Riaz's henchman, is badly burnt by firebombing a bookshop that sells *The Satanic Verses*. The novel ends with Shahid and Deedee escaping the aftermath of the book-burning and firebombing by going on a weekend trip to the countryside 'until it stops being fun' (*Album* 276).

Notwithstanding the lampooning of the derailed Left in the characterisation of the students' Marxist lecturer Brownlow, in this novel the 'debate' is so weighted against the Islamists, that Shahid's liberal individualism and decision to leave the 'paranoid' Islamic group is unequivocally presented as enlightened self-interest (*Album* 258).

Shahid's rejection of Islam is presented as a triumph of rationality and common sense over fanatic anti-intellectualism: '[h]ow narrow they were, how unintelligent, how . . . embarrassing it all was! . . . the thought of Riaz now made Shahid shudder in revulsion. What a dull and unctuous man he was; how limited and encased was his mind, how full of spite and acidity!' (*Album* 225, 240). (Kureishi's short story and screenplay *My Son the Fanatic* similarly contrasts the quasi-liberal, Westernised Pakistani taxi driver Parvez (Om Puri) who loves Scotch, Jazz, and bacon-butties, with his son Farid who embraces a radical sect of Islam. Parvez, characterised as the enlightened, down-to-earth voice of reason, realistic and humane, is defined against his deluded, indoctrinated and self-righteous son, although the screenplay is a more nuanced and ambitious work, as I have discussed at length in my book *Hanif Kureishi*.[51]) Kureishi rehearses stereotypes of Muslims as intrinsically violent: in *Black Album*, Chad is characterised as volatile and 'crazy', all 'bulk and suppressed violence' with 'the ferocity of a wild pig' (*Album* 78, 237). The posse's political activism soon 'inevitably' descends into extremism: book-burning, the firebombing of shops, and assault and so endorses dominant stereotypes of violent Islamic opposition.

If, as I have suggested, *Laundrette* is 'dialogic', making the reader or viewer provide the closure, in contrast this later text is excessively 'monologic', less complex, nuanced and therefore weaker. This is reflected in the novel's form; while *Black Album* is scattered with multiple perspectives and myriad subplots (such as the discovery of a divinely inscribed aubergine), they all appear to be marshalled in order to articulate the novel's central conflict. In his characterisation, Kureishi invents a polarity between radical orthodox Islam and detached liberal individualism with no recognition of the spectrum of attitudes in between. His Muslim characters tend to either scorn religion like Shahid's 'secular' father, brother Chilli, and his patrician wife Zulma in *Black Album*, and Parvez in *My Son the Fanatic*, or they are represented as extreme 'fundamentalists'—already a highly charged term in Britain. Kureishi's polarity ignores the wide range of different forms of Islam that are not extreme or aggressive. This implicitly positions Islamic beliefs as problematic in themselves and illustrates one of the ways in which practising Muslims are, as Tariq Modood argues, demonised and Islam

51 Ranasinha, *Hanif Kureishi*, 92–101.

perceived as a 'divisive' identity.[52] There is no suggestion that devout Muslims were not unequivocal about either Rushdie or the Ayatollah's *fatwa*, nor that not all of those offended by Rushdie's text supported the *fatwa* or the book-burnings.[53] I am not suggesting that Kureishi distorts 'real' Muslims or fails to provide positive images of a marginalised group, nor am I contesting the idea that there is a repressive strain in Islam that does not allow the possibility of dissent and is as intolerant as Kureishi suggests. In contrast to his earlier work, these later narratives do not articulate a range of heterogeneous voices on its central issues.

In *The Black Album,* we learn that the college principal had 'long been suspicious of Riaz's group, but, afraid of accusations of racism, she'd secured them a prayer room and otherwise avoided them, even when their posters were inflammatory' (*Album* 226). Here the novel suggests that fear of such accusations can lead to abstention from any form of critique. At one level this is a self-conscious construction of Kureishi's defiance of such censoring impulses, but at the same time his representations of British Muslims and my response raise an inevitable and important question. Is it possible to question the oppressive aspects of fundamentalism, most pertinently the way it is used to assert patriarchal authority and misogyny, without accusations of Eurocentrism or endorsing racist stereotypes?

In this context, I want to consider Bhabha's essay 'Unpacking my library . . . again', which is aligned in some respects to Kureishi's critique of fundamentalism, but points towards the possibility of a more nuanced examination and approach. Like Kureishi, Bhabha opposes the way fundamentalism 'limits choice to a pre-given authority or a protocol of precedence and tradition'.[54] However, in contrast, Bhabha also alerts us to the limits of liberalism as evidenced in some liberal responses to fundamentalism that emerged in the wake of the Rushdie affair. Bhabha observes that the 'trouble with concepts like individualism, liberalism or secularism' is that 'they seem "natural" to us: it is as if they are instinctive to our sense of what civil society or civil consciousness

---

[52] Tariq Modood, *Not Easy Being British: Colour, Culture and Citizenship* (London: Trentham Books 1992), 87.

[53] Nikos Papastergiadis, 'Ashis Nandy: Dialogue and Diaspora' *Third Text* 11 (1990): 100. See also Homi Bhabha, 'The Third Space' in Jonathan Rutherford (ed.), *Identity: Community, Culture, Difference* (London: Lawrence and Wishart, 1990), 214.

[54] Homi Bhabha, 'Unpacking my library . . . again', in Iain Chambers and Lidia Curti (eds.), *The Post-Colonial Question: Common Skies, Divided Horizons* (London: Routledge, 1996), 210.

must be'.[55] Bhabha cautions against such use of the term 'liberalism' as 'natural'. He suggests that it is the 'complex, self-contradictory history of "universal" concepts like liberalism, *transformed through their colonial and post-colonial contexts,* that are particularly important to our current social and cultural debates in a multicultural and multi-ethnic society'. Signalling the dangers implicit in the opposition between fundamentalism and traditional notions of 'secularism', Bhabha unpacks such constructions of secularism and suggests they can be imperialistic. He reveals the abuse of the term ' "secularism" . . . by many spokespersons of the Eurocentric liberal "arts" establishment who have used it to characterise the "backwardness" of migrant communities in the post-*Satanic Verses* cataclysm. Great care must be taken to "separate" secularism from the unquestioned adherence to a kind of ethnocentric and Eurocentric belief in the self-proclaimed values of *modernisation.*' Bhabha argues that the traditional claim to secularism is based on an 'unreconstructed liberalism' that pre-supposes an even playing field, a utopian notion of the self as sovereign and ' "free" choice as inherent in the individual'. This bears no relation to the experience of the marginalised. Such a 'secularism of the privileged' is differentiated from the secularism claimed by minority groups who struggle against inequities of race, class, gender or generation, as well as injustices 'exerted by state institutions against minority groups, or by patriarchal and *class* structures within minority communities themselves'.[56]

Kureishi's prescient observations on a Bradford Islamic school exclusively for girls, which restricts their education to a narrow range of subjects and to creation theories in science, when he visited it in 1986, illustrate Bhabha's point about the inadequacy of an unreconstructed liberalism. As Kureishi makes clear, for these female pupils' 'choice' is not simply individual but conditioned by the patriarchal religious structures within the community:

But Islamic schools like the one in Bately appeared to violate the principles of a liberal education, and the very ideas to which the school owed its existence. And because of the community's religious beliefs, so important to its members, the future prospects for the girls were reduced. Was that the choice they had made? Did the Asian community really want this kind of separate education anyway? And if it did, how many wanted it? Or was it only a few earnest

[55] Ibid. 208.     [56] Ibid. 209–10, emphasis in original.

and repressed believers, all men, frightened of England and their daughters' sexuality? (*Bradford* 133)[57]

Where Kureishi implicitly posits an unreconstructed secularism as an alternative to the way Islamic fundamentalists use religion to assert control over women, for Bhabha these kinds of oppression evidence the need to assert a redefined, 'subaltern' secularism, an ethical freedom of choice. This 'emerges from the limitations of "liberal" secularism and *keeps faith* with those communities and individuals who have been . . . excluded from the egalitarian and tolerant values of liberal individualism'.[58]

As I have argued, Kureishi never explores any forms of Islam that are not 'fundamentalist'. His rigidly dualistic approach reinforces what Modood describes as the assumption that 'religion divides, the secular unites . . . religion is "backward" and negative, secularism is progressive; religious people are the problem and secular rule is the solution'.[59] In contrast, reading Bhabha and Kureishi against each other, we see how Bhabha avoids this trap. Bhabha suggests that 'we need to "secularise" the public sphere so that, paradoxically, we may be free to follow our strange gods or pursue our much-maligned monsters, as part of a collective and collaborative "ethics" of choice.'[60]

Similarly in his work on British Muslims, Kureishi sets up an irresolvable opposition between community and individual: there is no representation of the communal that is not fundamentalist. Again, Bhabha shows us a way of thinking outside this dichotomy, drawing on Gita Sahgal's articulation of *Women Against Fundamentalism* as an 'emergent secular community'. Sahgal conceives of the space of the women's centre as a secular space 'to practice religion as well

---

[57] Although as Inderpal Grewal points out 'unfortunately [Kureishi] does not ask the Pakistani women of Bradford what they want', as she suggests, Kureishi's critique is important since such schools can 'concretize a reified "tradition" of the subordination of women' especially in the light of racism in Britain. For as Black British feminists argue this domination is sanctioned in terms of respecting Other cultures which is another problem of liberalism. Inderpal Grewal, 'Salman Rushdie: Marginality, Women and Shame', in M. D. Fletcher (ed.), *Reading Rushdie: Perspectives on the Fiction of Salman Rushdie* (Amsterdam: Rodopi, 1994), 133. See Saeeda Khanum for an insightful account of the female pupils' views and of the way these schools are used to produce dutiful wives in 'Education and the Muslim Girl', in Gita Sahgal and Nira Yuval-Davies (eds.), *Refusing Holy Orders: Women and Fundamentalism in Britain* (London: Virago, 1992). 'Faith schools' in relation to integration has become increasingly controversial.

[58] Bhabha, 'Unpacking my library . . . again', 209, emphasis in original.

[59] Modood, *Not Easy Being British*, 87.

[60] Bhabha, 'Unpacking my library . . . again', 211.

as challenge it'. She makes an important point that does not seem to occur to Kureishi: individuals opposed to fundamentalism can still be religious. Sahgal's secular space is an example of how secular choice, 'an ethical freedom of choice', can be communal without being fundamentalist. So where Kureishi positions the communal in opposition to the individual, Bhabha tries to maintain a notion of secularism that is communal. For Bhabha 'freedom is much more about the testing of boundaries and limits as part of a *communal collective* process, so that "choice" is less an individualistic desire than it is a public demand and *duty*.'[61]

## POLITICAL COMMITMENT AND IRONIC DISTANCE

Kureishi's anxiety about separatism, often elided in his work with other forms of political activism, reveals a conservative aesthetic that renders the liberal racial and gender politics in his work unthreatening and palatable, and reinforces his construction as privileged insider. A recurrent feature of his writings is the way his British-born protagonists of Asian origin face and make a choice between competing ways of surviving in white Britain. The arguments for and against separatism and political activism form the central debate in *Borderline*, and resurface in *The Buddha of Suburbia* as well as *The Black Album*. Kureishi's protagonists' ambivalence about 'belonging' to a community is presented as a healthy scepticism and assertion of independence or resistance to oppressive forms of identification stemming from notions of community based around ethnicity. However, Kureishi often elides such resistance with a rejection of political commitment.

While Kureishi's sympathy for the activists is clear, *Borderline* also signals an anxiety about separatist activism that inflects all his writing. Yasmin, the 'responsible' rebel and moral centre of the play, identifies positively with being British and cautions that rioting will adversely affect their community. Yasmin insists that she is not 'against things here. I want them to be improved' (*Outskirts* 167). Her position is one that a white liberal audience would find sympathetic. In an early interview, Kureishi positions himself as 'passing on life from people who really

---

[61] Ibid., emphasis in original.

experience the rough end of things to people who might possibly be able to do something about that'.[62] However, it is clear that the necessary dialogue with those who are far more alienated in Britain than Yasmin's portrayal suggests is not achieved in this play.[63] Yasmin's balanced view never faces an outright rejection of the possibility of progress. As Alan Fountain remarks of Channel 4's objections to Ceddo's film *The People's Account*, their discomfort stemmed from 'seeing teenage people saying, "this isn't going to work anymore, we are going to destabilise society until you take an interest in what we have got to say" '. Perhaps, in contrast, Kureishi's work was more amenable to the British arts establishment because it was less confrontational.

In *The Buddha of Suburbia*, in contrast to his soulmate Jamila, a feminist anti-racist, whose brand of individualism remains politically engaged, the protagonist Karim espouses a form of liberal individualism that evades political commitment to the anti-racist movement. In the same way, as we have seen in *The Black Album* Shahid chooses liberal sensualism over not only Islamic 'fundamentalism' but also anti-racist activism. Characteristically, given Kureishi's pervasive ironic distance, the critique of Karim is not so clear-cut. It appears intermittently in keeping with a liberal tradition of presenting alternative points of view. London's acting circles and the lure of drugs, sex, and excitement engage Karim and occupy the centre of the novel privileging Karim's pursuit of detached liberal individualism structurally and thematically. The self-deprecating Karim generates humour and sympathy, drawing us in to 'naturalise', if not endorse his selfishness: 'compared to Jammie I was, as a militant, a real shaker and a trembler.'[64] We are meant to admire Jamila, but we are subtly encouraged to identify with Karim, an identification encouraged by the first-person voice. It is almost as if Kureishi's comparison presents Jamila as how people should be, and Karim as how they are.

In terms of the polarities Kureishi sets up, the rejection of the group often involves a concomitant dismissal of modes of polit-ical solidarity. Yet, as Jamila's independence shows, as a member of a 'collective' based on ideological not ethnic ties, anti-racism does not necessarily involve an uncritical identification with an ethnic

---

[62] Cited in David Noakes, 'Anthem for Doomed Youth?', *Times Literary Supplement* (4 Dec. 1981), 1427.
[63] Alan Fountain, 'Channel 4 and Black Independents', in Mercer (ed.), *Black Film, British Cinema*, 43.
[64] Hanif Kureishi, *The Buddha of Suburbia* (London: Faber and Faber, 1990), 53.

community. Similarly, the problem in *The Black Album* is not that Shahid is uncertain about 'this matter of belonging' to 'his people', but the way in which Kureishi tends to define the terms of belonging between extreme polarities of unquestioning solidarity and complete conformity, or total rejection (*Album* 175). It is here that the comparison with Syal becomes especially relevant: in contrast to Kureishi's pervasive ironic distance and evasion of political commitment and all kinds of solidarity, Syal's anti-racist, feminist aesthetic is more politically nuanced and engaged.

## MEERA SYAL: RETHINKING AND CONTESTING GENDERED ETHNICITIES

Meera Syal is one of Britain's best-known Asians. She achieved a breakthrough to mainstream success with her role as writer and performer in the surprise hit TV comedy *Goodness Gracious Me* (the show started out on the radio and finally won 3.83 million viewers when it was moved to a 9.30 p.m. slot on TV), and more recently *The Kumars at No. 42*. The widespread appeal of these shows underlines how British Asian cultural forms currently make the greatest impact in popular culture beyond the confines of literary establishments. Although today Syal's work is not primarily accessed from a 'literary' perspective, she first came to the fore in the surge of British Asian women's writings in the 1980s. Alongside Ravinder Randhawa, Leena Dhingra, Rukhsana Ahmad, and others, she brought gendered questions of cultural identity to the fore, developing feminist themes, and challenging Eurocentric models of feminism by reformulating gendered ethnicities in her writings. As noted in the introductory chapter the Asian Womens Writer's Workshop (AWWW) (1984–97), founded by writer-activist Ravinder Randhawa, provided a platform for several Asian women writers who, like Syal, went on to become established writers.

During this period, diverse black and Asian feminists formed anti-racist, anti-sexist, and socialist collectives such as the Southall Black Sisters (1979), and later Women Against Fundamentalism (1990) that shared a common membership with the AWWW.[65] In comparison

---

[65] For an account of these movements, see Heidi Safia Mirza (ed.), *Black British Feminism: A Reader* (London: Routledge, 1997).

to Kureishi, Syal's involvement with these groups, and later with the Refugee Council and the Newham Asian Women's Project, impinges on her more politically-engaged responses, and helps explain why her early work in particular is more influenced by Asian community politics. *Bhaji on the Beach* (1993), for instance, provided a forum for debate on issues concerning British Asian women that did not exist in any media at that time.

Syal's intervention is not simply in placing Asian females at the centre of her narratives, but in her critique of the ways Asian women are defined as the object of the Eurocentric and non-Eurocentric male gaze. Syal's screenplays emerge in the context of the work of British Asian feminist director Pratibha Parma (*Khush* 1991), no longer concerned with simply contesting negative representations of women, but to 'find visually innovative ways that best reflect the complexity of experiences that Asian women in Britain have and . . . challenge mainstream film language that depicts minorities in anthropological ways'.[66] What is evident in their different films is the attempt to create a self-conscious audience of female spectators to re-imagine and reclaim female subjectivity (on screen) from the margins of hegemonic patriarchal discourses. As bell hooks argues, while film is a powerful site for creating space for a radical black female subjectivity, critical black female spectatorship emerges as a site of resistance only when individual black women actively resist the imposition of dominant gendered ways of knowing and looking.[67] In my discussion of Syal, we will see how her plays, prose, and films disrupt conventional racist and sexist representations of Asian women.

If Kureishi popularised British Asian experiences, it was through the perspectives of his male protagonists. Syal redresses the gender balance in British Asian dramatic, cinematic, and prose narratives, partly by creating roles not usually associated with or given to Asian women. 'The women I create are positive, rude and often antagonistic to men.'[68] Her early plays show that 'we doe-eyed maidens in saris walking five paces behind our husbands, could be rude, irreverent and ironic' (*PC* 125). In her early, unpublished play *Auntie's Revenge* (written in 1993 for the Royal Court Theatre), the protagonist is constantly

---

[66] Pratibha Parmar, interview, *Bazaar* (1992), 10.

[67] bell hooks, *Black Looks: Race and Representation* (Boston: South End Press, 1992), 128.

[68] Iqbal Wahab, 'Casting Aspersions' *Independent* (24 Oct. 1990), 15.

performing roles that subvert gendered and cultural notions of identity and satirise stereotypes of Asian women that the audience may bring to the viewing, particularly concerning older Asian matriarchs. Their impish humour and latent strength fascinate Syal as her portrayal of the feisty, devilish grandmother in BBC 2's *The Kumars at No. 42* suggests. Far from being the passive victim, Auntie pretends to have been beaten by her son Sanjay in order to incite the Asian women factory workers and so create trouble for her son.[69] Oppressed by the victim roles offered to her as an actor, Syal began to write to generate parts outside the clichéd victim of an arranged marriage, or a Mrs Patel in a corner shop. For Syal, the move from acting to writing marked an empowering movement allowing her to move from object to subject. She observed: 'I want to do funny stuff that reflects the women I know who have a sense of fun and irony. Actors have very little power so it has to come from creating your own work.'[70] She wanted to provide a greater range of roles for Asian women as 'rounded characters, real people who have layers, make mistakes' who were not created by the 'white fringe'. Like Kureishi, her achievement is to broaden the self-definition of the minority community, rather than to focus exclusively on the refutation of white stereotypes. In a statement that allows her to demarcate her own niche, Syal suggests she did not want to act as a mouthpiece for white liberal guilt during the era following the black uprisings of the 1980s:

To me, this was artistic freedom that I could turn inwards and look at the struggles within my community, rather than always examining how the host society saw and treated us. But I felt as if PC was now dividing itself into two separate stages. The first stage, in which racism was dragged into the open and rightly vilified, lent itself to angry, anti-white drama, an outpouring of our frustrations and white sympathy. The second, more interesting stage was beginning now the anger was abating, in which we could now explore deeper issues of identity with confidence and, we hope, humour. (*PC* 127–8)

While the sharp, satiric edge of her humour is blunted in her most recent *Bombay Dreams* (2002), bitter comedy lurks beneath the surface of the portrayal of the Kumars/Coopers in *Goodness Gracious Me* whose attempts at Anglicisation stem from a self-hatred partly induced by an outside world that does not accept them as they are.

---

[69] Meera Syal, *Auntie's Revenge*, unpublished play, 1993, 31.
[70] Rampton, 'No More Mrs. Patel for Meera', 45.

Syal is particularly insightful and inclusive in depicting the options available to British Asian women in relation to their cultures of origin and destination. This is where the comparison with Kureishi becomes especially relevant. To a greater extent than their predecessors, the British-born generation is positioned in a double bind between polarities of assimilation and abrogation vis à vis the dominant, white British culture, *and* the culture of origin. Kureishi embraces an aesthetic of ambiguity and attempts to transcend race, as Sammy's observation in his screenplay *Sammy and Rosie Get Laid* implies: 'Neither of us are English, we're Londoners you see.'[71] In this context, Kureishi's portrayals of going beyond race are a small step from affiliation to the dominant white culture. Syal attempts to blend aspects of both cultures together in a different way. What is distinctive about Syal's work is her disruption of these binary polarities projected for British Asians, women in particular. Assertions of cultural divergence from white British culture do not imply a complete acquiescence in all aspects of the culture of origin. Simultaneously, contesting and redefining what it means to be British Asian does not necessarily involve a total rejection of one's cultural heritage or suggest assimilation. This position of critique and redefining identities from *within* the British Asian community and home is a characteristic feature of Syal's aesthetic.

In Kureishi's *My Beautiful Laundrette* and *The Buddha of Suburbia*, rebellious Asian female protagonists Tania and Jamila find they cannot explore intellectual and sexual independence, while remaining within the family. Tania's departure leads Inderpal Grewal to argue that in *My Beautiful Laundrette* Kureishi 'does not do too well with feminist issues. The hero's cousin, a young girl who rejects the accepted role of women in both the English and Pakistani cultures, ultimately cannot be accommodated in the film. She disappears at a railway station, and this disappearance seems to be the only *solution* for a feminist Asian woman.'[72] Grewal's response points to the expectations of critics who seek overt political solutions, especially perhaps in a text authored by a minority artist. At one level, Tania's running away follows a clichéd trajectory of an Asian girl fleeing an oppressive family, although it can be argued that here Kureishi depicts the way some British Asian women are faced with such stark choices. Perhaps Kureishi suggests that leaving

---

[71] Hanif Kureishi, *Sammy and Rosie Get Laid* (London: Faber and Faber, 1988), 33.

[72] Inderpal Grewal, 'Salman Rushdie: Marginality, Women and *Shame*' in Fletcher (ed.), *Reading Rushdie*, 132 n. 12, emphasis mine.

home may be the 'solution' which underlines the way he gives you politics not in a way you want or expect. At the same time, responses such as Grewal's register an explicit disappointment that Kureishi fails to promote change or present alternative possibilities for circumventing cultural and sexual positioning. What Tania's disappearance makes clear is the way the film, and this is true of Kureishi's work in general, is not centrally interested in the women characters or what happens to them: Tania is already structurally marginalised in this narrative of the two male buddies. While Kureishi skilfully delineates complex, realistic Asian and white female characters and takes pains to empower them, often giving them the sharpest lines, they function primarily as foils to the men. His work is chiefly concerned with masculinity.[73]

In contrast Syal's work suggests that escape or exile is not the only alternative for British Asian women.[74] Although like Kureishi's, Syal's first play *One of Us* (1983) features a runaway Asian girl, her subsequent protagonists are all women who (like herself) have stayed close to the community while redefining what being an Asian woman means.[75] Yet this is not without cost. What becomes clear from Syal's female protagonists (and similar portrayals by contemporaries such as Gurinder Chadha) are the gendered and cultural expectations and roles from 'home' that are not merely rearticulated, but heightened in migration. These position some British Asian women in an especially painful intersection between the West and their ethnic background. Straddling these cultural divides, some live double lives, as Syal illustrates in her characterisation of young women in clandestine relationships like Hashida in *Bhaji on the Beach* and Tania in *Life isn't all Ha Ha, Hee Hee*. Or teenager Jes in Chadha's *Bend it Like Beckham*, who hides her football from her traditional parents, whilst negotiating the nightclub and undressing in the changing room with her peers with some trepidation.[76]

---

[73] For a contrasting view, see Elisabeth de Cacqueray, 'Constructions of Women in British Cinema: From Losey/Pinter's Modernism to the Postmodernism of Frears/Kureishi', *Caliban* 32 (1995), 109–20.

[74] This polarity used to be sometimes outlined for young Asian men as well as women, although it is increasingly challenged by subsequent generations. See Hiro's observation 'If an Asian youth wishes fully to adopt western values he has no alternative but to sever his connections with the family and totally disown his religious and cultural heritage.' Dilip Hiro, *Black British, White British* (London: Penguin, 1971), 170.

[75] Jacqui Shapiro and Meera Syal, *One of Us*, unpublished play, 1983.

[76] Non-South Asian filmmakers explore this straddling within British Muslim communities in *Yasmin*, dir. Kenny Glennan (2004) and *Ae Fond Kiss*, dir. Ken Loach (2004).

Syal's portrayals contest the patriarchal expectations imposed on Asian women by the majority community and their own communities. In the broader canvas of her second novel *Life,* a very different kind of novel to the autobiographical *Anita,* this is explored in the style of 'chick-lit' through the particular experiences of three very different middle-class thirty-something women from east London's British Asian community who have been childhood friends. The warm portrayal of their friendship is one way in which the text represents positive aspects of being Asian women. In distinct ways, they face the ways in which the socialisation of some British Asian women reproduces relations of domination and subordination. The novel charts naive Chila's growth to a feminist self-realisation as her marriage falls apart. Sunita's promising career as a lawyer seemed certain: now a dissatisfied mother she contemplates her vanished career, veering between guilt and the fear that she will end up like so many of her mother's friends, reeking of 'the sour, damp smell of unfulfilled potential' (*Life* 242). Tania, a chic TV producer with a white boyfriend, makes an analogous recognition of the way some British Asian women excel in the workplace and yet still attempt to fulfil certain ingrained expectations in the domestic space: 'We meet the world head up, head on, we meet our men and we bow down gratefully.... We hear our mothers' voices and heed them' (*Life* 145). Syal counters her emphasis on the performative nature of cultural and gendered identity with the insight that certain constructions of identity are harder to evade than others. Tania concludes: 'Everything else I can pick up or discard when I choose; my culture is a moveable feast. Except for this rogue gene which I would cauterize away if I could' (*Life* 146). Reconfiguring the patrilineal focus of the immigrant genre, Syal's sensitive portrait of the complexities of British Asian mother–daughter relationships depicts patriarchy, buttressed by tradition at its most insidious, effected not so much by sanctions and coercion, as by consent and compliance.

Syal presents these women's contestation of prescribed gender roles in ways that do not necessitate a self-distancing from one's culture. An example of the way this polarity is over-determined can be seen in the early British Asian film, *Majdhar* (1984), which depicts the 'progression' and 'independence' of the Asian female protagonist in terms of how Westernised she becomes.[77] British Asian women 'always proud to be who they were, but not scared to push back the boundaries' people Syal's texts (*Life* 84). This position is not confined to women.

[77] *Majdhar,* dir. Ahmed Jamal, Retake Film and Video Collective, 1984.

A sympathetic figure Dev, in her play *Blossom Time in Hanwell* (commissioned by the Royal Court Theatre in 1991), articulates a desire for the pursuit of individualism or 'personal selfishness' that does not involve an abrogation of culturally specific responsibilities: 'Putting the individual before the family, not in all cases, not neglecting the OAPs or that shit, but getting rid of this guilt we feel when we want to break the pattern our parents set up, challenge their beliefs.'[78]

Such balance, a perspective privileged in her writing, reflects Syal's own community, class, and religious background. Syal is anxious to emphasise her own family's progressive ethos: 'I found it a shock to hear about these families who treat their women in such a dogmatic way, and it is always the bad cases that get the most publicity.'[79] Kureishi depicts female characters from mostly working-class Pakistani Muslim families; their upbringing often contrasts with the relative freedom and autonomy allowed to other South Asian immigrant populations from various demographic groups, with differing cultural ideologies about women's roles. Stand-up comedian Shazia Mirza who mines her love–hate relationship with her Pakistani Muslim background in her comedy, observes how Syal 'had it easier'.[80]

## RE-THINKING GLOBAL SISTERHOOD: THE PROBLEMS OF EUROCENTRISM AND UNIVERSALISM

Nevertheless the assumption that an Asian feminist sensibility signifies a rejection of, or alienation from the culture of origin is a persistent one. In relation to Syal, it first surfaced in critical responses to her *My Sister-Wife* shown on BBC 2 in 1992, the first screenplay by an Asian female writer to be shown on British TV.[81] *The Times'* review suggests that 'Syal is clearly a feminist, certainly takes her ancestry pretty seriously, and is aware of the contradictions between those views.'[82] This kind of response needs to be contextualised with reference to the wider debates and contexts that operate on Syal's work, notably the Eurocentric, middle-class models of white feminism that began to be

---

[78] *Blossom Time in Hanwell*, unpublished play, 1991, 27. Hereafter *Blossom*.
[79] O'Connell, 'Meera Cracked', 16.     [80] Mirza, *The South Bank Show*.
[81] *My Sister-Wife*, dir. Lesley Manning, BBC 2, 24 Feb. 1992.
[82] Benedict Nightingale, 'A Wife in Two Worlds' *The Times* (24 Feb. 1992), 5.

questioned by black and Asian feminists in the 1980s. Syal also asserts the importance of Indian feminism. She cites *Manushi*, the first feminist journal published in India, as having one of the greatest influences on her political beliefs: 'each issue I tracked down was treasured. It made me realise that feminism was not a western invention.'[83] Hazel Carby's 'White Woman Listen! Black Feminism and the Boundaries of Sisterhood' (1982) is representative of the debates of this period. Carby writes: 'Feminist theory in Britain is almost wholly Eurocentric and, when it is not ignoring the experience of black women "at home", it is trundling "Third World women" onto the stage only to perform as victims of "barbarous" primitive societies.'[84]

Syal 'mirrors' both these specific local contexts and the particular nexus of problems facing black and Asian British feminists during this era. *My Sister-Wife* rehearses these debates and is a product of them. The screenplay was a co-operative production based on research by Asmaa Pirzada and Meera Syal with four sister-wives in London. The protagonist, Farah Khan (played by Syal), is an independent, articulate, young Westernised Pakistani businesswoman who falls obsessively in love with Asif, a married Muslim businessman, and agrees to become his second wife. The screenplay charts the gradual reversal of the two women's roles. The first wife, Maryam, becomes increasingly independent while Farah adopts the more traditional roles expected of South Asian women. *My Sister-Wife* attempts a delicate balance between de-centring ethnocentric models of love and marriage, critiquing competitive individualism, and Euro-American feminism, and relativist assumptions about polygamy, *without* reneging on the pain that arises from this arrangement. The tensions created by the situation are conveyed with subtlety and humour. The arrangement is impossible for British-born Farah, who married for love. But another more contented second wife contests the received idea that in such situations women are weak. Fawzia suggests that such a relationship needs reserves of strength: 'You think to share is a weak thing? . . . I understand. You have grown up in a selfish country. Me. Mine. This is all girls like you know' (*Sister-Wife* 140). The text exposes the hypocrisy of those who express horror at this arrangement, preferring to keep their 'mistresses' secret, hidden and separate. *The Times'* review

[83] Syal, 'Influences', 21.
[84] Hazel Carby, 'White Woman Listen! Black Feminism and the Boundaries of Sisterhood', in Mirza (ed.), *Black British Feminism*, 50.

phrases this point in such a way that it reinscribes the very hierarchy and abnormal/normal polarity that Syal's text attempts to subvert: 'The film . . . raises not just Muslim or Asian issues but much wider human ones. After all, extra unofficial wives are not unknown in *normal* British society.'[85] Asif rebukes both his Pakistani and white friends: '(Asif turns to first man) What take Glenda, the discipline Queen, home to meet Sufia? (Asif turns to the white man) Or maybe drag your secretary back for a game of strip scrabble with Susan? I am honest with my wife. Suppose that's my burden, coming from a primitive culture' (*Sister-Wife* 119). Interestingly, these scripted lines were excised from the version aired on BBC television.

At the same time, Asif is exposed as patriarchal, callous, and insensitive to both women, in making Maryam abort their female child and ignoring Farah's needs. It is Asif who has the 'best of both worlds', and the arrangement results in the two women fighting a self-destructive battle over him. Maryam and Farah compete for Asif's love by trying to produce a male heir, underlining the degree to which they are enmeshed in patriarchy. The text offers no solutions but tends towards a nuanced critique of polygamy. Syal suggests that the script 'took a polygamous set-up in a wealthy family as a metaphor for the painful adaptation processes facing women of my generation' (*PC* 127). Syal refers to the leap from arranged marriages to dating. This is the first generation of women who are faced with conflicting models of marriage, a clash that preoccupies Syal's narratives, influenced perhaps by her own Hindu father and Sikh mother's 'love' marriage, uncommon for their generation.[86] Asif's simultaneous attraction to Maryam's self-effacing behaviour, domesticity, and traditional dress (visualised in his fascination with her anklets) *and* to Farah's confidence as a working woman illustrates graphically the dual roles and conflicting expectations foisted on British Asian women today. The screenplay makes the point that minority women are affected by two sets of gender-relations, and gendered expectations; this is not the case for women of the dominant ethnic majority. These conflicts form the subject of her play *Blossom Time in Hanwell* (1991). The play provides a critique of aspects of arranged marriages while subverting dominant representations of the tradition, at the same time highlighting ethnocentric white feminism's blindness to the subordination of women in Western forms of courtship, preferring

---

[85] Peter Lewis, 'The Man with Two Wives', *The Times* (18 Feb. 1992), 5, emphasis mine.
[86] Meera Syal, *Who Do You Think You Are*? BBC 2, 24 Sept. 2004.

to focus exclusively on the control of women in arranged marriages. The play centres on two British Asian women in their thirties, who meet at Mrs Bagsheet's dating agency and decide to set up their own agency that will enable British Asian women of their generation to find partners who share their competing affiliations. The two women are financially independent 'career women', which undermines the traditional/modern (read Westernised) polarity vis à vis arranged marriages. Mrs Bagsheet observes:

'I see girls like you every day and know what conflicts are tearing you apart. . . . You girls come looking in here for love, or what you think is love. You read your *Cosmopolitans* and watch those soapy operas and think you can marry the man who makes your knees tremble and your heart go pit-a pat.' (*Blossom* 20)

This comment draws attention to the powerful influences of liberal ideologies of romance and courtship. *Blossom* is a critique of women as commodities in a 'free' consumer culture. These young women are positioned between two different forms of control. The play both satirises the way women are 'marketed' to men in the agency, and at the same time demonstrates that the positive relationship between Prem and Sweetie (whose marriage was arranged by Mrs Bagsheet) is far from the mainstream media's horror stories of arranged marriages.

## RE-FRAMING REPRESENTATIONS OF BRITISH ASIAN WOMEN

Syal's subsequent screenplay, *Bhaji on the Beach* (1993), articulates a wide range of gender issues. In the film *My Beautiful Laundrette*, Tania bares her breasts to her father's friends in an act of defiance of gendered expectations that nonetheless positions her literally in the voyeuristic gaze of white male fantasies of the sexually exotic other. In contrast *Bhaji* affirms the subjectivities of Syal's female protagonists, who are not the objects of a male phallocentric gaze. It primarily explores how women see themselves. *Bhaji* spans three generations, exploring the discoveries that nine Asian women experience during a day trip, organised by the earnest feminist Simi of the Saheli Women's Centre, to the quintessentially English seaside town of Blackpool (though its gaudiness instantly reminds the socialite Rekha of Mumbai). This setting has nothing of the exotic filter, which characterises the documentary's usually fetishistic approach to Other cultures. The film portrays the diversity of the community and the discrete ways in which Asian women of different generations have adapted to life in Britain. This is no simple 'sisterhood', despite Simi's invocation of female solidarity: 'This is your day. Have a female fun time!' (*Bhaji* 1). The characters range from boy-crazy teenagers Ladhu and Madhu, who are into bhangra and rap, to unfulfilled, middle-aged newsagents, and disapproving, small-minded old ladies in saris. On this eventful day, Hashida, an aspiring medical student, faces bigotry from this older generation of 'Aunties' when she discovers she is pregnant by her secret African-Caribbean boyfriend: 'Why a black boy? What's wrong with our men? And what will the child be? Dark and all mixed up!' (*Bhaji* 31). Characteristically, the film closes with the possibility that Hashida does not have to lose her boyfriend Oliver or her 'folks or them damn aunties either' (*Bhaji* 47).

As a self-conscious feminist statement, the film ridicules attempts to view women through stereotypical, patriarchal, ethnocentric ways of seeing. The way older Asian women are viewed as delicate, exotic and in need of protection is satirised in the encounter between Asha and the foppish 'actor, historian and ancient Blackpudlian' who tries to woo her (*Bhaji* 31). White male fetishising of South Asian women is a preoccupation of all Syal's work. *Blossom* contests white male perceptions of Asian women as 'untarnished by feminism' (*Blossom* 29). In *Life*, the novel form allows a glimpse into white male fantasises about Asian women 'serving him a home-made korma and then leading him to a silk-lined bedroom . . . taking him through a few positions in the *Kama Sutra*' (*Life* 54). This parody mocks the racialisation of gender relations in the Western world and shows how ideologies of race, gender, and sexuality reinforce each other. Patriarchal modes of seeing women within the Asian community are revealed as stemming from the desire to control and subordinate. *Life* juxtaposes the contradiction behind Deepak's colourful past and the pleasure he takes in his more conservative wife Chila, who is only accessible to his gaze, as his property. Like their female counterparts, two models of gender-relations affect Westernised Asian men, but the men occupy a more empowered position in relation to these models, as Syal examines in this novel.

In *Bhaji*, Ginder has taken refuge from her abusive husband Ranjith in a shelter for women. Ranjith is goaded into 'reclaiming' his wife, who is perceived by his family as the receptacle of their honour. The treatment and impact of domestic violence is particularly complex and nuanced.

The pressures (and the appeal of family) exerted by the presence of children, the interference of the extended families and the expectation for women 'to put up and shut up', are subtly delineated (*Bhaji* 444). This makes Ginder's final reconciliation with her husband the film's most ambivalent aspect. At the close of the film, Ranjith is publicly shamed when Ginder's previously concealed bruises are accidentally exposed, and his Aunt Asha chastises him. Nevertheless, Ginder is persuaded to return to him and to the institution of marriage and family that has been revealed as oppressive and patriarchal. In this way, *Bhaji* stops short of a radical reconceptualisation of gender-relations, reflecting a compromised form of feminism, shaped perhaps by the desire of the filmmakers to pitch this film to a broad-based audience.

## BRITISH ASIAN WOMEN, COMMUNITY, AND THE POLITICS OF REPRESENTATION

Although on the whole British Asian responses to *Bhaji* were positive, certain reactions highlight the implications of the shift Syal's work embodies: moving from the problems of how Asians are perceived to an examination of problems in the community, making her comparable to Kureishi.[87] As Syal suggests, the two are interrelated because 'how you are seen forces you to question what and who you are' (*PC* 127). The issues are linked in another way in relation to audience: giving the inner struggles a wider political platform affects how the community is seen and treated by the majority community. This is the essence of the hostile response of an Asian man to *Bhaji*, whom Syal cites in her essay as 'Mr. Angry of Luton' (*PC* 131). He censures Syal for showing 'our women doing such things. Showing them as frustrated when we are fighting to hold on to our culture? Painting our men as violent when the *real* violence is against us by white people?' (*PC* 131, emphasis mine). At one level these objections can be refuted easily. This response invites a reversal of the very point of departure that her work marks: a shift from a focus on white racism to the threats women face from within the community

---

[87] Farrah Anwar's review compares *Bhaji on the Beach* favourably to Kureishi's televised *Buddha of Suburbia*. Farrah Anwar, 'Bhaji on the Beach (review)', *Sight and Sound* 4.2 (1994), 48. However, Syal refers to criticisms she received because she tackled taboo subjects of violence, sex, and pregnancy in 'Interview with Alison Oddey', in Alison Oddey (ed.), *Performing Women: Stand-ups, Strumpets and Itinerants* (Basingstoke: Macmillan, 1999), 61.

in terms of sexist and violent practices. An exclusive focus on white racism deflects attention from the critique of masculinist violence. His response hierarchises domestic violence as less 'real' than racial violence. At the same time, it advances a similar argument as Jamal's regarding *My Beautiful Laundrette*: interrogating the implications of exposing certain sexist forms of oppression or racism within black communities in a context where they can be manipulated by a racist society. This epitomises the dilemma of the black or Asian feminist: required to say nothing about such practices, or expose what could be used to pathologise the community. There is no safe position from which you can condemn such forms of oppression (especially culturally specific ones) *and* racist portrayals. Syal thematises this very problem in her novel *Life*. While she creates characters that adopt forms of self-censorship, Syal does not. Sunita plans to expose hospitals that refuse to tell pregnant Asian women the sex of their baby. Then she hears about a special clinic advertised in an Asian community newspaper where they guarantee you can have a boy: 'And there I was, back in the grey area again, caught out by the enemy within. There wasn't any point pursuing it after that' (*Life* 231).

## THE CONTRASTING RECEPTIONS OF KUREISHI AND SYAL

Although more careful not to dismiss such hostile responses to her work, Syal is no less compromising on issues of censorship than Kureishi leading her to ask somewhat rhetorically: '. . . maybe trying to have an honest dialogue about what is happening within our community while it is being attacked from outside is foolish. But what are the alternatives? Writing the safe characters that offend no one and say nothing? Or, in this atmosphere of fear, is the real alternative silence?' (*PC* 132). Yet Syal's portrayals have not provoked nearly the same degree of hostility amongst minority audiences. There are several factors that contribute to their different reception. Kureishi's mixed-race background has structured some culturally specific responses to his work. Paradoxically, especially at the outset, Kureishi was enough of an insider to be seen by his Western readers as an authoritative translator and an authentic 'voice from the ghetto'.[88] For some white (largely American) critics the objectivity

---

[88] Noakes, 'Anthem for Doomed Youth?', 1427.

and clarity of his perceptions and his outsider/insider position is doubly determined by his mixed parentage: 'Kureishi's liminal position betwixt and between British and Pakistani worlds enables him to see through each with dangerous clarity.' An early review in the *New York Times* underlines how Kureishi's mixed descent immediately positions him as objective: 'Had *My Beautiful Laundrette* been written by anybody but the London-born Mr. Kureishi, whose father was Pakistani and mother was English, the film would possibly seem racist.'[89] Conversely some British Asian filmmakers and critics such as Chadha suggest that 'he's quite isolated from the Asian side of himself . . . one criticism is that he's used that side of him without real cultural integrity. He's used it to fulfil the briefs of the Max Stafford Clarkes.'[90] Such anxiety over the 'cultural integrity' of the mixed-race writer and cultural ownership suggest that disputes over representation include such proprietorial attempts to demarcate who should profit from the wavering value of minority culture.

Notwithstanding Syal's ironic narrative tone, her portrayals of Asian communities characterised by a warmth and depth make her criticisms more palatable. In contrast to Kureishi, she maintains a critique laced with penetrating humour that does not become ironic distance. Anita Roy suggests that unlike *The Buddha of Suburbia*, in *Anita and Me* 'Meena's journey to worldly wisdom never descends to bleak, biting satire, and the characters from both communities are portrayed with affection.'[91] At times Kureishi's ironic detachment in his work that ostensibly deals with the objectification of ethnic minorities, underlines his own objectifications. Syal's explicitly feminist thrust contrasts with Kureishi's ambivalent treatment of women and identifies a constituency of Asian and other women readers that Kureishi may not share. The popularity of Syal's novels is part of the proliferation of novels by women for increasingly lucrative female readerships over the last decade. Her novels are also less literary and more accessible than Kureishi's.

Other contextual factors play a large role in their contrasting receptions. For Syal, writing in the 1990s, Britain (in terms of cultural representation and literary fashion at least) is very different from the mid-1980s when Kureishi first came to the fore and British Asian identity

[89] Donald Weber, ' "No Secrets Were Safe from Me": Situating Hanif Kureishi', *The Massachusetts Review* 38.1 (1997),127. Vincent Canby, ' "Laundrette" Social Comedy Sleeper', *New York Times*, (7 Mar. 1986), 31.
[90] Cited in Farrah Anwar, 'Is There a Sodomite in the House?' *Guardian* (7 Aug. 1992), 29.
[91] Anita Roy, 'rev. of *Anita and Me*', *Times Literary Supplement* (5 Apr. 1996), 26.

was considered problematic. To an extent this wider representation makes the issue of representation less fraught than it was over a decade before. Furthermore, as Judith Williamson observes, 'the more power any group has to create and wield representations, the less it is required to *be* representative.'[92] So the relative positions of the different sections of the Asian community described by Syal and Kureishi must be taken into account when evaluating their different receptions. Syal's writings and that of her co-writers on *Goodness Gracious Me* and *The Kumars* primarily satirise their Punjabi Hindu community, who are on the whole more prosperous and less alienated than the Pakistani and Bangladeshi Muslim communities that are Kureishi's subject.[93]

As certain responses to Monica Ali's Booker-nominated portrayal of a cross-section of east London's Bengalis in her first novel *Brick Lane* (2003) suggest, the correlation between disempowerment, alienation, and disputes over the burden of representation remains very much alive, almost two decades after Kureishi's *Laundrette*. Speaking on behalf of some members of the neighbourhood in the East End of London that inspired the novel, the Greater Sylhet Welfare and Development Council (GSWDC), branded it as a 'despicable insult' to Bangladeshis living in the area, and in Bangladesh, particularly the Sylhetis. Tellingly, their main point of contention is their perception that the novel portrays Bangladeshis as 'backward, uneducated and unsophisticated'. As we saw with Kureishi, the reception of mixed-race Monica Ali's novel appears to fall into similar polarities of 'Tell us about them' and 'What gives you the right to write about us?'[94] For instance D. J. Taylor assumes that 'If Monica Ali wants to write about Brick Lane, *which as a Bangladeshi she presumably knows a good deal about*, then she should be free to do so.' On the other hand, the GSWDC argue 'It is a completely stereotypical view of Bangladeshis living in Brick Lane and one we simply do not recognise.'[95]

However, such media attention on the conservative views of the vocal, mostly male, self-appointed 'community leaders' erases the spectrum of diverse responses of distinct class, ethnic, regional, and gendered

[92] Cited in Kobena Mercer 'Recoding Narratives of Race and Nation', in Mercer (ed.), *Black Film, British Cinema*, 12.

[93] Unemployment stands at 8% for Indians and at 21% for Pakistanis and Bangladeshis: the highest of all Britain's ethnic minorities. Office for National Statistics, Labour Force Survey (1992–9).

[94] Monica Ali, 'Where I'm coming from', *Guardian* (17 June 2003), online edition.

[95] Cited in Matthew Taylor, 'Brickbats fly as community brands novel "despicable"', *Guardian* (3 Dec. 2003), online edition, emphasis mine.

British Asian groupings. Ali's unadorned, moving portrait of her young Muslim female protagonist Nazneen's gradual transformation from self-abnegation to self-possession is very popular amongst young Asian women, and has won warm praise from artists Shazia Mirza and Syal. Again, the mostly male Sikh community leaders' violent protests against Gurpreet Kaur Bhatti's play *Behzti* (*Behzti* means Dishonour in Punjabi) depicting rape and murder in a *gurdwara* led to its closure in Birmingham in December 2004. While the politics of representation stems from the politics of race, perhaps the wider rise of the cult of the author in Britain, and elsewhere, also contributes to the continued positioning of minority writers as representative of their communities by both majority and minority readerships.

With reference to the largely positive response from the Asian community to the parody of Asians in *Goodness Gracious Me*, Syal claims that 'it is a sign of maturity, confidence and security when a community is able to laugh at itself and acknowledge some truth in certain stereotypes'.[96] 'It . . . shows a community is able to come to a point of settlement and some degree of contentment with themselves that they are able to take a parody.'[97] Clearly certain groupings within the British Asian population are in a better position to be confident and secure than others. In a recent Commission for Racial Equality (CRE) survey of young black and Asian peoples' perceptions of racism, the majority felt they faced less intolerance than their parents' generation, which partly endorses Syal's statement. However, the report also showed that the younger Muslims in the group were acutely aware of the stereotypes of Islam that prevail in British society. They were at pains to emphasise the positive aspects of their religion. Syal suggests that subsequent generations of British Asians are more confident about their own cultural heritage than her own: 'They are defying all the predictions about the poor, lost mongrel generation. Many of them are sticking very firmly to the good bits of the culture and are very proud of who they are, much more than my generation.'[98] In *Life*, Tania reinforces this progressive trajectory, although her observation is framed by the ironic self-awareness that every generation thinks they had it tough and were 'pioneers':

The teenagers lounged easily against each other, the girls in customized Punjabi suits, cut tight, set off by big boots and leather jackets; others in sari blouses

---

[96] Randeep Ramesh, 'British, Asian and Hip', *Independent* (1 Mar. 1998), 20.
[97] Jasper Rees, 'Asian Screen Cred', *Times* (30 Oct. 1999), 29.
[98] O'Connell, 'Meera Cracked', 16.

twinned with khakis and platform trainers. Some of them smoked. They weren't looking over their shoulders wondering who was watching. When did it become easier? Tania wondered with a sharp stab of envy. She had a powerful urge to tell them that if it hadn't been for her and the mini-wars she had fought on this road, maybe they wouldn't be loafing in their mix and match fashions listening to their masala music with not a care in the world . . . when she realised she sounded like her dead mother. (*Life* 42–3)

Such confidence eludes the second-generation Muslims cited above. More recently, *Brick Lane* and Nadeem Aslam's *Maps for Lost Lovers* (2004) recreate self-enclosed, separate British Muslim communities, a world apart, that modifies the perspectives developed in novels like Syal's, suggesting the range of different experiences. Like Ali's novel, Tanika Gupta's play *Fragile Land* (2002) set in a post-9/11 political landscape, explores British Asian teenagers' experiences of disaffection, radical Islam, and Islamophobia marking a shift to Asian identities rooted in religion, rather than race.

Although the CRE survey supports Syal's claim regarding *Goodness Gracious Me*'s popularity among Asian viewers, significantly, the satire of religion remained fraught. The Broadcasting Standards Commission upheld 'in part' the complaints of twelve viewers who said that the 'religious symbol of the Hindu faith was unacceptably mocked' in one episode.[99] Equally, some Catholic viewers objected to the parody of the Kumars/Coopers taking communion in church. Moreover anxieties over how the comedy would be interpreted by the white population persist:

Goodness Gracious Me was liked . . . it showed Asian people in a wide range of roles without taking itself too seriously. The only concern expressed about using humour in this way was that, while Black and Asian people might see the joke, White people might take it to be a true representation of the group in Britain.[100]

The comedy directed at both majority and minority communities may make the satire of the white British more palatable for the latter. The comedy of reversal in the now legendary satirical sketch of drunken Asians 'going for an English' at the Mount Batten Restaurant in Mumbai, harassing the English waiter and asking for 'the blandest thing on the menu', has become a classic, searing the national consciousness,

[99] Randeep Ramesh, 'Goodness Gracious Me! Heard the One about the Funny Asian?', *Independent* (29 June 1998), 11.

[100] CRE, 'Stereotyping and Racism in Britain: An Attitude Survey', *Impact* (Oct./Nov. 1999), 41.

whilst entering the comic lexicon: effective without being didactic.[101] The producer, Anil Gupta, delineates the strategy behind the comedy of reversal: 'If we'd done it as white people that would just put people's backs up; they don't want to be lectured. This way you make the Indian angle more accessible. It's easier to see the absurdities of what you do when you watch other people doing it.'[102] At the same, challenging the complacencies of the Asian viewers appears equally important. But, as with Kureishi, the question remains, can parody be subversive? This is inextricably entwined with questions of audiences and reception. The impacts of portrayals are still determined by the group's relative power and position in society, because they are released into a context where there has been a history of systematic discrimination against Asians in Britain and not the other way round. This must be taken into account, however much the comedy show may laugh at white British paternalism and shallowness. The inroads into mainstream popular culture and the 'hideously white' BBC and publishing industry should not be overstated; we need to examine the extent to which such inroads have initiated meaningful shifts in cultural hierarchies. For instance, Chadha's films *What's Cooking* (2000) and *Bend it Like Beckham* (2003) produced in the wake of *Goodness Gracious Me*'s mainstream success draws not only on its sitcom aesthetic—the three Asian girls' disdain for Jess's lack of interest in clothes and men recall similar sketches from *Goodness Gracious Me*—but also on the conventions that structure this kind of ethnic comedy: humour generated from generational conflicts, and directed particularly at the responses of older Asian characters. *Bend it Like Beckham*'s melodramatic mother figure comes across as a tired caricature: yet such conventions make these filmic texts familiar, decipherable, and popular with mainstream audiences. In this way, as I suggested in the opening chapter, questions of literary fashion remain relevant to contemporary British South Asian cultural forms which are in part produced for the market.

A comparison of Kureishi and Syal points to the broad, fluid spectrum of opinion, identity and experiences that constitute being of Asian origin in Britain. This is reinforced in turn by the different concerns, forms, and styles adopted by younger British-born writers. The magic realist flourishes of Hari Kunzru's postmodern satire *The Impressionist* contrast with slow pace, concern for character, and commitment to narrative

---

[101] *Goodness Gracious Me*, dir. Anil Gupta, BBC 2, 21 Oct. 1998.
[102] Rampton, 'A Message to Take Away', 68.

in Ali's *Brick Lane*. The diverse spectrum of identity and multiple affiliations amongst the new crop of writers, actors, and musicians underlines that 'British Asian' has as many identities as its constituents, and points to the new directions in British Asian cultural production that have challenged the earlier models developed in the 1980s and 1990s. Neil Biswas/Jon Sen's TV drama *Second Generation* (2003) represents a recent manifestation of a younger, emergent, and vigorous British Asian culture, entwining the club and music-obsessed world of a new breed of British Asians, various shades of generational and racial clash, with the specific experiences of young British Asians growing up bi-culturally in the twenty-first century. These new cultural formations often acknowledge the weight of the past whilst mapping new alignments of the future.

These British writers' cultural production is not necessarily 'Asian'. They justifiably resent being courted only to represent and popularise British Asian experiences. Like their forerunners they wish to transcend race, religion, class, and culture and tell 'universal' stories, an aspiration that is no longer synonymous with 'white', thanks in great measure to their predecessors.

# Afterword: Made in Britain

SALMAN RUSHDIE: 'I never thought of myself as coming from any race, let alone an inferior one, until I arrived in Britain.'

JATINDER VERMA: 'Growing up in British-ruled Kenya, despite speaking Punjabi at home, my education and literary references were English. Suddenly I arrived in Britain and realised it's not who you are in particular that's important, it's what you represent—the unwanted black mass. This pushed me towards a fascination with India . . . gave me freedom. Britain made me—my work is unashamedly exotic, foreign, alien.'

MEERA SYAL: 'When people ask you "Why don't you go back to where you come from?" You need to know the answer . . . whether it's historically, emotionally, spiritually you need to know . . . because you'll be asked that question all your life.'[1]

What connects these diverse South Asian diasporic writers most prominently appears to be their encounter with mainstream, mostly white British culture: spurring them to create, artistically express, and explore their cross-cultural identities. Across the generations, these writers define their cultural identity in direct response to their cultural contact or various receptions in Britain. From Tambimuttu's writings to Kureishi's and Syal's we have seen that the process of cultural translation involves, not simply the selective transfer from one culture to another, but a cross-cultural confrontation that often includes an invention, imitation or creation of identity for these writers. This impacts on different generations in diverse ways.

Situating succeeding generations of South Asian diasporic writers and their reception culturally and historically, illustrates the shifting processes of cultural translation, that both historicise *and* shape distinct perceptions of cultural difference, and moments of potential

[1] Rushdie, interview with Joan Bakewell, *Heart of the Matter*, BBC 2, 10 July 1988, BBC TV Archives. Jatinder Verma, interview with Rukhasana Mosam, *Bazaar* (1991), 18, 20. Syal, *Who Do You Think You Are*? BBC 2, 24 Sept. 2004.

integration negotiated on specific terms. Tracing such changes enables us to chart a history of the ideological construction of racial Others. Broadly speaking, the dynamics of colonial constructions of racial Others impact most obviously, but not exclusively, on the early, culturally colonised migrants like Chaudhuri and Markandaya. Their work and reception reveal the colonial mindset of absolute difference: an outlook internalised by Chaudhuri and Markandaya as evinced by their differing internalisations of racial inferiority, and efforts to assimilate into monocultural English literary traditions. Other writers such as Anand contested this outlook in a bid to achieve moral equivalence. At the same time, Tambimuttu's reception reflects a version of primitivism, a valorising of authentic differences to provide a critique of the host society's limitations. Tambimuttu's imitative or 'false' self-translation enacts 'the trap of specularity'. Younger writers for their part firmly repudiate older forms of racism, exploring and celebrating permeable cultural boundaries rather than fixed differences. Bhabha and Rushdie reciprocally argue that cultural identities cannot be ascribed to pre-given, irreducible, scripted, ahistorical cultural traits that define the conventions of ethnicity. Nor can 'coloniser' and 'colonised' be viewed as separate entities that define themselves independently. Self-consciously contesting originary notions of authentic culture, their theoretical insights on the construction of culture, and the invention of tradition, were particularly serviceable to the first generation of British-born Asians. In contrast to first-generation migrant writers, this generation knew no other home: schooled in 1970s Britain and often marginalised, with little cultural representation of their backgrounds, they 'had to construct themselves from scratch' as Dhondy's protagonist suggests. Kureishi's Karim similarly concludes: 'if I wanted the additional personality bonus of an Indian past, I would have to create it' (*Buddha* 213). With an imaginative range uncontained by the colonial past, the British-born writers convey how these negotiations of cultural identity are played out by minority communities, involving a continual interface and exchange of cultural performances that in turn produce a mutual and mutable recognition or representation of cultural difference. Kureishi's contrasting representations of British Muslim identity as fixed and not open to renegotiation, by contrast, uncritically mirror destructive hierarchies of race, class, and religion inscribed in contemporary British culture.

Within and across the generations we see a simultaneous desire to domesticate the foreign and savour its exotic Otherness, a desire to which these migrant texts conform but which they also contest.

Markandaya's novels emphasise commonality and a 'normative' universality while reproducing the culture of origin as an exotic object for Western consumption. Sivanandan's representations of Sri Lanka are less straightforwardly shaped to meet the demands of metropolitan publishers and consumers. Rushdie tilted at the mythology of a homogenous English culture by insisting on and asserting the processes of cultural hybridisation, creatively exploring the way 'English' cultural identity is being transformed by encounters with transnational migrant communities, and that we are all plural beings. The hybridity of 'home'-colonised cultures is different in kind, rather than degree, to that of the British-born generation. First-generation migrant authors like Rushdie self-consciously mediate between and translate cultures, and in different ways constantly refer back to a point of origin, unlike the British-born generations who foreground networks rather than roots. Entering a context that has already been transformed by migrants, Syal and Kureishi are not actively hybridising British culture in the manner of Rushdie. Instead they turn their attention to exploring the diversity of immigrant lives in Britain and to aspects such as conflicts within British Asian communities. The British-born writers' integration is symbolised by their lighter humour and their shift to popular culture, which is above all what distinguishes this generation's cultural production. This move underscores the degree to which they are working from *within* mainstream British culture and the degree to which they have adopted the resources of British cultural traditions. Their use of satire contrasts with Sivanandan's oppositional practices, rooted in older terms of anti-colonial struggle and liberation. Analogously, while Kureishi and Syal penetrated mainstream media, creating a niche for minority arts within mainstream institutions, Sivanandan had literally to create an institutional space from which to articulate his critiques of British society.

This study identifies the anomalies of individual historical moments as well as the salient literary themes and preoccupations, such as the complex relationship between acculturation and assertion of cultural difference, and formulation of alternative models of identity and belonging that have crossed time and space. Juxtaposing the array of writers makes explicit chains of influences, illuminating affinities and literary echoes across and within the different generations. Kureishi both parodies and repeats Tambimuttu's deployment of and resistance to cultural difference. Chaudhuri's preoccupations reverberate in Naipaul; his idiosyncrasies are fictionally recreated in Rushdie's Saladin Chamcha. Chaudhuri's formal experiments with the auto-biographical form are played out differently in Rushdie's literary experimentation with versions of himself in his characterisation of Chamcha and *Shame*'s author-narrator. Naipaul's sense of rootlessness had a decisive effect on Rushdie's and Bhabha's ideas about dislocation and cosmopolitanism. Rushdie casts the widest shadow. Tensions in his work have bred a range of narratives. Writers such as Aamer Hussein, Sunetra Gupta, and Romesh Gunesekera adopt and modify his concern to create an aesthetic out of homelessness, and to explore the complexity of difference, assimilation, and modernity. In diverse ways, they too fictionalise the interplay between countries of origin and destination as separate but interconnecting worlds, amalgamating a desire for a certain kind of homeland with the brutal recreations of aspects of modern Indian, Pakistan, and Sri Lanka.

In contrast, Sivanandan and Dhondy were at first primarily engaged with effecting social and political change in Britain before imaginatively reclaiming their former homelands in fictional narratives that intersect with certain typologies of Rushdie's fiction. Rushdie's essays and especially *Satanic Verses*, Dhondy's stories, and Kureishi's and Syal's plays and films suggest other shared, reciprocal agendas formed by the cultural experience of the 1980s: the race politics and the fracturing of common black identity theorised by Stuart Hall and Homi Bhabha amongst others. As Bhabha observes: 'How do strategies of representation or empowerment come to be formulated in the competing claims of communities where, despite shared histories of deprivation and discrimination, the exchange of values, meanings and priorities may not always be collaborative and dialogical, but may be profoundly antagonistic, conflictual and even incommensurable?'[2] Generational differences are not straightforward. Juxtaposing Chaudhuri and Syal, who though living and writing contemporaneously remain ideologically decades apart, provides an index of the range and diversity of Asian writers in Britain. At the same time, Tagore's wry observations (made during a visit to London in 1879) lampooning 'the ingabanga—the England-worshipping Bengali' who would have to 'use smelling salts . . . if he saw you happen to use the wrong knife to eat fish', have a curious afterlife over a century later in *Goodness Gracious Me*'s satirical

---

[2] Homi Bhabha, *The Location of Culture* (London: Routledge, 1990), 2.

spoof of the Kumars'/Coopers' extreme, spectacularly hopeless brand of assimilation.[3]

While I argue that figures like Rushdie, Dhondy, and Kureshi have had an enormous impact on succeeding generations of writers, this is less true for the earlier figures. In this context this study calls for a reassessment of the term 'South Asian' as a generic category, particularly given the complexity and diversity of these texts as I suggested in Chapter 1. While 'South Asian' enables the cluster of texts to be discussed together in this study, it also begs the question of a formative literary tradition and history. Yet to some extent 'South Asian' is a categorisation that does not assume literary continuity and tradition but is rather a marketing and conceptual category that enables the analysis of texts and consumption of texts, including criticism, in particular ways.

Recent commentators argue persuasively against reading black and Asian writing as 'a species of journalism'.[4] Undoubtedly, considering these writers solely in extra-literary terms would constitute a form of ethnic 'pigeon-holing', sidelining them as only speaking to minority readerships and interests. Yet what emerges from this history of production and consumption is the connection of these narratives, often stitched out of real life stories, not only to political realities, but also to changing social climes, fashions, and publishing trends. If the mainstream media foregrounds representational rather than textual complexity, at present, postcolonial literary criticism remains confined within the parameters of the textual paradigm, evading the significance of the material historical contexts of literary production and consumption. My analysis of these writers' literary products as a sociological phenomenon unmasks the complicity of publishing and review apparatuses in their selection, dissemination, and consumption, attesting how these texts were and continue to be informed and shaped by the demands of the mainstream. My study shows the ways in which publishers' ideas of public taste in the book market governed the kind of material they would accept and how it led them to encourage different kinds of writing from their authors, according to the shifting interests and cultural expectations of different periods. At the same time, my discussion of the complex and non-obvious ways in which some of

---

[3] Tagore, Letters and Notes, reprinted in *Away*, ed. Amitava Kumar (Routledge: London, 2004), 75.

[4] Sukhdev Sandhu, *London Calling: How Black and Asian Writers Imagined A City* (London: HarperCollins, 2003).

these writers respond to changing national politics and to progressive ideologies within Britain disrupts homogenising notions of 'dominant' expectations and unsettles assumptions of the centre's unity and fixity.

If, as is argued here, the production and consumption of South Asian cultural production is contingent on a situational ethic that is constantly changing, this raises deeply vexed questions about the 'representative' role of such a migrant or minority writer. My study of the imbrication of fiction and cultural history in the shifting constructions of South Asian Anglophone cultural identity delineates the transformation of the role of the postcolonial writer of South Asian origin. Up to the time of Independence, South Asian Anglophone writers were clearly positioned: Anand versus Chaudhuri for instance. In the transitional period that followed Independence, other issues emerge, particularly over the author's geopolitical location, audience, and writing in English. What kind of writer are you? What gives you the right to write the nation? Who are you writing for, and as? Anthropological specimen? Native informant? Cultural ambassador? Anti-racist activist? Questions over the moral, ethical duties and political roles of the South Asian Anglophone writer straddling cultural boundaries impinge, albeit in different ways, on the younger first- and second-generation writers, with the desire to confound and invert stereotypes becoming eclipsed in their representations of Asians with particular histories. Some of these cultural productions marked the British Asian community's dialogue with itself, raising the question 'South Asia for whom?' Equally, their individual stories with wider resonance shift perceptions of what constitutes contemporary British writing. Early writers negotiated their designation as cultural translators to break into cloistered Western literary establishments, and reach an international audience. Decades later, seeking to tap the rich vein of his British Asian background, Kureishi adopted the role of translator in his early plays. Yet he insists on his right to examine wider society: 'I want to feel free to not only be an Asian writer' but 'a writer who is also Asian'.[5] The difficulties in achieving this aim become apparent in the critical puzzlement that first greeted Kureshi's move away from ethnic or racial themes. Reviews of the short stories *Love in a Blue Time* (1997) that first marked this shift frequently single-out for praise the few stories that deal with race: 'only the stories which relate personal dilemmas to

[5] Colin McCabe, 'Interview: Hanif Kureishi on London', *Critical Quarterly*, 41.3 (1999), 52 , 49, 52.

the larger contexts of race achieve a choked, baffled power.'[6] Similarly, a review favourably contrasts Kureishi's autobiographical essay *The Rainbow Sign,* for its 'elliptical brilliance about being at once English and Asian', with *The Buddha of Suburbia* where 'such challenging topics bob tantalizingly into view . . . and as quickly vanish'.[7] His recent exclusive focus on relationships and modern urban experiences mark his refusal to remain within the confines of the designation, a cultural shift reflected in his successors.

Regardless of such transformations, this history of their reception has shown how South Asian migrant and minority writers continue to be positioned as authoritative insiders, an integral part of the burden of representation. Paradoxically they are simultaneously heralded as 'objective' outsiders on cultural borders 'looking in': observing their countries and cultures of 'origin' and destination with the detachment of distance and revealing 'true' insights. Local South Asian critics and minority readerships vociferously contest this notion. Such a construction does not take into account the ways in which these writers' perceptions of all these subjects are themselves shaped by dominant ways of knowing: successive generations become increasingly integrated within Britain, which compromises the degree to which they can claim external perspectives. Finally, this historicised account of the contexts of South Asian Anglophone literary production and reception testifies to the importance of the achievement, however ambivalent, of the early, now generally overlooked, migrants who wrote in inimical climates and paved the way for younger writers like Rushdie, and who deserve greater recognition than is customarily given by those living in the very different conditions of the twenty-first century.

[6] Sean O'Brien, 'Love in a Blue Time', *Times Literary Supplement,* (28 Mar. 1997), 20.
[7] Neil Berry, 'Conquerors of the Capital', *Times Literary Supplement,* (30 Mar. 1990), 339.

# Bibliography

## UNPUBLISHED ARCHIVAL MATERIAL

**Allen and Unwin Ltd., MS 3282, University of Reading**
Allen and Unwin, letter to Raja Rao, 6 Feb. 1939.
———, letter to Iqbal Singh, 26 Apr. 1939.
———, letter to Mulk Raj Anand, 22 March 1949.
———, letter to Mulk Raj Anand, 11 Oct. 1949.
Anand, Mulk Raj, letter to Allen and Unwin, 17 Mar. 1949.
Barnes, Malcolm, letter to Raja Rao, 3 Mar. 1937.
———, letter to Raja Rao, 19 May 1937.
———, letter to Raja Rao, 12 June 1937.
———, letter to Raja Rao, 10 Nov. 1937
Rao, Raja, letter to Philip Unwin, 24 Feb. 1937.
———, letter to Philip Unwin, 5 Mar. 1937.
———, letter to Malcolm Barnes, 6 Nov. 1937.
———, letter to Malcolm Barnes, 15 Nov. 1937.
Rao, Raja, and Iqbal Singh, letter to Stanley Unwin, 12 Jan. 1939.
Unwin, Philip, letter to Raja Rao, 20 Feb. 1937.
Unwin, Rayner, Report on Raja Rao's *Indian Nation*, 1954.


**BBC Written Archives Centre**
Bokhari, Z. A., letter to Mulk Raj Anand, 4 Dec. 1941.
———, letter to Mulk Raj Anand, 9 Sept. 1942.
Chaudhuri, Nirad, interview, *Everyman*, 26 June 1983, 1–30.
———, interview with D. Barlow, BBC *Profile*, 3 Oct. 1974.
Hiro, Dilip and Stuart Hall, *Asian Teenagers 2*, Radio 4 (28 Feb. 1968).
Hosain, Attia, *Writing in a Foreign Tongue*, Third Programme, 8 May 1956.
Hughes, P. and Mollie Greenmalgh, Memo to Script Editor, 9 Nov. 1956, Narayan R cont 4.
Lowe, K. F., letter to Prince Tambimuttu, 17 May 1944, Contributors Talks File 1 (1941–62).
Naipaul, V. S., letter to Grenfell Williams, 14 May 1954, File R cont 1 (1950–62).
Narayan, R. K., interview with Hallam Tennyson, 4 Oct. 1961, File R cont 1 (1950–62).
Tambimuttu, *The Man in the Street*, 17 Oct. 1941, Contributors Talks File 1 (1941–62), 4.

Tambimuttu, *Mind the Traffic*, 2 Dec. 1941, Contributors Talks File 1 (1941-62).

———, *How it Works: The British Press*, 21 Dec. 1941, Contributors Talks File 1 (1941-62), 5.

———, *Open Letter to a Marxist*, 20 Sept. 1942, Contributors Talks File 1 (1941–62).

**British Library**

Chaudhuri, B. B., letter to George Bernard Shaw, 27 July 1944, Add. 50524, f. 109.

Harrod, Roy, letter to Nirad C. Chaudhuri, 21 May 1968, Add. 71620 f. 11.

Tambimuttu Papers, Add. 10028.

Grigson, Geoffrey, letter to Tambimuttu, 11 Dec. 1947.

Tambimuttu, letter to Ralph Pieris, 22 Apr. 1947.

———, letter to Fredoon Kabraji, 14 Mar. 1946.

**Chatto and Windus Archive, MS 2444, University of Reading**

File Aubrey Menen, 1947–8 University of Reading:

Aubrey Menen, letter to Peter Cochcrane, 16 Oct. 1947.

File Chaudhuri 1964–7:

Chaudhuri, Nirad, letter to Gabrielle Smith, 20 June 1964.

———, letter to Peter Calvocoressi, 22 Mar. 1965.

Lindley, Denver, letter to Peter Calvocoressi, 5 May 1965.

Wint, Guy, letter to Ian Parsons, June 10 1964.

File Chaudhuri 1971–4:

Chaudhuri, letter to Laurens Van der Post, 10 June 1974.

File Chaudhuri 1979–83:

Anonymous, report of Hinduism, undated.

The International Society for Krishna Consciousness, letter to David Attwooll, 23 May 1981.

Voice of India, letter to David Attwooll, 27 May 1981.

File Markandaya 1954–60, Chatto and Windus Archive:

Lubbock, Roger, letter to Richard Walsh, Oct. 15 1954.

———, letter to Richard Walsh, 1 Feb. 1960.

File Markandaya 1970–6:

Markandaya, letter to D. J. Enright, 26 May 1975.

Walsh, Richard, letter to Kamala Markandaya, 24 Aug. 1973.

———, letter to Norah Smallwood, 17 Jan. 1974,

File Markandaya 1976–82:

Markandaya, Kamala, letter to Smallwood, 11 Aug. 1976.

———, letter to Norah Smallwood, 17 Oct. 1976.

———, letter to Norah Smallwood, 8 Nov. 1976.

Varten, Cynthia, letter to Norah Smallwood, 20 Sept. 1976.

**Colombo Municipal Library Archives, Sri Lanka**

Dunstan de Silva, 'A Myth that Sustains an Empire', *Young Ceylon* 4. 1 (May 1935).

**Columbia University Rare Book and Manuscript Library, New York**

Raine, Kathleen, letter to Tambimuttu, 22 Nov. no year, MS Coll. Poetry London-New York Records, 1943–68.
——, letter to Tambimuttu, 15 Apr. 1951, MS Coll. Poetry London-New York Records, 1943–68.

**Harvard University Library**

Laughlin, James, letter to the US Immigration Department, 22 Apr. 1959, James Laughlin Correspondence, 1942–72, BMS Am 2077 (1635), Folder 2.
MacGregor, Robert M., letter to Tambimuttu, 13 Dec. 1971, James Laughlin Correspondence, 1942–72, BMS Am 2077 (1635), Folder 2.

**Jonathan Cape Archive, University of Reading**

Calder, Liz, letter to Claire Tomalin, 30 Apr. 1981.
Cooke, Judy, Reader's Report on *Madame Rama*, undated.

**Lake House Newspaper Archives, Sri Lanka**

Anonymous, 'Of Cabbages and Kings', *Ceylon Daily News* (20 July 1955), 31.

**Macmillan Publishers Ltd. Archive**

Squire, J. C., Reader's Report on *A Passage to England*, undated.
Swithunbank, B. W., Reader's Report on *A Passage to England*, undated.
Watson, Francis, First Reader's Report on *Circe*, 28 June 1961.
——, Second Reader's Report on *Circe*, 15 May 1963.

**Penguin Correspondence, Special Collections, University of Bristol**

Anand, Mulk Raj letter to Mr Maynard, 30 Oct. 1940, Penguin 00.0312.6 [DM 1107].
Markandaya, letter to John Guest at Longman, 21 Jan. 1972, 'The Nowhere Man' File, Allen Lane: Penguin Press, 7139.0467.4 [DM 1852].
Penguin, letter to Innes Rose, 6 Aug. 1977, 'The Nowhere Man' File, Allen Lane: Penguin Press, 7139.0467.4 [DM 1852].
Rosenburg, Elizabeth, to John Guest, Reader's Report on *Nowhere Man*, 17 Sept. 1973 'The Nowhere Man' File, Allen Lane: Penguin Press, 7139.0467.4 [DM 1852].

**Oxford University Press Archive**

Chester, P. J., memo to Ron Heapy, 13 Apr. 1972.

Dayal, Ravi, letter to Ron Heapy, 14 Apr. 1972.

Ravenscroft, Arthur, Reader's Report on Rao, 2 Oct. 1973.

**Tambimuttu Archive, Northwestern University, Chicago**

Dickins, Anthony, letter to Tambimuttu, 18 Dec. 1949, Box 35 folder 6.

IAC, letter to the GLC, 24 July 1982, Box 42 folder 17.

Leary, Timothy, *How to Start Your Own Religion,* unpublished pamphlet, Box 2 folder 3, 2.

Mackenzie, Anthony, letter to Tambimuttu, 14 Jan. 1983, Tambimuttu Archive, Box 34 folder 2.

Tambimuttu, *Return Journey to Ceylon,* undated, Box 2 folder 6

———, letter to Indian Ministry of External Affairs, 15 Nov. 1971, Box 7 folder 1.

———, letter to Safia Tyabjee, 27 July 1978, Box 3 folder 1.

———, letter to President J. R. Jayewardene, 2 Feb. 1982, Box 42 folder 17.

West, V., letter to Tambimuttu, 24 June 1973, Box 3 folder 1.

*Television and screenplays*

*Bhaji on the Beach,* dir. Gurinder Chadha. Films on Four. 1993.

*Bend it Like Beckham,* dir. Gurinder Chadha, 2003.

*Goodness Gracious Me,* dir. Anil Gupta. BBC 2. 21 Oct. 1998.

*Majdhar,* dir. Ahmed Jamal. Retake Film and Video Collective. 1984.

*My Beautiful Laundrette*, dir. Stephen Frears. Films on Four. 1986.

*My Sister-Wife,* dir. Lesley Manning. BBC 2. 23 Feb. 23 1992.

*Unpublished interviews or lectures*

Ash, Ranjana, address, Launch of Asian Writers Series at Asian Literature in Translation Conference, Commonwealth Institute, 19 Nov. 1993.

Gunesekera, Romesh, lecture, University of London, 1 Dec. 1998.

Kureishi, Hanif, address, Cheltenham Literary Festival, 17 Oct. 1997.

Niven, Alistair, address, Culture and the Literary Prize Conference, Oxford Brookes University, 5 Oct. 2003.

Rushdie, Salman, lecture, Oxford University, 20 May 1999.

*Broadcast interviews*

Abedayo, Diran, interview, *Newsnight,* BBC 2, 2 Dec. 1999.

Bakewell, Joan, interview with Tambimuttu, *Late Night Line Up,* BBC 2, 26 Feb. 1971.

Rushdie, Salman, *The Booker Prize,* BBC 2, 20 Oct. 1981.

———, interview with Joan Bakewell, *Heart of the Matter,* BBC 2, 10 July 1988.

Syal, Meera, *The South Bank Show,* ITV, 3 Mar. 2002.

———, *Who Do You Think You Are?* BBC 2, 24 Sept. 2004.

Sivanandan, A. Interview with Jonathan Dimbleby, *This Week, Next Week*, BBC 2, 3 Nov. 1985.

——, *Refugee Tales*, Channel 4, 24 May 2000.

*Personal interviews and communications*

Aloysius, Joe, interview with the author, 2 Jan. 2001.

Chaudhuri, Nirad C. interview with the author, 27 Oct. 1997.

Kureishi, Hanif, letter to the author, 20 Jan. 2001.

Sivanandan, A., interview with the author, 12 Apr. 1999.

Syal, Meera, letter to the author, 12 Feb. 2000.


PUBLISHED MATERIAL

*Primary texts*
*Date in Square brackets is year of original publication.*

Ali, Monica, *Brick Lane* (London: Doubleday, 2003).

Anand, Mulk Raj, *Untouchable* (London: Lawrence and Wishart, 1935).

——, *Coolie* (London: Lawrence and Wishart, 1936).

——, *Two Leaves and a Bud* (London: Lawrence and Wishart, 1937).

——, *Conversations in Bloomsbury* (London: Wildwood House, 1981).

Asian Women Writers' Workshop, *Rights of Way: Prose and Poetry* (London: Women's Press, 1988).

Aslam, Nadeem, *Maps for Lost Lovers* (London: Faber, 2004).

Centerprise, *Breaking the Silence: Writing by Asian Women* (London: Centerprise Trust 1984).

Chaudhuri, Nirad C., *The Autobiography of an Unknown Indian* [1951] (Bombay: Jaico Publishing House, 1997).

——, 'The Western Influence in India, *The Atlantic Monthly* 193.3 (1954), 70–4.

——, *A Passage to England* [1959] (Delhi: Orient Paperbacks, 1971).

——, *The Continent of Circe* [1965] (Bombay: Jaico Publishing House, 1996).

——, Chaudhuri, Letters to the Editor, *The Statesman* (20 Mar. 1965).

——, *The Intellectual in India* (Delhi: Associated Publishing House, 1967).

——, 'Indian England', *London Magazine* 10.8 (1970), 66–75.

——, 'The Vicious Spiral of Hindu-Muslim Hatred', *The Times* (21 Dec. 1971), 10.

——, 'Tagore the True and the False', *Times Literary Supplement* (27 Sept. 1974), 1029–31.

——, *Scholar Extraordinary: The Life of Friedrich Max Müller* (New Delhi: Orient, 1976).

——, 'Woman of the World', *Times Literary Supplement* (16 Jan. 1976), 55.

——, 'The Wolf without a Pack', *Times Literary Supplement* (6 Oct. 1978), 1121.

Chaudhuri, Nirad C., *Hinduism: A Religion to Live By* [1979] (Delhi: Oxford UP, 1997).

_____, 'Why I Write in English', *Kunapipi* 3.1 (1981), 1–3.

_____, 'Opening Address', in Maggie Butcher (ed.), *The Eye of the Beholder: Indian Writing in English* (London: Commonwealth Institute, 1983), 8–20.

_____, *Thy Hand, Great Anarch! India, 1921–52* [1987] (London: Hogarth Press, 1990).

_____, 'Why I Mourn for England', *Daily Telegraph* (20 Feb. 1988), 1.

_____, 'My Hundreth Year', in Ian Jack (ed.), *Granta 57 India! The Golden Jubilee* (London: Granta, 1997), 205-11.

_____, *Three Horsemen of the New Apocalypse* (Delhi: Oxford UP, 1997).

Corner, Caroline, *Ceylon the Paradise of Adam* (Bodley Head, 1908).

Desani, G.V., *All About H. Hatterr* (London: Bodley Head, 1970).

Dhondy, Farrukh, *East End at Your Feet* (Basingstoke: Macmillan 1976).

_____, *Siege of Babylon* (Basingstoke: Macmillan, 1978).

_____, *Come to Mecca and Other Stories* (London: Macmillan, 1978).

_____, *Poona Company* (London: Gollancz, 1980).

_____, *Romance, Romance and The Bride* (London: Faber and Faber, 1985).

_____, *Vigilantes* (London: Hobo, 1988).

_____, *Bombay Duck* (London: Cape, 1990).

_____, Comment, *The Times* (21 June 1995), online edition.

_____, 'Speaking in Tongues' in Ferdinand Dennis and Naseem Khan (eds.), *Voices of the Crossing* (London: Serpent's Tale, 2000), 163–73.

_____, *C. L. R. James: a Life* (London: Weidenfield and Nicholson, 2001).

_____, 'The Death of Multiculturalism', *Guardian* (8 Nov. 2002), online edition.

_____, 'Different Strokes', (13 Mar. 2004), www.mid-day.com, online edition.

_____, (ed.), *Ranters, Ravers and Rhymers: Poems by Black and Asian Poets* (London: Collins, 1990).

Eliot, T. S., *Collected Poems 1909–1962* (London: Faber and Faber, 1963).

Ezekiel, Nissim, *Selected Prose* (Delhi: Oxford UP, 1992).

Forster, E. M., *A Passage to India* (London: Penguin, 1935).

Gunesekera, Romesh, *Reef* (London: Granta, 1994).

Hosain, Attia, *Sunlight on a Broken Column* (London: Chatto and Windus, 1961).

Kureishi, Hanif, *Sammy and Rosie Get Laid* (London: Faber and Faber, 1988).

_____, *The Buddha of Suburbia* (London: Faber and Faber, 1990).

_____, *Outskirts and Other Plays* (London: Faber and Faber, 1992).

_____, *The Black Album* (London: Faber and Faber, 1995).

_____, *My Beautiful Laundrette and Other Writings* (London: Faber and Faber, 1996).

_____, *My Son the Fanatic* (London: Faber and Faber, 1997).

_____, *My Ear at his Heart: Reading my Father* (Faber and Faber, 2004).

_____ and Jon Savage (eds.), *The Faber Book of Pop* (London: Faber, 1995).

Mamdani, Mahmood, *From Citizen to Refugee* (London: Francis Printer 1973).

Markandaya, Kamala, *Nectar in a Sieve* [1954] (New York: Signet, 1982).

_____ , *Some Inner Fury* (London: Putnam, 1955).

_____ , *A Silence of Desire* (London: Putnam, 1960).

_____ , *Possession* (London: Putnam, 1963).

_____ , *The Coffer Dams* (London: Hamilton, 1969).

_____ , *The Nowhere Man* (London: Allen Lane, 1972).

_____ , *Two Virgins* (London: Chatto and Windus, 1974).

_____ , 'One Pair of Eyes: Some Random Reflections' in Alastair Niven (ed.), *The Commonwealth Writer Overseas: Themes of Exile and Expatriation* (Brussels: Didier, 1976), 23–32.

_____ , *The Golden Honeycomb* (London: Chatto and Windus, 1977).

_____ , *Pleasure City* (London Chatto and Windus, 1982).

Mukta, Parita, *Shards of Memory: Woven Lives in Four Generations* (London: Weidenfeld and Nicolson, 2002).

Narayan, R. K., *Swami and Friends* [1935] (London: Mandarin, 1990).

_____ , *My Days* (New York: Viking Press, 1974).

Nehru, Jawaharlal, *The Discovery of India* (London: Meridian Books, 1946).

Naipaul, Shiva, 'Passports to Dependence', *Sunday Times Magazine* (30 Dec. 1973).

_____ , *Beyond the Dragon's Mouth: Stories and Pieces* (London: Abacus, 1988).

Naipaul, V. S., *The Mimic Men* (London: Penguin, 1967).

Randhawa, Ravinder, *A Wicked Old Woman* (London: The Women's Press, 1987).

Rao, Raja, *Kanthapura* (London: Allen and Unwin, 1938).

Rushdie, Salman, *Midnight's Children* (London: Picador, 1981).

_____ , 'An Interview', *Literary Review* 63 (1983), 31.

_____ , *Shame* [1983] (London: Vintage, 1995).

_____ , '*Midnight's Children* and *Shame*', *Kunapipi* 7.1 (1985), 1–19.

_____ , *The Jaguar Smile: A Nicaraguan Journey* (London: Picador, 1987).

_____ , *The Satanic Verses* (London: Viking, 1988).

_____ , *Imaginary Homelands, 1981–1991* (London: Granta, 1991).

_____ , 'Minority Literatures in a Multi-cultural Society' in Kirsten Holst Peterson and Anna Rutherford (eds.), *Displaced Persons* (Sydney: Dangaroo Press, 1992), 33–42.

_____ , *The Wizard of Oz* (London: British Film Institute, 1992).

_____ , *The Moor's Last Sigh* [1995] (London: Vintage, 1996).

Sahgal, Nayantara, *Prison and Chocolate Cake* (London: Victor Gollancz, 1954).

_____ , *From Fear Set Free* (London: Victor Gollancz, 1962).

_____ , *Rich Like Us* (London: Sceptre, 1983).

_____ , 'The Schizophrenic Imagination' in Anna Rutherford (ed.), *From Commonwealth to Post-Colonial* (Sydney: Dangaroo Press, 1992), 30–6.

Scott, Paul, *Staying On* (London: Heinemann, 1977).

Sidhwa, Bapsi, *Cracking India* (Minneapolis: Milkweed, 1991).

Sivanandan, A. 'White Racism & Black', *Encounter* 31.1 (1968), 95–6.

——, 'The Liberation of the Black Intellectual', *Race and Class* 18.2 (1977), 329–43.

——, 'Imperialism and Disorganic Development in the Silicon Age', *Race and Class* 21.2 (1979), 1–26.

——, *Asian and Afro-Caribbean Struggles in Britain* (London: Institute of Race Relations, 1986).

——, *Communities of Resistance: Writings on Black Struggles for Socialism* (London: Verso, 1990).

——, 'European Commentary: Racism, the Road from Germany', *Race and Class* 34.3 (1993), 67–73.

——, 'Race Against Time', *New Statesman and Society* (15 Oct. 1993), 16.

——, 'Fighting our Fundamentalisms: An interview with A. Sivanandan by CARF', *Race and Class* 36.3 (1995), 73–81.

——, 'La trahison des clercs', *New Statesman and Society* (14 July 1995), 20–1.

——, *When Memory Dies* (London: Arcadia Books, 1997).

——, *Where the Dance is: Stories from Two Worlds and Three* (London: Arcadia Books, 2000).

Syal, Meera, 'My Sister-Wife', in Rukhsana Ahmad and Kadija George (eds.), *Six Plays by Black and Asian Women Writers* (London: Aurora Metro Press, 1993), 111–59.

——, 'PC: GLC', in Sarah Dunant (ed.), *The War of Words: The Political Correctness Debate* (London: Virago, 1994), 116–32.

——, *Anita and Me* (London: Flamingo, 1996).

——, 'Influences', *New Statesman and Society* (19 Apr. 1996), 21.

——, *Life Isn't All Ha Ha, Hee Hee* (London: Doubleday, 1999).

Tagore, Rabindranath, *The Home and the World* (Leipzig: Bernhard Tauchnitz, 1921).

Tambimuttu, M. J., *Tone Patterns* (Colombo: Slave Island Printing Works, 1936).

——, 'First Letter', *Poetry London* 1.1 (1939), n.p.

——, 'Four Ceylonese Love Poems', *Poetry London* 1.2 (1939), n.p.

——, 'Second Letter', *Poetry London* 1.2 (1939), n.p.

——, 'Third Letter', *Poetry London* 1.3 (1940), 65–6.

——, *Out of this War* (London: The Fortune Press, 1941).

——, 'From *Out of this War*', *Kingdom Come* (Spring 1941), 70–1.

——, 'Sixth Letter', *Poetry London* 1.6 (1941), 160–5.

——, 'Eighth Letter', *Poetry London* 2.7 (1942), 3–7.

——, *Natarajah: A Poem for Mr. T.S. Eliot's Sixtieth Birthday* (London: Editions Poetry London, 1948).

——, 'Preface', *Poetry London* 4.13 (1948), 3.

——, 'Poetry in India: Its Heritage and New Directions' *The Atlantic Monthly* 192.4 (1953), 147–8.

_____, 'Elizam: A Reminiscence of a Childhood in Ceylon', *The Reporter* 11.12 (1954), 38–41.

_____, 'Uncle Gamini and the British', *The Reporter* 10.3 (1954), 44–5.

_____, 'Woman in India' in T. Tambimuttu (ed.), *India Love Poems* (New York: Peter Pauper Press, 1954), 7–30.

_____, 'The Tree Climber: A Short Story Set in Ceylon', *The Reporter* 13.4 (1955), 38–42.

_____, 'Editorial', *Poetry London-New York* 1.4 (1960), 3–5.

_____, 'Fitzrovia' [1974] in Jane Williams (ed.), *Tambimuttu: Bridge Between Two Worlds* (London: Peter Owen, 1989), 223–35.

_____, 'Swami Rock, Raga Rock' [n.d.] in Jane Williams (ed.), *Tambimuttu: Bridge Between Two Worlds* (London: Peter Owen, 1989), 28–45.

_____, (ed.), *Poems from Bangla Desh: The Voice of a New Nation* (London: The Lyrebird Press, 1972).

Vakil, Ardashir *Beach Boy* (London: Hamish Hamilton, 1997).

Vijaya-Tunga, J., *Grass for My Feet* (London: Edwin Arnold, 1935).

Woolf, Leonard, *The Village in the Jungle* [1913] (Delhi: Oxford University Press, 1992).

Zilwa, Lucian de, *The Dice of the Gods* (London: Heath Cranston, 1917).


*Secondary Material*

Achebe, Chinua, *Hopes and Impediments* (London: Doubleday, 1988).

Ahmad, Aijaz, *In Theory: Classes, Nations and Literatures* (London: Verso, 1992).

_____, 'Out of the Dust of Idols' *Race and Class* 41.1/2 (1999), 1–21

Ahmad, Rukhsana, 'In Search of a Talisman' in Ferdinand Dennis and Naseem Khan (eds.), *Voices of the Crossing* (London: Serpent's Tale, 2000), 101–15.

Alderson, Brian, 'Children's Fiction', *The Times* (7 Jan. 1981), 7.

Ali, Monica, 'Where I'm coming from', *Guardian* (17 June 2003), online edition.

Alibhai, Yasmin, 'Satanic Betrayals', *New Statesman and Society* (24 Feb. 1989), 12.

Allen, Richard, 'A Post-Colonial World: *Look Back in Anger* and *The Enigma of Arrival*' in Richard Allen and Harish Trivedi (eds.), *Literature and Nation: Britain and India, 1800–1990* (London: Routledge in association with the Open University, 2000), 138–53.

Amarasinghe, Y. Ranjith, *Revolutionary Idealism and Parliamentary Politics* (Colombo: Social Scientists' Association, 1998).

Anonymous, 'Review of *Untouchable*', *Times Literary Supplement* (2 May 1935), 298.

_____, 'Review of *Kanthapura*', *Times Literary Supplement* (26 Mar. 1938), 122.

Anonymous, 'Editorial', *Sunday Times* (7 Oct. 1951), 1.

———, 'Of Cabbages and Kings', *Ceylon Daily News* (20 July 1955), 31.

———, 'New Magazine in Manhattan', *Time* (14 May 1956), 64.

———, 'Review of *Nowhere Man*', *Yorkshire Post* (20 Apr. 1973).

———, 'Review of *Nowhere Man*' *The Times* (26 Apr.) 1973.

———, 'Review of *When Memory Dies*', *Socialist Worker* (10 May 1997), 31.

———, San Diego State University Women and Development Syllabus. <http://www.inform.umd.edu/EdRes/Global/international-development>

———, Teacher's Guide to *Nectar in a Sieve*. <http://www.penguinclassics. com/CAN . . . rs_guides/t_markandaya_nectar.html.

Anwar, Farrah, 'Is There a Sodomite in the House?' *Guardian* (7 Aug. 1992), 29.

———, '*Bhaji on the Beach* (rev.)' *Sight and Sound*, 4.2 (1994), 47–8.

Asad, Talal, 'The Concept of Cultural Translation in British Social Anthropology' in J. Clifford and G. E. Marcus (eds.), *Writing Culture: The Poetics and Politics of Ethnography* (Berkeley and Los Angeles: University of California Press, 1986), 141–64.

———, *Genealogies of Religion: Discipline and Reasons of Power in Christianity and Islam* (Baltimore: Johns Hopkins University Press, 1993).

Ash, Ranjana, 'Remembering India: Homeland, Heritage or Hindrance in the Writings by Women of the Indian Diaspora' in Kathleen Firth and Felicity Hand (eds.), *India: Fifty Years after Independence* (Leeds: Peepal Tree Press, 2001), 90–109.

Ashcroft, Bill, Gareth Griffiths, and Helen Tiffin, *The Empire Writes Back: Theory and Practice in Post-Colonial Literatures* (London: Routledge, 1989).

———, *Key Concepts in Post-Colonial Studies* (London: Routledge, 1998).

Bassnett, Susan and Harish Trivedi (eds.), *Post-colonial Translation: Theory and Practice* (London: Routledge, 1999).

Basu, Tapan Kumar, 'Class in the Classroom: Pedagogical Encounters with *Nectar in a Sieve*', in Rajeswari Sunder Rajan (ed.), *The Lie of the Land: English Literary Studies in India* (Delhi: Oxford UP, 1992), 105–12.

Baker, Samuel, *Eight Years Wandering in Ceylon* (London: Longmans, 1890).

Bakewell, Michael, *Fitzrovia: London's Bohemia* (London: National Portrait Gallery Publications, 1999).

Bayly, Christopher, *Imperial Meridian: The British Empire and the World, 1780–1830* (London: Longman, 1989).

Benjamin, Walter, 'The Task of the Translator (1923)', trans. Harry Zohn in *Illuminations* Hannah Arendt (ed.), (New York: Schocken, 1969), 69–82.

Benn, Melissa, 'Island in the Stream of History', *Independent* (11 Jan. 1997), online edition.

Bhabha, Homi, 'The Third Space' in Jonathan Rutherford (ed.), *Identity: Community, Culture, Difference* (London: Lawrence and Wishart, 1990), 207–22.

_____, *The Location of Culture* (London: Routledge, 1994).

_____, 'Unpacking my library . . . again' in Iain Chambers and Lidia Curti (eds.), *The Post-Colonial Question: Common Skies, Divided Horizons* (London: Routledge, 1996), 199–212.

_____, 'Paean for Pluralism' *India Today International* (29 Dec. 1997), 24k.

_____, 'The Vernacular Cosmopolitan', in Ferdinand Dennis and Naseem Khan (eds.), *Voices of the Crossing* (London: Serpent's Tale, 2000), 133–42.

Bilgrani, Akeel, 'What is a Muslim? Fundamental Commitment and Cultural Identity', *Critical Inquiry* 18 (1992), 821–43.

Boehmer, Elleke, *Colonial and Post-Colonial Literatures: Migrant Metaphors* (Oxford: Oxford UP, 1995).

_____, (ed.), *Empire Writing: An Anthology of Colonial Literature 1870–1918* (Oxford: Oxford UP, 1998).

Bottrall, Ronald, 'Letter to the Editor' *London Magazine* 5.8 (1965), 101–2.

Bowen, David (ed.), *The Satanic Verses: Bradford Responds* (Bradford: Bradford and Ilkley Community College, 1992).

Brah, Avtar, *Cartographies of Diaspora: Contesting Identities* (London: Routledge, 1996).

Braybrook, Neville, 'rev. of *All About Mr. Hatterr*', *Times Literary Supplement* (15 May 1948), 273.

Breit, Harvey, 'Editorial', *Atlantic Monthly* 192.4 (1953), 1–3.

Brennan, Timothy, *Salman Rushdie and the Third World* (Basingstoke: Macmillan, 1989).

Brockes, Emma, 'Laughing all the Way to the Bank', *Guardian* (19 July 2004), online edition.

Brooks, David, 'Interview with Salman Rushdie', *Helix* 19/20 (1984/5), 55–69.

Brown, Hilton, 'Review of *The Village*', *Times Literary Supplement* (15 Apr. 1939), 215.

Bryden, Ronald, 'Kinship', *The Listener* (12 Apr. 1973).

Cacqueray, Elisabeth de, 'Constructions of Women in British Cinema: From Losey/Pinter's Modernism to the Postmodernism of Frears/Kureishi', *Caliban* 32 (1995), 109–20.

Canby, Vincent, 'Laundrette: Social Comedy Sleeper' *New York Times*, (7 March 1986), 31.

Carby, Hazel, 'White Woman Listen! Black Feminism and the Boundaries of Sisterhood' in Heidi Safia Mirza (ed.), *Black British Feminism* (London: Routledge, 1997), 45–53.

Chakrabarty, Dipesh, 'Postcoloniality and the Artifice of History: Who Speaks for "Indian Pasts?"', in Padmini Mongia (ed.), *Contemporary Postcolonial Literary Theory* (London: Arnold, 1996), 223–47.

_____, *Provincializing Europe: Postcolonial Thought and Historical Difference* (Princeton: Princeton UP, 2000).

Chatterjee, Partha, *Nationalist Thought and the Third World: A Derivative Discourse?* (London: Zed Books, 1986).

——, 'The Nationalist Resolution of the Women's Question' in Kumkum Sangari and Sudesh Vaid (eds.), *Recasting Women: Essays in Colonial History* (Delhi: Kali, 1989), 233–53.

——, *The Present History of West Bengal: Essays in Political Criticism* (Delhi: Oxford UP, 1997).

Chatterjee, P. C., *The Adventure of Indian Broadcasting* (Delhi: Konarck Press, 1998).

Chatterjee, Rimi, 'Macmillan in India' in Elizabeth James (ed.), *Macmillan: a Publishing Tradition* (Houndmills: Palgrave, 2001), 153–70.

Chaudhuri, Amit, 'Lure of the Hybrid', *Times Literary Supplement*, (3 Sept. 1999), 5–6.

Chellappan, K., 'The Discovery of India and the Self in Three Autobiographies', in H. H. Anniah Gowda (ed.), *The Colonial and the Neo-Colonial: Encounters in Commonwealth Literature* (Mysore: University of Mysore, 1983).

Chew, Shirley and Anna Rutherford (eds.), *Unbecoming Daughters of the Empire* (Sydney: Dangaroo Press, 1993).

Cheyfitz, Eric, *The Poetics of Imperialism: Translation and Colonization from The Tempest to Tarzan* (Oxford: Oxford UP, 1991.

Chisholm, Anne, 'Changing the Anglo-Indian Literary Landscape', *National Times* (4 Oct. 1981), 13.

Church, Michael, 'Nein Danke', *The Times* (12 Nov. 1983), 6.

Chow, Rey, *Primitive Passions: Visuality, Sexuality, Ethnography and Contemporary Chinese Cinema* (New York: Columbia UP, 1995).

Clarke, J. J., *Oriental Enlightenment: The Encounter between Asian and Western Thought* (London: Routledge, 1997).

Cleverdon, Douglas (ed.), *Verse and Voice: Poems and Ballads of the Commonwealth* (Commonwealth Arts Festival, 1965).

Cole, W. Owen (ed.), *Religion in Multi Faith Schools* (The Yorkshire Community Council, 1973).

Collins, Glenn, 'Screen Writer Turns to the Novel to Tell of Race and Class in London' *New York Times*, (24 May 1990) 17.

Commission for Racial Equality, 'Stereotyping and Racism in Britain: An Attitude Survey', *Impact* (Oct./Nov. 1999), 40–8.

Cooke, Judy, 'Review of *The Crow Eaters*', *The New Statesman* (19 Sept. 1980), 23.

Curtis, Nick, 'Radical Islam meets Ecstasy', *Financial Times* (11 Mar. 1995), p. xii.

Dasgupta, Swapan (ed.), *Nirad C. Chaudhuri: The First Hundred Years: A Celebration* (Delhi: HarperCollins, 1997).

Davison, Peter (ed.), *The Complete Works of George Orwell: All Propaganda is Lies* (London: Secker and Warburg, 2001).

_____ (ed.), *The Complete Works of George Orwell: Two Wasted Years* (London: Secker and Warburg, 2001).

Dhillon-Kashyap, Perminder, 'Locating the Asian Experience', *Screen* 29.4 (1988), 120–6.

Dickins, Anthony, 'Tambimuttu and *Poetry London*', *London Magazine* 5.8 (1965), 53–7.

Dix, Carol, 'Reaching a Wider Audience', *Times Education Supplement* (3 June 1977), 29.

Donnell, Alison, *Twentieth Century Caribbean Literature: Critical Moments in Anglophone Literary History* (London: Routledge, 2005).

Eagleton, Terry, *Criticism and Ideology* (London: Verso, 1978).

Easthope, Antony, *British Post-Structuralism Since 1968* (London: Routledge, 1988).

Editorial, 'Goodness, Gracious, Laugh: Good Comedy Helps Good Race-Relations', *The Times* (9 Jan. 1999), 21.

Engels, Frederick and Karl Marx, *The German Ideology, Parts I and III* (London: Lawrence and Wishart, 1940).

Enright, D. J. (ed.), *The Oxford Book of Contemporary Verse, 1945–1988* (Oxford: Oxford UP, 1988).

Ewart, Gavin, 'Tambi the Great', *London Magazine* 5.9 (1965), 57–60.

Fallowell, Duncan, 'Nirad C. Chaudhuri: At Home in Oxford', *The American Scholar* 60.2 (1991), 242–6.

Fanon, Frantz, *Black Skin, White Masks* [1952], trans. Charles Lam Markmann (London: Pluto Press, 1986).

_____ , *The Wretched of the Earth* [1961], trans. Constance Farrington (London: Penguin, 1967).

Fausset, Hugh I'Anson, 'Rabindranath Tagore: Mediator Between East and West: Divine Visionary', *Times Literary Supplement* (16 Aug. 1941), 394-5.

_____ , 'Three Poets', *Times Literary Supplement* (13 Sept. 1941), 457.

Forbes, Geraldine, *Indian Women and the Freedom Movement: A Historian's Perspective* (Bombay: Research Centre for Women's Studies, 1997).

Foster, Paul, *The Buddhist Influence in T. S. Eliot's 'Four Quartets'* (Frankfurt: Haag und Herschen, 1977).

Fountain, Alan, 'Channel 4 and Black Independents' in Kobena Mercer (ed.), *Black Film, British Cinema* (London: Institute of Contemporary Arts, 1988), 42–4.

Fraser, G. S., *A Stranger and Afraid: The Autobiography of an Intellectual* (Manchester: Carcanet Press, 1983).

Frears, Stephen, 'Keeping His Own Voice: An Interview with Lester Friedman and Scott Stewart' in Wheeler Winston Dixon (ed.), *Re-Viewing British Cinema, 1900–1992* (Albany: State University of New York Press, 1994), 221–40.

Fryer, Peter, *Staying Power* (London: Pluto Press, 1984).

Fusco, Coco, 'Fantasies of Oppositionality—Reflections on Recent Conferences in Boston and New York', *Screen* 29.4 (1988), 80–96.

Gardner, Jessica, 'Where is the postcolonial London of London Magazine?' *Kunapipi* 21.2 (1999), 93–101.

Geetha, P., 'The Novels of Kamala Markandaya: Reassessing Feminine Identity' in Kamini Dinesh (ed.), *Between Spaces of Silence: Women Creative Writers* (Delhi: Sterling, 1994).

George, T. J. S., *Krishna Menon* (London: Jonathan Cape, 1964).

Gilroy, Paul, 'Steppin' Out of Babylon—Race, Class and Autonomy' in *The Empire Strikes Back: Race and Racism in 70s Britain*, ed. Centre for Contemporary Cultural Studies (Birmingham: Hutchinson in association with the Centre for Contemporary Cultural Studies University of Birmingham, 1982), 276–315.

——, *After Empire: Melancholia or Convivial Culture* (London: Routledge, 2004).

Glendinning, Victoria, 'The Naked and the not so Naked' *Sunday Times* (26 Apr. 1981) 42.

Goldberg, David Theo, *Multiculturalism: A Critical Reader* (Oxford: Blackwell, 1994).

Gordon, Kim, C. L. R. James, and Anthony Bogues, *Black Nationalism and Socialism* (London: Socialists Unlimited for Socialist Workers Party, 1979).

Graham, Douglas (ed.), *Keith Douglas: The Letters* (Manchester: Carcanet Press, 2000).

Gramsci, Antonio, *Selections from Prison Notebooks*, ed. and trans. Q. Hoare and G. Nowell Smith (London: Lawrence and Wishart, 1971).

Grant, Damian, *Salman Rushdie* (Plymouth: Northcote House in association with the British Council, 1999).

Grewal, Inderpal, 'Salman Rushdie: Marginality, Women and *Shame*' in M. D. Fletcher (ed.), *Reading Rushdie: Perspectives on the Fiction of Salman Rushdie* (Amsterdam: Rodopi, 1994), 123–44.

Guha, Ranajit (ed.), *Subaltern Studies I: Writings on South Asian History and Society* (Delhi: Oxford UP, 1982).

Gupta, Suman, *V. S. Naipaul: Writers and their Works* (Plymouth: Northcote House Publishers, 1999).

Gurr, Andrew, *Writers in Exile: The Identity of Home in Modern Literature* (Sussex: The Harvester Press, 1981).

Haffenden, John, 'An Interview with Salman Rushdie', *Literary Review* 63 (1983), 31.

Hall, Stuart, 'Cultural Identity and Diaspora' in Jonathan Rutherford (ed.), *Identity: Community, Culture, Difference* (London: Lawrence and Wishart, 1990), 222–37.

——, 'New Ethnicities' in Kobena Mercer (ed.), *Black Film, British Cinema* (London: Institute of Contemporary Arts, 1988), 27–31.

_____, 'Review of *Imaginary Homelands*', *Sight and Sound* 1 (1991), 32.

Hamilton, Ian, 'Bonny Prince Charlatan', *Times Literary Supplement* (1 Dec. 1989), 1335.

_____, *The Little Magazines: A Study of Six Editors* (London: Weidenfield and Nicholson, 1976).

_____, *Oxford Companion to Twentieth Century Poetry in English* (Oxford: Oxford UP, 1994).

_____, 'Sohoitis', *Granta* 65 (1999), 291–303.

Hare, Steven, *Portrait of a Publisher* (Harmondsworth: Penguin, 1970).

Harrison, James, *Salman Rushdie* (New York: Twayne, 1992).

Hayman, Ronald, interview, *Books and Bookmen* (Sept. 1983).

Heath, Stephen, *Questions of Cinema* (Basingstoke: Macmillan, 1981).

Heath-Stubbs, John and David Wright (eds.), *Faber Book of Twentieth Century Verse* (London: Faber and Faber, 1953).

Heber, R. *Hymns, Ancient and Modern* (London: William Clowes, 1924).

Hiro, Dilip, *Black British, White British* (London: Penguin, 1971).

Holmström, Lakshmi (ed.), *The Inner Courtyard: Stories by Indian Women* (London: Virago, 1990).

hooks, bell, *Yearning: Race, Gender and Class Politics* (Boston: South End Press, 1991).

_____, *Black Looks: Race and Representation* (Boston: South End Press, 1992).

Huggan, Graham, *The Postcolonial Exotic: Marketing the Margins* (London: Routledge, 2001).

Hunter, Alan, 'Fate of an Indian in London', *Eastern Daily Press* (18 May 1973).

Hutcheon, Linda, *A Poetics of Postmodernism* (London: Routledge, 1988).

Innes, C. L., *A History of Black and Asian Writing in Britain 1700–2000* (Cambridge: Cambridge UP, 2002).

Jack, Ian, 'The World's Last Englishman' in Swapan Dasgupta (ed.), *Nirad C. Chaudhuri: The First Hundred Years: A Celebration* (Delhi: HarperCollins, 1997), 39–51.

Jacquemond, Richard, 'Translation and Cultural Hegemony' in Lawrence Venuti (ed.), *Re-thinking Translation: Discourse, Subjectivity and Ideology* (London: Routledge, 1992), 139–58.

Jamal, Mahmood, 'Dirty Linen' in Kobena Mercer (ed.), *Black Film, British Cinema* (London: Institute of Contemporary Arts, 1988), 21–2.

Jameson, Fredric, 'Third-World Literature in the Era of Multinational Capitalism', *Social Text* 15 (1986), 65–88.

JanMohamed, Abdul, 'Worldliness-Without-World, Homelessness-as-Home: Towards a Definition of the Specular Border Intellectual' in Michael Sprinker (ed.), *Edward Said: A Critical Reader* (Cambridge, Mass.: Blackwell, 1992), 96–120.

Jayawardena, Kumari, *Feminism and Nationalism in the Third World* (London: Zed Books, 1986).

_____, *The Origins of the Left Movement in Sri Lanka* (Colombo: Sanjiva Books, 1988).

Jayawardena, Kumari, *'Nobodies to Somebodies': The Rise of the Colonial Bourgeoisie in Sri Lanka* (Colombo: Social Scientists' Association and Sanjiva Books, 2000).

Jensen, Lars, Anna Rutherford, and Shirley Chew (eds.), *Into the Nineties: Post-Colonial Women's Writing* (Sydney: Dangaroo Press, 1994).

Jha, Rama, 'Kamala Markandaya: The Woman's World' in Robert L. Ross (ed.), *International Literature in English: Essays on the Major Writers* (London: St. James, 1991).

Johnson, Marigold, 'Unhappy Love Affairs', *Times Literary Supplement* (23 Dec. 1955), 773.

——, 'Living by Faith', *Times Literary Supplement* (2 Dec. 1960), 783.

——, 'Long Race', *Times Literary Supplement* (20 Apr. 1973), 437.

Joshi, Priya, *In Another Country: Colonialism, Culture and the English Novel in India* (New York: Columbia UP, 2002).

Jussawalla, Adil (ed.), *New Writing in India* (Harmondsworth Penguin, 1974).

Katrak, Ketu, 'Indian Nationalism, Gandhian Satyagraha and Representations of Female Sexuality', in Andrew Parker et al. (eds.), *Nationalisms and Sexualities* (London: Routledge, 1992), 395–406.

Kavanagh, P. J., 'Enoch's England', *Guardian* (19 Apr. 1973).

Kermode, Frank, 'Voice of the Almost English', *Guardian* (10 Apr. 1990) 42.

Khair, Tabish, *Babu Fictions: Alienation in Contemporary Indian English Novels* (Delhi: Oxford UP, 2001).

Khan, Naseem, *The Art Britain Ignores: The Art of Ethnic Minorities in Britain* (London: Community Relations Commission, 1976).

——, 'Interview with Kamala Markandaya: The Maharajah's Pomp without Power', *Guardian* (26 Apr. 1977), 11.

Khilnani, Sunil, *The Idea of India* (London: Hamish Hamilton, 1997).

Kymlicka, Will, *Multicultural Citizenship: A Liberal Theory of Minority Rights* (Oxford: Clarendon Press, 1996).

Lazarus, Neil, 'The Prose of Insurgency: Sivanandan and Marxist Theory' *Race and Class* 41.1/2 (1999), 35–47.

Lehmann, John, *Poems from New Writing, 1936–1946* (London: John Lehmann, 1946).

Lejeune, Philippe, *On Autobiography* (Minneapolis: University of Minnesota Press, 1989).

Lewis, Peter, 'The Man with Two Wives', *Times (Arts)* (18 Feb. 1992), 5.

Lewis, Russell, *Anti-Racism: A Mania Exposed* (London: Quartet Books, 1988).

MacCabe, Colin, 'Realism and the Cinema: Notes on some Brechtian themes' *Screen* 15.2 (1974), 7–27.

——, *James Joyce and the Revolution of the Word* (Basingstoke: Macmillan, 1978).

——, *The Eloquence of the Vulgar* (London: British Film Institute, 1999).

——, 'Interview with Hanif Kureishi on London', *Critical Quarterly* 41.3 (1999), 37–56.

McClintock, Anne, *Imperial Leather: Race, Gender and Sexuality in the Colonial Context* (London: Routledge, 1995).

McGowan, William, *Only Man is Vile: The Tragedy of Sri Lanka* (London: Picador, 1992).

McGuinness, Frank, 'Review of *A Handful of Rice*', *London Magazine* (May 1966), 106.

Maclaren-Ross, J., *Memoirs of the Forties* (London: Alan Ross Ltd., 1965).

McLeod, John, *Beginning Postcolonialism* (Manchester: Manchester UP, 2000).

——, *Post-Colonial London: Re-Writing the Metropolis* (London: Routledge, 2004).

Malik, Kenan, *The Meaning of Race: Race, History and Culture in Western Society* (Houndmills: Macmillan, 1996).

Mannoni, O. D., *Prospero and Caliban: The Psychology of Colonisation* (New York: Praeger, 1964).

Marcus, Laura, *Auto/biographical Discourses: Theory, Criticism and Practice* (Manchester: Manchester UP, 1994).

Markham, E. A. and Arnold Kingston (eds.), *The Ugandan Asian Anthology: Merely a Matter of Colour* (London: Q books, 1973).

Memmi, Albert, *The Colonizer and the Colonized* (London: Earthscan Publications, 1990).

Mercer, Kobena, 'Diaspora Culture and the Dialogic Imagination: The Aesthetics of Black Independent Film in Britain' in Mbye B. Cham and Claire Andrade-Watkins (eds.), *Black Frames: Critical Perspectives on Black Independent Cinema* (Cambridge, Mass.: MIT Press, 1988), 50–61.

——, *Welcome to the Jungle: New Positions in Black Cultural Studies* (London: Routledge, 1994).

Miller, J. B., 'For His Film, Hanif Kureishi reaches for a "Beautiful Laundrette"', *New York Times* (2 Aug. 1992) 16.

Miller, Karl (ed.), *Writing in England Today: the Last Fifteen Years* (Harmondsworth: Penguin, 1968).

Minh-ha, Trinh T., *Cinema Interval* (London: Routledge, 1999).

Mirza, Heidi Safia (ed.), *Black British Feminism: A Reader* (London: Routledge, 1997).

Modood, Tariq, 'British Muslims and the Rushdie Affair', in James Donald and Ali Rattansi (eds.), *Race, Culture and Difference* (London: Sage Publications in association with the Open University, 1992), 260–77.

——, *Not Easy Being British: Colour, Culture and Citizenship* (London: Trentham Books Ltd. 1992).

——, ' "Difference", Cultural Racism and Anti-Racism', in Pnina Werbner and Tariq Modood (eds.), *Debating Cultural Hybridity: Multi-Cultural Identities and the Politics of Anti-Racism* (London: Zed Books, 1997), 154–72.

Modood, Tariq, 'Introduction: The Politics of Multiculturalism in the New Europe' in Tariq Modood and Pnina Werbner (eds.), *The Politics of Multiculturalism in the New Europe: Racism, Identity and Community* (London: Zed Books, 1997), 1–25.

Mohanty, Chandra Talpade, 'Under Western Eyes: Feminist Scholarship and Colonial Discourses' *Boundary* 2 (1984), 333–58.

——, 'Cartographies of Struggle', in Ann Russo,Torres Lourdes, and Chandra Talpade Mohanty (eds.), *Third World Women and the Politics of Feminism* (Bloomington: Indiana UP, 1991), 1–47.

Molony, John Chartres, 'Review of *Two Leaves and a Bud*', *Times Literary Supplement* (15 May 1937), 379.

——, 'Review of *Bachelor of Arts*', *Times Literary Supplement* (12 June 1937), 446.

——, 'Review of *The Dark Room*', *Times Literary Supplement* (22 Oct. 1938), 679.

Moore-Gilbert, Bart, *Postcolonial Theory: Contexts, Practices, Politics* (London: Verso, 1997).

——, *Hanif Kureishi* (Manchester: Manchester UP, 2001).

Mortimer, Raymond, 'The Square Peg', *Sunday Times* (9 Sept. 1951), 3.

Mukherjee, Meenakshi, *The Twice Born Fiction: Themes and Techniques of the Indian Novel in English* (Delhi: Heinemann, 1971).

——, 'Introduction' in Meenakshi Mukherjee (ed)., *Midnight's Children: A Book of Readings* (Delhi: Pencraft International, 1999), 1–20.

——, *The Perishable Empire: Essays on Indian Writing in English* (Delhi: Oxford UP, 2000).

Mukherjee, Shika, 'Bengal's Love-Hate for Niradbabu', *Times of India* (3 Aug. 1999), 8.

Murphy, Dervla, 'In the Chowk Tea-house', *Times Literary Supplement* (21 Nov. 1980), 1322.

Naik, M. K., *A History of Indian English Literature* (Delhi: Sahitiya Akademi, 1982).

——, 'Tributes', *Journal of Commonwealth Literature* 35.1 (2000), 179.

Naipaul, V. S., *The Overcrowded Barracoon and other Articles* (London: Andre Deutsch, 1972).

Nandy, Ashis, *The Intimate Enemy* (Delhi: Oxford UP, 1983).

——, *The Savage Freud and Other Essays on Possible and Retrievable Selves* (Delhi: Oxford UP, 1995).

Narasimhaiah, C. D. *Essays in Commonwealth Literature: Heirloom of Multiple Heritage* (Delhi: Pencraft International, 1995).

Narayan, Shyamala A. and Jon Mee, 'Novelists of the 1950s and 1960s', in Arvind Krishna Mehrotra (ed.), *A History of Indian Literature in English* (London: Hurst and Co., 2003), 219–31.

Nasta, Susheila, 'Homes Without Walls: South Asian Writing in Britain' in Ralph J. Crane and Radhika Mohanram (eds.), *Shifting Continents/Colliding Cultures: Diaspora Writing of the Indian Subcontinent* (Amsterdam: Rodopi, 2000), 83–101.

———, *Home Truths: Fictions of the South Asian Diaspora in Britain* (Houndmills: Palgrave, 2002).

——— 'Between Bloomsbury, Gandhi and Transcultural Modernities: the Publication and Reception of Mulk Raj Anand's *Untouchable* (1935)', unpublished paper, The Colonial and Postcolonial Lives of the Book Conference, 3–5 Nov. 2005.

Natarajan, Nalini, 'Woman, Nation, and Narration in *Midnight's Children*' in Meenakshi Mukherjee (ed.), *Midnight's Children: A Book of Readings* (Delhi: Pencraft International, 1999), 165–82.

Nazareth, Ho, 'Handcuffed to History', *Time Out* (8–14 May 1981), 20.

Nelson, Emmanuel, 'Troubled Journeys: Indian Immigrant Experience in Kamala Markandaya's *Nowhere Man* and Bharati Mukherjee's *Darkness*', in Anna Rutherford (ed.), *From Commonwealth to Post-Colonial* (Sydney: Dangaroo Press, 1992), 53–9.

Ngugi, Wa Thiong'o, *Decolonising the Mind: The Politics of Language in African Literature* (London: James Currey, 1986).

Nicholson, Norman (ed.), *The Penguin Anthology of Religious Verse* (London: Penguin, 1942).

Nightingale, Benedict, 'A Wife in Two Worlds', *The Times* (24 Feb. 1992), 5.

Niranjana, Tejaswini, *Siting Translation: History, Post-Structuralism, and the Colonial Context* (Berkeley and Los Angeles: University of California Press, 1992).

Noakes, David, 'Anthem for Doomed Youth?', *Times Literary Supplement* (4 Dec. 1981), 1427.

O'Connell, Alex, 'Meera Cracked', *The Times* (16 Oct. 1999), 16.

Papastergiadis, Nikos, 'Ashis Nandy: Dialogue and Diaspora', *Third Text* 11 (1990), 99–108.

Oddey, Alison, 'Interview with Meera Syal', in Alison Oddey (ed.), *Performing Women: Stand-ups, Strumpets and Itinerants* (Basingstoke: Macmillan, 1999), 56–65.

Office for National Statistics. Labour Force Survey, 1992–9.

Orwell, George, 'Anand's *The Sword and the Sickle*', *Horizon* (1942).

Owesu, Kwesi (ed.), *Black British Culture and Society* (London: Routledge, 2000).

Pandey, Gyanedra, 'In Defence of the Fragment: Writing about Hindu–Muslim Riots in India today', *Economic and Political Weekly* (1991), 559–73.

Parakrama, Arjuna, *De-Hegemonizing Language Standards: Learning from (Post)Colonial Englishes about 'English'* (Basingstoke: Macmillan, 1995).

Paranjape, Marakand R., 'Inside and Outside the Whale: Politics and the New Indian English Novel', in Viney Kirpal (ed.), *The New Indian Novel in English: A Study of the 1980s* (Delhi: Allied Publishers, 1990), 213–26.

Parma, Pratibha, 'Sammy and Rosie Get Laid' (review), *Marxism Today* 32 (1988), 39.

Parry, Benita, 'Problems in Current Theories of Colonial Discourse', *Oxford Literary Review* 9.1/2 (1987), 27–58.

———, 'Signs of Our Times: Discussion of Homi Bhabha's *The Location of Culture*', *Third Text* 28/29 (1994), 5–24.

Patke, Rajeev, 'Poetry Since Independence' in Arvind Krishna Mehrotra (ed.), *A History of Indian Literature in English* (London: Hurst and Co., 2003), 243–75.

Payne, Robert, 'Review of *Possession*', *Saturday Review* (25 May 1963), 34.

Perera, Suvendrini, 'Unmaking the Present, Remaking Memory: Sri Lankan Stories and a Politics of Co-existence', *Race and Class* 41.1/2 (1999), 189–96.

Poologasingham, P., *Poet Tambimuttu: A Profile* (Colombo: P. Tambimuttu, 1993).

Prescod, Colin and Hazel Waters, *A World to Win: Essays in Honour of Sivanandan, Race and Class* 41.1/2 (1999).

Price, David, 'Salman Rushdie's Use and Abuse of History in *Midnight's Children*', *Ariel* 25.2 (1994), 91–107.

Proctor, James, *Dwelling Places: Post-war Black British Writing* (Manchester: Manchester UP, 2003).

Quennell, Peter, 'Review of *The Prevalence of Witches*', *Daily Mail* (22 Nov. 1947).

Rafael, Vincente, *Contracting Colonialism: Translation and Christian Conversion in Tagalog Society* (Ithaca, NY: Cornell University Press, 1988).

Raine, Kathleen, *India Seen Afar* (Devon: Green Books, 1990).

Rajan, Rajeswari Sunder, *Real and Imagined Women: Gender, Culture and Postcolonialism* (London: Routledge, 1993).

Ram, Mohan, *Sri Lanka: The Fractured Island* (Delhi: Penguin, 1989).

Ramesh, Randeep, 'British, Asian and Hip', *Independent* (1 Mar. 1998), 20.

———, 'Goodness Gracious Me! Heard the One about the Funny Asian?' *Independent* (29 June 1998), 11.

Rampton, James, 'No More Mrs Patel for Meera', *Independent* (12 Apr. 1997), 45.

———, 'A Message to Take Away', *Independent* (17 Jan. 1998), 68.

Ranasinha, Ruvani, *Hanif Kureishi: Writers and their work* (Plymouth: Northcote House in association with the British Council, 2002).

Rao, A. V. Krishna, 'The Golden Honeycomb: a Brief Study' in G. S. Balarama Gupta (ed.), *Studies in Indian Fiction in English* (Gulbarga: JIWE Publications, 1987), 77–84.

Rattansi, Ali, 'Changing the Subject: Racism, Culture and Education', in James Donald and Ali Rattansi (eds.), *Race, Culture and Difference* (London: Sage Publications in association with the Open University, 1992), 11–49.

Ray, Sangeeta, *En-Gendering India: Woman and Nation in Colonial and Postcolonial Narratives* (Durham: Duke University Press, 2000).

Rees, Jasper, 'Asian Screen Cred', *The Times* (30 Oct. 1999), 24–9.

Richardson, Al (ed.), *Blows Against the Empire: Trotskyism in Ceylon: The Lanka Sama Samaja Party, 1935–1964* (London: Revolutionary History Porcupine Press, 1997).

Richardson, Maurice Lane, 'Review of *The Prevalence of Witches*: Tribal Affairs', *Times Literary Supplement* (6 Dec. 1947), 625.

Root, Jane, 'Scenes from a Marriage', *Monthly Film Bulletin* (1985), 333.

Rowe-Evans, Adrian, 'V.S. Naipaul: A Transition Interview 1971', in Feroza Jussawalla (ed.), *Conversations with V.S. Naipaul* (Jackson: University Press of Mississippi, 1997), 24–36.

Roy, Anita, 'Review of *Anita and Me*', *Times Literary Supplement* (5 Apr. 1996) 26.

Rubin, Gareth, 'Meera's Image', *Independent* (19 Dec. 1999), 11–12.

Rushdie, Salman and Elizabeth West (eds.), *The Vintage Book of Indian Writing in English, 1947–1997* (London: Vintage, 1997).

Rustomji-Kerns, Roshini, 'Introduction' in Urvashi Butalia and Ritu Menon (eds.), *In Other Words: New Writing by Indian Women* (Delhi: Kali for Women, 1992).

Sahgal, Gita and Nira Yuval-Davies (eds.), *Refusing Holy Orders: Women and Fundamentalism in Britain* (London: Virago), 1992.

Said, Edward, *Orientalism* (London: Routledge, 1978).

———, *The World, the Text and the Critic* (Cambridge, Mass.: Harvard UP, 1983).

———, 'Reflections on Exile', *Granta* 13 (1984), 159–72.

———, *Culture and Imperialism* (London: Chatto and Windus, 1993).

———, *Representations of the Intellectual* (London: Vintage, 1994).

Sampson, George and R. Churchill, *The Concise Cambridge History of English Literature* (Cambridge: Cambridge UP, 1961).

Sandford, Budick and Wolfgang Iser (eds.), *The Translatability of Cultures: Figurations of the Space Between* (Stanford: Stanford University Press, 1996).

Sandhu, Sukhdev, *London Calling: How Black and Asian Writers Imagined a City* (London: HarperCollins, 2003).

Sangari, Kumkum, 'The Politics of the Possible', *Cultural Critique* 7 (1987), 157–86.

Sangari, Kumar and Sudesh Vaid (eds.), *Recasting Women: Essays in Colonial History* (Delhi: Kali, 1989).

Sarkar, Sumit, *Modern India, 1885–1947* (Basingstoke: Macmillan, 1989).

Schwarz, Bill (ed.), *West Indian Intellectuals in Britain* (Manchester: Manchester UP, 2003)

Scott, Paul, 'Bitter Potion for Circe's Swine', *Times Literary Supplement* (2 Dec. 1965), 1093.

——— 'Fiction' *The Times* (28 Apr. 1977), 22.

Sergeant, Howard (ed.), *Commonwealth Poems of Today* (London: John Murray 1967).

Seshadri-Crooks, Kalpana, 'Surviving Theory: a Conversation with Homi K. Bhabha' in Fawzia Afzal-Khan and Kalpana Seshadri-Crooks (eds.), *The Pre-occupation of Postcolonial Studies* (Durham: Duke UP, 2000), 369–79.

Sethi, Rumina, *Myths of the Nation: National Identity and Literary Representation* (Oxford: Clarendon Press, 1999).

Shahani, Ranjee Gurdasing, 'Review of Anand's *The Sword and the Sickle*', *Times Literary Supplement* (2 Apr. 1942), 221.

Sharma, S., J. Hutnyk, and A. Sharma (eds.), *Dis-orienting Rhythms: the Politics of New Asian Dance Music* (London: Zed Books, 1996).

Sheppard, Samuel Townsend, 'Review of *Coolie*', *Times Literary Supplement* (20 June 1936).

Shills, Edward, 'Citizen of the World', *The American Scholar* 57 (1988), 549–73.

Shohat, Ella, ' "Notes on the Post-colonial" ', *Social Text* 31.32 (1993), 99–113.

Sidhwa, Bapsi, 'Interview with Julie Rajan', *Monsoon* magazine, online edition.

Singer, Elyse, 'Hanif Kureishi: A Londoner, But Not a Brit', in Melissa Biggs (ed.), *In the Vernacular: Interviews at Yale with the Sculptors of Culture* (Jefferson, NC: McFarland and Co., 1991), 103–9.

Singhe, Jyotsna G., *Colonial Narratives Cultural Dialogues: Discoveries of India in the Language of Colonialism* (London: Routledge, 1996).

Siriwardene, Regi, 'Review of *When Memory Dies*', *Nethra* 1.2 (1997), 74–81.

Spaeth, Anthony, 'Rushdie's Children', *Time* (16 Dec. 1991), 98–100.

Spengler, Oswald, *The Decline of the West* (London: Allen and Unwin, 1961).

Spivak, Gayatri Chakravorty, *Outside in the Teaching Machine* (London: Routledge, 1993).

———, *The Spivak Reader: Selected Works of Gayatri Chakravorty Spivak* ed. Donna Landry and Gerald MacLean (London: Routledge, 1996).

———, *A Critique of Postcolonial Reason: Towards a History of the Vanishing Present* (Cambridge, Mass.: Harvard UP, 1999).

——— and Sneja Gnew, 'Questions of Multiculturalism' in Mary Broe and Angela Ingram (eds.), *Women's Writing in Exile* (Chapel Hill: University of North Carolina Press, 1989), 413–20.

Squire, J. C., 'A Bridge between England and India', *Illustrated London News* (3 Nov. 1951), 706.

Srivastava, Sharad, *The New Woman in Indian English Fiction: A Study of Kamala Markandaya, Anita Desai, Namita Gokhale and Shoba De* (Delhi: Creative Books, 1996).

Stam, Robert and Ella Shohat, *Unthinking Eurocentrism* (London: Routledge, 1994).

Stanford, Derek, *Inside the Forties: Literary Memoirs, 1937–1957* (London: Sidgwick and Jackson, 1977).

Stevenson, Randall, *Modernist Fiction: An Introduction* (London: Harvester Wheatsheaf, 1992).

Stocking, George, *Victorian Anthropology* (New York: The Free Press, 1987).

Stokes, Eric, 'Generally Ravishing', *Times Literary Supplement* (29 Apr. 1977), 507.

Suleri, Sara, *The Rhetoric of English India* (Chicago: University of Chicago Press, 1992).

Tarlo, Emma, *Clothing Matters: Dress and Identity in India* (Chicago: University of Chicago Press, 1996).

Taylor, Charles, 'The Politics of Recognition', in Amy Gutman (ed.), *Multiculturalism: Examining the Politics of Recognition* (Princeton: Princeton UP, 1994).

Taylor, Matthew, 'Brickbats fly as community brands novel "despicable"', *Guardian* (3 Dec. 2003), online edition.

Tharu, Susie and K. Lalitha (eds.), *Women Writing in India: 600 B.C. to the Present*, 2 vols. (London: Pandora, 1993), ii.

Thurlow, Richard C., 'Satan and Sambo: The Image of the Immigrant in English Racial Populist Thought since the First World War', in Kenneth Lum (ed.), *Hosts, Immigrants and Minorities* (Folkestone: Dawson and Sons, 1980), 39–63.

Todd, Richard, *Consuming Fictions: the Booker Prize and Fiction in Britain Today* (London: Bloomsbury, 1996).

Towheed, Shafquat, 'Two Paradigms of Literary Production: a brief comparison of the production, distribution, circulation and legal status of Rudyard Kipling's *Departmental Ditties* (1886) and Indian Railway Library Texts', unpublished paper, The Colonial and Postcolonial Lives of the Book 1765–2005 Conference, Institute of English Studies, University of London, 3–5 Nov. 2005.

Treneman, Ann, 'Revelations; I Thought, I'll be a Writer', *Independent* (15 Apr. 1997), 10.

_____, and _____ (eds.), *Interrogating Post-Colonialism: Theory, Text and Context* (Shimla: Institute of Advanced Study, 1996).

Trivedi, Harish, and Meenakshi Mukherjee (eds.), 'Salman the Funtoosh: Magic Bilingualism in *Midnight's Children*' in Meenakshi Mukherjee (ed.), *Midnight's Children: A Book of Readings* (Delhi: Pencraft International, 1999), 69–95.

Unwin, Stanley, *The Truth about a Publisher: An Autobiographical Record* (Allen and Unwin, 1960).

Veer, Peter Van der (ed.), *Nation and Migration: The Politics of Space in the South Asian Diaspora* (Philadelphia: University of Pennsylvania Press, 1995).

Venuti, Lawrence, 'Translation as Cultural Politics: Regimes of Domestication in English', *Textual Practice* vii (1993), 208-33.

Visram, Rozina, *Ayahs, Lascars and Princes* (London: Pluto, 1986).

———, *Asians in Britain: Four Hundred Years of History* (London: Pluto, 2002).

Viswanathan, Gauri, *Masks of Conquest: Literary Study and British Rule in India* (New York: Columbia University Press, 1989).

Wagle, N. K. and Milton Israel (eds.), *Ethnicity, Identity, Migration: The South Asian Context* (Toronto: University of Toronto Press, 1993).

Wahab, Iqbal, 'Casting Aspersions', *Independent* (24 Oct. 1990), 15.

Wakeman, John, *World Authors, 1950–1970: A Companion Volume to Twentieth Century Authors* (New York: Wilson, 1975).

Walsh, William, 'The Meeting of Language and Literature and the Indian Example' in Guy Amirthanayagam (ed.), *Writers in the East–West Encounter* (Basingstoke: Macmillan, 1982), 100–37.

Wardle, Irving, 'Review of *Borderline*', *The Times* (6 Nov. 1981), 18.

———, ' "Us and Them . . . and Those" ', *The Times* (17 Sept. 1983), 9.

Weber, Donald, ' "No Secrets Were Safe from Me": Situating Hanif Kureishi', *The Massachusetts Review* 38.1 (1997), 119–35.

West, W. J. (ed.), *George Orwell: The War Commentaries* (Harmondsworth: Penguin, 1987).

———, *George Orwell: The War Broadcasts* (Harmondsworth: Penguin, 1987).

Wickremasinghe, Nira, *Ethnic Politics in Colonial Sri Lanka, 1927–1947* (Delhi: Vikas, 1995).

Williams, Jane (ed.), *Tambimuttu: Bridge Between Two Worlds* (London: Peter Owen, 1989).

Wilson, Amrit, *Finding a Voice: Asian Women in Britain* (London: Virago, 1978).

Wolf, Rita, 'Beyond the Laundrette', *Guardian* (14 Feb. 1987), 14.

Young, G. M (ed.), *Macaulay: Prose and Poetry* (London: Hart-Davis, 1952).

Young, Robert, *White Mythologies: Writing History and the West* (London: Routledge, 1990).

———, *Postcolonialism: An Historical Introduction* (Oxford: Blackwell, 2001).

Yuval-Davies, Nira, *Woman-Nation-State* (London: Sage, 1997).)

# Index